How to Make
Sewing Patterns

Also by Don McCunn

Text Only e-Books

An Introduction to Pattern Design

How to Make Custom-Fit Bras

How to Make Bikinis and Bandeaux

Interactive e-Books

How to Make Custom-Fit Slopers

How to Make A Custom Dress Form

How to Make Custom-Fit Corsets

How to Make Bust Sling Bras

Interactive e-Books include
embedded demonstration videos
website: Pattern-Design-Guides.com

Patterns for Fashion Dolls

website: Patterns-for-Fashion-Dolls.com

How to Make

Sewing Patterns

Second Edition

Don McCunn

Design Enterprises of San Francisco

To Dr. Paul D. Reinhardt whose
inspiration is the cornerstone of this book.

To my students both in the classroom and in my online classes
whose questions and enthusiasm have kept me going and led me forward.

To my models who have made my
ongoing research and development possible.

To Feather and John King
who have helped keep this book alive.

And to my wife whose continued support has
made all my endeavors possible.

Model on Cover: Alexandra Matthew

Library of Congress Control Number: 2016902273

Hardback Edition ISBN: 978-0-932538-20-8
Paperback Edition ISBN: 978-0-932538-21-5

Publisher's Cataloging-in-Publication
(Provided by Quality Books, Inc.)

McCunn, Donald H., author.
How to make sewing patterns / Don McCunn. -- Second edition.
pages cm
Includes index.
LCCN 2016902273
ISBN 978-0-932538-20-8
ISBN 978-0-932538-21-5

1. Dressmaking--Pattern design. I. Title.

TT520.M15 2016 646.4'072
QBI16-600025

DESIGN ENTERPRISES OF SAN FRANCISCO
1007 Castro Street, San Francisco, CA 94114
Website: deofsf.com

Available to the trade from Ingram Book Company

Acknowledgments

I learned the principles of pattern drafting from Dr. Paul D. Reinhardt at the University of Texas Drama Department, and I am indebted to him for the content and inspiration of his excellent teaching which has informed every edition of this book.

I wish to thank Harold H. Hart for publishing the first edition. In the forty plus years since, I have presented its content in many pattern design classes. Whether in academia or online, people in these classes have improved this approach to pattern drafting immeasurably through penetrating questions and by applying these techniques to a wide variety of figure shapes. Additionally, I have worked with models who opened doors to ideas and techniques that would not have been possible otherwise, and I am grateful to them all, in particular Alexandra Matthew, who was instrumental in much of the work I did in developing my online classes.

When I first started teaching, I noticed how quickly people could grasp a topic when seeing it demonstrated. Thanks to 21st century technology, I can now share those demonstrations with close ups, time compression, and the ability for people to watch them as often and whenever they want through my Interactive e-Books at Pattern-Design-Guides.com.

Bill Jones introduced me to quarter scale fashion dolls, which opened my eyes to how pattern making techniques could be tried, ideas explored, and designs prototyped with small scale garments. I dedicate the Mini-Me Dress Form described in this book to him.

Feather and John King of Blue Feather Products kept the book alive when my own energy flagged. Their dedication to the first edition made it possible for me to develop the second edition, and I am deeply grateful.

Finally, everything I am able to do is because of the incredible support I receive from my wife Roxey.

Table of Contents

Introduction

Creating the Sloper . . . 10
Designing from a Sloper. . . . 11
Fabric and the Body . . . 12
How to Use This Book . . . 15
Patternmaking Tools and Materials . . . 16

Creating the Sloper Patterns

Basic Body Contours and Lines. . . . 17
Measurements . . . 19
 Girth Measurements 21
 Length Measurements 23
The Skirt Sloper . . . 27
 The Body and the Skirt. 27
 Drafting the Skirt Pattern 29
 Initial Fitting of the Skirt 31
The Pants Sloper. . . . 43
 Drafting the Pants Pattern 44
 Optimizing the Pattern for a Tummy. 48
 Fitting the Pants 50
 Styling Pants 53
The Bodice Sloper. . . . 57
 A Man's Body and the Front Pattern. 57
 The Back of the Body and the Pattern 60
 A Woman's Body and the Front Pattern 63
The Sleeve Sloper . . . 79
 The Body and the Sleeve. 79
 The Sleeve Pattern 79

Pattern Alteration Techniques

Changing Seam Locations. . . . 85
 Changing External Lines. 85
 Changing Internal Lines 87
Changing Dart Locations . . . 90
 Side Seam Bust Dart 90
 Center Front Dart. 92
 French Dart. 92
 Curved Dart 92
 Shoulder Darts 93
Changing Darts To Seams. . . . 95
 Princess Seams. 95
 Front Yoke 98
 Changing Back Darts to Seams 100
Principles of Adding Fullness . . . 101
 Location Of Fullness. 101
 Changing Darts To Fullness 101
 Determining Fullness. 103
The Procedures for Adding Fullness . . . 105
Sleeve Variations 111
 Flounced Sleeve 112
 Gathered Sleeve Top 112
 Gathered Sleeve Cap 113
 Leg-Of-Mutton Sleeve 114

Puffed Sleeve 115
Bell Sleeve 116
Cape Sleeve 117
Raglan Sleeve 118
Tunic Sleeve 120
Collars 121
Mandarin Collar 122
Shirt Collar I 124
Shirt Collar II 125
Flat Collars 126
Adding Fullness to Collars 128

Designing Garments
Skirts 130
Skirt Waistbands 130
Fitted Pencil Skirt 131
Full Skirt 132
Wrap Around Skirt 133
Dirndl Skirt 133
Pants 135
Pants Waistbands 135
Plackets 137
Pockets 137
Cuffs 140
Shirts and Blouses 141
The Body of the Shirt 141
The Shirt Sleeve 143
The Cuff 143
Full Sleeves and Tapered Cuffs 144
Dresses and Tops 145
Peasant Top 145
High Waistlines 146
Low Necklines 146
Cowl Necklines 147
Wrap Around Closings 148
Working with Knits 149
Handkerchief & Circular Skirts 149
Knit Tops 150
Raglan Sleeve 151
Leggings 152
Jackets and Coats 153
Creating the Body of the Jacket 154
Lapels and Collars 156
The Two Piece Sleeve 157
Fabric 159

Appendix
The Dress Form 163
Scale Rulers 169
Working in Quarter Scale 178
Scaling Patterns 178
Making a Mini-Me Dress Form 179

Index 180

Introduction

Pattern drafting may seem like a complex and mystifying art, but it is basically a simple process. In essence, a two-dimensional piece of material is shaped and altered so that it will cover a three-dimensional body.

To create patterns for a specific body and a variety of different designs requires three steps:

1. Measuring the body.
2. Making fitted patterns called Slopers.
3. Creating designs from the Slopers.

In this book, the steps are explained conceptually so that once you understand the process, you can easily change the sequence of steps based on the needs of individual projects.

Basic Patternmaking Approaches

The fashion industry makes patterns for a "standardized body" in order to fit as many people as possible. But Mother Nature never makes the same shape twice, and this book shows you how to make custom-fit patterns for a specific body.

For example, Donna Karan created a fitted skirt pattern for Vogue Patterns (V2893) that uses a 3" (7.5 cm) fitted, contoured waistband. This portion of a woman's body can vary quite a bit. The illustrations below show the waist-to-hip region of four models, the shape of the Vogue pattern, and the shape of the custom-fit patterns for each model.

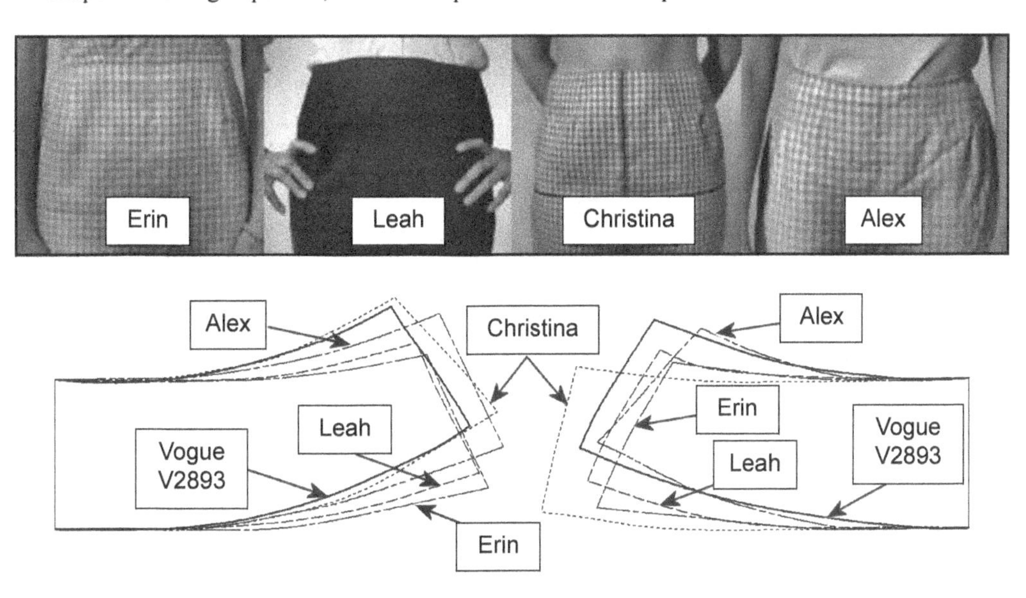

Creating the Sloper

Measurements

Taking measurements of the body is the first step in creating patterns. While it is important to take these measurements as accurately as possible, they merely serve as guides. Why? Fabric has give and needs to move and flow with the body. Furthermore, the body is a series of contours. There are no points or sharp angles to establish exact locations. Pattern shapes are therefore best verified by fitting fabric to the body, and measurements accurate to 1/2" (12 mm) are more than adequate.

Drafting the Initial Patterns

The initial pattern drafted establishes lines on paper that can be matched to a body's reference lines. For example, the vertical Center Front and Center Back lines establish the location of the spine on the pattern. The waist, bust, and hip lines set basic horizontal locations.

Since the vertical and horizontal lines for patterns are drawn at right angles, the marking paper used by the fashion industry is convenient. It has blue dots every 1" and comes in rolls the same width as fabric: 36", 45", 48", and 60".

The location and size of darts required for a custom fit cannot be determined from measurements. They need to be established by fitting fabric to the body.

Fitting Shells

The initial patterns must be transferred to fabric for a fitting. During the fitting, the size and shape of the darts and location of the seams is established. This fitting is done for half of the body.

Fitting shells can be made from a variety of fabrics. Muslin is commonly used. Gingham, however, is a fabric that is woven with two different colored threads in a pattern of squares, making it easy to align the grain of the fabric to the basic reference lines of the body, resulting in an accurate fit that would be difficult, if not impossible, to achieve any other way. For this book, the fitting shells for the bodice and skirt are made from gingham. The fitting shell for pants is made from muslin as explained on page 43.

Finalizing the Sloper

Once the fabric has been fitted, the resulting shapes can be used to finalize the paper patterns referred to here as Slopers. Since the initial fitting is done for only half the body, the fitting shell should be sewn for both sides of the body to determine any asymmetrical contours.

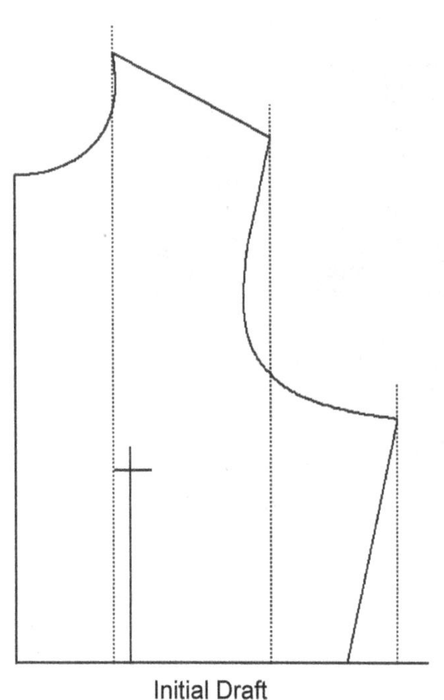

Initial Draft

Gingham fitting matches the fabric grain to reference lines of the body.

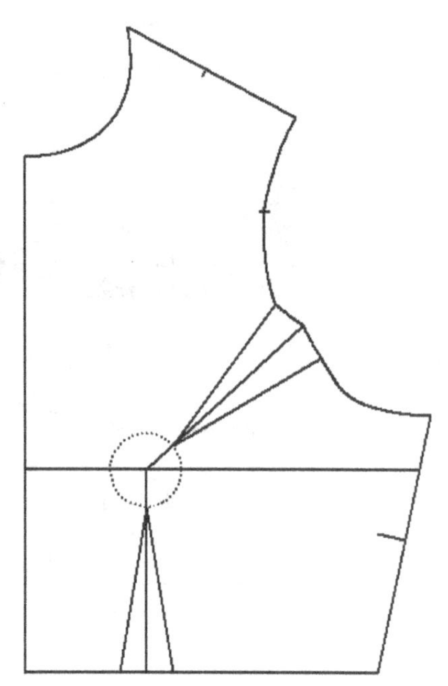

Final Sloper

Designing from a Sloper

The Concept of the Design

In conceiving a design, the first consideration must be the garment's function. Is it to be for a formal occasion, work, or play?

Once the garment's purpose has been established, the specific design can be developed. Inspiration may be from the imagination, a sketch in a clothing catalog, a garment viewed in a store window or on a person. Diverse designs can be created by combining different sleeve and collar patterns with basic body styles.

To evaluate the design, make a sketch. Make sure the different elements complement each other. Individual touches may also be added to increase the originality of the idea or to compensate for any special qualities in the shape of the wearer so that the garment will be as flattering as possible.

After this, the material to be used must be examined for its properties of draping, weight, and flexibility.

Creating the Pattern

Before creating a pattern, such things as seam and dart placements as well as the types of openings for the garment (lacings, buttons, hooks, eyes, zippers, etc.) must be determined. With these considerations in mind, drafting the actual patterns can begin.

When working from Slopers that have gone through the fitting process, new seam lines and dart placement can be made on a copy of the Sloper. Always maintain a master copy of the Sloper that remains unchanged.

There are only a few techniques that are required to change a Sloper for a specific design:

- Change dart locations.
- Change darts to seams.
- Change seam locations.
- Add fullness.

A brief illustration of these techniques is shown below. The second part of this book provides step-by-step instructions.

Fittings

Even working from fitted Slopers, it is always a good idea to baste a garment together for a trial fitting. A fitting session not only allows you to correct the patterns if necessary but also provides an opportunity to devise variations in the shape of the seams and the darts that can further enhance the design. Once the garment has been carefully fitted, it is ready for sewing.

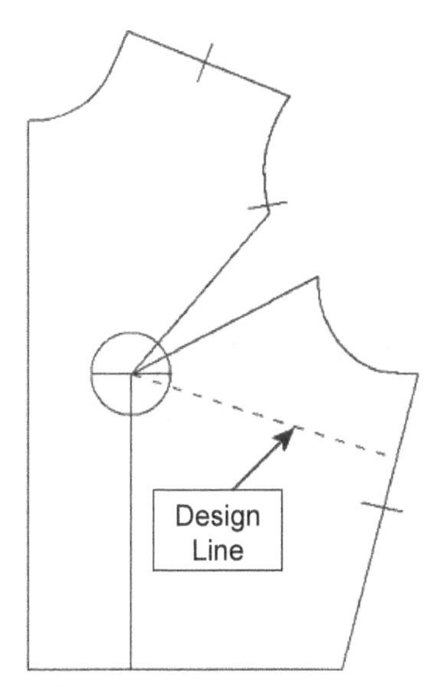

Draw a Design Line

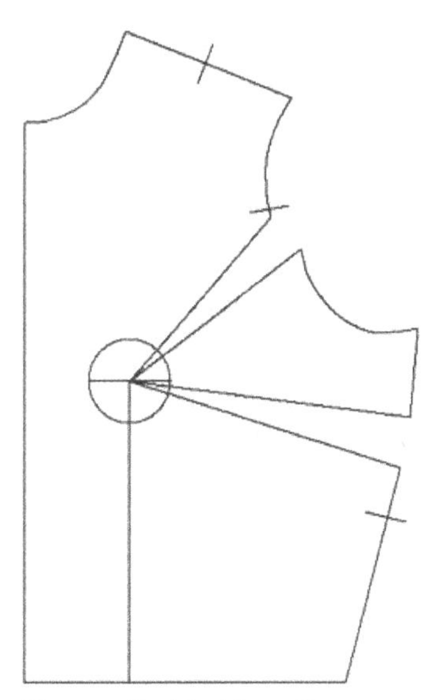
Change the Dart Location

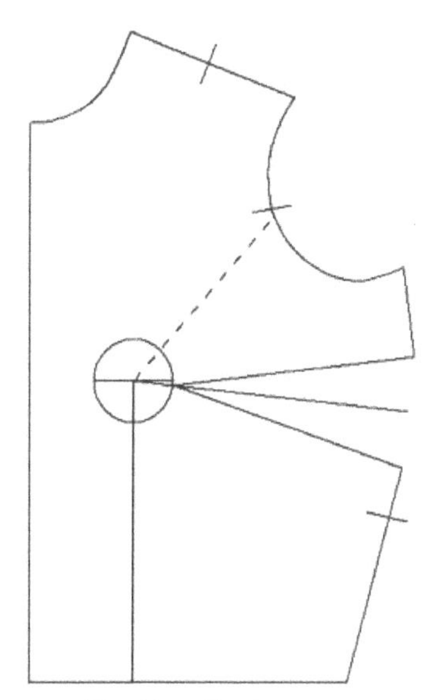
The New Design

Fabric and the Body

Understanding the body's contours and then learning how to shape flat fabric to fit these contours is essential. With these two principles in mind, individual problems and mistakes can be corrected. Not understanding these two concepts is the source of all errors in measuring, drafting, and fitting.

The Body

The body is a marvellous combination of many different shapes and curves. Most people are aware of the obvious shapes. Pattern drafters must become aware of every shape and how movement affects them.

There are so many variations in body shapes that it is impossible to describe them all in this introduction. The first part of this book is dedicated to an understanding of a body's contours by describing how to take measurements, draft Slopers, and fit patterns to the body.

The important point is to start looking at the body now. The body has the three dimensions of height, width, and depth. It is a combination of continuously changing curves.

Look at each individual part of the body, comparing the front to the side to the back. There is the main torso. Connected to it are the arms, legs, and neck. Each of these joints requires special consideration in the pattern drafting process.

For instance, look at how the neck joins the body. The front view shows an abrupt angle as the neck meets the shoulder. The side view shows an almost straight line where the neck meets the front and the back of the body. The curve of the body is in one direction. The curve of the neck is in another.

The human body is exceedingly complex to describe. But by carefully looking at the body, the most complex variations become immediately obvious. Similarly, if any step in the measuring or pattern drafting procedure should become unclear, look at the body to see which of the contours is being used. This will make the whole process much easier.

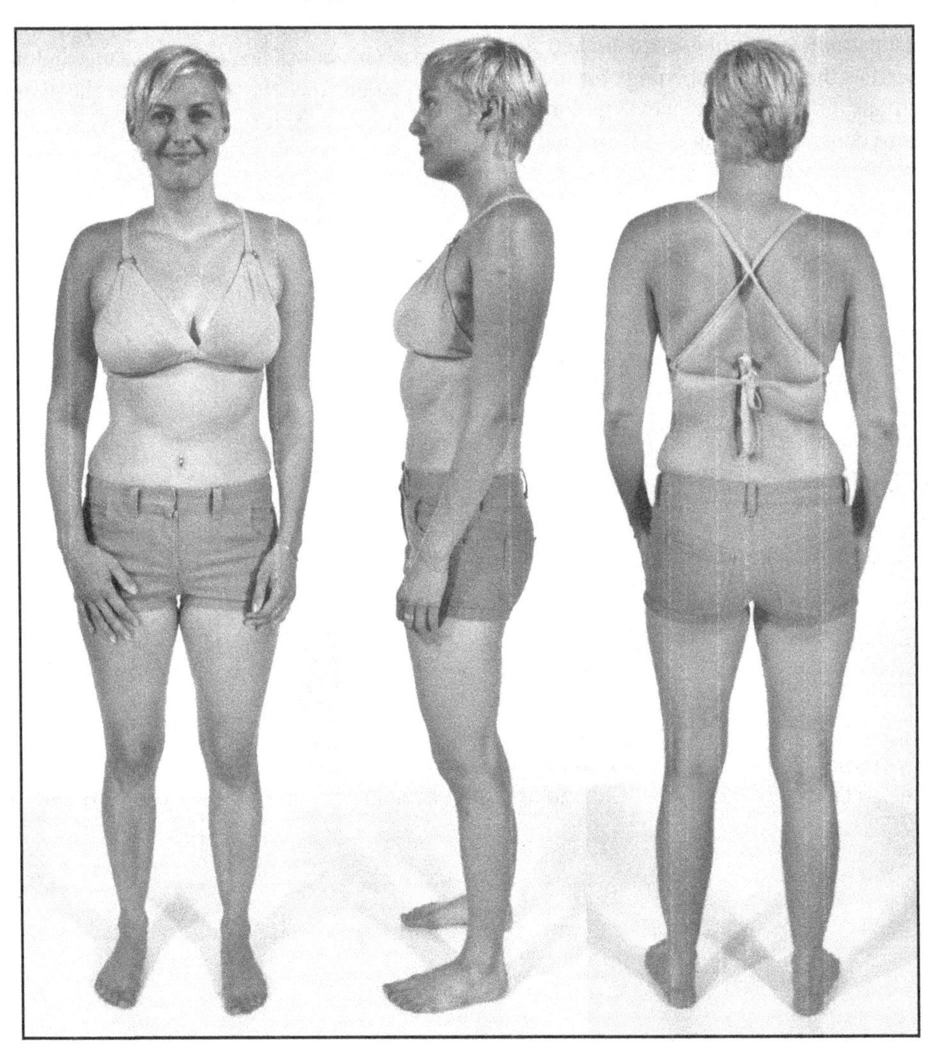

Shaping Fabric

For the purposes of understanding patternmaking, the following descriptions apply to woven fabric and not knits. This is because woven fabric is essentially flat. Knits can take on a three-dimensional shape. Patterns for woven fabric can be easily converted for knits. But patterns for knits cannot be reliably converted for woven fabric.

Woven fabric has the two dimensions of length and width. The third dimension of depth is negligible. It may be shaped to fit the three-dimensional human form just as paper may be used to wrap a box.

Studying paper is a good way of understanding how woven fabric responds to shaping. Paper is stiffer than fabric but it responds the same in all other ways.

For example, take a piece of paper and bend it from top to bottom. It bends easily. Now bend it from side to side. Once again it will bend easily in that one direction. But try bending it from top to bottom and from side to side at the same time. It cannot be done without wrinkling the paper.

Woven fabric, like paper, will bend smoothly in only one direction at a time. Many of the body's contours bend several directions at once. Fabric therefore must be shaped to follow the contours of the body.

The shaping devices in garment construction are darts and seams. Pattern drafting is the process of locating these darts and seams so that the fabric will lay flat where the body is flat and bend where the body bends. If the contours of the body are successfully followed, there will be no unsightly bulges or wrinkles.

Darts

A dart is a "V" shaped wedge that is removed from the fabric, allowing it to bend in two directions at the same time. Paper may be used to demonstrate the basic idea of the dart.

1. Take a piece of paper and draw a "V" shaped dart on it with the point near the center of the paper and the two legs running off one edge.
2. Number the edges of the paper.

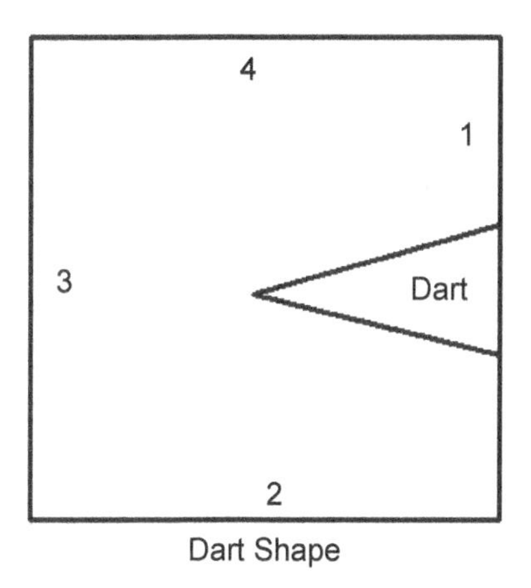

Dart Shape

Now cut out the dart and tape the two cut edges together. Notice how the paper now bends in two directions. One bend in the paper follows the line of the dart from edge #1 to edge #3. The paper also bends from edge #2 to edge #4.

In fabric, the wedge of the dart is normally sewn out rather than cut out but the principle of removing a wedge of the material and the resulting shape are the same.

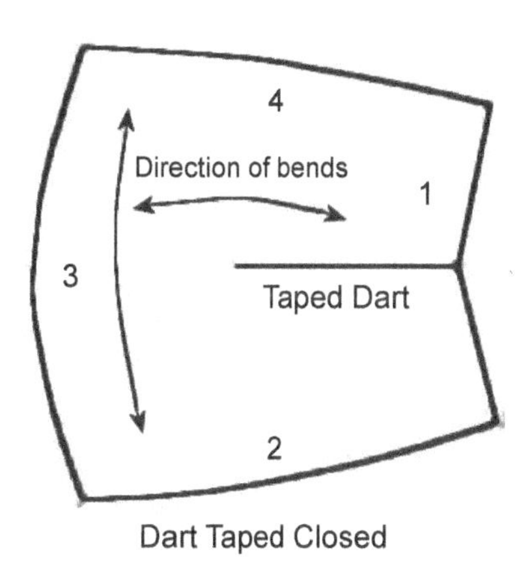

Dart Taped Closed

Seams

A seam joins two separate pieces of fabric together. Seams can affect the shape in three different ways.

1. Seams may be added to fabric without changing the shape of the fabric. For example, cut a piece of paper in half and tape it back together. There is no change in the shape.

This is a decorative seam. It may be used to join together two pieces of different colored fabric as in patchwork quilts.

2. Seams may be used instead of darts to bend fabric in two directions at the same time. For example, take the piece of paper that was used for the dart. Cut from edge #3 to the dart's point, then tape it back together.

This seam replaces the dart. The shape of the fabric is the same whether the dart or the seam is used to do the shaping.

3. Seams may be used to shape fabric so it will bend in more than two directions at the same time. A mandarin collar is shaped to fit both the neck and the body smoothly. Notice how many different directions the fabric is going.

Putting darts and seams in fabric so it will fit the body is what pattern drafting is all about.

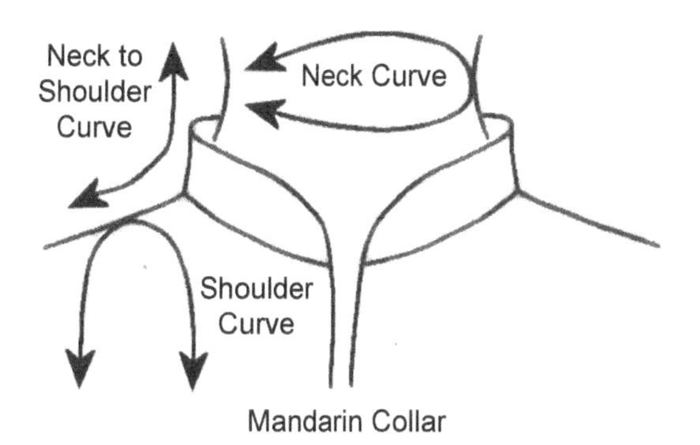

Mandarin Collar

Fabric Grain Lines

Just as the body has horizontal and vertical lines, fabric has horizontal and vertical lines. To ensure the best possible fit for a finished garment, a pattern must match the lines of the body to the fabric's grain lines.

Woven fabric starts with vertical threads on a loom. These vertical threads are held parallel to each other and a series of horizontal threads is woven between them. The two sets of threads are at perfect right angles to each other. The direction of the threads is the direction of the fabric's grain. There is both a horizontal grain and a vertical grain.

The way to determine a fabric's grain is to select a single thread and follow it for its entire length. Or, pull a single thread out of the fabric leaving an empty space between the adjacent threads.

When shaping fabric to fit a body's contours, it is not always possible to keep the grain lines in vertical and horizontal directions. So the most important locations for the grain lines to remain horizontal and vertical must be determined for each pattern piece.

Ease

Patterns cannot be made for a body's exact size because clothing from such patterns would be uncomfortable and restrict movement. The extra width added to a body's measurements for patterns is called Ease.

There are two kinds of Ease. The first is Fitting Ease. This is the amount of Ease added to patterns to make the resulting garments wearable. The second is Design Ease. This is the amount that a pattern is expanded to create the desired fullness for a given design.

Design Ease is variable. It can be adjusted to the taste of the person wearing the clothes and/or the designer. The amounts of Ease given in this book are only intended to be a starting point for individual preference.

How to Use This Book

This book has been developed to show when, where, why, and how to place darts and seams to achieve any desired design. Instructions are given in steps. Each new step is based on the previous ones. To benefit the most from this book, try out each step as it is described.

Measurements, which provide the distances from given reference lines to basic seam locations, are described first. They are used to analyze the size and shape of the body.

Then Slopers, which show the three-dimensional shape of the body on two-dimensional paper, are drawn by establishing the reference lines on paper and measuring the distances to the seam locations. To give a better understanding of the underlying principles and techniques, the easiest patterns are presented first.

Finally, the Slopers are transferred to fabric, such as gingham or muslin, and checked for accuracy in fittings because even when measurements are taken accurately and drafting is done correctly, further adjustment may be necessary to adapt the patterns to the individual shape of the wearer.

The first part of this book will show you how to measure, draft, and fit the Slopers. If you are developing these patterns for yourself, it is best to have someone help you with the measuring and fitting. However, if you do not have anyone, do-it-yourself (DIY) instructions have been included.

After the Slopers have been drafted, they can be changed to achieve any style desired. Remember, Slopers are the shape of the body. All clothes are designed to fit certain parts of the body, hang from other parts, and be full in other areas. Slopers can be altered to achieve this.

The second section of this book shows techniques that can be used to alter Slopers. Most contemporary clothes are based on a few standard variations of sleeve, collar, and body patterns. Most of these variations are described in the section on pattern alterations.

The third section of this book shows how patterns can be put together to achieve diverse designs. Examples are given to show some of the many different variations that are possible.

One of the greatest thrills is to design, draft, sew, and wear your own creations. To create an original design, start with a sketch. You do not have to be a great illustrator to be a good designer, so try it. The best way is to draw the desired design over a body silhouette that shows the correct proportions of the body. Photographs of an individual's body are a great resource for making these sketches. Other silhouettes may be achieved by tracing fashion illustrations.

The final part of this book presents additional information to make designing, drafting, and sewing as rewarding as possible. There is a section which describes the way fabric relates to pattern drafting. Another shows how to make a custom dress form accurately and inexpensively from the Slopers.

Working in Quarter Scale

It will be easier to follow along with the book if the patterns are drafted in quarter scale first. Purchase a tablet of 8½" x 11" (A4) graph paper that is lined off in quarter inch squares. When a measurement calls for 3", for example, instead of measuring 3", count 3 squares. A quarter scale ruler is also useful, see page 169. Once the patterns are drafted to quarter scale, it is easier to make full size patterns. Quarter scale patterns can also be used to practice pattern alteration.

You can also make garments out of fabric in quarter scale. To see how these garments hang on a body, instructions are included for how to make a Mini-Me Dress Form, see page 179. This dress form can be made from the Slopers you create. Or you can use the sample quarter scale patterns on page 83.

Squared-off graph paper is suggested because pattern drafting frequently requires drawing parallel lines and right angles. Graph paper already indicates these.

Two important drafting terms may be defined as follows: Parallel lines are two lines that are the same distance from each other for their entire length; they never touch. A right angle is a square corner: Two lines intersect, forming a 90 degree angle. A plastic triangle may be used to help draw right angles. The corner of a piece of paper or of a book may also be used.

Another step that is frequently necessary in pattern drafting is dividing measurements into fourths and halves. To facilitate this, you can use the scale ruler described on page 169 which automatically divides these measurements.

For ease of use, it may be helpful to "unbind" this book and insert its pages in a three ring binder. To "unbind," open the book to the middle, say around page 90. Spread it open at the spine, then cut through the spine with a sharp knife. Next, pull off one page at a time. The pages will come off the same way paper may be torn off a tablet of scratch paper. Once the pages are removed, they may be punched and put in a three ring binder.

Video Instruction

If you like to learn through demonstrations, many of the instructions in this book are included as embedded videos in Interactive e-Books found at Pattern-Design-Guides.com.

Patternmaking Tools and Materials

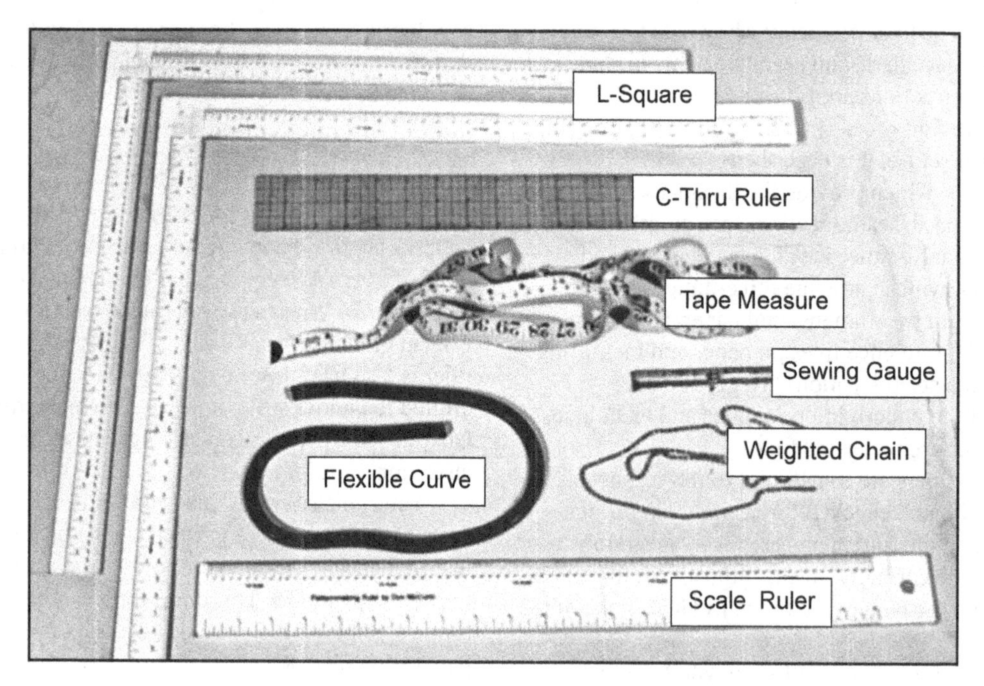

The following tools and supplies can be used to create patterns. Some of these are optional. You will also need basic sewing supplies such as scissors, thread, etc.

- Tape measure - for taking measurements and marking off lengths.
- Pencil and eraser - for recording measurements and drawing patterns,
- 2 yards of velcro - to establish reference lines around the body such as the waist.
- Weighted chain - for measurements and fittings.
- 2 L-Squares - for measurements from one side of the body to another.
- Pattern paper - to create the patterns (marking paper is recommended).
- Yard stick - for drawing lines and marking off lengths.
- Scale ruler - for dividing measurements, see page 169.
- Flexible curve - for drawing curved lines.
- Sewing gauge - for adding seam allowances.
- C-Thru ruler - for adding seam allowances.
- Gingham and muslin - for creating fitting shells. (Gingham with 1/4" pastel colors works best.)

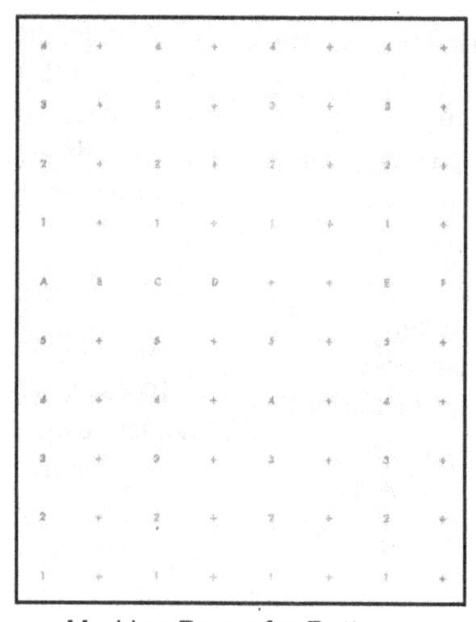

Marking Paper for Patterns

Creating the Sloper Patterns

Basic Body Contours and Lines

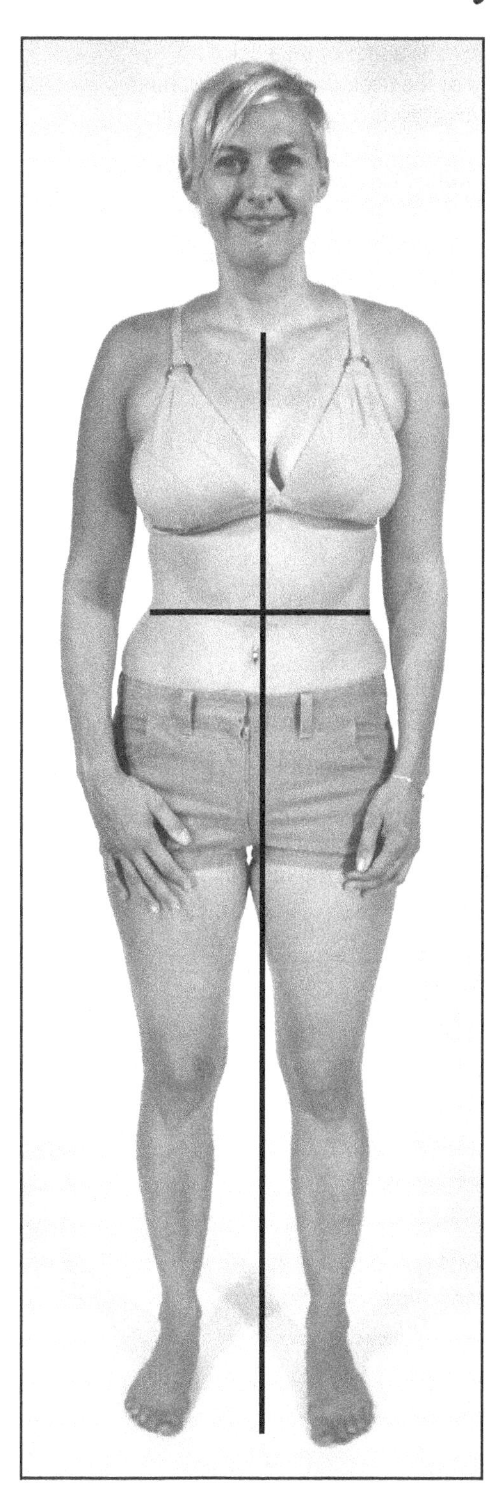

This approach to pattern drafting starts with the body. The basic lines of the body must be determined and understood if the patterns are going to be accurately drafted.

To draw the body as a two-dimensional shape, a vertical reference and a horizontal reference line must be established.

The most natural vertical line of the body is the spinal column. It is in the center of the body and it reaches from the top to the bottom of the torso. An imaginary line may extend it to the floor.

Center Front

The vertical line used for drafting patterns for the front part of the body will follow a line that is directly in front of the spinal column. It is referred to as the Center Front.

Center Back

The vertical line that follows the spinal column is used for drafting patterns for the back. It is referred to as the Center Back.

Once the vertical line is established, a horizontal line must be determined. The Waist is the basic horizontal line used for this approach to pattern drafting.

Waist

Find the Waist by putting a string around the body and pulling it tight. This string must be kept parallel to the floor at all times.

At the side of the body, the Waist is half way between the bottom of the rib cage and the top of the hip bone. In men the distance between the rib cage and the hip bone is less than 1" (2.5 cm) but for women, this distance is between 2" to 3" (5 to 7.5 cm).

Important Note - The Waist used for measuring and drafting the Slopers may or may not be the waist used in the final design. For example, men's pants are almost never designed to fit at the natural waist. They are 3" to 4" (7.5 to 10 cm) lower.

The next step is to determine the seam lines that will be used to measure, draft, and fit the Slopers. These lines will follow the natural contours of the body. These contours are gradual curves. There are not any definite points or lines to look for, but some locations are better than others.

Neckline

The best way to determine the Neckline in the back and to the side of the body is to use a weighted chain around the neck as it will follow the natural curves of the body.

The chain at Center Back is just above a large vertebrae in the spinal column. Put a finger at this point and tip the head up and down. The large vertebrae does not move. It is a part of the body. The vertebrae just above it does move. It is a part of the neck.

The chain then crosses over the shoulder at the base of the neck. In some cases, this neck to shoulder area will have three planes. The chain crosses the center of the middle plane.

From the shoulder, the Neckline should follow the hollow between the neck and the collar bone around to the Center Front.

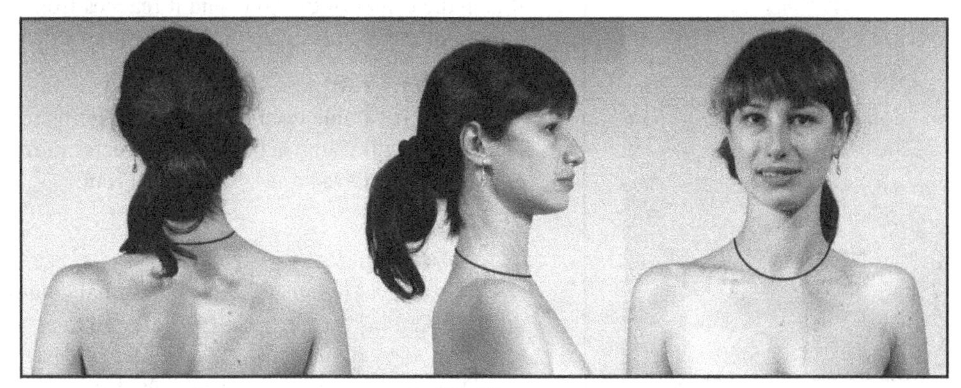

Neckline

Shoulder Seam

The Shoulder Seam for the Sloper is located on the top of the shoulder. It runs from the neckline to the sleeve seam dividing the front of the body from the back of the body.

To determine the best location for the Shoulder Seam, place a book on top of the shoulder and hold it parallel to the floor as seen from the side. The Shoulder Seam should be directly under the book.

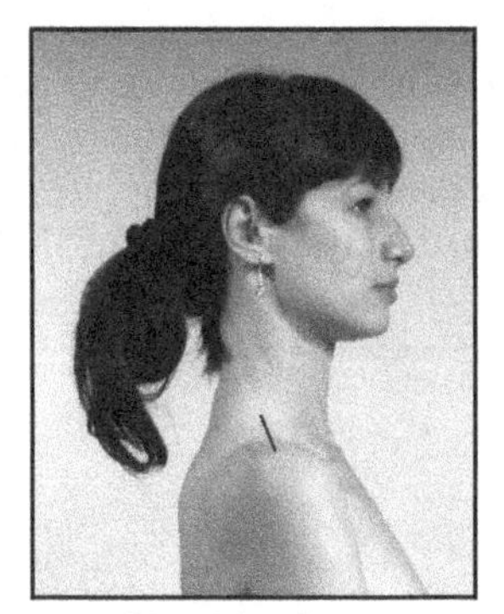

Shoulder Seam

Shoulder Point

The Shoulder Point is where the Shoulder Seam meets the Sleeve Seam. It is the separation point between the body and the arm.

To determine the best location for the Shoulder Point, raise the arm straight out from the side of the body. You can feel the bones in the arm move. The bones in the body do not move.

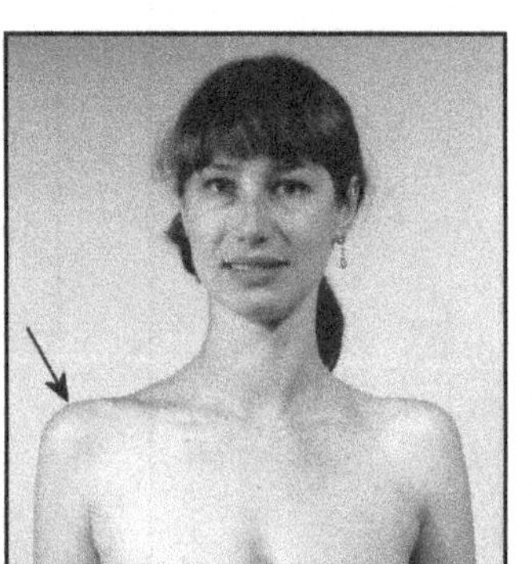

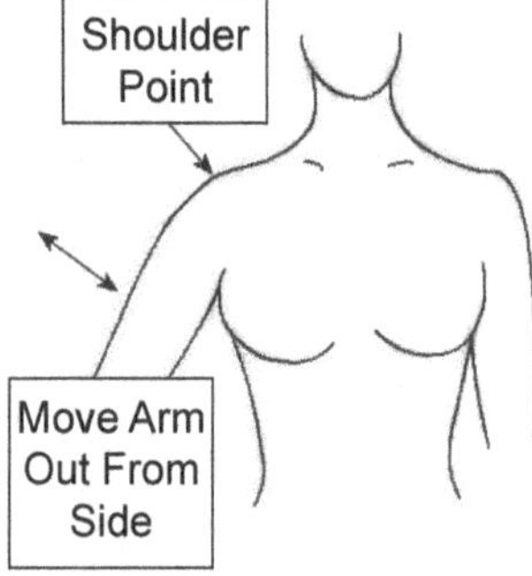

Shoulder Point

Measurements

Measurements are the foundation of pattern drafting. They determine the distances from the basic reference lines to the basic seam lines, and they are used to reconstruct the shape of the body on paper.

There are different ways to take measurements and also many different measurement charts. The pattern drafting instructions in this book are based on the specific measurements and the method for taking them described in this section.

The Measurement Chart is divided into two basic groups of measurements, Girth and Length. Girth measurements are taken horizontally and most of them go around the entire circumference of the body. They should be taken parallel to the floor except where otherwise noted.

Length measurements are taken vertically. They should be at right angles to the floor, except where otherwise noted. Their main purpose is to give the distances between the individual Girth measurements and also the distances from these measurements to the floor.

Several measurements are taken from the same point on the body. These points should be clearly indicated so that the exact same location can be used each time.

Waistline

It is very important to mark the waistline clearly by using velcro or tying a string securely around the waist to maintain a consistent reference around the entire body. Make sure the string is parallel to the floor.

Shoulder Seam /Neckline Point

This is the point where the Shoulder Seam intersects with the Neckline. Mark this with either tape on the body or with a pin through the clothes. If a pin is used, make sure the clothes do not shift as the measurements are taken.

Shoulder Point

In the same manner, clearly mark the point where the Shoulder Seam meets the Sleeve Seam.

The measurements should be taken snugly but not tightly (unless otherwise specified) with the subject standing in a relaxed, upright position. The measurements should be taken over any foundation garments that are going to be worn such as bras, corsets, or padding. They should not be taken over bulky clothing, such as knitted sweaters, as that would distort the measurements.

The approximate length of various measurements are given in brackets [ ]. If the measurements you take do not agree with those in brackets, recheck them carefully.

The list of measurements in the Measurement Chart are all numbered. These numbers will be used throughout the book for easy reference.

While it can be easier to take measurements as a two person process, the images in this book show how you can take your own by tying a string at one end of the tape measure.

Measurement Chart

Body Girth

1. Neck:
2. Neck Width:
3. Shoulder Width:
4. Above Bust (w):
5. Chest (m):
6. Bust (w):
7. Bust to Bust (w):
8. Rib Cage (w):
9. Waist

Body Length

20. Center Front to Waist:
21. Center Front to Rib Cage (w):
22. Center Front to Knee:
23. Center Front to Floor:
24. Side Front to Bust (w):
25. Side Front to Rib Cage (w):
26. Side Front to Waist:
27. Bust to Shoulder (w):
28. Center Front/Waist to Shoulder (m):
29. Center Back:
30. Side Back:
31. Center Back/Waist to Shoulder:
32. Armpit to Waist:

Arm Girth

10. Biceps:
11. Wrist:
12. Palm:

Arm Length

33. Arm Length:
34. Shoulder to Elbow:
35. Sleeve Cap:

Leg Girth

13: Hips:
14. Thigh:
15. Leg Width:
16. Knee:
17. Calf:
18: Ankle:
19. Heel:

Leg Length

36. Waist to Hips:
37. Waist to Knee:
38. Waist to Calf:
39. Waist to Ankle
40. Waist to Floor:
41: Inseam:
42. Crotch Depth:

(w) measurement only applies to women.
(m) measurement only applies to men.

Girth Measurements

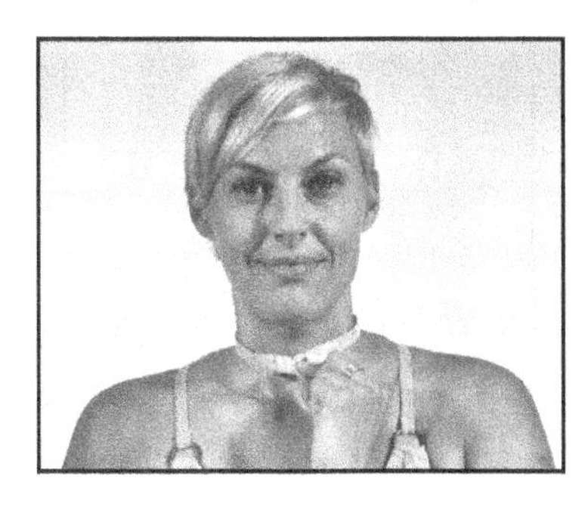

1) NECK - The circumference of the neck should be taken just over the large vertebrae at Center Back and over the collar bone in the front. The tape measure should follow the Neckline as described on page 18. The measurement should be snug but not tight.

2) NECK WIDTH - To take this measurement, put a string around the neck so it hangs down the front of the body. Measure from one side of the string to the other. [For women, this measurement should be between 4" and 5" (10 and 13 cm). For men, it can be up to 6" (15 cm).]

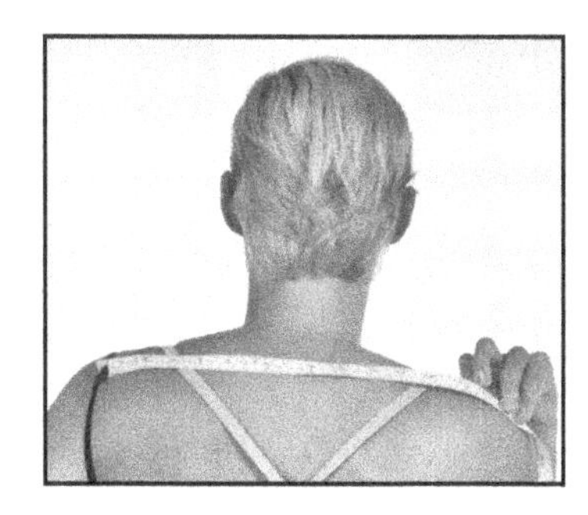

3) SHOULDER WIDTH - This measurement is the distance between the left Shoulder Point and the right Shoulder Point, see page 18. This measurement should be taken across the back. Be sure the tape measure is parallel to the ground.

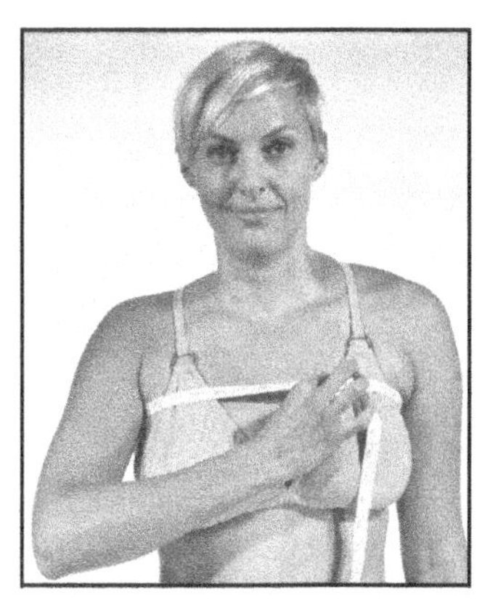

4) ABOVE BUST (Women only) This is the circumference of the rib cage above the bust.

Note: The location of the arm makes it impossible to keep the tape measure parallel to the floor for this measurement. Take this measurement very snugly.

5) CHEST (Men only) - This measurement should be taken around the fullest part of the chest. The tape measure should cross over the shoulder blades in the back.

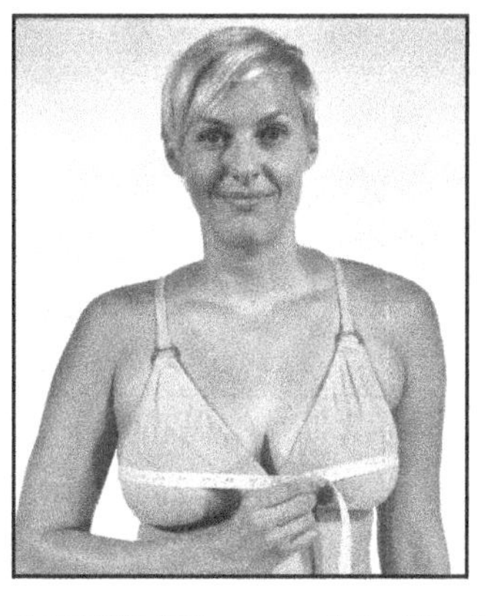

6) BUST (Women only) - The Bust measurement is taken around the fullest part of the bust. It will be over the shoulder blades in the back. Keep the tape measure parallel to the ground.

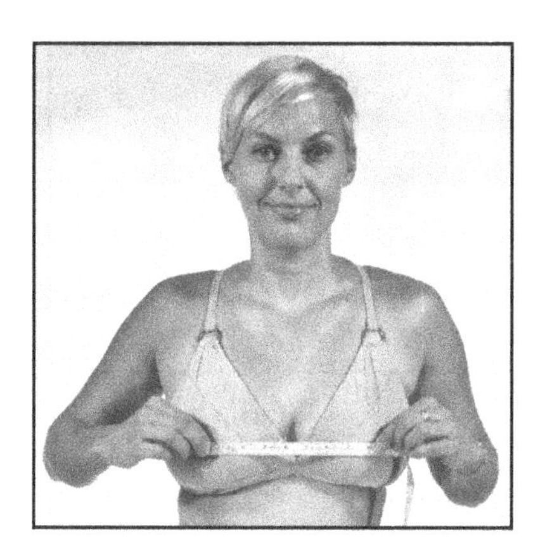

7) BUST TO BUST (Women only) - This measurement is taken from the apex of one bust to the apex of the other.

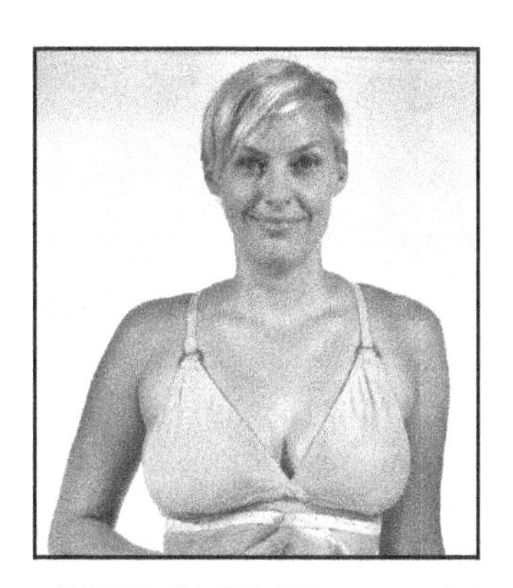

8) RIB CAGE (Women only) - The Rib Cage measurement is taken just below the bust. It does not go over the shoulder blades in back.

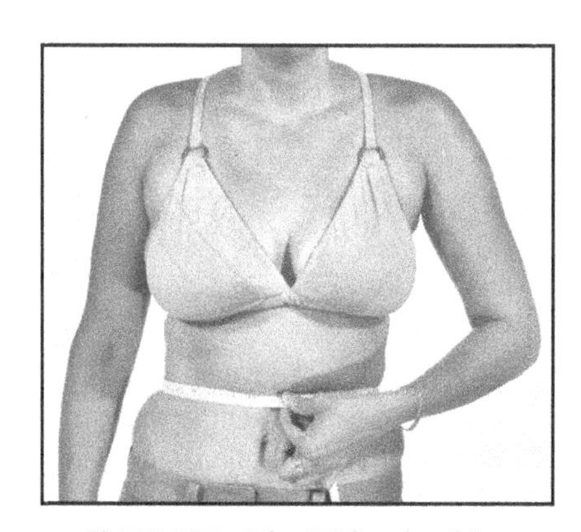

9) WAIST - The Waist should already have a string around it as described earlier. Take the Waist measurement directly over the string.

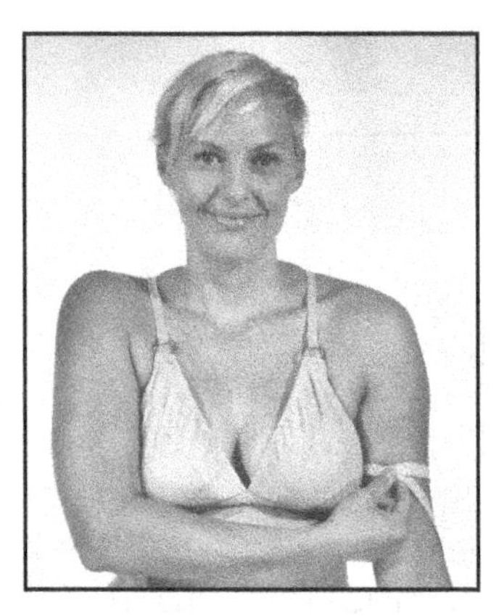

10) BICEPS - The Biceps measurement is around the fullest part of the upper arm.

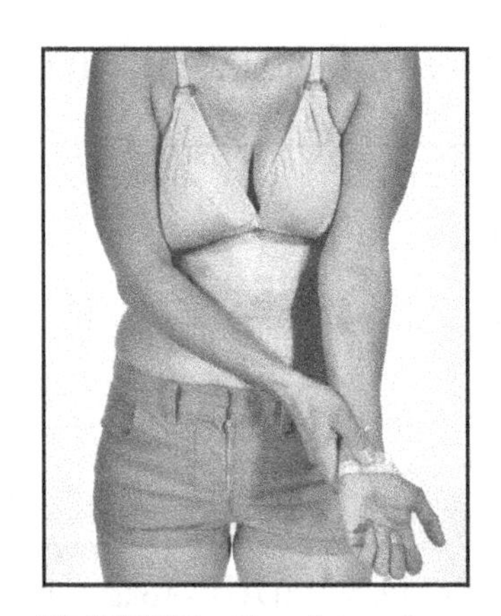

11) WRIST - The circumference of the Wrist is just below the large wrist bone.

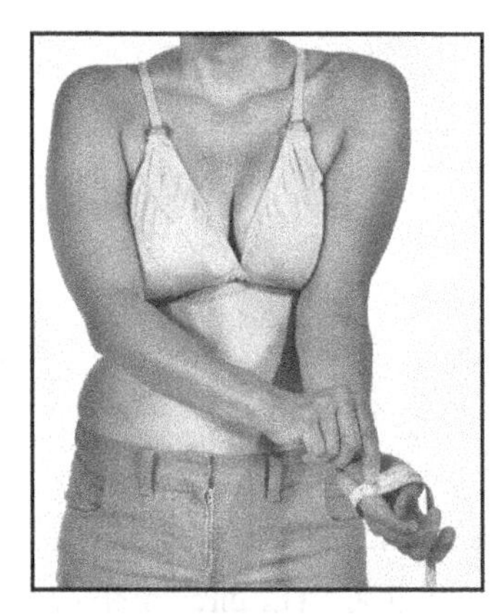

12) PALM - This circumference measurement is taken around the largest part of the hand. This measurement is used to check finished patterns to make sure the hand will be able to get through the finished sleeve.

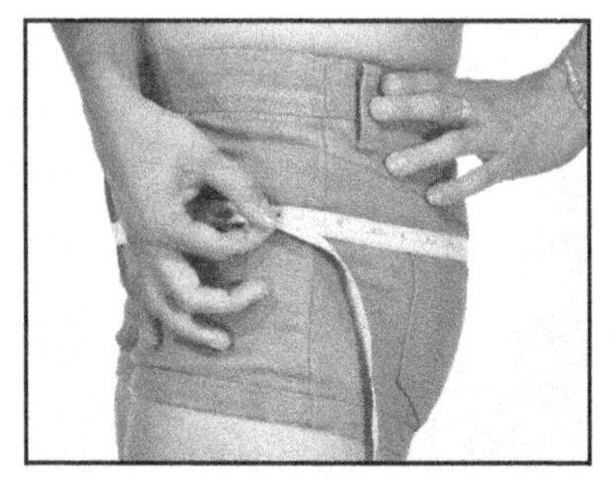

13) HIPS - The Hip measurement is taken over the fullest part of the hips as seen from the side. For some people, the Hip measurement is larger when they sit. So take the Hip measurement both standing and sitting and record the larger of the two measurements.

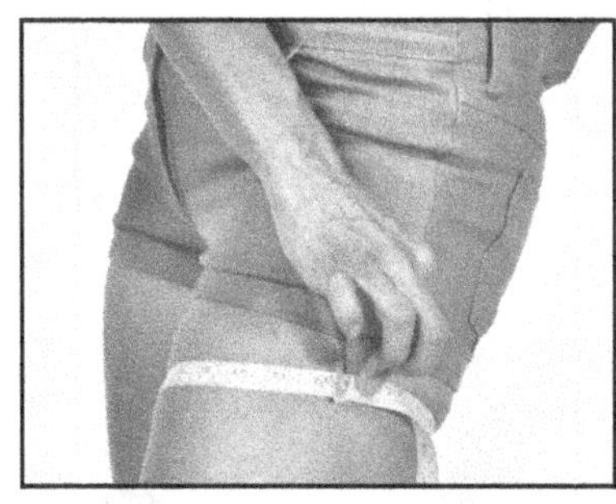

14) THIGH - The Thigh measurement is the circumference of the largest part of the leg near the crotch.

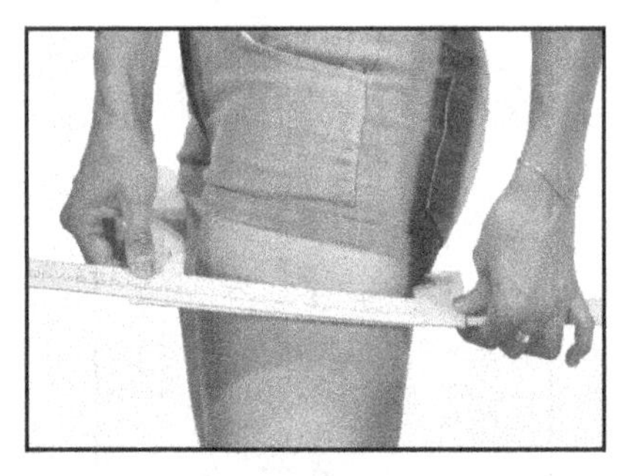

15) LEG WIDTH - The Leg Width is the distance from the front of the leg to the back of the leg. This measurement is taken straight. Two L-squares are used in this photo. [For women, this distance is between 6" and 8" (15 and 20 cm). For men, it is between 7" and 9" (18 and 23 cm).]

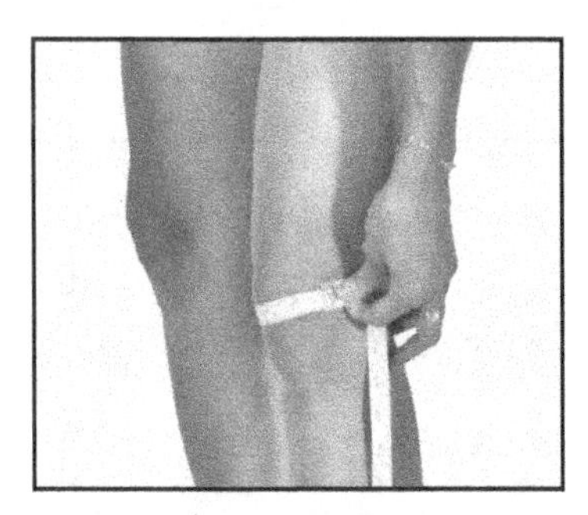

16) KNEE - The Knee measurement is the circumference of the knee directly over the knee cap.

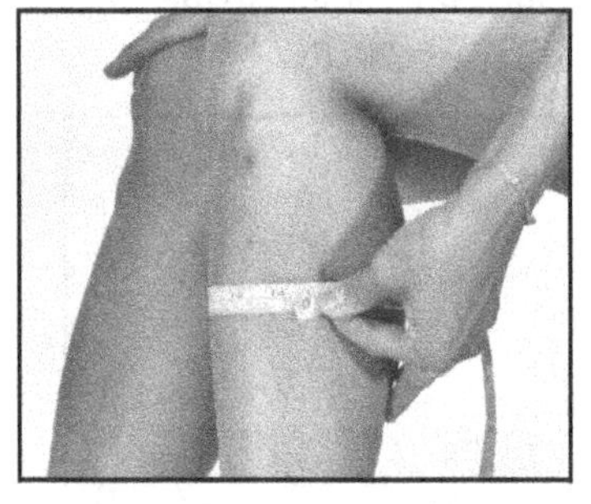

17) CALF - The Calf measurement is the circumference of the calf at the fullest part.

18) ANKLE - The Ankle measurement is the circumference of the ankle at the fullest part.

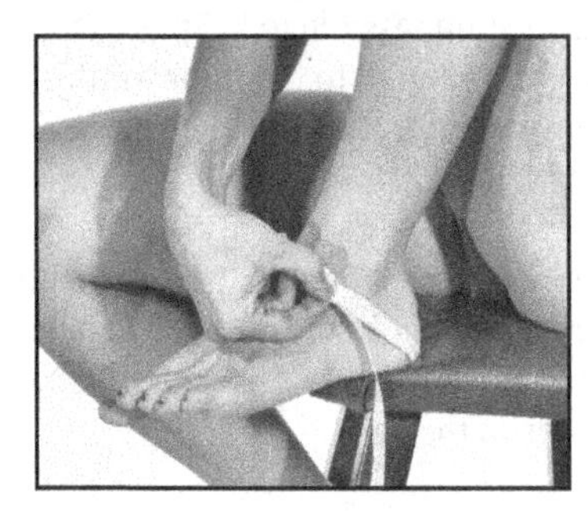

19) HEEL - The Heel measurement is the circumference of the heel at the fullest part. This measurement is used to check finished patterns to make sure the foot will be able to get through the finished garment.

Length Measurements

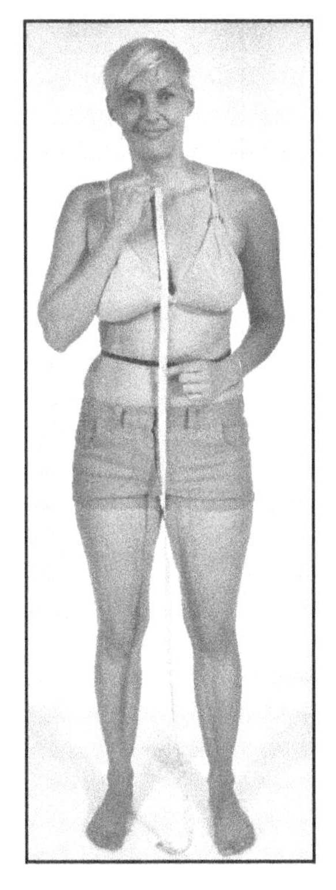

20) CENTER FRONT TO WAIST (Men & Women),
21) CENTER FRONT TO RIB CAGE (Women),
22) CENTER FRONT TO KNEE, and
23) CENTER FRONT TO FLOOR

The Center Front measurements are taken down the middle of the front of the body, starting at the hollow just above the two collar bones. These measurements should establish the locations of the earlier Girth measurements.

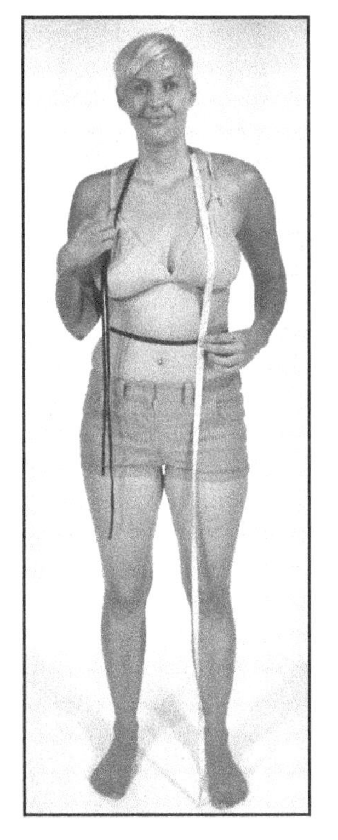

24) SIDE FRONT TO BUST (Women),
25) SIDE FRONT TO RIB CAGE (Women), and
26) SIDE FRONT TO WAIST (Men & Women)

The Side Front measurement starts from the point where the Shoulder Seam meets the Neckline as described on page 18. The tape measure should be kept parallel to the Center Front while these measurements are being taken. [The Side Front to Waist measurement, #26, is usually 3" (8 cm) longer than Center Front to Waist measurement #20.]

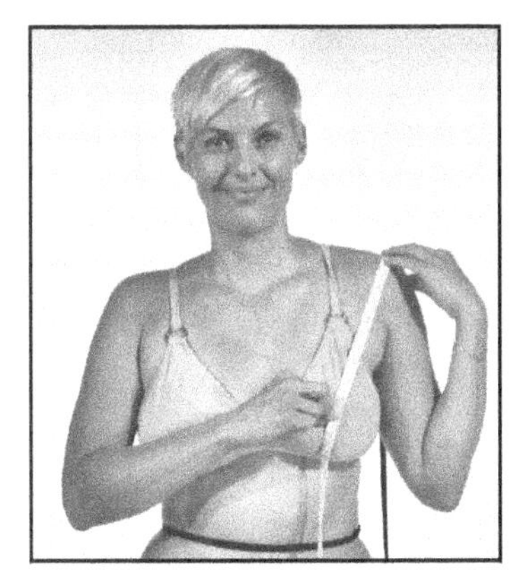

27) BUST TO SHOULDER (Women only) - The Bust to Shoulder measurement is taken diagonally from the Bust Apex to the Shoulder Point.

28) CENTER FRONT/WAIST TO SHOULDER (Men only) - This measurement is taken diagonally from the intersection of the Center Front and the Waist (the navel) to the Shoulder Point.

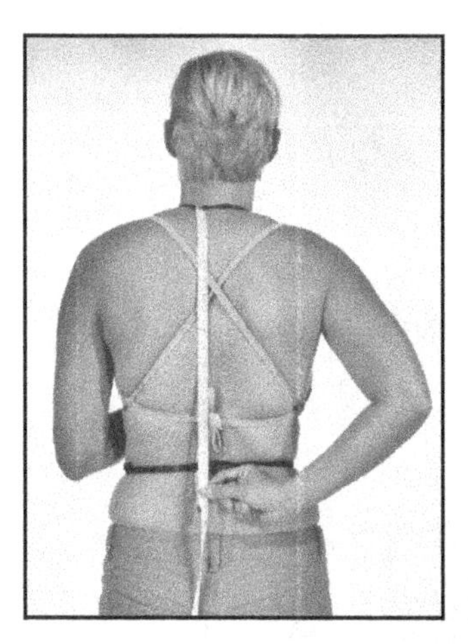

29) CENTER BACK - The Center Back measurement is taken from the top of the large vertebrae on the spinal column to the Waist. In other words, from the Neckline to the Waist.

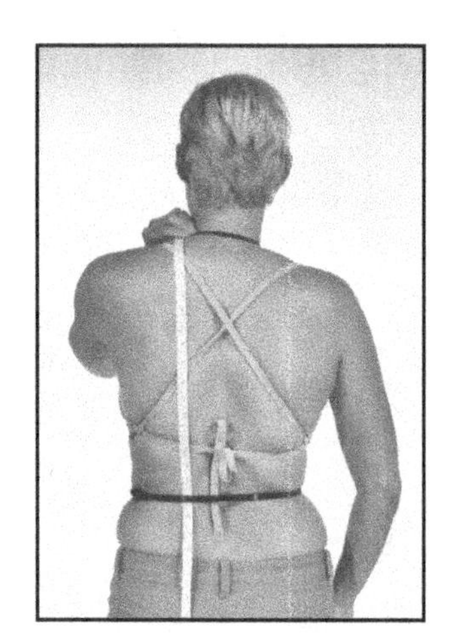

30) SIDE BACK - Starting from the intersection of the Shoulder Seam and the Neckline, measure down to the Waist. The tape measure should be kept parallel to the Center Back. [The Side Back measurement and the Side Front measurement are usually the same length within 1" (2.5 cm) or so. The Side Back measurement is usually 1" (2.5 cm) longer than the Center Back measurement.]

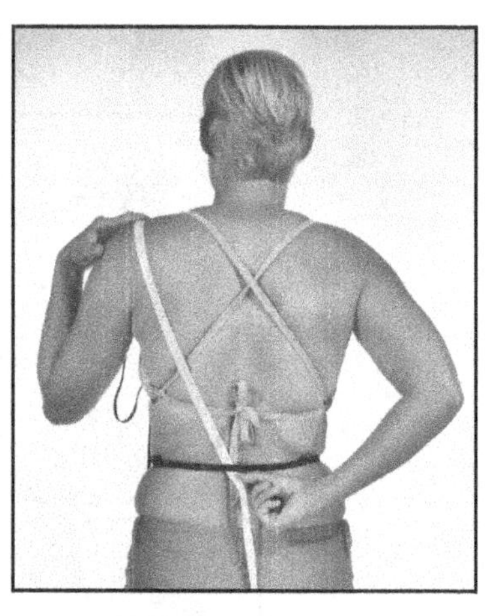

31) CENTER BACK/WAIST TO SHOULDER Measure diagonally from the intersection of the Center Back and the Waist to the Shoulder Point.

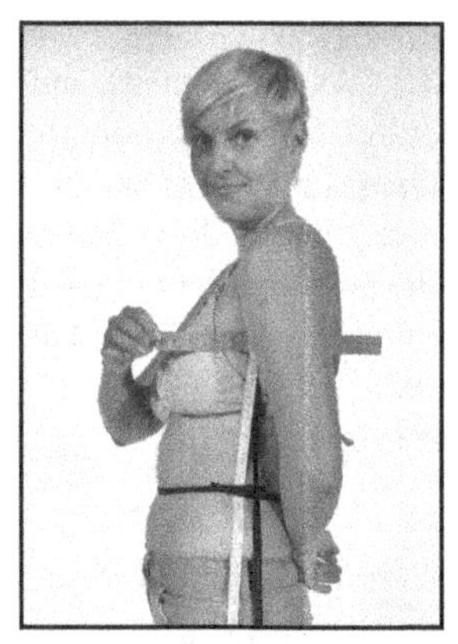

32) ARMPIT TO WAIST - This measurement is taken down the side of the body from under the arm to the Waist. The best way to take this measurement is to attach the tape measure to the middle of a ruler. Place the ruler under the arm so that it is at a comfortable height, but not too low, then measure to the Waist.

33) ARM LENGTH - This measurement is taken from the Shoulder Point to the bottom of the large wrist bone. The arm should be bent to at least a right angle at the elbow. Make sure the tape measure goes over the back of the elbow.

34) SHOULDER TO ELBOW - Measure from the Shoulder Point to the elbow.

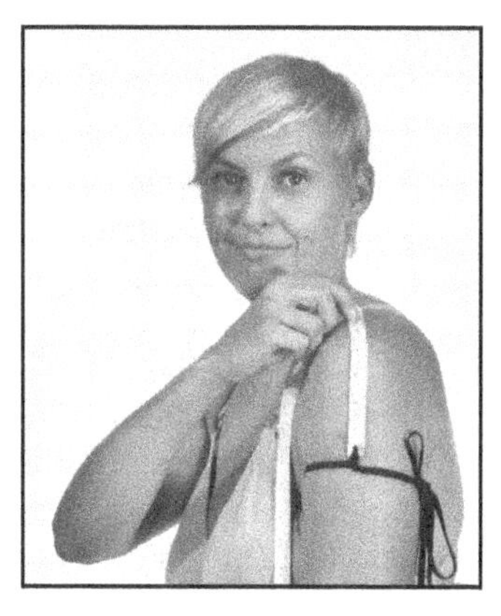

35) SLEEVE CAP - To measure the Sleeve Cap, secure one end of the tape measure to a string at the highest point under the arm. With the arm down at the side of the body, make sure the string is parallel to the floor. Now measure up to the Shoulder Point. [The Sleeve Cap is usually 5" (13 cm).]

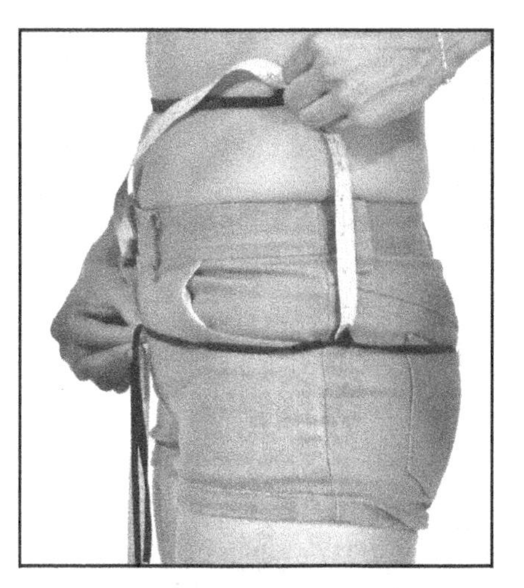

36) WAIST TO HIPS - This measurement is the distance from the Waist to the fullest part of the hips. Take this measurement down the side of the body.

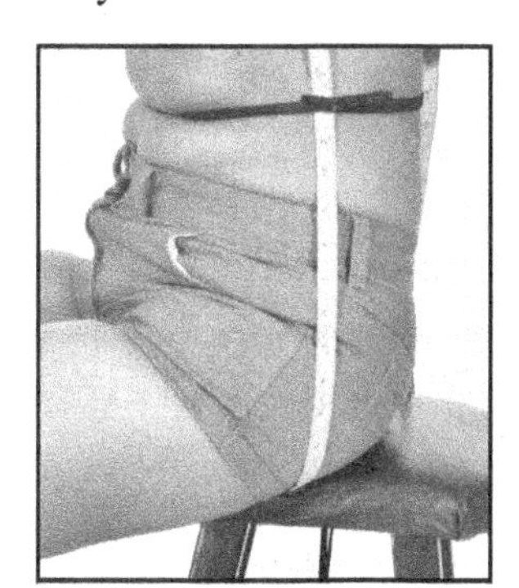

42) CROTCH DEPTH - Have the person being measured sit in a chair and measure up from the chair to the Waist.

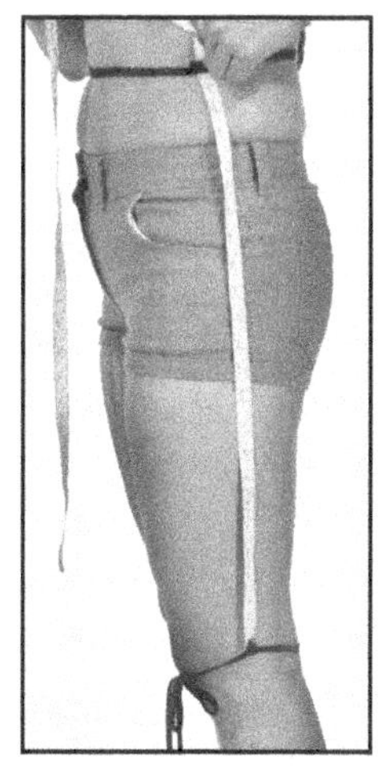

37) WAIST TO KNEE,
38) WAIST TO CALF,
39) WAIST TO ANKLE, and
40) WAIST TO FLOOR

Tie the end of the tape measure to the locations on the body where the Girth measurements were taken, then measure from the knee, calf, ankle, and the floor up the side of the body to the waist.

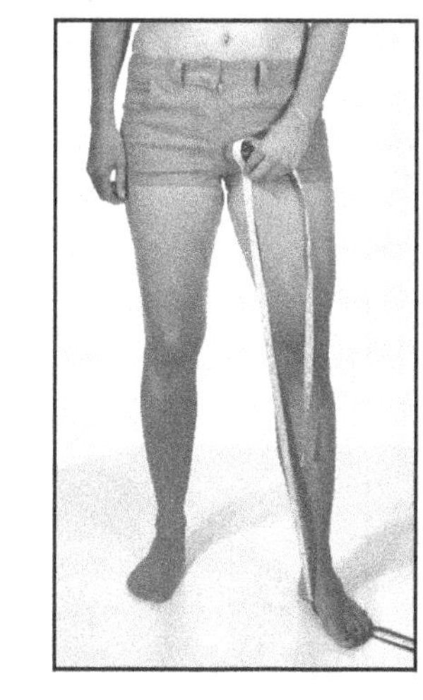

41) INSEAM - This measurement is taken up from the floor to the inside of the leg at the crotch. If you are measuring someone else, have the person who is being measured hold the tape measure in a comfortable position in the crotch.

Using Scale Rulers

When you are drafting the Slopers, you will be creating patterns for either the front half or the back half of the body. Since the Girth measurements are for the full circumference of the body or from one side of the body to the other, you will only need a quarter or a half of each measurement.

You can calculate these fractions in your head or use a calculator. However, an easy and efficient way to determine the necessary dimensions is to use one of the scale rulers in the back of this book. You can either copy the pages for instant use as paper rulers. Or you can make the rulers as described. You can see below how these scale rulers automatically divide the measurements during the drafting process.

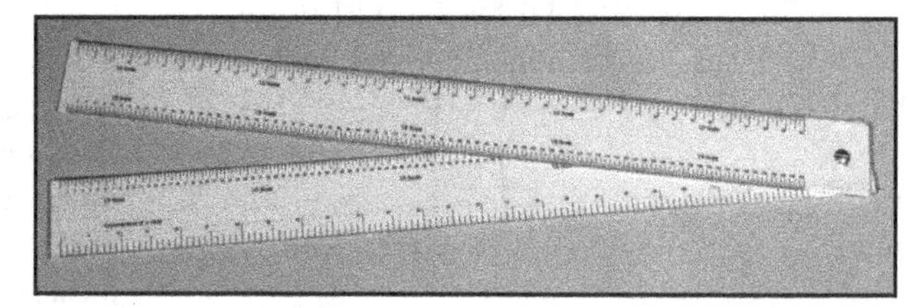

Scale Ruler

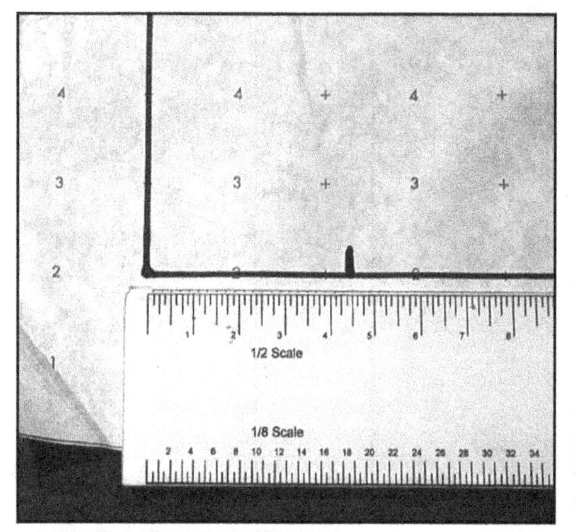

Marking 1/2 Neck Width Measurement (#2)

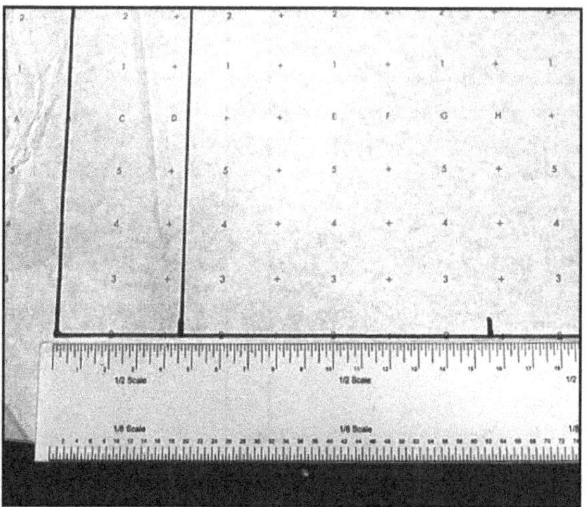

Marking 1/2 Shoulder Width Measurement (#3)

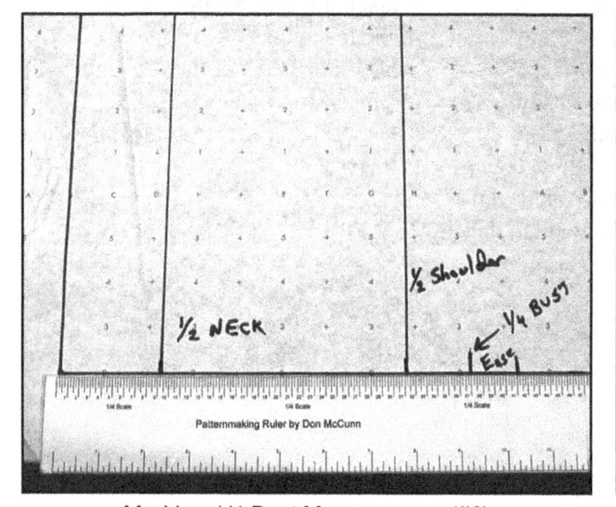

Marking 1/4 Bust Measurement (#6)

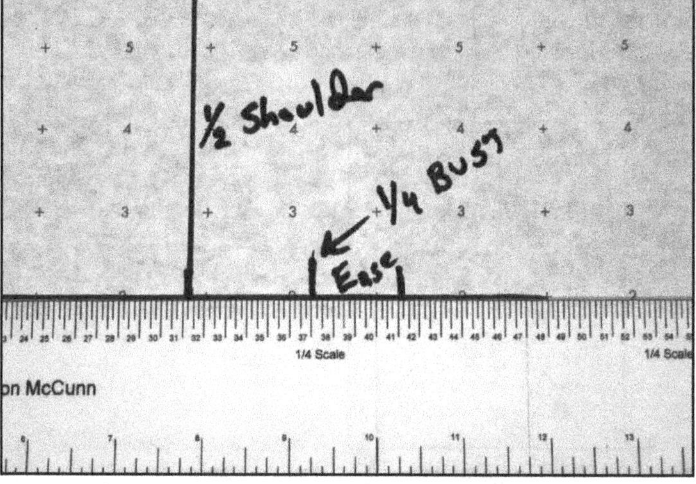

Close Up of Marking 1/4 Bust Measurement (#6)

The Skirt Sloper

This Sloper is presented first because it is the simplest of all the basic patterns. Although skirts are primarily of interest to people making women's clothes, this Sloper records the shape of the waist-to-hip region, so it is also used to create pants and dress forms (aka body doubles) for men as well as women. This Sloper is sometimes referred to as a Lower Torso Sloper.

The Body and the Skirt

The fundamental concept behind this Sloper is that the shape of the waist-to-hip contour can vary widely from person to person. Therefore neither the Side Seam nor the position, size, and shape of the darts should be established when initially drafting the pattern but during the fitting; and the fitting shell made from the pattern must be made wide enough to allow for shaping. For the pattern, establish the basic vertical reference lines: Center Front (CF) and Center Back (CB). Then the horizontal reference lines: Waist, Hip, and Hem (or Knee).

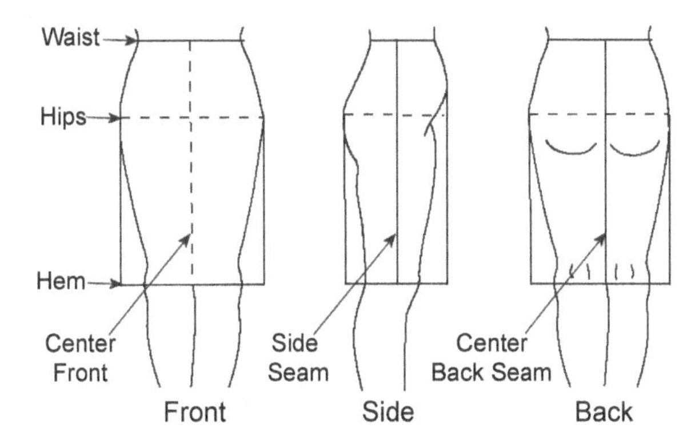

The Hip is the line that follows the horizontal grain of the fabric. If the grain of the fabric is kept parallel to the ground at this point the skirt will hang correctly. If the grain is not parallel to the ground around the entire body, the skirt will pitch forward, backwards, or side ways.

To keep the Hip line parallel to the ground, the skirt must be carefully shaped to follow the contours of the body in the hip-to-waist region. An accurate fit in this region will keep skirts and pants hanging correctly.

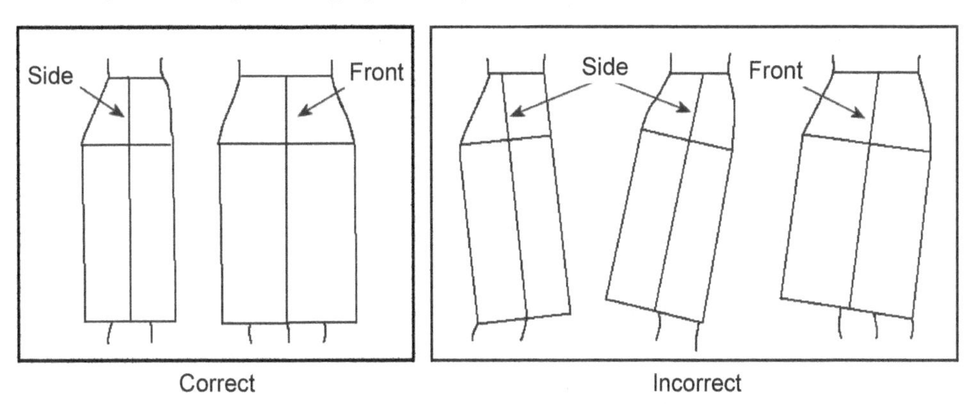

Waist-to-Hip Contours

The shaping of the waist-to-hip region can include several distinct curves. The most obvious ones are the shape of the buttocks and the side where the seam is commonly found. These two shapes at the back and the side are similar in women and men except that men do not have as much of a curve at the side of the body as women.

Women have three other areas for shaping that are less obvious. Since not all women are shaped the same in these areas either, each skirt should be shaped to fit the individual contours of the wearer.

Buttocks

If you look at the body from the side, you can see it curves out from the Waist to the Hips. If you look straight down at the hips you see that the hips also curve around from the Center Back to the side of the body. These two curves of the body at the hips mean that if the fabric is to fit the body, it must have a dart (or a seam).

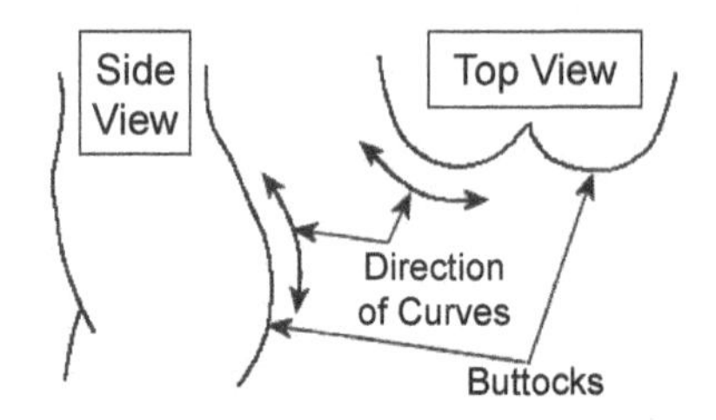

The fullest part of the hips is a gradual curve. If a straight vertical line is drawn at this point, the hips would coincide with it for about 3" (8 cm) of its length. This means that the Hip line can be established anywhere in this area. The recommended area is in the middle of the fullness. The hip dart should stop at the top of this fullness.

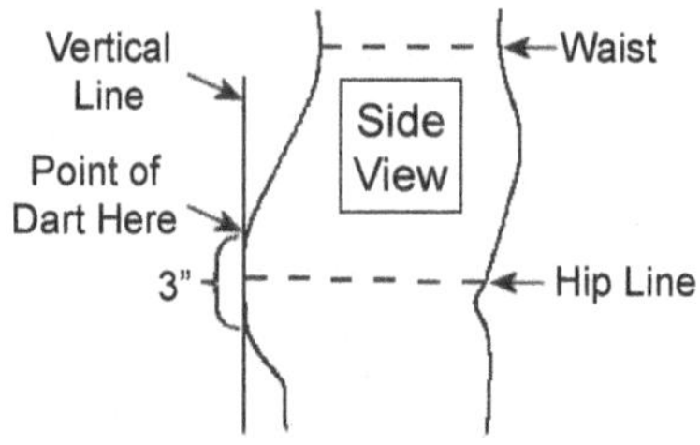
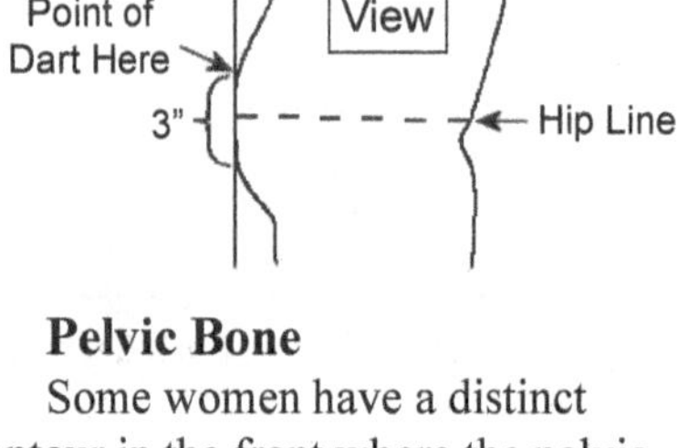

Side of Body

Another obvious set of curves is the side of the body. The body curves out from the Waist down to the Hips. From a top view you can see it also curves around from Center Front to Center Back. If the fabric is to fit smoothly, a dart or seam must be placed here.

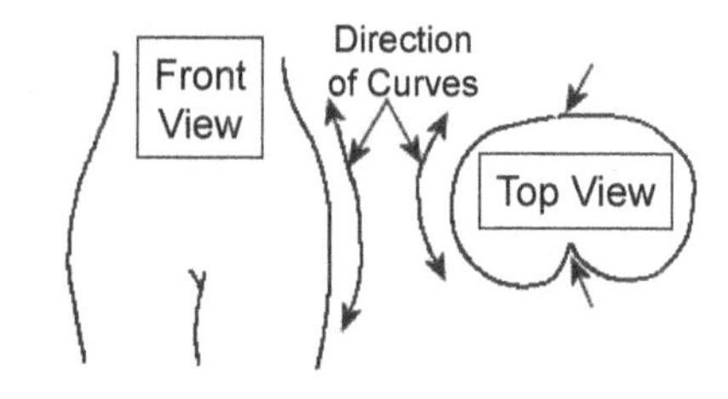

Tummy to Waist

Some women have an indentation above the tummy in to the Waist. This may require a dart about 3" (8 cm) out from the Center Front towards the Side Seam.

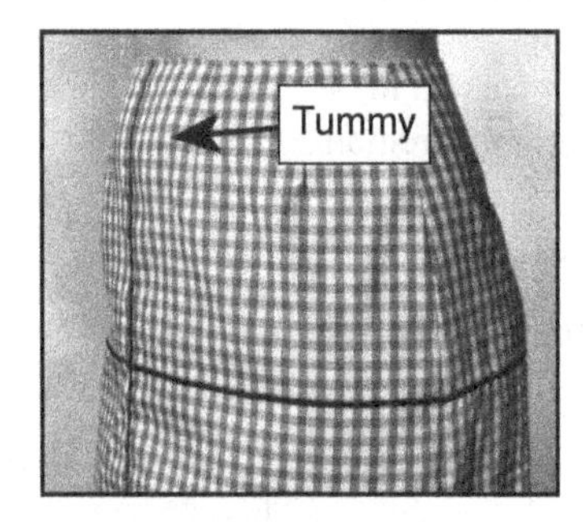

Pelvic Bone

Some women have a distinct contour in the front where the pelvic bone is located. Depending on how much the Waist is indented, this could require a dart.

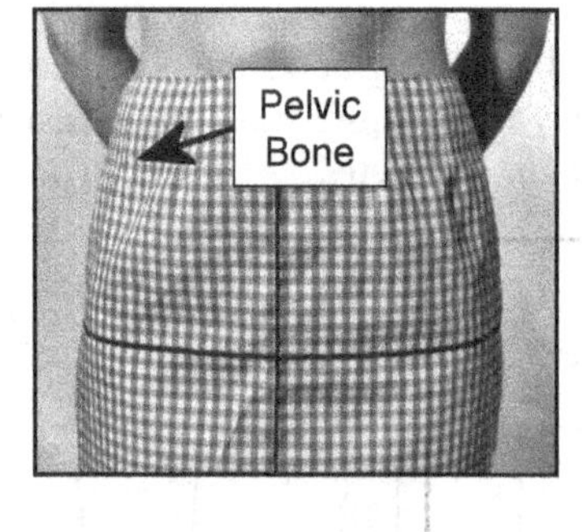

High Hip

Some women have a high hip in the back near the side of the body. This might require an additional dart.

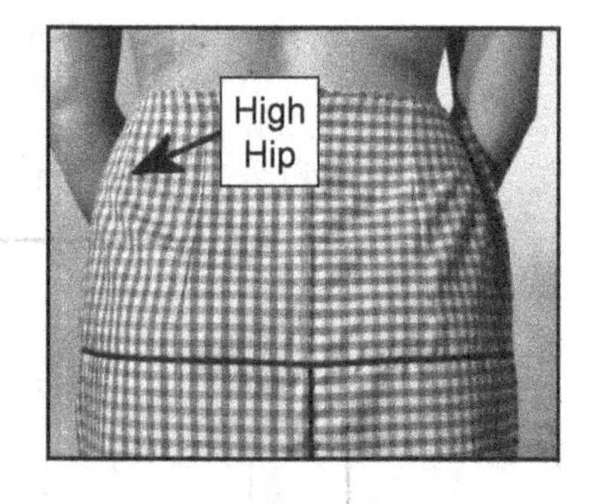

Sway Back Posture

A standard hip dart is a "V" shape. This fits a body that angles straight out from the natural waist to the buttocks. The Sway Back posture is flat from the natural waist down before angling out toward the buttocks. The distance that this contour remains flat varies with each individual's posture.

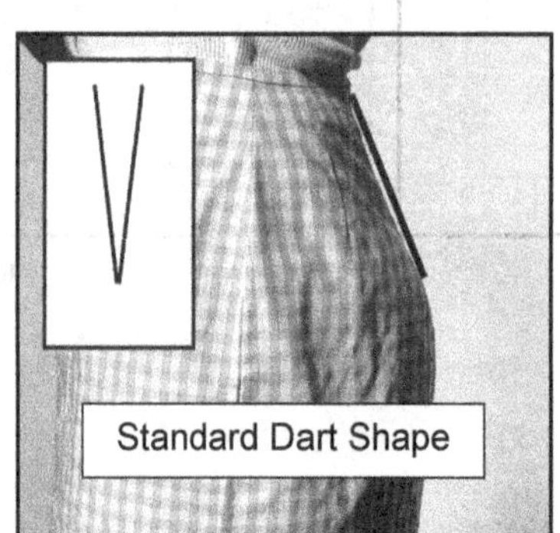

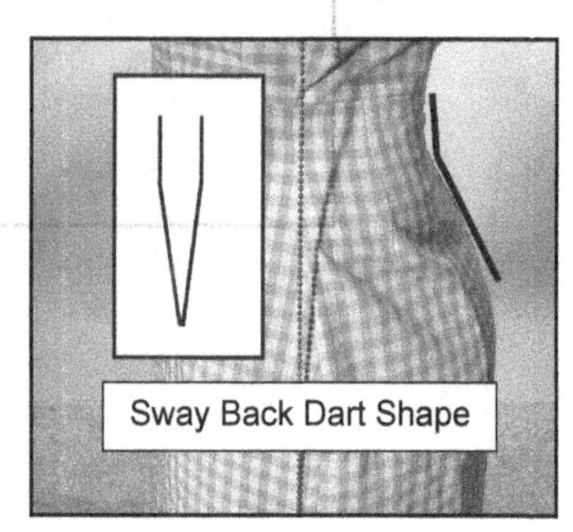

Drafting the Skirt Pattern

The Skirt Sloper is drafted to fit one-fourth of the body. There will be a Side Seam dividing the front from the back. And there will be a Center Front/Center Back line dividing the left side from the right side.

The difference between the front skirt pattern and the back skirt pattern is in the length, size, and location of the darts and the shaping of the Side Seams. These factors will be established in the fitting because it is too difficult to determine the exact shapes from measurements. For the initial draft, the Side Seam is located half way between Center Front and Center Back. Separate patterns for the front and back will be established after the initial fitting. Any adjustments for assymetrical bodies should be made during a subsequent fitting.

The images below show the relationship between the lines of the body and the drafting process.

Step 1 - Draw Waist, CF, & Hem Lines

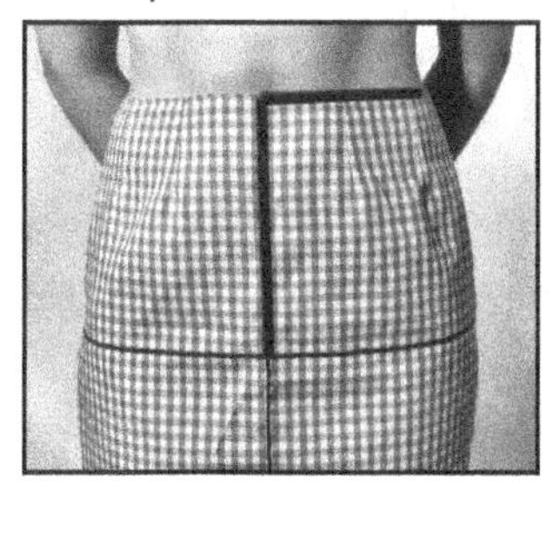

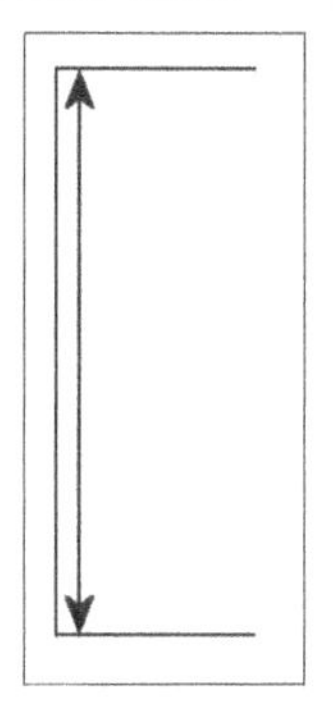

Step 2 - Draw Hip Line

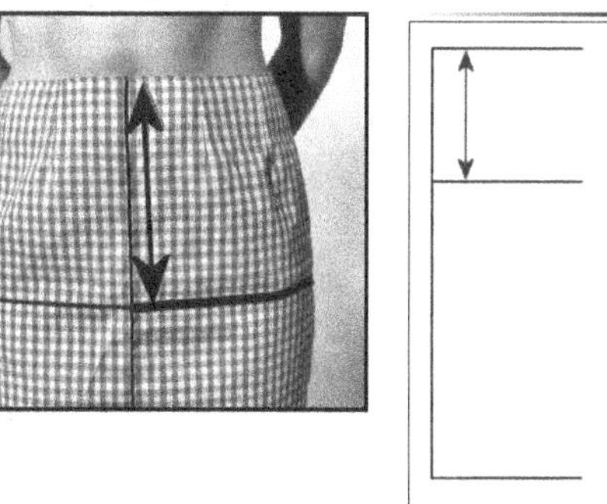

Step 3 - Mark 1/4 Hip Circumference

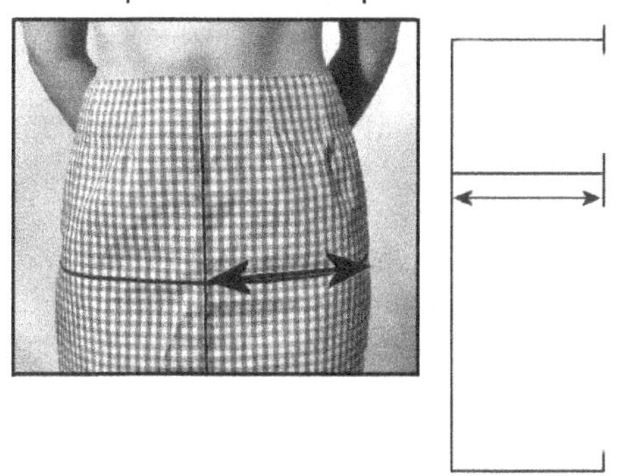

Step 4 - Mark 1/4 Waist Circumference

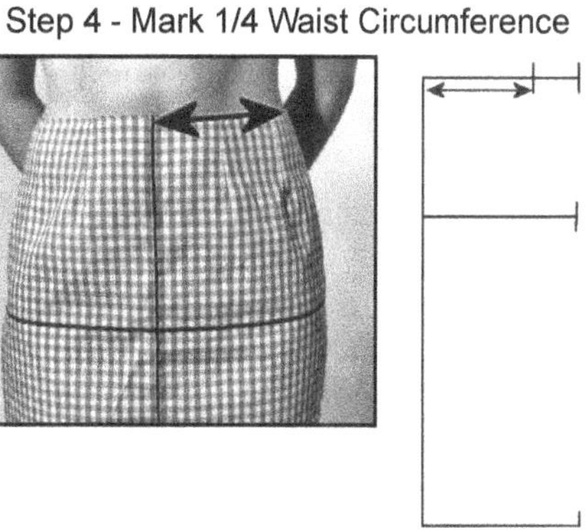

Step 5 - Add Ease & Draw Side Seam

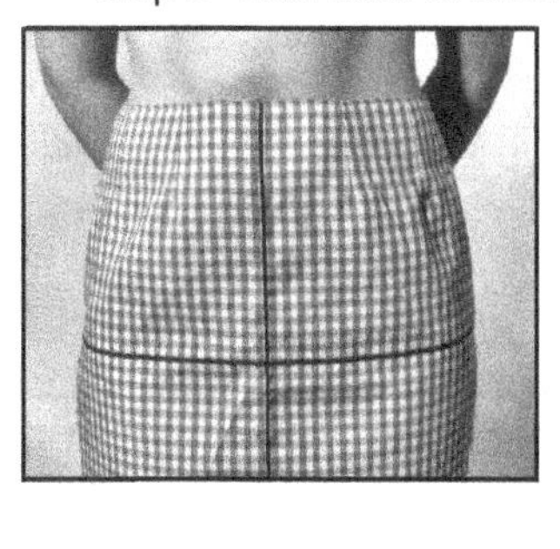

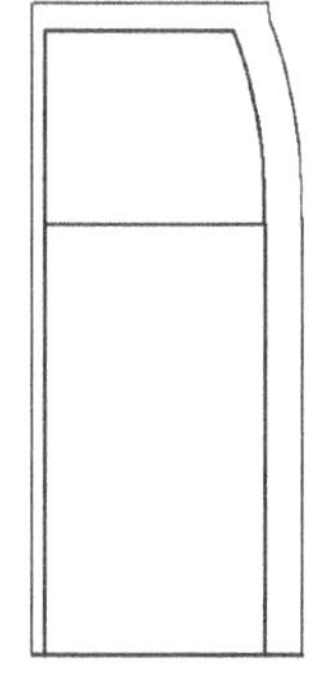

9: Waist:		36. Waist to Hips:	
13. Hips:		37. Waist to Knee:	

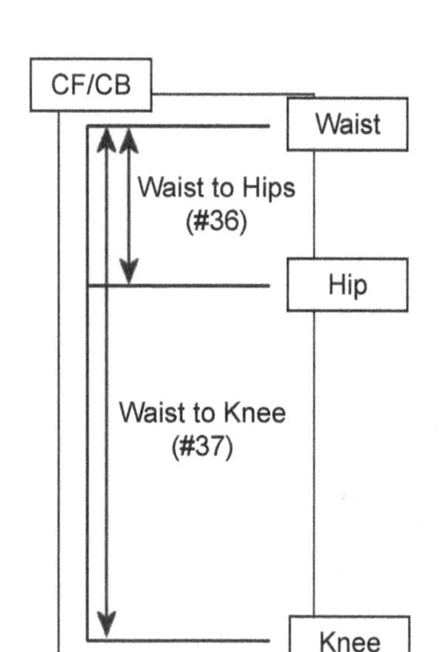

The Basic Reference Lines

Step 1. Cut out a piece of pattern paper that is at least 4" (10 cm) wider than one-fourth the Hip measurement (#13). It should also be 5" (12 cm) longer than the Waist to Knee measurement (#37), or the desired Waist to Hem length.

Step 2. Draw a vertical line 1" (25 mm) in from the edge of the paper. Mark off the Waist to Knee measurement (#37) on this line. This line is the Center Front/Center Back (CF/CB) line of the skirt.

Step 3. At the top of the Waist to Knee length, draw a line at right angles to the Center Front/ Center Back line. This will be the Waist line.

Step 4. At the bottom of the Waist to Knee length, draw another line at right angles to the Center Front/Center Back line. This is the Hem line.

Step 5. On the Center Front/Center Back line, measure down from the Waist line the Waist to Hip measurement (#36). At this point, draw another line at right angles to the Center Front/Center Back line. This is the Hip line.

This establishes the basic reference lines for the skirt pattern. Measurements may now be made from the Center Front/Center Back line to establish the location of the Side Seam.

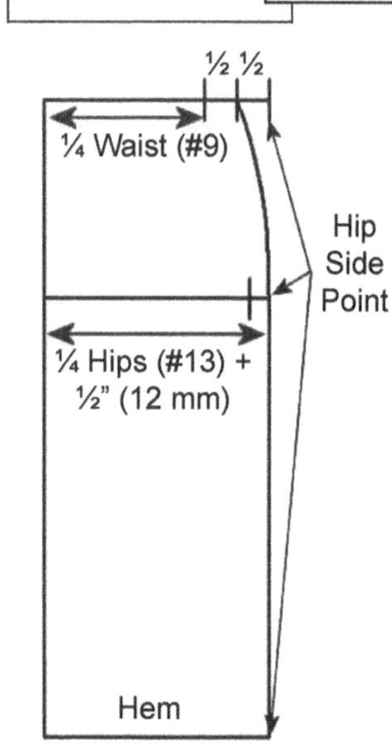

The Side Seam

Step 6. Measure out from the Center Front/Center Back line one-fourth of the Hip measurement (#13) plus ½" (12 mm) on the Waist, Hip, and Hem lines, making a mark on each line. These will be the Side Hip points.

The Hip measurement is divided into fourths because the pattern is to cover one-fourth of the body. A ½" (12 mm) is added to this measurement to allow for ease of movement.

Step 7. On the Waist line, mark off one-fourth of the Waist measurement (#9). This will be the Side Waist mark.

Step 8. To shape the Side Seam, find a point on the Waist line that is half way between the Side Waist point and the Side Hip point. The Side Seam will start here. Curve this out and down toward the Side Hip point on the Hip line.

This line should curve out the most in the top 3" (76 mm) of the Side Seam because women's bodies have the greatest amount of curve from the Waist to the hip bone on the side of the body.

The Side Seam is not curved all the way into the Waist measurement because some allowance must be left in the fabric for the darts. Only part of the body's curve is at the side. The rest is in the front and back and this will be shaped with darts. The specific shape of this curve will be adjusted during the fitting.

Step 9. From the Side Hip point on the Hip line continue the Side Seam straight down to the Side Hip point on the Hem line.

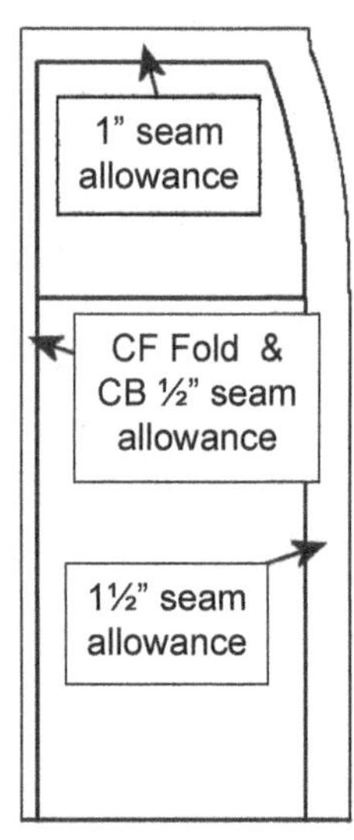

Seam Allowances

The pattern is created using seam lines. For the fabric fitting shell, seam allowances need to be added. The seam allowances for the fitting shell need to be wide enough that adjustments can be made during the fitting.

Step 10. In a skirt of this type, the front section is normally cut out of a single piece of fabric. The Center Front line will therefore be a fold line, so no seam allowances are added. The Center Back, on the other hand, is usually a seam. It will not be shaped so the seam allowance can be a standard sewing seam allowance.

Step 11. Add a 1½" (38 mm) seam allowance to the Side Seam.

Step 12. Add a 1" (25 mm) seam allowance to the Waist line.

Initial Fitting of the Skirt

This initial pattern is based on a body's circumference and length measurements. But these measurements do not reveal where the contours of the body change and every body is unique. So the only way to accurately determine where these contours occur is to fit fabric to the body.

The instructions in this section show how to use a gingham fitting shell made from the initial patterns to convert the two-dimensional pattern to the three-dimensional shape of the body. This is achieved by keeping the vertical grain of the fabric at Center Front and Center Back at right angles to the floor and the horizontal grain of the fabric at the hips parallel to the floor. Adjust the darts and the Side Seam so the vertical grain of the fabric is maintained at right angles to the floor at different locations around the body.

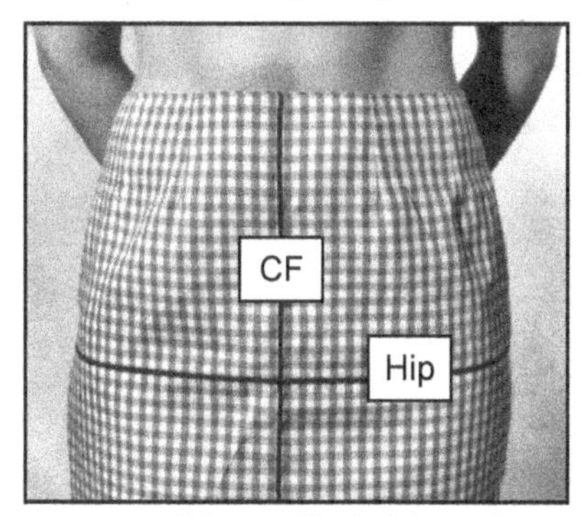

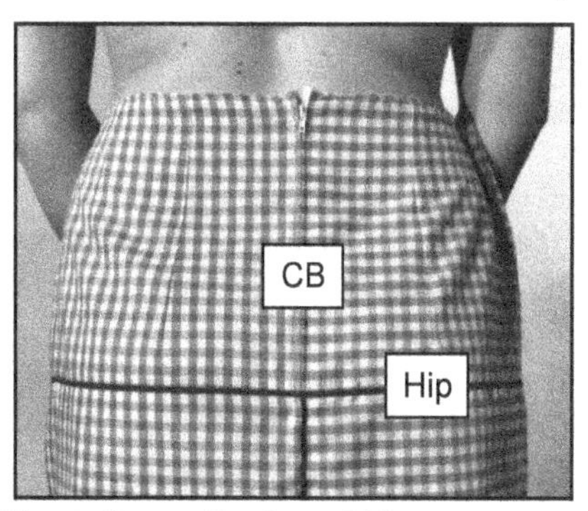

Primary Grain Lines: Center Front, Center Back, and Hips

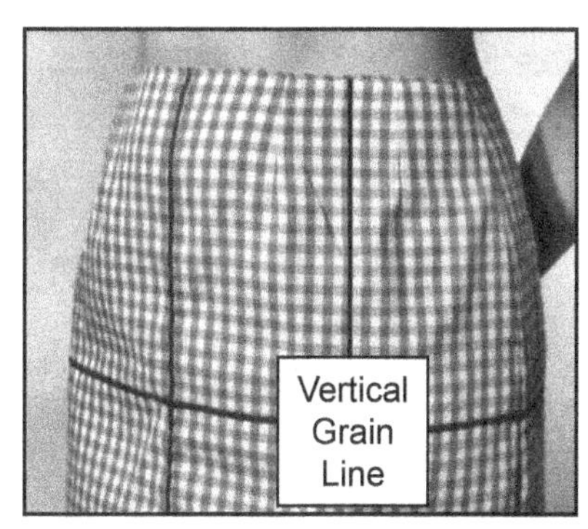

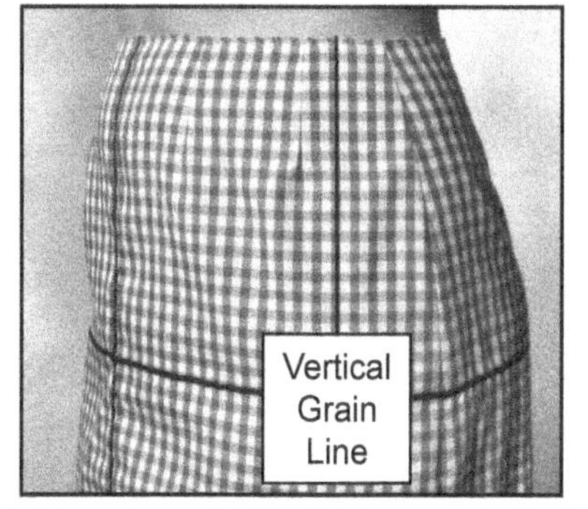

Darts Keep the Vertical Grain Aligned

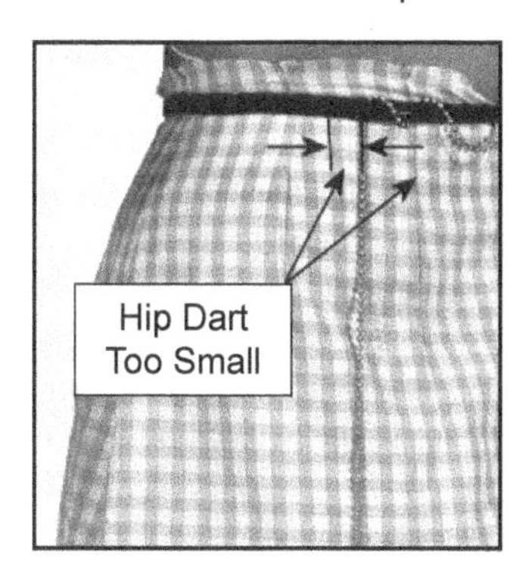

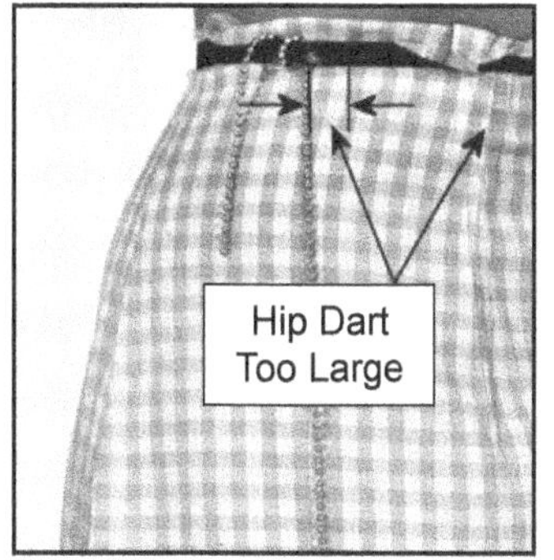

The two examples above show what the grain looks like when a dart is not adjusted to the contours of the body. The weighted chain in the photo indicates a line that is at right angles to the floor. When the dart is too small at the waist, the vertical grain will be too close to the Side Seam. When the dart is too large, the grain is pulled toward Center Back.

Create a Fitting Shell for the Skirt

Use the paper pattern to cut a fitting shell. The front can be cut on the fold. The back should have a seam. Sew the back from the hip to the hem. You can either leave the top of the back seam open or sew in a 7" (18 cm) zipper. Do not sew the Side Seam at this time. You can mark the Center Front and the Hip line on the fitting shell.

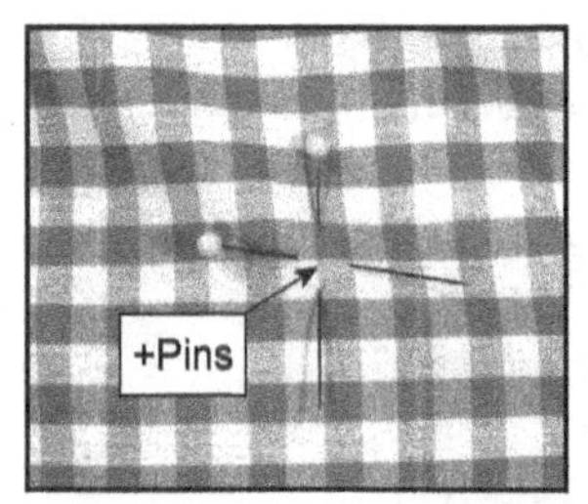

Pins to Mark Dart Point

Initial Skirt Fitting Process

During the initial fitting, mark the point of each dart indicating a vertical and horizontal position, then mark the width of the darts at the waist. It is easier to establish the lines of the darts when you record them on the paper pattern. Don't overwork the darts during the first fitting.

Fit only one side of the body. If the body is asymmetrical, fit the larger or higher side first. Adjust for the asymmetrical shape during subsequent fittings. This prevents over emphasizing the difference in the two sides of the body.

Fit the Hip (Buttocks) Dart (men and women)

The hip dart is a good one to start with because this contour is the easiest to identify. A good way to determine where the point of the hip dart should be located is to back up against a wall. The dart's point should be where the body breaks away from the wall in both a vertical and a horizontal direction.

If you are doing the fitting as a Do-It-Yourself process, see the instructions found on page 35.

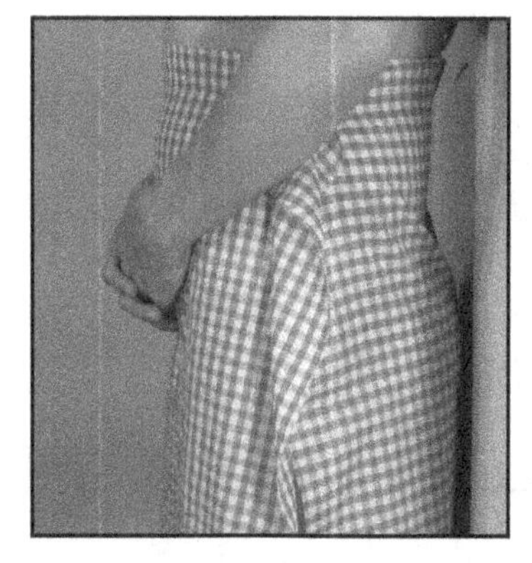

Step 1. Put the fitting shell on and secure it at the waist.

Step 2. Verify that the Center Front and Center Back are at right angles to the floor.

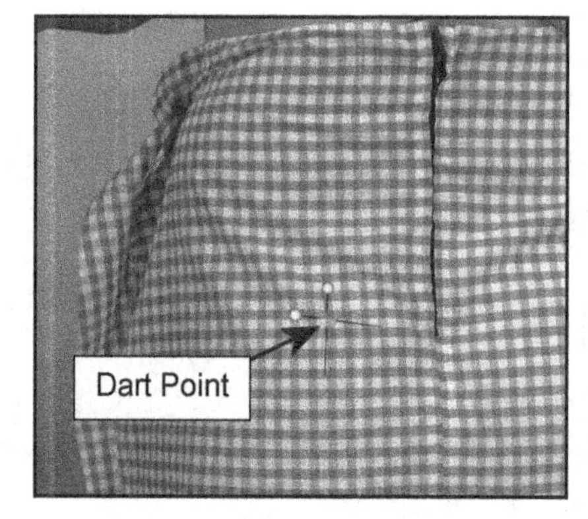

Step 3. Locate where the top of the hips angle in toward the waist, then mark with a horizontal pin.

Step 4. Locate where the hips angle away from Center Back and toward the side of the body, then mark with a vertical pin.

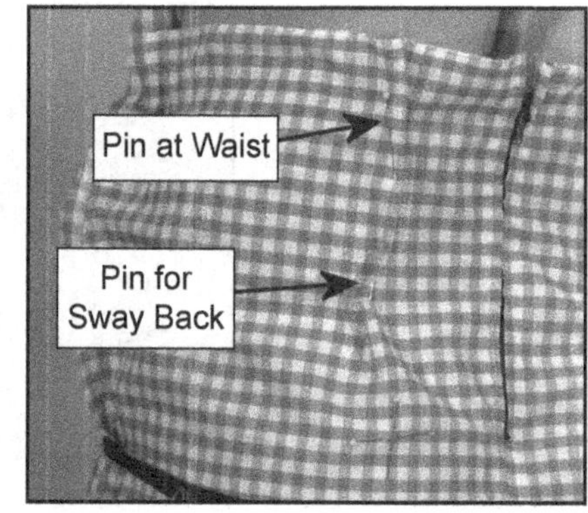

Step 5. At the waist, adjust the fabric so the vertical grain at the side back is at right angles to the floor, then pin the dart width.

Step 6. If the body has a sway back, determine the location where the flat back angles out to the hips. Use a horizontal pin to indicate the distance down from the waist and a vertical pin to pin the dart width at this location.

Fit the High Hip Dart (women only)

If you are doing the fitting as a DIY process, see the instructions on page 35.

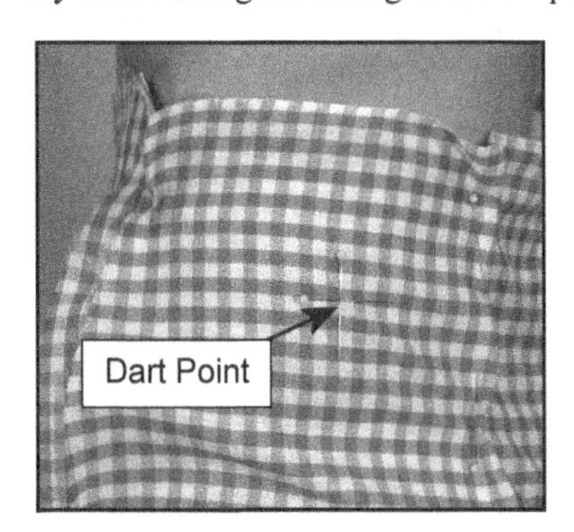

Step 1. If the body does not have a high hip shape, proceed to the shaping for the front of the fitting shell.

Step 2. Locate where the high hip shape angles in toward the waist, then mark with a horizontal pin.

Step 3. The High Hip dart can be located half way between the hip dart and the Side Seam. Mark this location with a vertical pin.

Step 4. At the waist, adjust the fabric so the vertical grain at the side is at right angles to the floor, then pin the dart width.

Fitting the Front Tummy Dart (women only)

The contour of a woman's front is a more gradual shape than the hips. This means the darts will be shorter and smaller than the hip dart. Establishing these darts requires a certain amount of discretion. Some women need two darts, others only one or none. Generally, it is a good idea to locate darts so they divide the distance from the Center Front to the Side Seam into thirds. It is easiest to establish these locations when transferring the darts to a paper pattern.

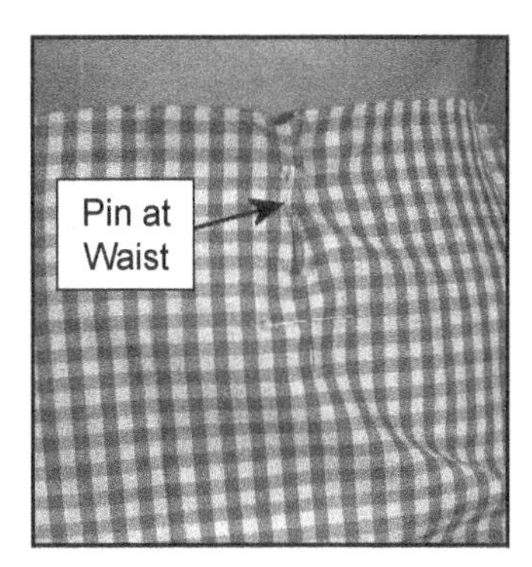

Step 1. If there is a contour near Center Front at the tummy, locate where the tummy angles in toward the waist, then mark with a horizontal pin.

Step 2. Darts for the tummy should be located approximately 1/3 of the way between the Center Front and the Side Seam. Use a vertical pin to mark this location.

Step 3. At the waist, adjust the fabric so the vertical grain at the side front is at right angles to the floor, then pin the dart width.

Fitting the Front Pelvic Bone Dart (women only)

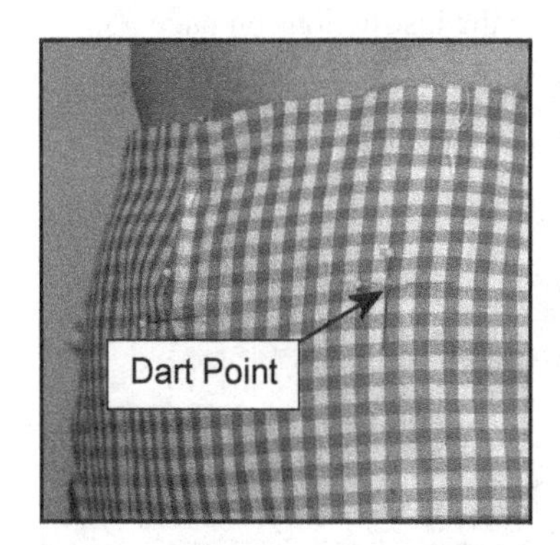

Step 1. If there is a contour at the pelvic bone, locate where the pelvic bone shapes in toward the waist, then mark with a horizontal pin.

Step 2. The shape for the pelvic bone dart can be located 2/3 of the way between Center Front and the Side Seam. Use a vertical pin to mark this location.

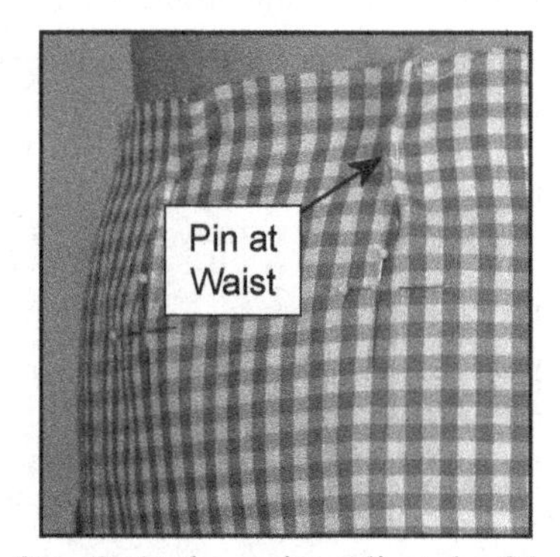

Step 3. At the waist, adjust the fabric so the vertical grain at the side is at right angles to the floor, then pin the dart width.

The Side Seam (men and women)

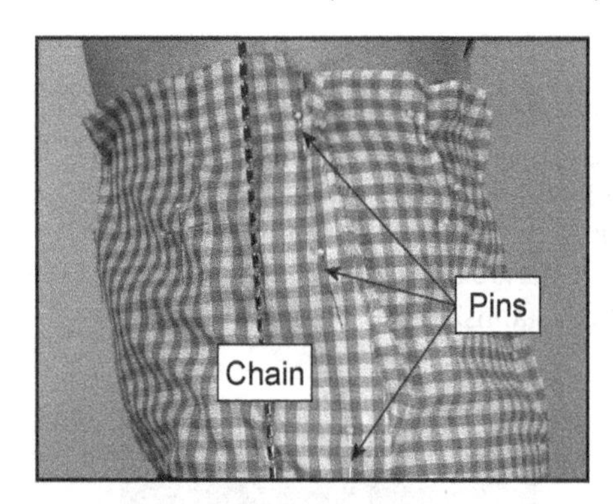

Step 1. To determine the location of the Side Seam, use two L squares to find a point that is half way between the front and the back of the body at the fullest part of the hips. Use a pin to mark this location.

Step 2. Pin the Side Seam close to the body straight up from the hips to the waist.

Step 3. Use a weighted chain to verify that the Side Seam is at right angles to the floor.

Initial Do-It-Yourself Fitting

When two people are doing a fitting, the entire pinning process can be accomplished without removing the fitting shell. When fitting yourself, follow the sequence below:

1. Fit the back as described below.
2. Remove the fitting shell and record the darts, see page 37.
3. Fit the front, see page 33.

Pinning requires the use of two hands; taping can be done with one. So an alternative to pinning during fittings is to use tape, such as masking tape, to hold the darts and seams together.

Modify the Fitting Shell

To fit the back, use two lengths of bias tape as a second pair of hands. Cut these bias tapes so they are 24" (60 cm) longer than your Waist Measurement (#9). Use a zigzag stitch to sew one of the bias tapes for about 3" (8 cm) just to one side of the Center Back seam. Sew the other bias tape to the back close to the Side Seam.

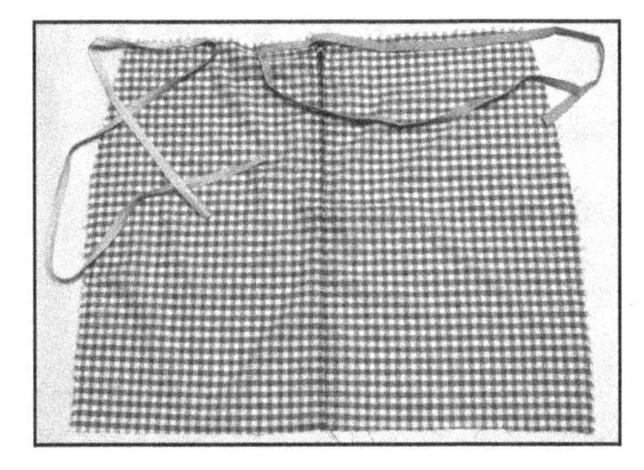

Fitting the Hip Dart

The hip dart is the easiest to identify. If you back up to a wall, you can see and feel where the hip breaks away from the wall in both horizontal and vertical directions. This identifies the location for the dart's point.

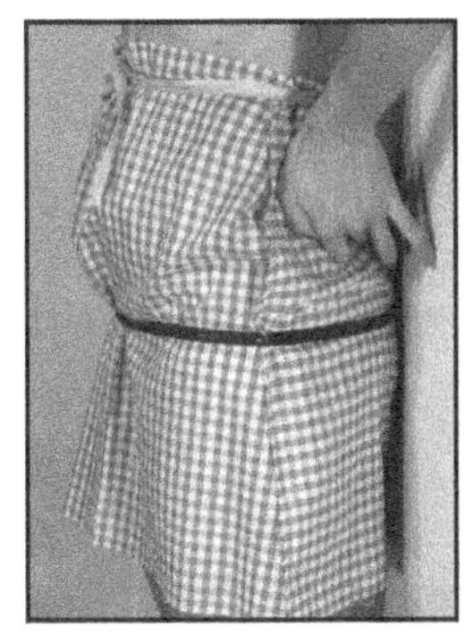

Step 1. Put the fitting shell on and use bias tapes to secure it at the waist.

Step 2. Verify that the Center Back is at right angles to the floor.

Step 3. Back up to a wall to locate where the hips angle away from the wall in both the horizontal and vertical directions, then make a mark. This will be the dart's point.

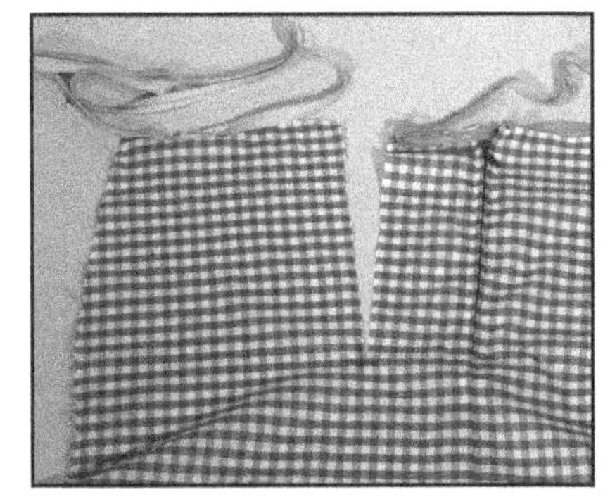

Step 4. Remove the fitting shell, then draw a line following the vertical grain from the dart's point to the waist.

Step 5. Cut the fitting shell along the line drawn in Step 4, then put the fitting shell back on.

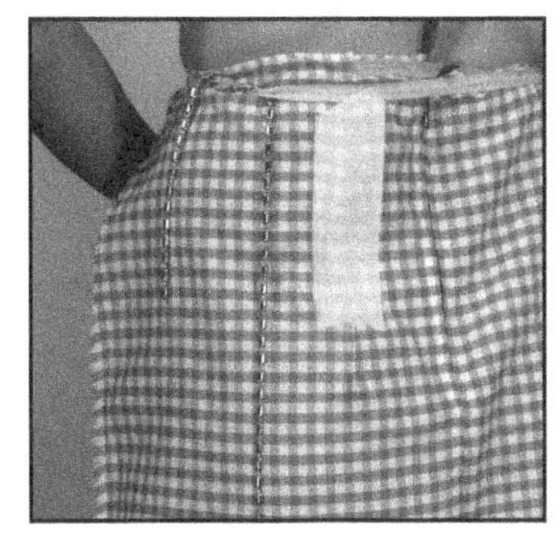

Step 6. Use a weighted chain to adjust the vertical grain on the side of the dart closest to the Side Seam.

Step 7. Smooth the fabric so the vertical grain is correct on both sides of the dart, then tape the dart closed.

Fitting the High Hip Dart

Not all women will require a High Hip dart. When in doubt, it is easier to check this during a second fitting after the more obvious darts are sewn.

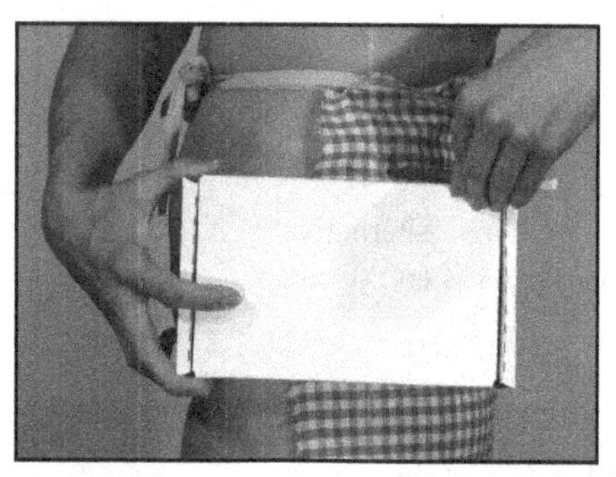

Step 1. Use a flat object such as a book to locate where the high hip shape angles up toward the waist.

Step 2. Make a mark and remove the fitting shell.

Step 3. The High Hip dart can be located half way between the hip dart and the Side Seam. Mark this location for the dart's point.

Step 4. Draw a line following the vertical grain from the dart's point to the waist.

Step 5. Cut the fitting shell along the line drawn in Step 4, then put the fitting shell back on.

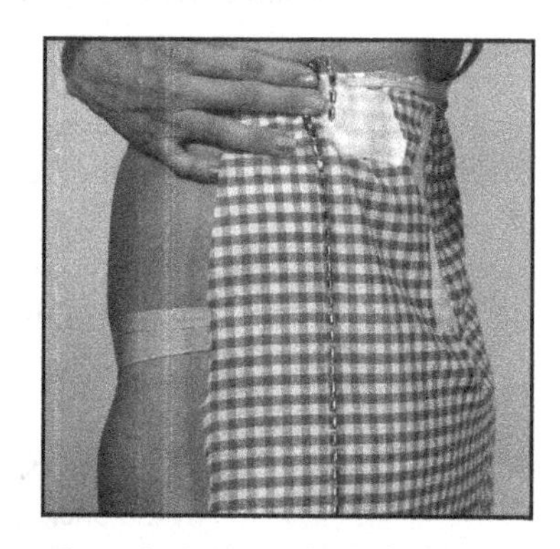

Step 6. Use a weighted chain to adjust the vertical grain close to the Side Seam.

Step 7. Smooth the fabric so the vertical grain is positioned correctly on both sides of the dart, then tape the dart closed.

Record the Skirt Darts

After you have established the locations of the darts in the initial fitting, they should be recorded on paper patterns so you can fine tune their shaping as well as their locations. For example, no matter how careful you are in the fitting, it is possible that you will not have the dart width centered over the dart's point. To perfect this placement during the fitting can be very time consuming. Doing it when the dart markings are transferred to paper is quick and easy.

Record the Back Skirt Darts

The back darts for the DIY fitting were created by overlapping the fabric for the dart and taping it in place. The dart width is determined by measuring how much the fabric overlaps at the waist. Use half this width for each side of the dart centerlines for Step 7 below.

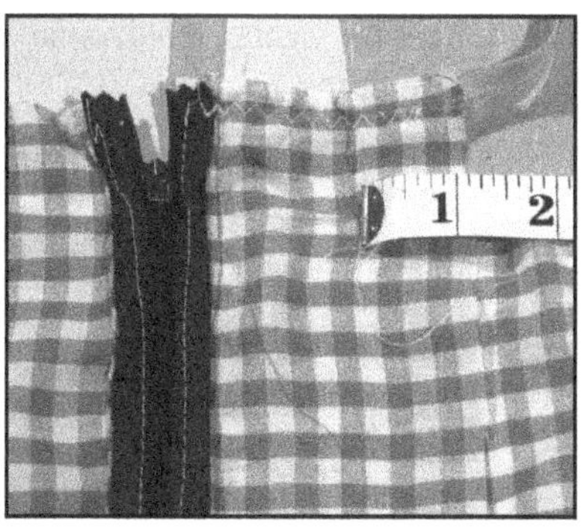

Measuring Width of Taped Dart

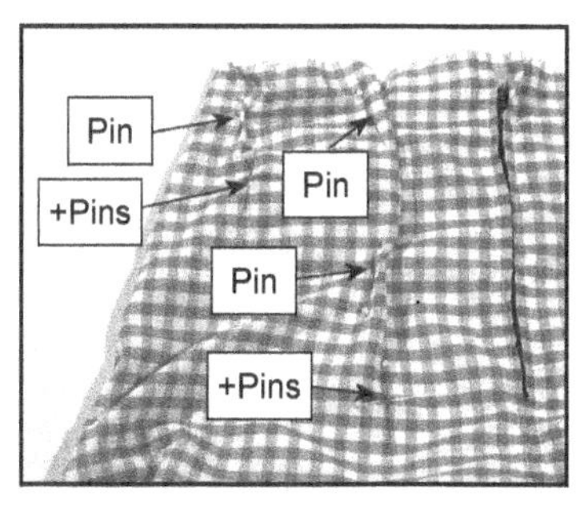

Step 1. On the fitting shell, mark the locations of the pins for both darts. If the dart was pinned for a sway back, mark the location where the change in the dart occurs.

Step 2. On the fitting shell, mark the dart widths at the waist.

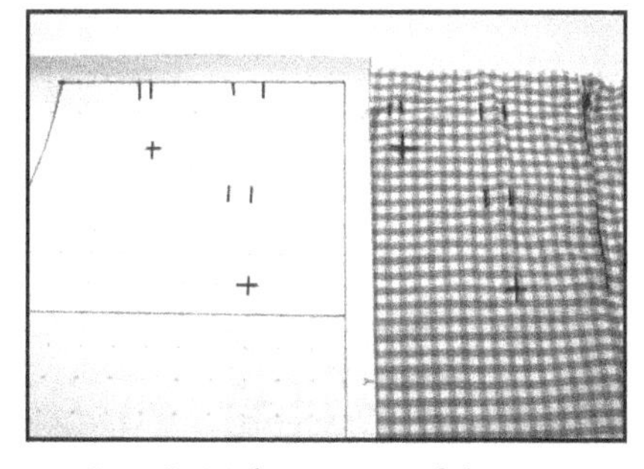

Step 3. Make a copy of the paper pattern.

Step 4. Transfer the marks from the fitting shell to the back pattern.

Step 5. The High Hip dart can be adjusted so it is located half way between the hip dart and the Side Seam.

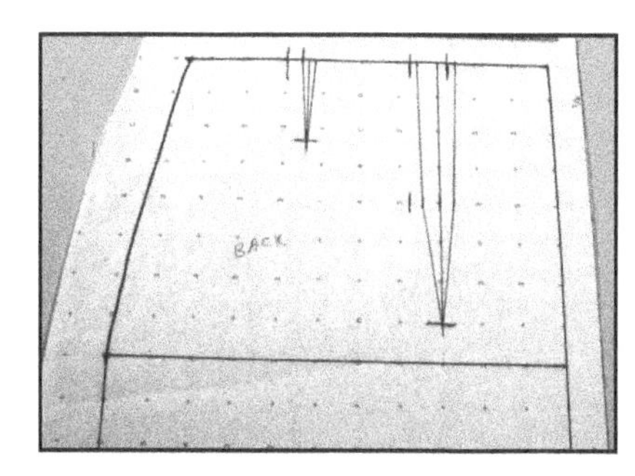

Step 6. On the paper pattern, draw a centerline for the dart from the dart points to the waist. These centerlines should be parallel to the Center Back.

Step 7. Measure the dart widths and mark half the dart width on each side of the dart's centerlines. If necessary, adjust the dart width for a sway back.

Step 8. Draw in the darts.

Step 9. Transfer the dart shapes from the paper pattern to the other side of the fitting shell.

If you have not fit the Front Darts, proceed to page 33.

Record the Front Darts

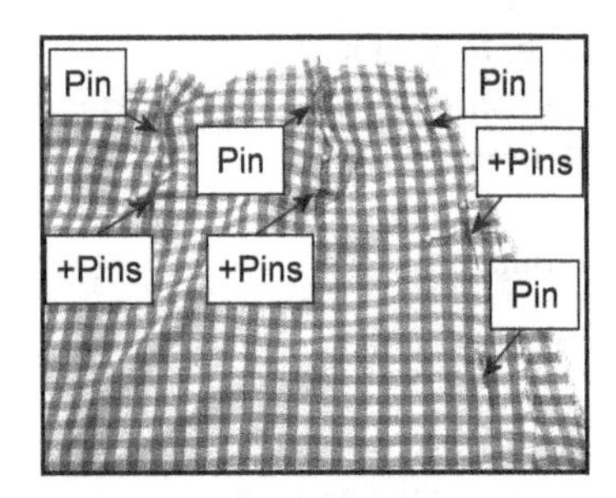

Step 1. On the fitting shell, mark the location of the pins for the darts.

Step 2. On the fitting shell, mark the dart widths at the waist.

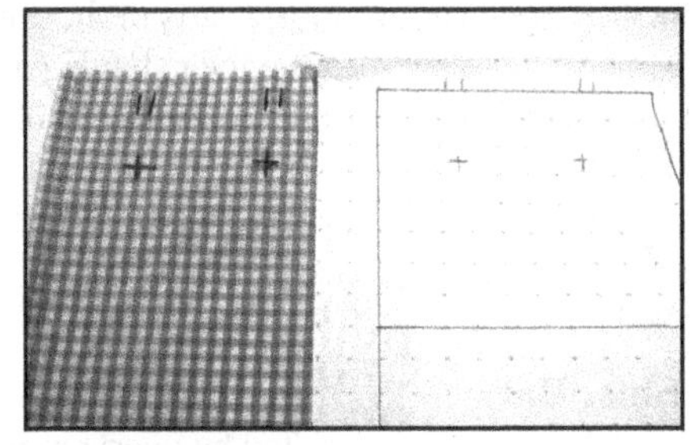

Step 3. Transfer the marks from the fitting shell to the front pattern.

Step 4. The locations of the darts can be adjusted so they divide the distance from the Center Front to the Side Seam in thirds.

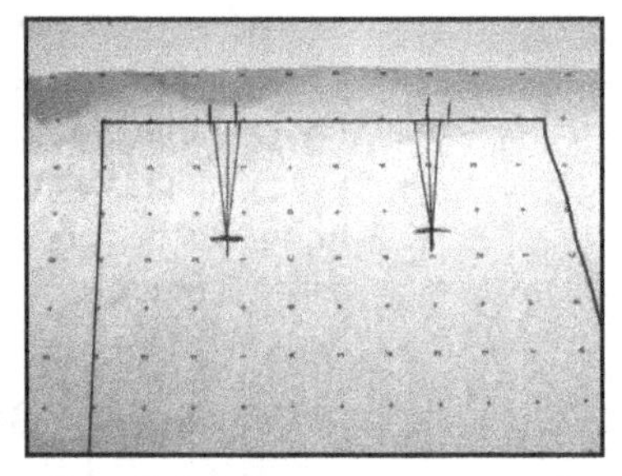

Step 5. On the paper pattern, draw a centerline for the darts from the dart points to the waist. These centerlines should be parallel to the Center Front.

Step 6. Measure the dart widths and mark half the dart width on each side of the dart's centerlines.

Step 7. Draw in the darts.

Step 8. Transfer the dart shapes from the paper pattern to the other side of the fitting shell.

If you have not yet established the Side Seam, proceed to page 34.

Verify Ease in the Side Seam

When the Side Seam is fitted, the Ease required for movement may not have been retained. As the shaping of the Side Seam is recorded on the paper pattern, the pattern should be checked to verify the Ease is still included at the hips and the waist.

Place the paper pattern on top of the fitting shell and mark the location where the pins indicate the Side Seam on both the front and back patterns.

Verify the Hip Ease

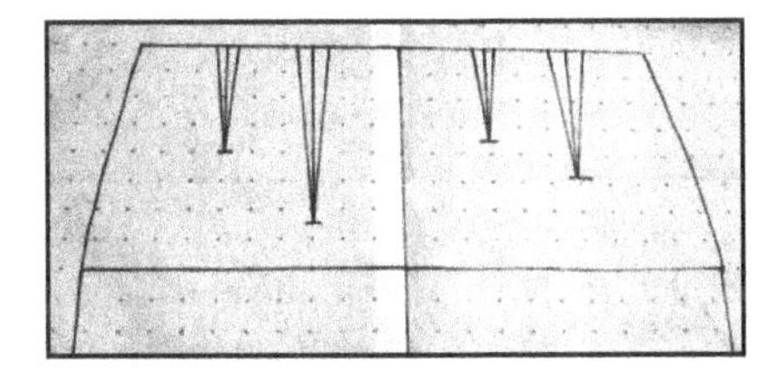

Step 1. Fold the back pattern along the Center Back line.

Step 2. Place the back pattern on top of the front pattern with the Center Back line touching the Center Front line.

Step 3. Tape in place.

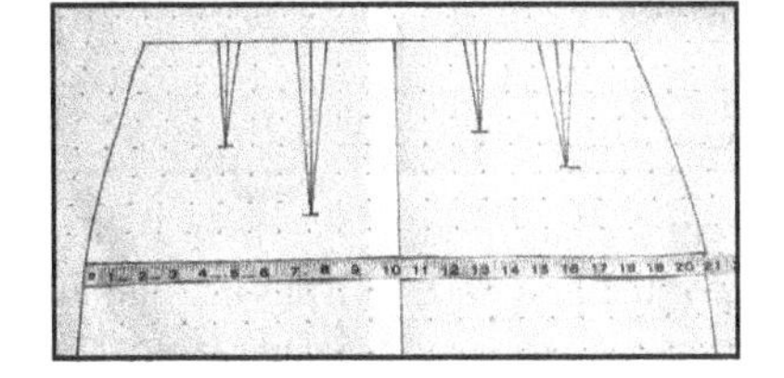

Step 4. Measure from the Side Seam on the back pattern to the Side Seam on the front pattern and record in (a) below.

Step 5. Perform the calculations as shown.

Step 6. Adjust the length of the Hip line at both Side Seams using (d) below.

Enter the width of the pattern from Step 4: (a) ______

Enter Hip measurement #13 + 2" (5 cm): ______ Divide by 2: (b) ______

Difference between (a) and (b): (c) ______

Divide (c) by 2: (d) ______

If (a) is greater than (b), then move the front and back Side Seams in at the hips by the amount shown in (d).

If (b) is greater than (a), then move the front and back Side Seams out at the hips by the amount shown in (d).

Verify Ease at the Skirt's Waist

When you are measuring the waist, you need to exclude the width of the darts as shown in the steps below. The number and position of the darts on your pattern may vary from the ones shown below.

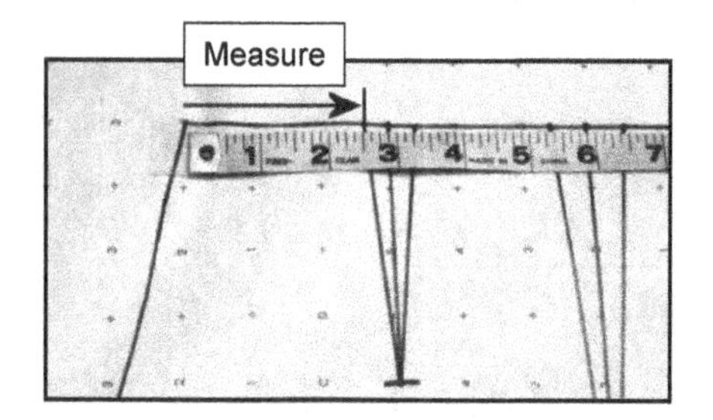

Step 1. Measure from the back Side Seam to the outside leg of the first dart.

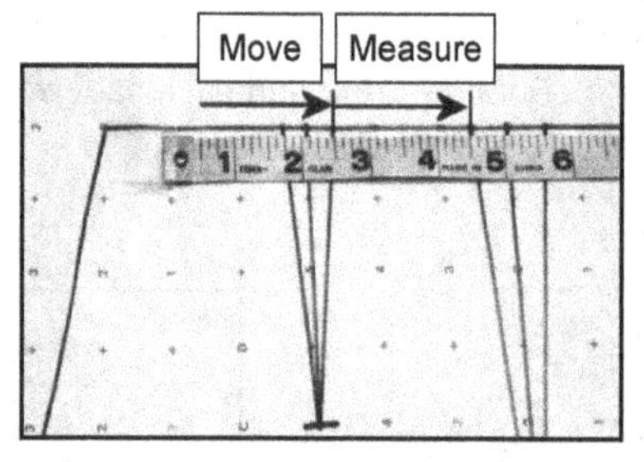

Step 2. Move the tape measure from the outside leg of the dart to the inside leg of the dart.

Step 3. Measure to the outside leg of the Hip dart.

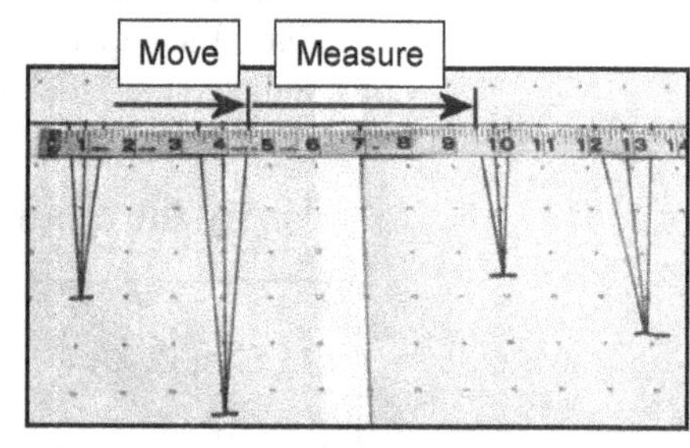

Step 4. Move the tape measure from the outside leg of the Hip dart to the inside leg of the Hip dart.

Step 5. Measure to the inside leg of the first front dart.

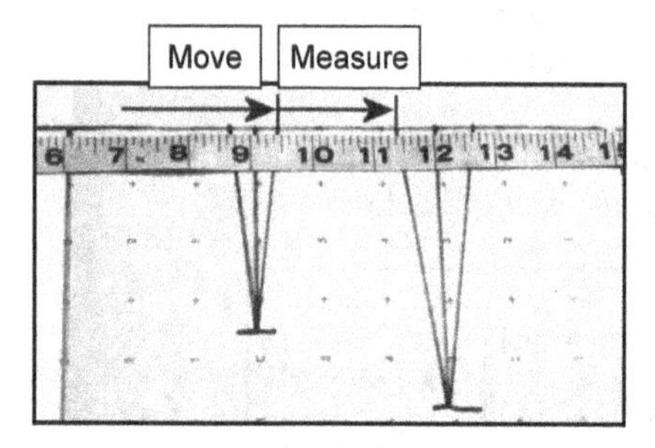

Step 6. Move the tape measure from the inside leg of the first dart to the outside leg of this dart.

Step 7. Measure to the inside leg of the second dart.

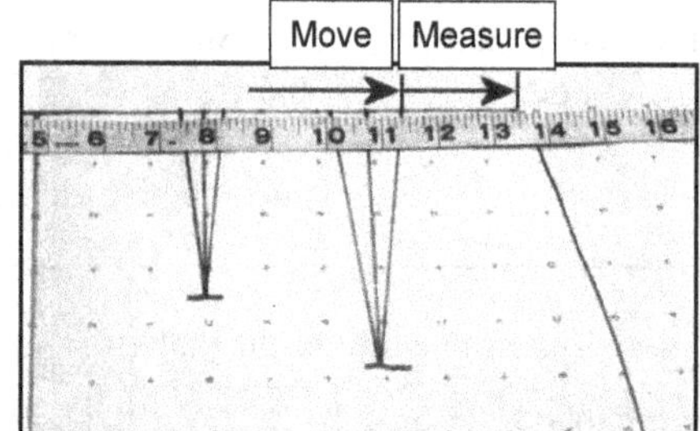

Step 8. Move the tape measure to the outside leg of the second dart and measure to the Side Seam of the front pattern and record in (a) below.

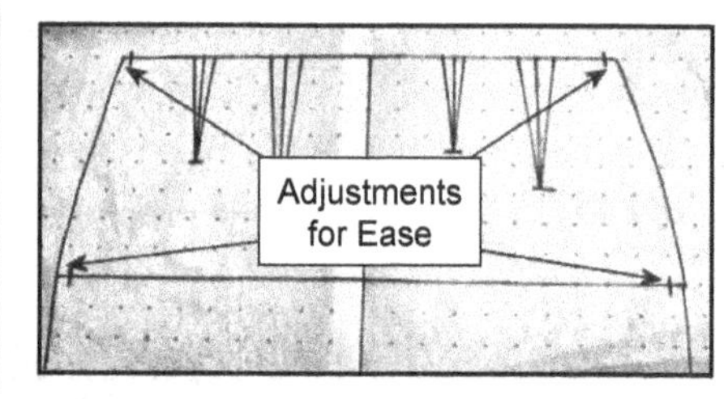

Step 9. Perform the calculations as shown.

Step 10. Using (d) below, adjust the length of the waist line at both Side Seams.

Step 11. Redraw the Side Seams and adjust the seam allowances as necessary.

Enter the width of the pattern from Step 8: (a) ______

Enter Waist measurement #9 + 1" (2.5 cm): ______ Divide by 2: (b) ______

Difference between (a) and (b): (c) ______

Divide (c) by 2: (d) ______

If (a) is greater than (b), then move the front and back Side Seams in at the waist by the amount shown in (d).

If (b) is greater than (a), then move the front and back Side Seams out at the waist by the amount shown in (d).

Verify the Sloper with a Second Fitting

For the second fitting, sew the darts and Side Seams on both sides of the fitting shell. Use a medium stitch length such as 4 mm. This allows you to remove the stitching for subsequent changes if necessary.

Put the fitting shell on and with the horizontal grain at the hip parallel to the floor, use a weighted chain to verify the Center Front, Center Back, and key grain lines are at right angles to the floor, see page 42.

Using Photos to Verify Fit

You can use photographs to accurately determine necessary adjustments to the patterns. The photos below show two different variations of Hip Dart fit that need adjustment. The weighted chain shows where the vertical grain should be located at the waist.

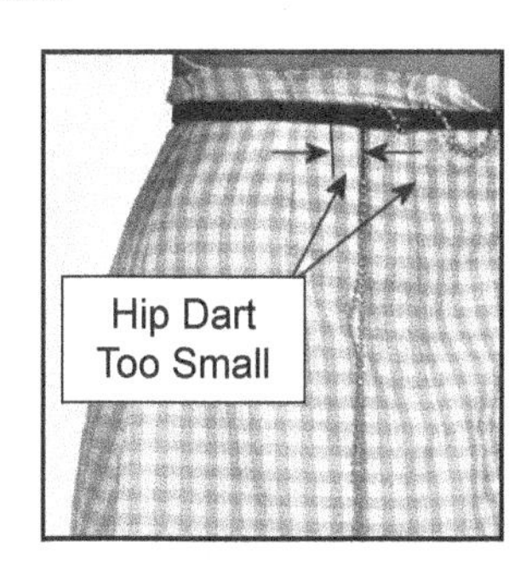

Hip Dart Too Small

The weighted chain shows the vertical grain is not close enough to the dart. This means the dart width is too small and needs to be made larger. The grain is off by two gingham squares at the waist. So the dart width needs to be made larger by half an inch.

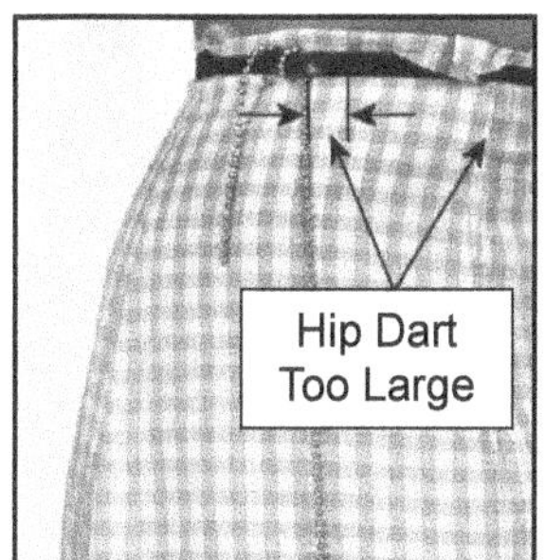

Hip Dart too Large

The weighted chain shows the vertical grain is too close to the dart. This means the dart width is too large and needs to be made smaller. The grain is off by two gingham squares at the waist. So the dart width needs to be made smaller by half an inch.

The Camera Equipment

Almost any kind of camera can be used to take these fitting photos. The camera needs some form of support and, for DIY applications, a timed shutter delay or a remote shutter release. The setup shown below is a smart phone mounted on a tripod with a Bluetooth Remote Shutter Release.

The camera needs to be at hip level and the person needs to be photographed from different angles as shown on page 42.

For the DIY process, the remote shutter release allows you to take pictures from different directions without twisting your body.

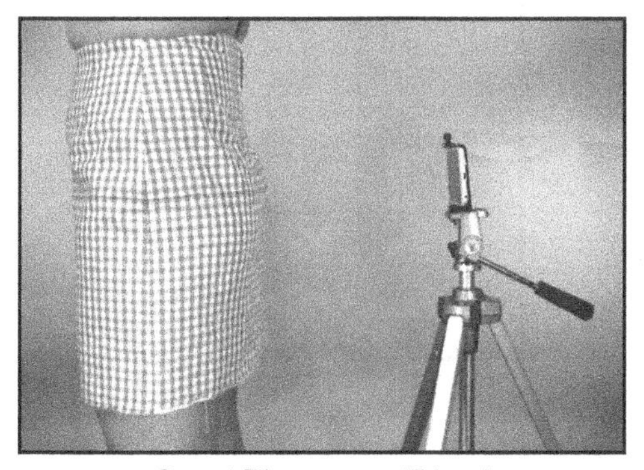

Smart Phone on a Tripod

Bluetooth Remote Shutter Release

Angles for Verifying the Fit of the Skirt

To verify the fit of the skirt, the vertical grain needs to be viewed at hip level from the different angles shown below. This can be done either by eye or with a photograph. The drawings below each photo indicate the body as viewed from above.

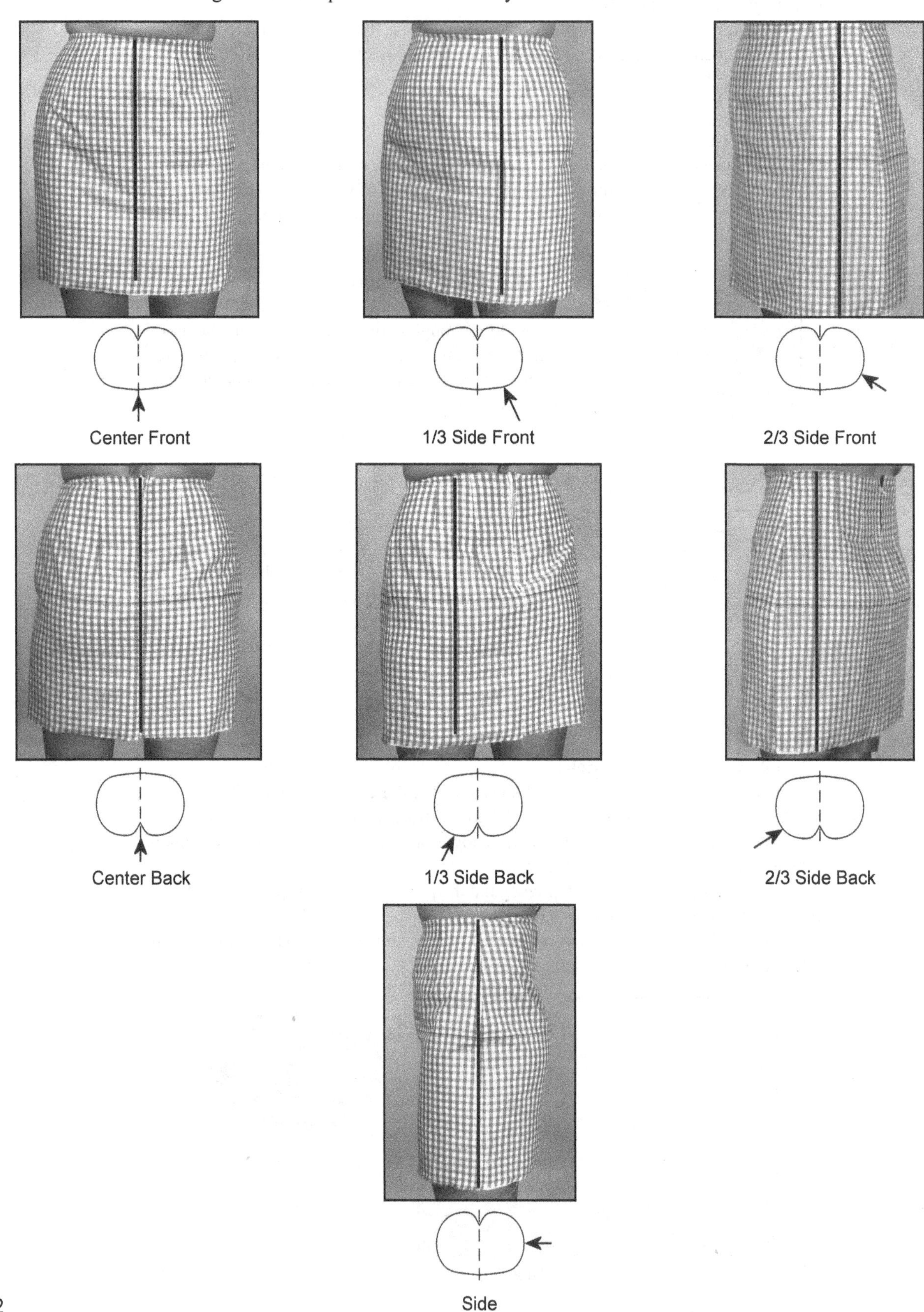

The Pants Sloper

The Pants Sloper is for a slacks cut: the torso portion is designed to fit so the pants legs will hang straight down. With loose-cut legs, the accuracy of the torso and Crotch Curve can be verified. After the Pants Sloper is completed, a description of how it can be modified for closer fit legs is described starting on page 55.

Even without the pattern alteration techniques described later in this book, the Pants Sloper may be styled into many different variations and some suggestion are included starting on page 53.

The Body and the Pants

The Pants Sloper, like the Skirt Sloper, is designed to fit the waist-to-hip region closely. From the hips, legs hang straight down to the floor. The Side Seam follows the same line as the Skirt Sloper. To shape for the leg, a Crotch Curve and Inseam are added to the Center Front and Center Back locations.

The basic vertical reference line for the Pants Sloper follows the center of the leg rather than the center of the body. The basic horizontal reference line is once again the Hip line.

The same techniques may be used to draft pants for men and women. The patterns can then be individualized to the shape of the wearer with the shaping of the Side Seam, dart sizes, and locations.

Important Note - The fitting shell for the Skirt Sloper uses gingham to optimize the accuracy of the fit. For pants, muslin is used because the grain of the back pattern's torso portion is cut on the bias. To fit muslin, you must rely on the fabric fitting the body smoothly rather than studying the direction of the grain.

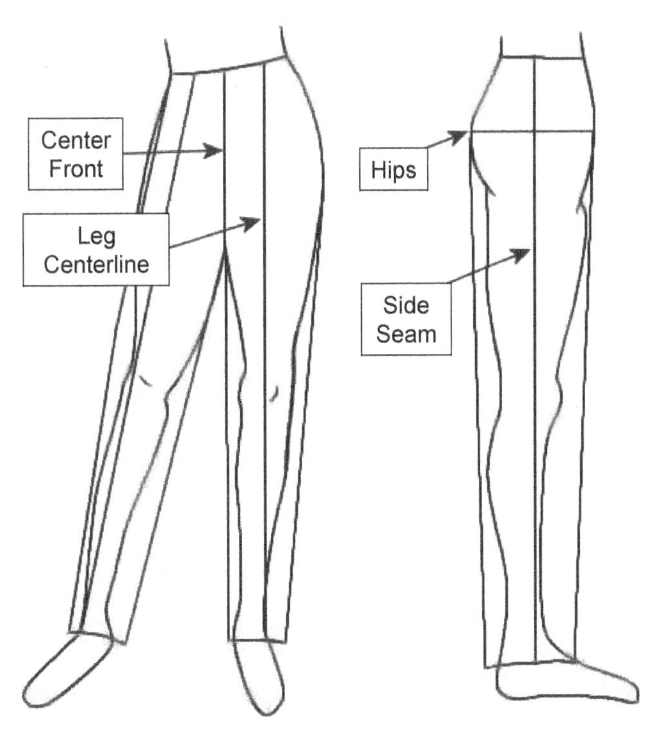

Pants and the Body

Drafting the Pants Pattern

9. Waist:		36. Waist to Hips:	
13: Hips:		37. Waist to Knee:	
14. Thigh:		40. Waist to Floor:	
15. Leg Width:		41: Inseam:	
		42. Crotch Depth:	

The initial pattern is for the front of the leg. The pattern for the back of the leg is created starting on page 45.

¼ Thigh
#14
Thigh
Line
Waist
to Floor
#40
Inseam
#41
Cuff
4" 4"

The Basic Reference Lines for the Leg

Step 1. Draw a vertical line of the Waist to Floor length (#40). This is the Leg Centerline.

Step 2. At the bottom of this line, draw a line at right angles to it. Mark off 4" (10 cm) on each side of the Leg Centerline. This is the Cuff line.

The 4" (10 cm) width is used as a standard measurement to show the general taper of the leg. The pants cannot fit the leg tightly at this point because there must be an allowance for getting the foot through the finished garment.

Step 3. Measuring up from the Cuff line, mark the Inseam length (#41) on the Leg Centerline. At this point, draw a line at right angles to the Leg Centerline. This is the Thigh line.

Step 4. Mark off one-fourth of the Thigh measurement (#14) on the Thigh line on each side of the Leg Centerline.

The Leg Girth measurements are divided in half for the front section of the leg pattern. These measurements are then bisected by the Leg Centerline, hence the one-fourth measurement.

⅛ Waist
#9
Waist
Line
CF
Waist to
Hips #36
¼ Hips
#13
Hip
Line
Leg
Centerline

The Basic Reference Lines for the Torso

Step 5. Draw a line at right angles to the top of the Leg Centerline. This is the Waist line.

Step 6. From that point, measure down the Leg Centerline the Waist to Hip measurement (#36), then draw another line at right angles to the Leg Centerline. This is the Hip line.

Step 7. Mark off one-eighth of the Waist measurement (#9) on both sides of the Leg Centerline at the Waist. Draw a line from the left Waist mark to the Thigh line keeping it parallel to the Leg Centerline. This line is the Center Front, CF, line of the pants.

The Waist measurement is divided into eighths because this section of the pants is for one-fourth of the body. The Leg Centerline divides this measurement in half, thus one-eighth of the total Waist measurement.

Step 8. Measuring out from the Center Front line, mark off one-fourth of the Hip measurement (#13) on the Hip line.

Important - Notice the Hip measurement is taken from the Center Front line rather than the Leg Centerline as the other measurements were.

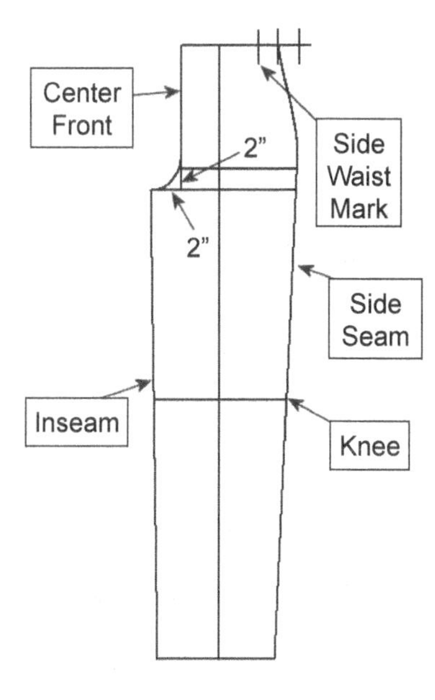

The Front Crotch Curve and Inseam Lines

Step 9. Measure from the Center Front line to the left mark on the Thigh line. This distance should be 1¾" to 2" (4.5 to 5 cm). If it is less, extend the Thigh line out to 1¾" (4.5 cm) for women and 2" (5 cm) for men.

Step 10. Measure up 2" (5 cm) from the Thigh line on the Center Front line. From this point, curve in the Front Crotch curve to the left mark on the Thigh line. This curve should be almost a quarter of a circle in shape.

Step 11. Draw a line straight down from the left mark on the Thigh line to the left mark on the Cuff line. This is the Inseam.

The Side Seam

Step 12. If you have a fitted Skirt Sloper, use this pattern to draw the Side Seam from the waist to the hips, then proceed to Step 13. You can also add the darts from the Skirt Sloper.

On the Waist line, find the mark that is one-fourth the Waist measurement from Center Front. This is the Side Waist mark.

For men, the Side Seam will start from this point.

For women, make a mark on the Waist line that is one-fourth the Hip measurement from Center Front. The Side Seam for women will start half way between this point and the Side Waist point just as it did for the Skirt Sloper, see page 30.

Step 13. Starting from the appropriate mark described in Step 12, draw the Side Seam. Curve the Side Seam out from the Waist to the mark on the right side of the Hip line. Then extend the Side Seam straight down from the Hip to the mark on the right side of the Cuff line. For larger thighs, the mark on the Thigh line is to the right of the Side Seam. If this is the case, curve the Side Seam out to this mark, then down to the Cuff line.

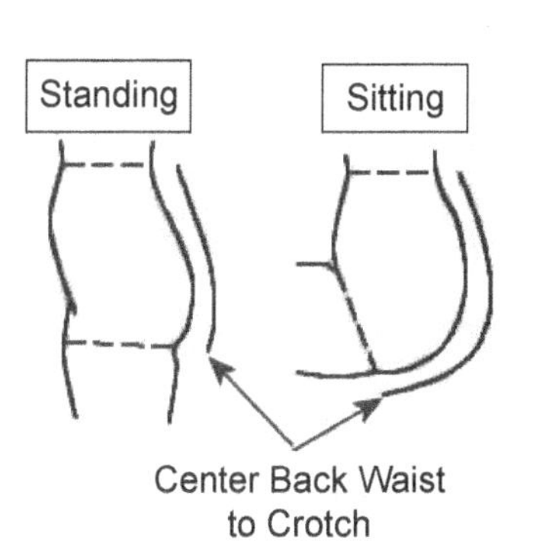

The pants, as they are now drafted, show the basic taper of the leg. For aid in styling pants, add the location of the knee.

Step 14. For the Waist to Knee length (#37), measure down the Leg Centerline. Draw a line at right angles to the Leg Centerline at this point.

The Back Pants Pattern

The back pants pattern is different from the front pants pattern in two ways. First, Ease will be added to the back measurements to allow for the body's movement. Secondly, the back pattern must be adjusted for sitting.

The distance from the Waist to the crotch is longer when a person is sitting than when a person is standing. This must be compensated for by adding a "hinge" to the back pattern at the Hip line.

The back pattern may be drafted by tracing the front pattern, then making adjustments.

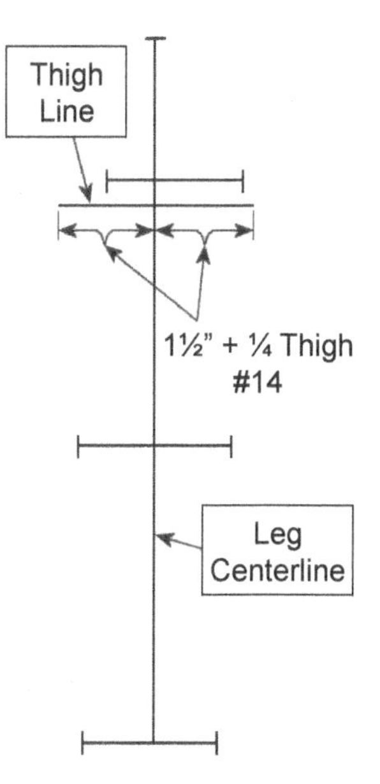

The Basic Reference Lines for the Back Pants

Step 1. Use a clean sheet of paper to trace the locations of the Leg Centerline, Hip line, Thigh line, Knee line, and Cuff line from the front pattern. Trace the two marks at the Cuff line for the Inseam and the Side Seam. Include a mark on the Hip line where the Center Front line coincides with the front Hip line. This mark is the Center Back Hip point.

The tracing may be made by placing semi-transparent paper, such as the recommended marking paper, on top of the front pants pattern. Or by placing the front pants pattern on top of another sheet of paper and transferring the marks with a tracing wheel and tracing paper.

Step 2. On the Thigh line, mark off 1½" (4 cm) plus one-fourth of the Thigh measurement (#14) on each side of the Leg Centerline.

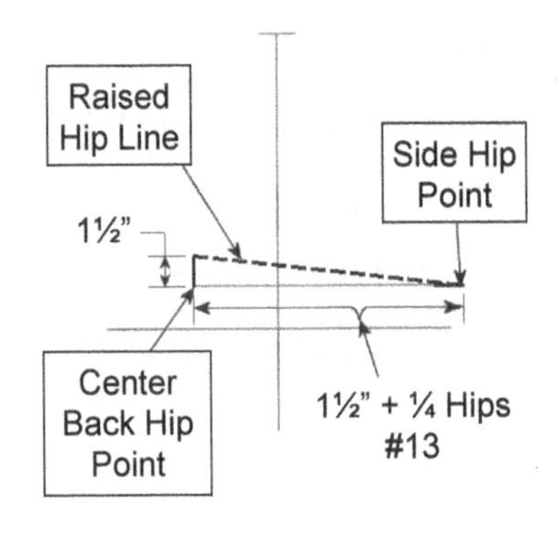

Step 3, For Men: Measure out from the Center Back Hip point on the Hip line 2" (5 cm) plus one-fourth of the Hip measurement (#13). This mark is the Side Hip point.

For Women: Measure out from the Center Back Hip point on the Hip line 1½" (4 cm) plus one-fourth of the Hip measurement (#13). This mark is the Side Hip point.

Step 4. For Men: Measure straight up from the Center Back Hip point 2" (5 cm) and make a mark. Connect this point to the Side Hip point with a dotted line. This is the Raised Hip line.

For Women: Measure straight up from the Center Back Hip point 1½" (4 cm) and make a mark. Connect this point to the Side Hip point with a dotted line. This is the Raised Hip line.

The Raised Hip line creates the "hinge" at Center Back that provides the extra fabric required for sitting.

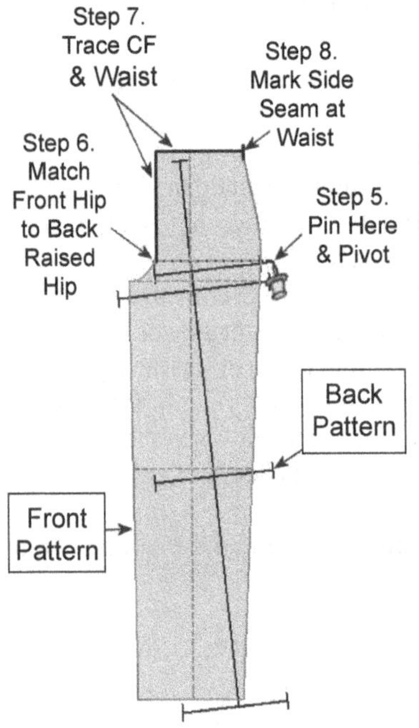

The Pivot

Step 5. Keep the back and front patterns aligned at the Leg Centerline and the Hip line. Put a pin through both patterns at the back Side Hip point.

Step 6. Pivot the patterns at the pin so the front Hip line coincides with the back Raised Hip line.

Step 7. Trace the Center Front line and the Waist line from the front pattern onto the back pattern.

Step 8. Also mark the location of the front Side Seam at the Waist on the back Waist line.

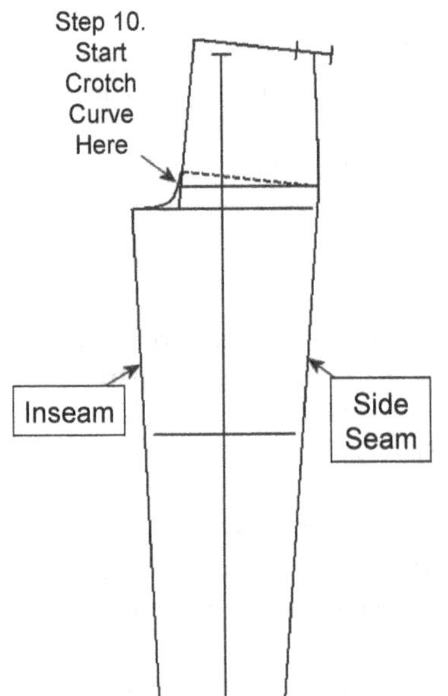

The Back Side Seam Lines

Step 9. Remove the back pattern from the front pattern. If you have a fitted Skirt Sloper, use this pattern to draw the Side Seam from the waist to the hips. You can also add the darts. Then proceed to Step 11.

For Women: Start drawing in the back Side Seam from the point established in Step 8. Curve the Side Seam out to the Side Hip point, then down to the mark on the Cuff line.

For Men: Find the point on the back Waist line where the front Side Seam started (Step 8). Measure out on the Waist line from this point 2" (5 cm) and draw in the Side Seam starting from this new point. Curve it to the Side Hip point and down to the Cuff line. The 2" (5 cm) added at the back Waist line is a dart allowance for the Hip dart.

Step 10. Extend the Center Back line straight down to the Thigh line. Measure up from the Thigh line 2" (5 cm) and make a mark. From this point, curve the back Crotch Curve out to the left mark on the Thigh line.

Step 11. Draw in the Inseam from the left mark on the Thigh line to the left mark on the Cuff line. The Inseam can curve in between the Knee and the Thigh lines.

The pattern as it is now drafted may fit with no problem at all. However, some body shapes will require an additional check to make sure the Crotch Curve will provide a comfortable fit.

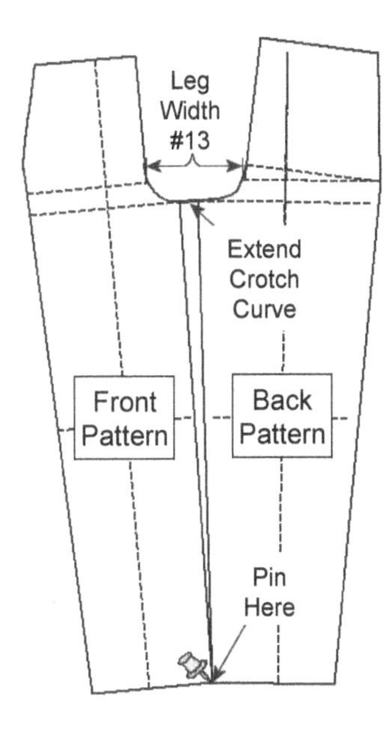

Extend the Back Crotch Curve

Step 10. Place the front and the back pants patterns so that the Inseams overlap.

Step 11. Put a pin through the back Inseam and the front Inseam at the Cuff lines. This pin is to act as a pivot for the patterns.

Step 12. Pivot the patterns so that the front Inseam at the Thigh line touches the back Inseam at the Thigh line.

Step 13. Measure from the top of the front Crotch Curve to the top of the back Crotch curve. This measurement should be the Leg Width length (#15).

Step 14. If it is not the Leg Width measurement, pivot the patterns until this measurement is reached.

Step 15. Shorten or lengthen the back Crotch Curve.

The following chart gives approximate Leg Width measurements for men and women.

	Small	Medium	Large
Men	6" (15 cm)	7 to 8" (18 to 20 cm)	9" (23 cm)
Women	6" (15 cm)	7" (18 cm)	8" (20 cm)

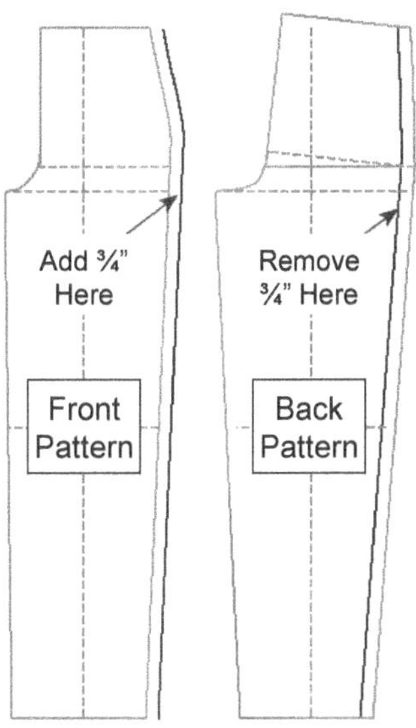

Women's Side Seams

If the Skirt Sloper was not used to draw the Side Seam for the pants, the following adjustment may be made on women's pants. This adjustment usually makes it easier to fit the pants.

Step 16. Move the Side Seam on the front pattern out ¾" (19 mm) for its entire length. Move the Side Seam on the back pattern in ¾" (19 mm) for its entire length.

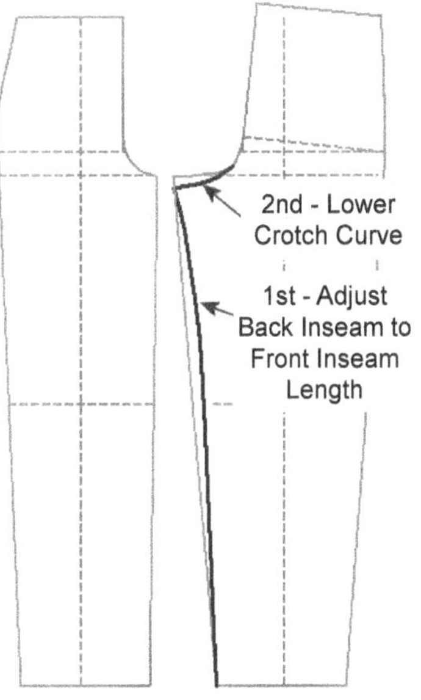

Inseam Length

Step 17. On the front pattern, measure the Inseam from the knee to the crotch. Next measure the curved Inseam of the back pattern from the knee to the crotch. If the back pattern is longer due to the curved seam, drop the back Crotch Curve to the correct length. Do not shorten the width of the Crotch Curve. Just drop the height.

Seam Allowances

Before the patterns are cut for a fitting, add the following seam allowances. The Side Seam and the Inseam should have a 1½" (38 mm) seam allowance. The Waist should have a 1" (25 mm) seam allowance. The Center Front, Crotch Curve, and Center Back should have a ½" (12 mm) seam allowance. A larger seam allowance on the Crotch Curve will make it difficult to achieve an accurate fit.

Optimizing the Pattern for a Tummy

The photos below illustrate what the muslin pants fitting shell looks like using the patterns up to this point. You will save time and effort by developing a larger front pattern before doing a fitting.

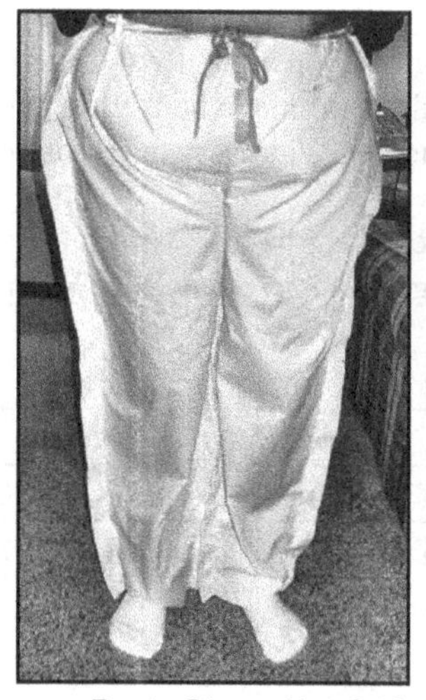

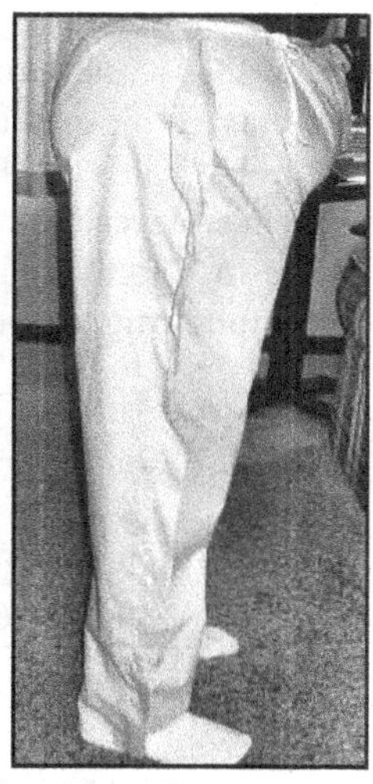

Pants Sloper Not Optimized for a Tummy

To optimize the Pants Sloper for a tummy, the first thing to keep in mind is that a good fit doesn't mean tight. It means having the fabric follow the contours of the body in an attractive manner. One of the underlying concepts of the Pants Sloper is that it is a slacks cut. In other words, it fits the lower torso so the fabric will hang nicely down the leg. Once this fit is optimized, you can adjust the pattern for other designs.

To add room in the front pattern for the tummy, extend the Front Crotch Curve. This is similar to the procedure used to modify the Back Crotch Curve, see page 47.

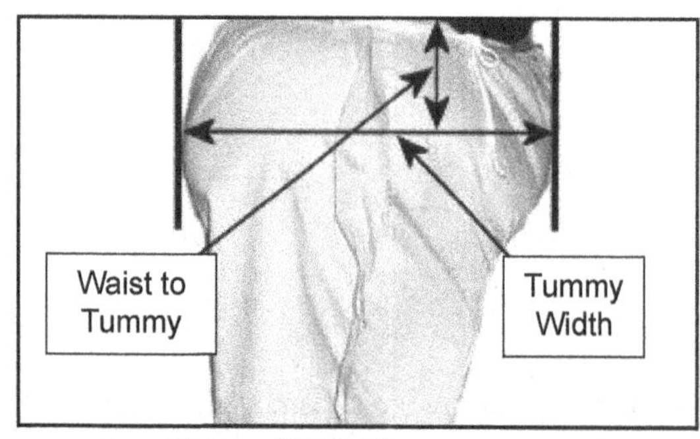

Tummy Width Measurement

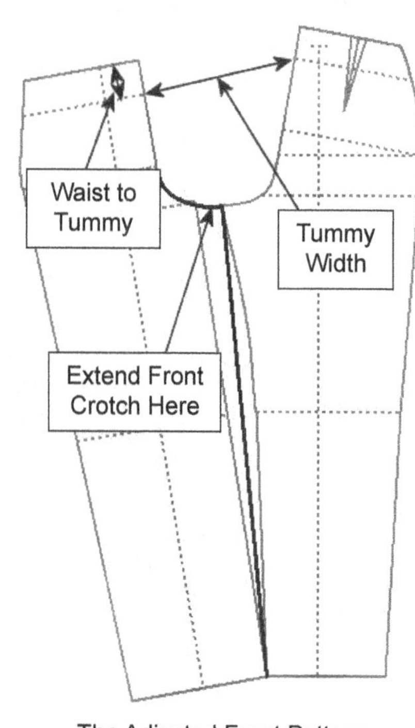

The Adjusted Front Pattern

Step 1. Measure the Tummy Width and record the results below.
Step 2. Measure the Waist to Tummy distance and record the results below.

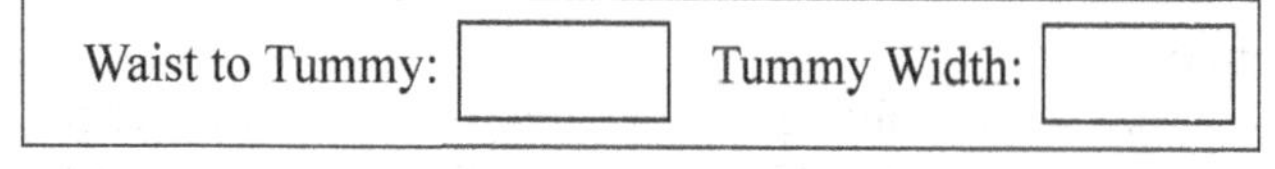

Step 3. On the front and back patterns, draw lines parallel to the waist at the Waist to Tummy height.

Step 4. Place the patterns together at the cuff, then spread them for the Tummy Width measurement.

Step 5. Extend the Front Crotch Curve to meet the back Crotch Curve.

Step 6. Redraw the Inseam.

Step 7. Verify that the combined Crotch Curves create a smooth curve particularly at the junction of the Inseam.

Leg Shape

A tummy can result in a tapered leg that draws the eye to the top of the pants. Adjust by adding to the front pattern's width at the cuff.

Step 1. Measure around the foot from Side Seam to Inseam shaping the tape measure to the desired look for the cuff.

Step 2. Adjust the front leg pattern to the desired cuff width by adding the same amount to the Side Seam and the Inseam.

Step 3. Draw in new Side Seams and Inseams for the front pattern.

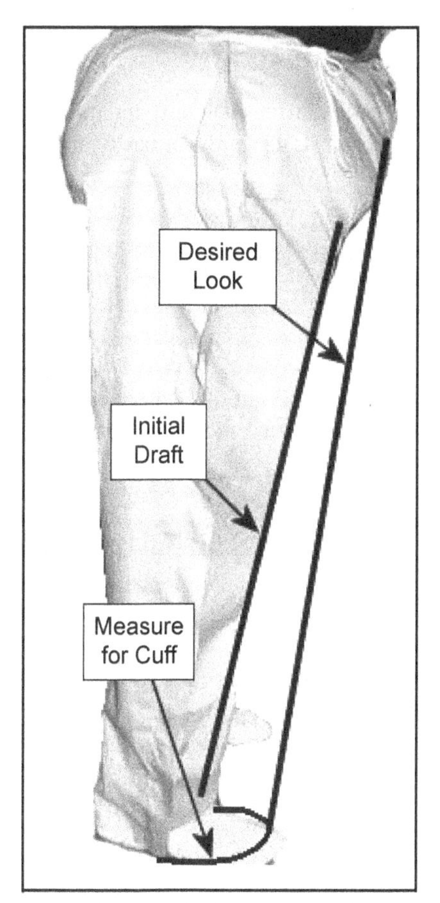

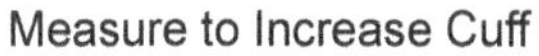

Measure to Increase Cuff

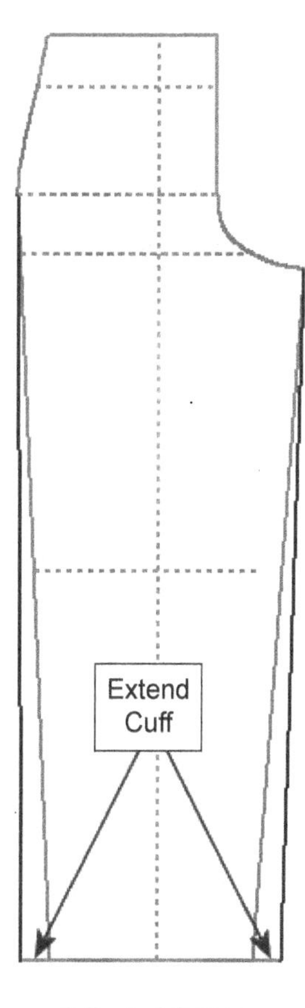

Adjusted Pattern

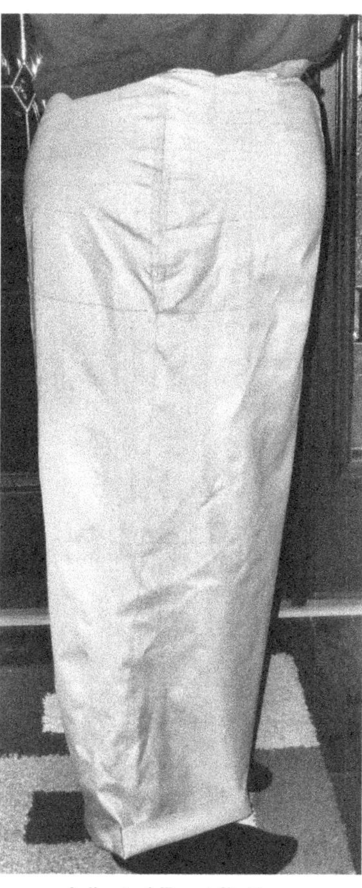

Adjusted Front Pattern

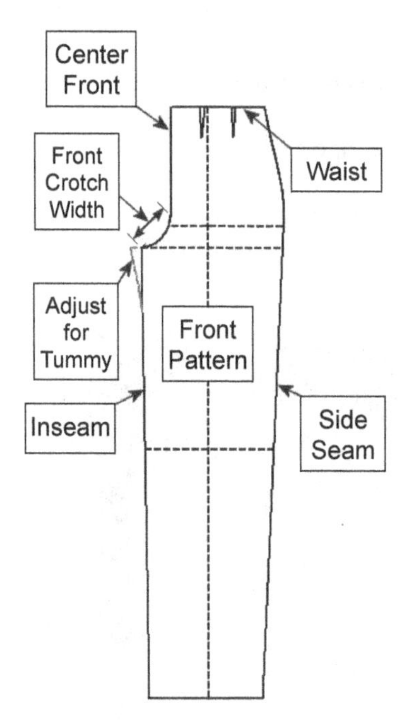

Fitting the Pants

The pants pattern is now ready to be cut out of muslin and fitted. The pattern drafting approach described here in combination with the methods used to check the patterns minimize fitting time. However, individual figures vary and it may be necessary to check the Crotch Curve then shape the waist-to-hip region to the particular shape of the wearer.

Each seam in the pants has its own particular function in making pants fit well. It is important to understand these functions not only for fitting the basic patterns but also for styling and designing any pants pattern.

Waist

The Waist must fit the body closely. Pants hang from the waist and must be adjusted so that they fall correctly, without pitching sideways, forwards, or backwards.

Side Seam

The Side Seam is responsible for the overall fit of the pants. It may be adjusted so that the pants are either close fitting or loose.

Center Front

The Center Front seam should follow the Center Front of the body. It should follow the grain of the fabric. The Center Front is a straight seam not a shaped seam.

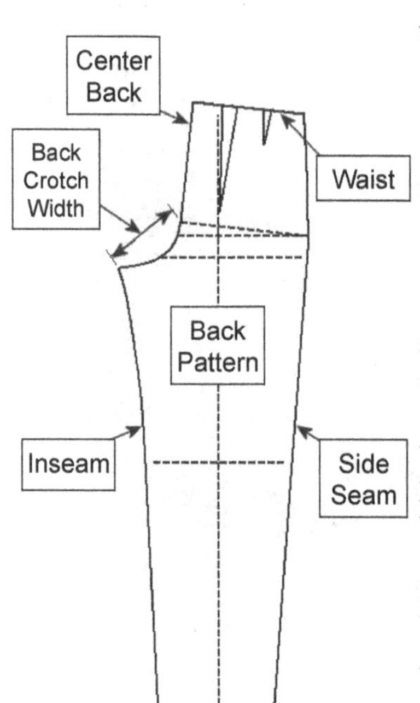

Center Back

This seam is slightly off the grain of the fabric in order to provide give at the back for sitting. It is straight, not shaped.

Crotch Curve

The Crotch Curve is shaped to fit between the legs. This seam cannot be seen when a person is standing in an erect position with the feet together. It must be shaped to the contour of the individual.

The Front Crotch Width determines the distance of the Inseam from the front of the body. For most people, 1¾" to 2" (4 to 5 cm) will place the Inseam in the correct position. However, if a woman has a pronounced tummy, this length may be extended so the pants can hang straight down the front, see page 48.

The Back Crotch Width establishes how close fitting the pants will be at the buttocks. If this length is short, the Center Back seam will pull into the separation between the buttocks. If this length is too long, the pants will be baggy in the seat.

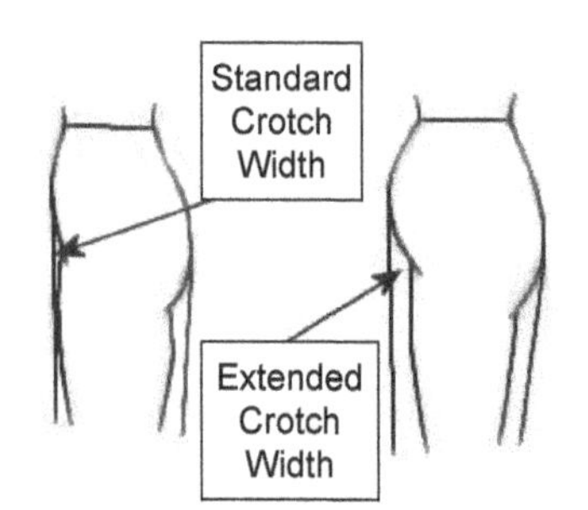

Front Inseam

The front Inseam must remain fairly straight. It may follow the leg taper established by the basic pattern and then flare out below the knee. To prevent excessive fullness between the legs, it should not flare out too much.

Back Inseam

The back Inseam determines how close the pants will fit at the thigh. The more the back Inseam curves in, the closer the pants will fit. If the pattern is closer than the allotted 3" (7.5 cm) of Ease, there may be horizontal wrinkles under the buttocks.

The Fitting Procedure for the Pants

Step 1. If a Skirt Sloper has already been fitted, it may be used to establish the darts and Side Seams. Match the front skirt pattern up with the front pants pattern at the Center Front and Waist. Transfer the dart and Side Seam shapes to the pants pattern. Repeat the procedure for the back pattern.

If the skirt pattern has not been previously fitted, the darts and the Side Seams are established in Step 5 below.

Step 2. Cut the patterns out of muslin. To fit the pants, the seams should be basted for the first fitting. Sew each leg separately. Turn one leg right side out and place it inside the other leg. Sew around the Center Back and the Crotch Curve. Leave the Center Front open for getting in and out of the pants.

Step 3. Put the pants on with the seam allowances out. Adjust the pants from the side so that the pants legs hang straight down. The fabric should not break at the front or the back of the leg.

Step 4. Check the Crotch Curve for a comfortable fit. The Crotch Curve as drafted will fit most people without any further adjustment. To keep the pants from pivoting forward and buckling at the knee, however, some people may need to curve the Back Crotch lower, see page 52.

Crotch Curve
Needs Adjusting

If the Crotch Curve needs to be adjusted, take the pants off and baste the curve lower. Trim the seam allowance down to ½" (12 mm) and try the pants on once again.

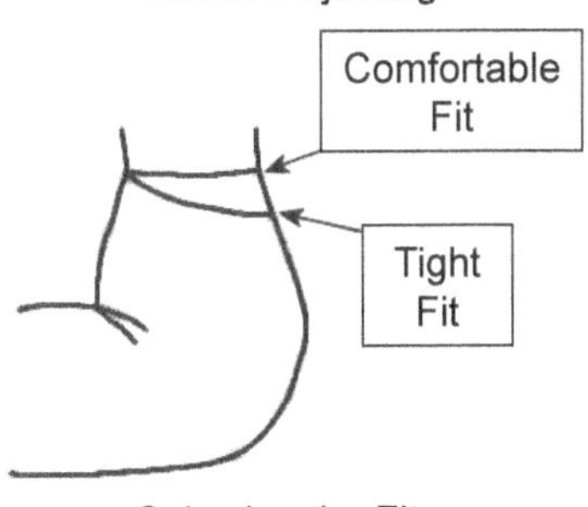

Selecting the Fit
at the Waist

Step 5. After the pants have been adjusted to hang straight down the body, the darts and the Side Seam can be added to the pants. The same procedure used to fit the skirt is used to fit the waist-to-hip region of the pants. See the instructions starting on page 31. Remember, men will only have one dart, a dart for the buttock.

Step 6. Tie a string around the Waist. Adjust the pants so they hang straight down the body. Check them from the front, the side, and the back.

Step 7. The Side Seam may now be adjusted to establish how close fitting or loose the pants are going to be. The Waist will usually have about ½" (12 mm) of Ease. The following chart lists the amount of Ease at the Hips for fitted pants.

	Tight	Snug	Comfortable
Women	1" (2.5 cm)	2" (5 cm)	3" (7.5 cm)
Men	1" (2.5 cm)	2" to 3" (5 to 7.5 cm)	3" (7.5 cm)

Finished Sloper

Step 8. Have the person wearing the pants sit sideways on a chair and mark the Waist height at Center Back.

For the pants to look their best in a standing position, the Waist at Center Back should be held as low as is comfortably possible while the person is sitting.

If the wearer is more interested in comfort of movement, the Waist mark at Center Back should be at the natural waist line while the person is sitting.

Step 9. Have the person stand and mark the Waist just above the string. While marking the back, make sure the string stays at the mark established in Step 8 above.

For Men – Measure down from this waist to the desired top of the pants. This lower waist should be used for the second fitting.

Adjusting the Back Crotch Curve

Getting pants to fit may require adjusting the Crotch Curve. When the buttocks drop below the top of the Inseam, the Back Crotch Curve needs to be lowered. The instructions in Step 4, page 51 show how to adjust this during the fitting.

Adjusting the Back Crotch Using Measurements

This contour may become evident when taking measurements. Use the chart below to determine if the back pattern should be adjusted. Keep in mind that measurements are not infallible.

Enter Waist to Floor (#40): (a)	
Enter Inseam (#41): (b)	
Subtract (b) from (a): (c)	
Enter Crotch Depth (#42): (d)	

If (c) is smaller than or equal to (d), then no adjustment is necessary.
If (d) is greater than (c), then adjust the pattern by adding a Crotch Depth line.

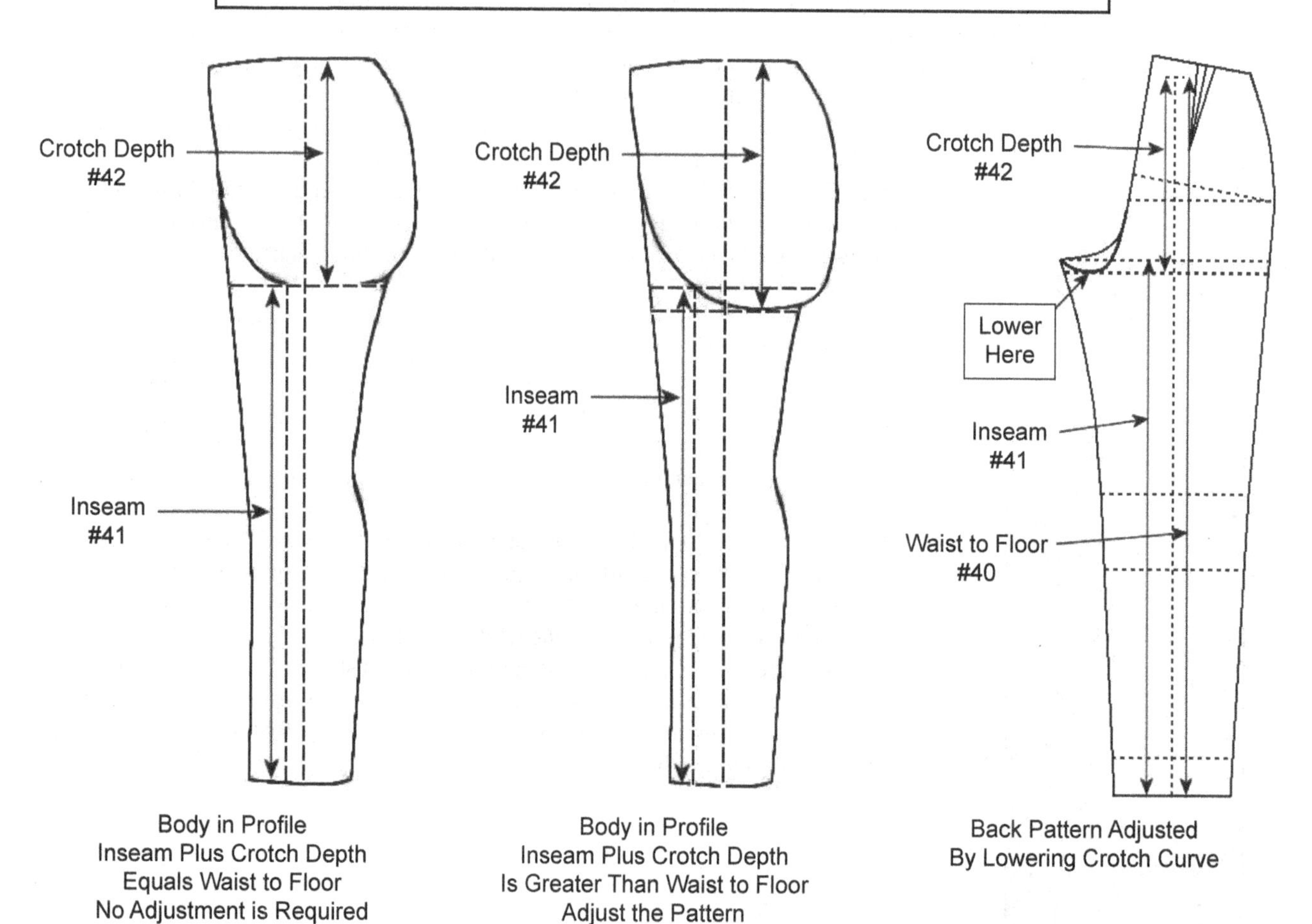

Body in Profile
Inseam Plus Crotch Depth
Equals Waist to Floor
No Adjustment is Required

Body in Profile
Inseam Plus Crotch Depth
Is Greater Than Waist to Floor
Adjust the Pattern

Back Pattern Adjusted
By Lowering Crotch Curve

Adjusting the Pattern

After the darts and Side Seams have been shaped during the initial fitting, transfer the marks back to the paper pattern. During this stage, draw the centerline of the darts so they are parallel to either the Center Front or Center Back lines. Then center the width of the dart at the waist on the dart centerline. This is the same procedure described for the skirt, see page 37

The Side Seam is the final check on the pattern. During the fitting process, it is easy to remove the initial Ease added to the pattern. It is very important to make sure that you adjust the pattern based on the wearer's waist (#9) and Hip (#13) measurements, see the instructions starting on page 39.

After correcting the pattern, transfer the darts and Side Seams to the other side of the fitting shell and do another fitting to verify that the grain of the fitting shell is correct. During this fitting you can determine whether you want additional Ease or less. Adjust the Side Seams to achieve the exact amount of Ease desired. Be sure to check this final shape by sitting as well as standing.

Styling Pants

Different styles of pants may be created by changing the shape of the Inseam and Side Seam and/or by altering the height of the Hem.

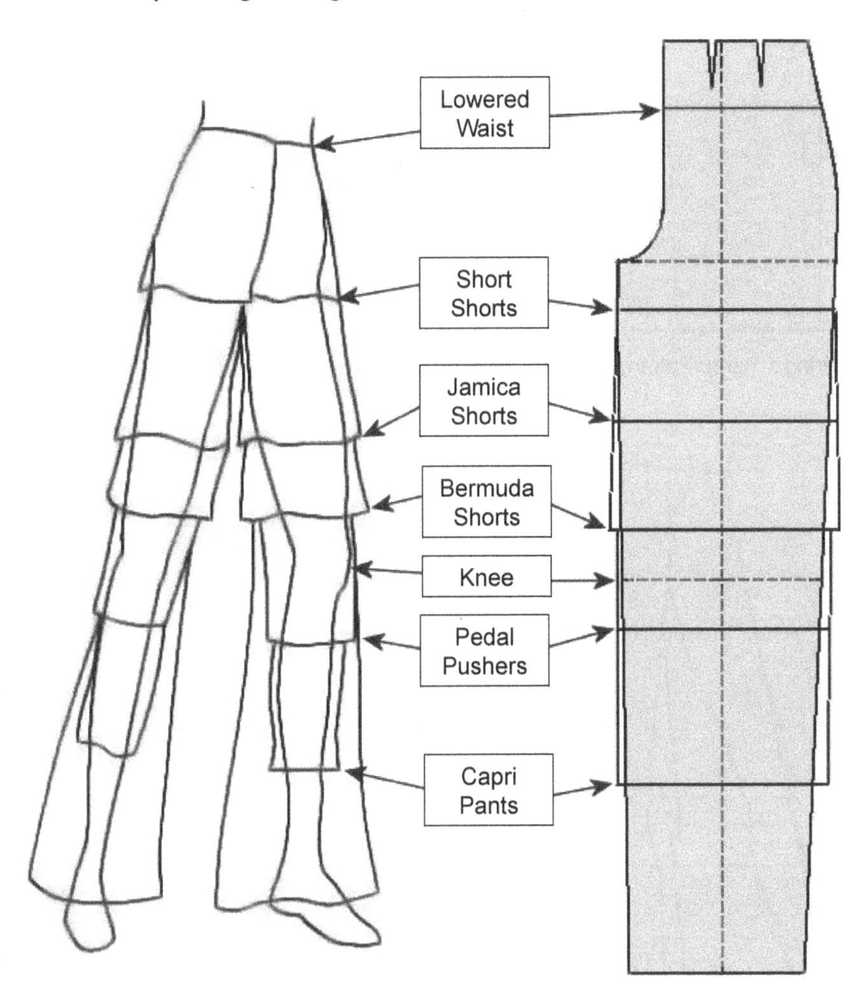

Pants with Fullness

Full-length pants can have either a straight leg or some flare. Flaring from the mid thigh level is frequently used to minimize the bulk around the upper thigh. You can determine the amount of fullness to add by placing a tape measure on the ground and shaping it to the size of the desired hem. For the Culotte style of pants, the front Crotch Curve needs to be extended so the garment will hang away from the body at Center Front.

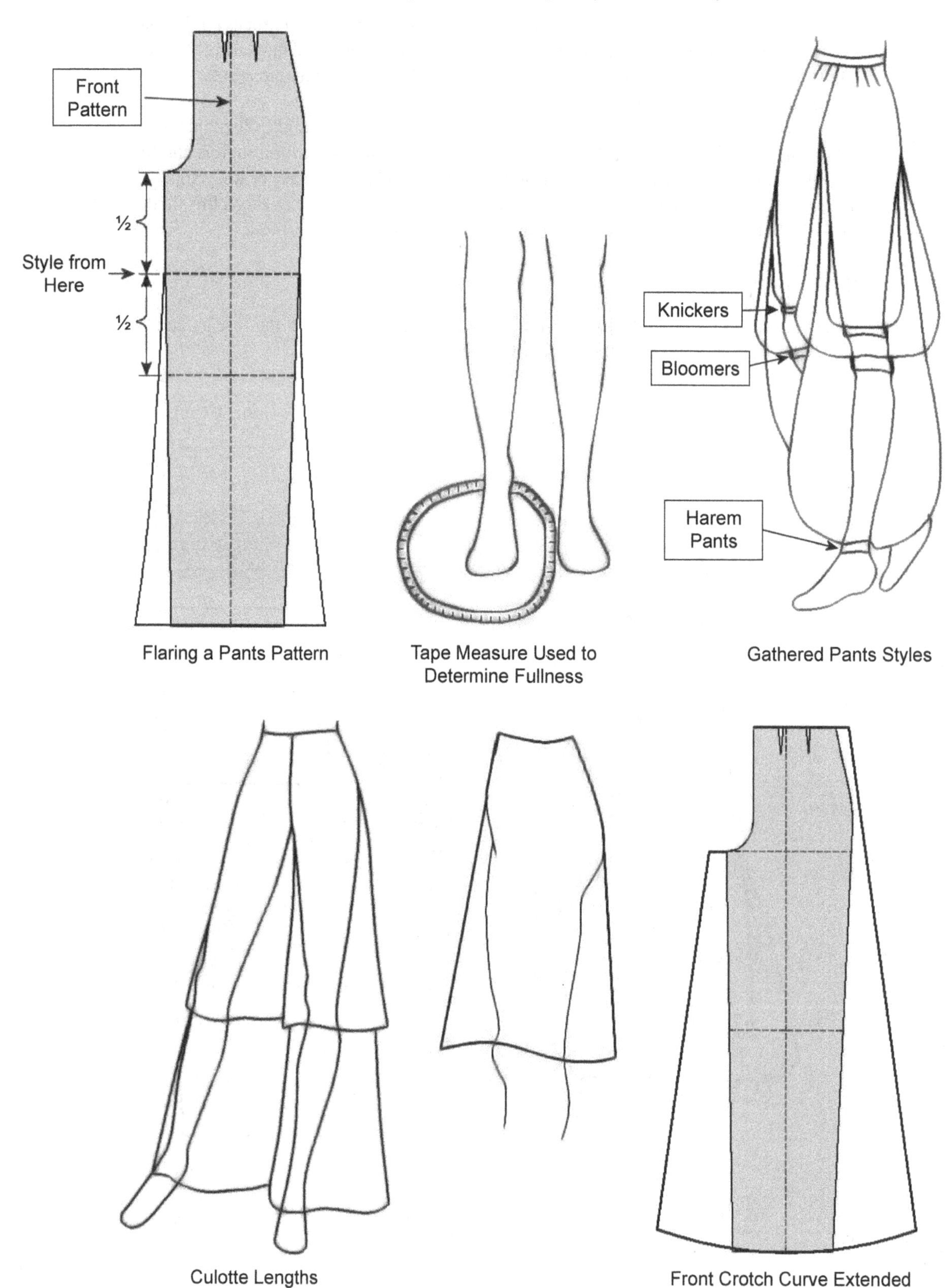

Flaring a Pants Pattern

Tape Measure Used to Determine Fullness

Gathered Pants Styles

Culotte Lengths

Front Crotch Curve Extended

Close Fitting Pants

After the Pants Sloper is fitted, the pattern can be used to cut closer fitting pants by indicating the actual size of the body on the leg portion. If the pants are to be made of stretch fabric, no Ease may be needed. For woven fabric, leave a wide 1½" (4 cm) seam allowance at the Side Seam and Inseam so the pants can be adjusted for the fit desired.

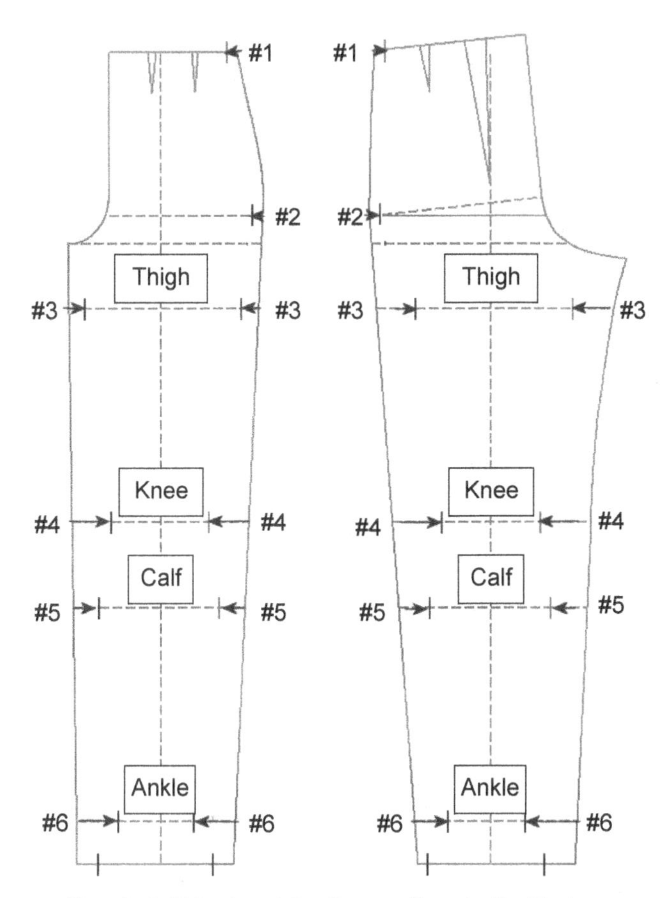

Step 1. Add horizontal reference lines to the Pants Sloper indicating the Thigh, Calf, and Ankle.

Step 2. Subtract the body measurement (b), see page 20, from the total pattern width (a) and record in (c).

Step 3. Divide (c) as shown to determine how much to subtract from each Side Seam and Inseam location, record in (d).

Step 4. Add marks on the pattern as shown above.

Step 5. Draw in the lines for the body.

	a. Pattern	From Chart	b. Body	c. Difference	Divide		d. Subtract
Waist		Divide Waist #9 by 2:			by 2	#1	
Hips		Divide Hips #13 by 2:			by 2	#2	
Thigh		#14:			by 4	#3	
Knee		#16:			by 4	#4	
Calf		#17:			by 4	#5	
Ankle		#18:			by 4	#6	

Shorts

The Pants Sloper is for a slacks cut with the back of the pants falling straight down the leg. The Pants Sloper can be modified for shorts to make the back fabric follow closer to the contour at the bottom of the buttocks. This is achieved by reducing the length of the back Crotch Curve.

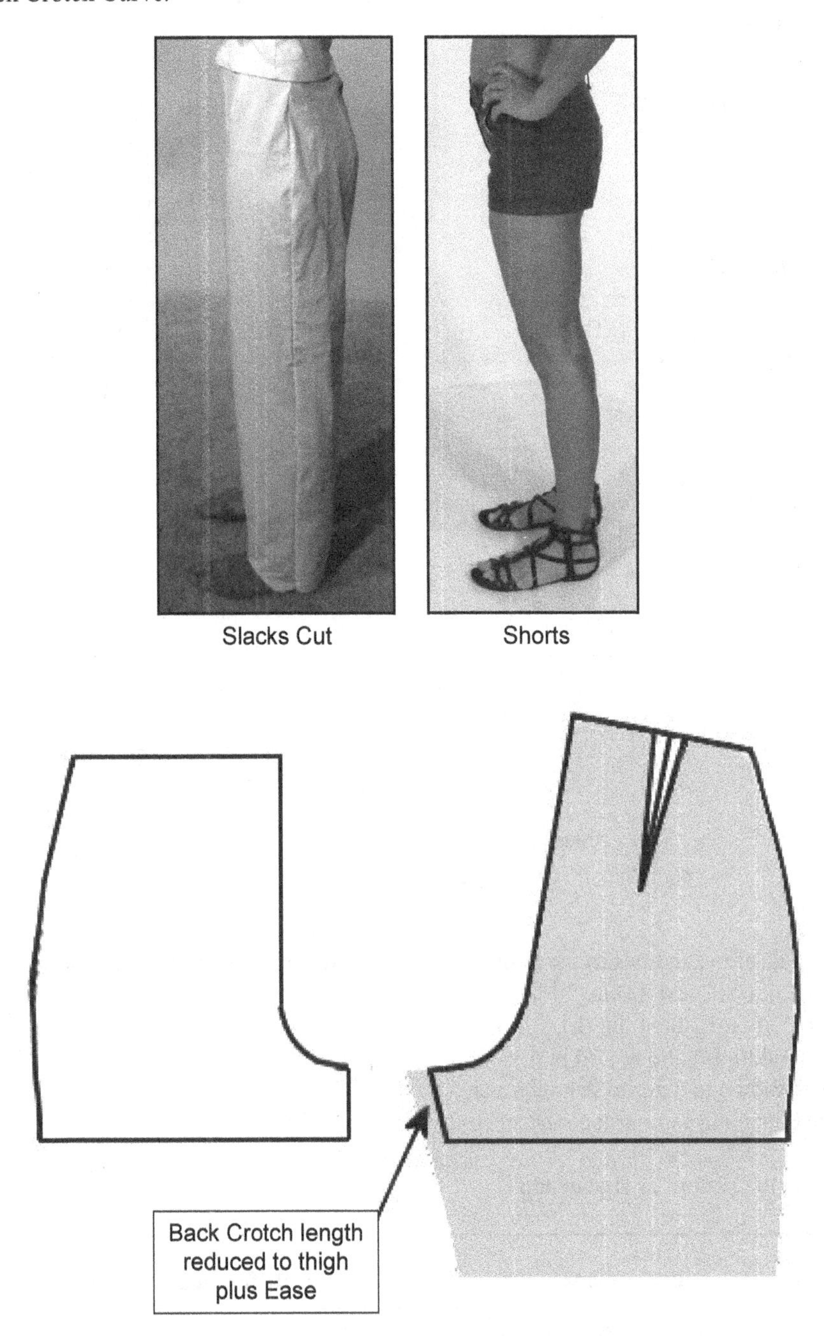

The Bodice Sloper

This description of the Bodice Sloper covers three patterns: a man's front pattern; a back pattern for men and women; the woman's front pattern. This approach presents the easiest patterns first.

The body is divided between the front and the back by the Shoulder Seam, see page 18, and the Side Seam. The basic reference lines are the Center Front or the Center Back lines and the Waist line. The Bodice Sloper is also referred to as the Upper Torso Sloper.

A Man's Body and the Front Pattern

A man's body in front is a fairly simple form. The chest to waist area is straight up and down. The body curves at the shoulder and at the side.

The curves of a man's body in front bend in only one direction at a time. The curve from the chest up to the shoulder is higher than the curve from the front to the side. Fabric can bend in these two independent directions without being shaped by a dart or a seam.

This describes the standard shape of men's bodies, the shape that is used to design conventional men's clothes. Some men's bodies differ from this standard. Variations, such as a barrel chest, present fitting and styling issues that are discussed in the design section.

The Man's Front Pattern

A man's Sloper is drafted for half the front. The Center Front and Waist are the basic reference lines. The location of the Shoulder Seam and the Side Seam are determined by measuring out from the basic reference lines. Then the neck curve and the armscye (armhole) curve are drawn in.

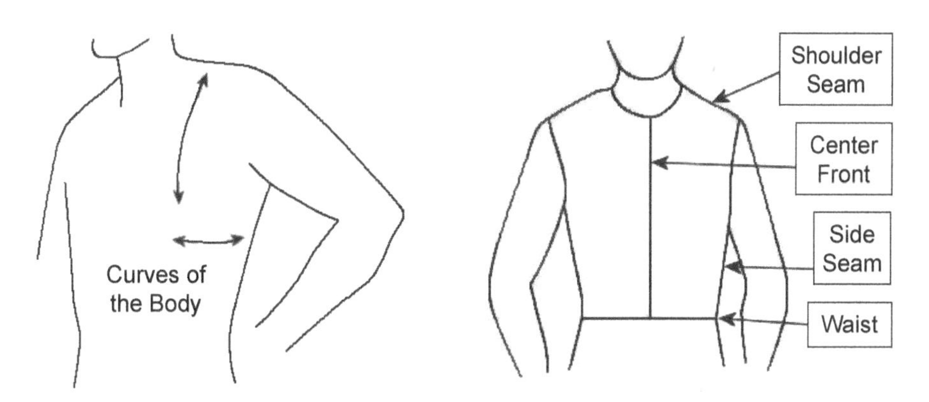

A Man's Body and Front Pattern

2. Neck Width:		20. Center Front to Waist:	
3. Shoulder Width:		26. Side Front to Waist:	
5. Chest:		28. Center Front/Waist to Shoulder:	
9. Waist:		32. Armpit to Waist:	

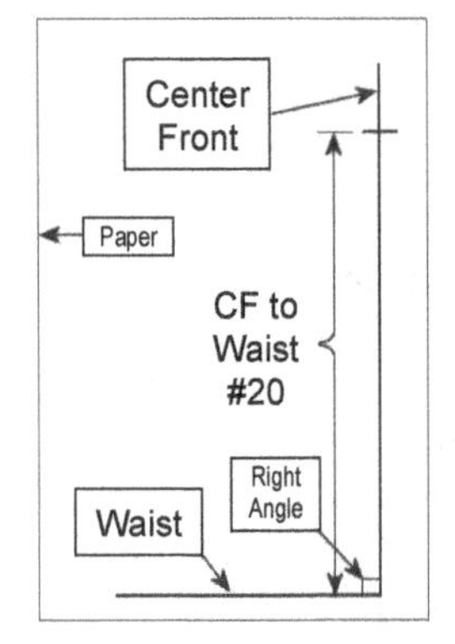

The Basic Reference Lines

Step 1. On a sheet of paper approximately 24" by 24" (60 by 60 cm), draw a vertical line approximately 5" (12 cm) in from the right side of the paper. This is the Center Front line (CF).

Step 2. About 5" (12 cm) from the bottom of the paper draw a line at right angles to the Center Front line. This is the Waist line.

Step 3. Mark off the Center Front to Waist measurement (#20) on the Center Front line.

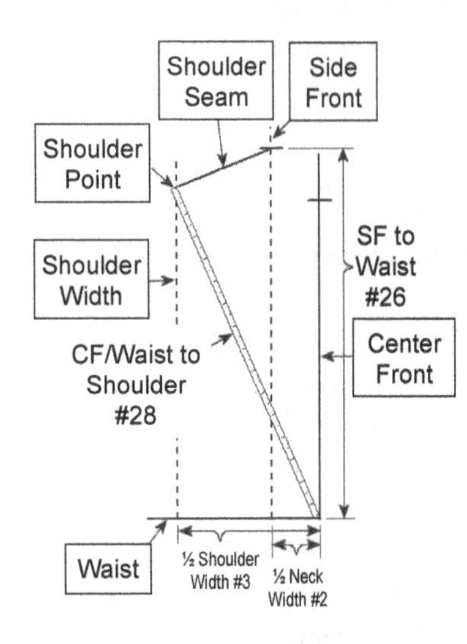

The Shoulder Seam

Step 4. On the Waist line, measure out from the Center Front half the Neck Width measurement (#2), then make a mark. From this point, draw a line that is parallel to the Center Front line. This is the Side Front line. On this line, mark off the Side Front to Waist measurement (#26) .

Step 5. On the Waist line, measure out from the Center Front half of the Shoulder Width measurement (#3), then make a mark. From this point, draw a second line parallel to the Center Front line. This is the Shoulder Width line.

Step 6. To find the Shoulder Point, use the Center Front/Waist to Shoulder length (#28) to strike an arc from the Center Front at the Waist to the Shoulder Width line.

To strike this arc, take a tape measure and find the Center Front/Waist to Shoulder length. Put one end of this length on the Center Front at the Waist and place the other end on the Shoulder Width line, holding the tape straight and taut.

Step 7. Draw a line from the top of the Side Front length (Step 4) to the Shoulder Point to form the Shoulder Seam.

The Side Seam

Step 8. On the Waist line, measure out from the Center Front one-fourth of the Waist measurement (#9) and make a mark. This is the Side Waist point.

One half of the Waist measurement would be the distance from the Center Front to the Center Back. To establish the location of the Side Seam, this measurement is divided into half again (one-fourth of the total Waist measurement). The same thing will be done to the Chest measurement.

Step 9. On the Waist line, measure out from the Center Front line 1" (2.5 cm) plus one-fourth of the Chest measurement (#5), then make a mark. From this point, draw a line parallel to the Center Front line. This is the Chest Width line.

1" (2.5 cm) of Ease is added to this measurement to compensate for the movement of the arms in relation to the body and for the movement of the chest.

Step 10. Use the Armpit to Waist measurement (#32) to strike an arc from the Side Waist point until it intersects the Chest Width line. Mark this point and draw a line connecting it to the Side Waist point. This is the Side Seam.

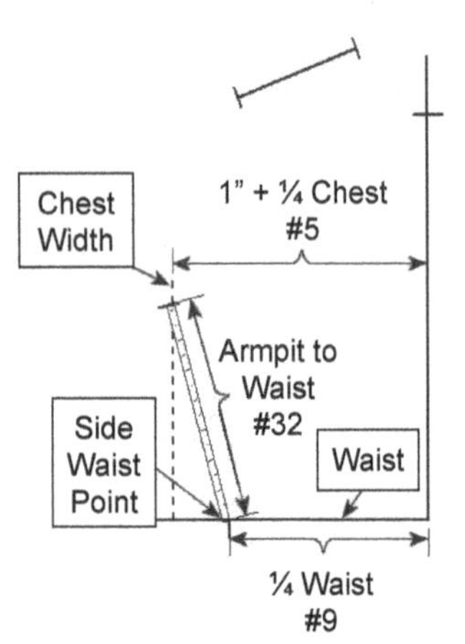

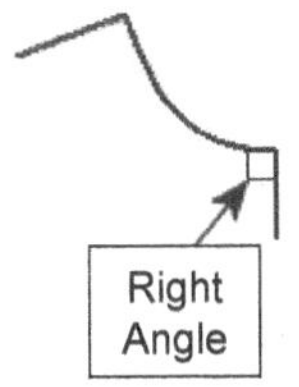

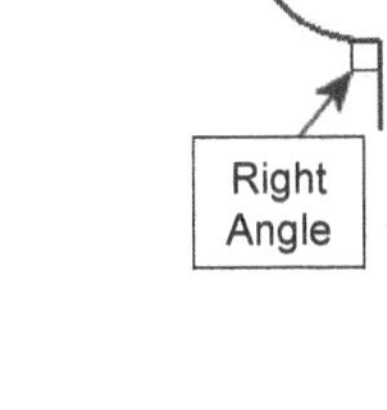

The Neck Curve

Step 11. The Neck curve is sketched in freehand. It is almost semi-circular in shape. The intersection of the Neck curve with the Center Front should be a right angle. If this is not done, there will be an uneven shape at Center Front.

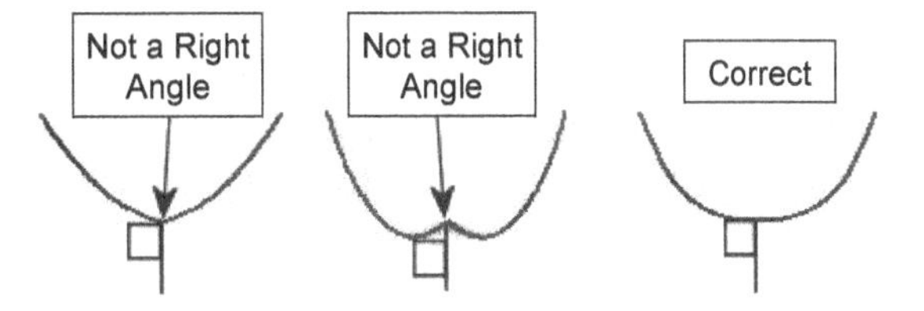

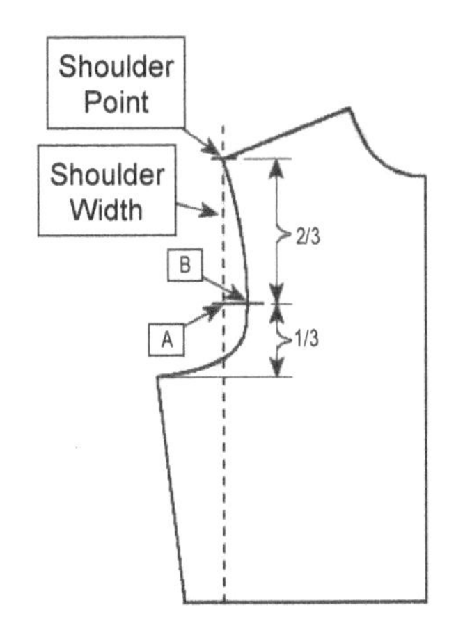

The Armscye (Armhole) Curve

Step 12. The Armscye curve is also sketched in freehand. Measure down from the Shoulder Point two-thirds of the distance from the Shoulder Point to the top of the Side Seam and mark point A on the Shoulder Width line. Measure ¾" (2 cm) in from point A toward the Center Front line and mark point B.

The Armhole curve is drawn straight from the Shoulder Point to point B. From here, it curves out to the top of the Side Seam.

The shape of the Neck curve and the Armhole curve are approximated in the drafting process. The exact shape will be determined by the contours of the individual body during the fitting.

Seam Allowances

Add a 1½" (4 cm) seam allowance to the Side Seam and the Shoulder Seam. Add 1" (2.5 cm) seam allowance to the Armhole and Neck curves and add 1" (2.5 cm) seam allowance to the Center Front for pinning the garment closed during the fitting. Add a 2" (5 cm) seam allowance to the Waist.

The Back of the Body and the Pattern

Men's and women's backs have the same fundamental structure, and there are two basic back shapes that may be found: the flat shouldered back; the rounded shouldered back. To determine which shape you are working with, look at the body from the side.

On a flat shouldered back, the back of the arm is even with the shoulder blades. Place a yardstick across the shoulder blades so that it is parallel to the floor. Notice that both the back of the arms and the shoulder blades touch the yardstick. The fabric covering this back shape may hang from the Shoulder Seam without any need for a dart at the shoulder.

Round shouldered backs have arms that pitch forward from the shoulder blades. If a round shouldered person were to back up flat against a wall, the backs of their arms would not touch the wall, only their shoulder blades. Rounded shoulders require a dart or seam to shape the fabric as it must bend in two directions at the same time: in a vertical direction from the Shoulder Seam down to the shoulder blade; and in a horizontal direction from the Center Back around to the Armscye (Armhole) seam.

All bodies bend in two directions in the lower back. From the shoulder blades to the waist, bodies bend horizontally from Center Back to the Side Seam and vertically from the bottom of the shoulder blades into the Waist. Hence the need for a dart or seam to shape this contour.

The Back Pattern

The back pattern is drafted for the flat shouldered back. The adjustment for round shouldered backs is made during the fitting.

The back pattern is drafted in almost the same way as the man's front pattern. The main difference is adding additional allowance for the lower back darts.

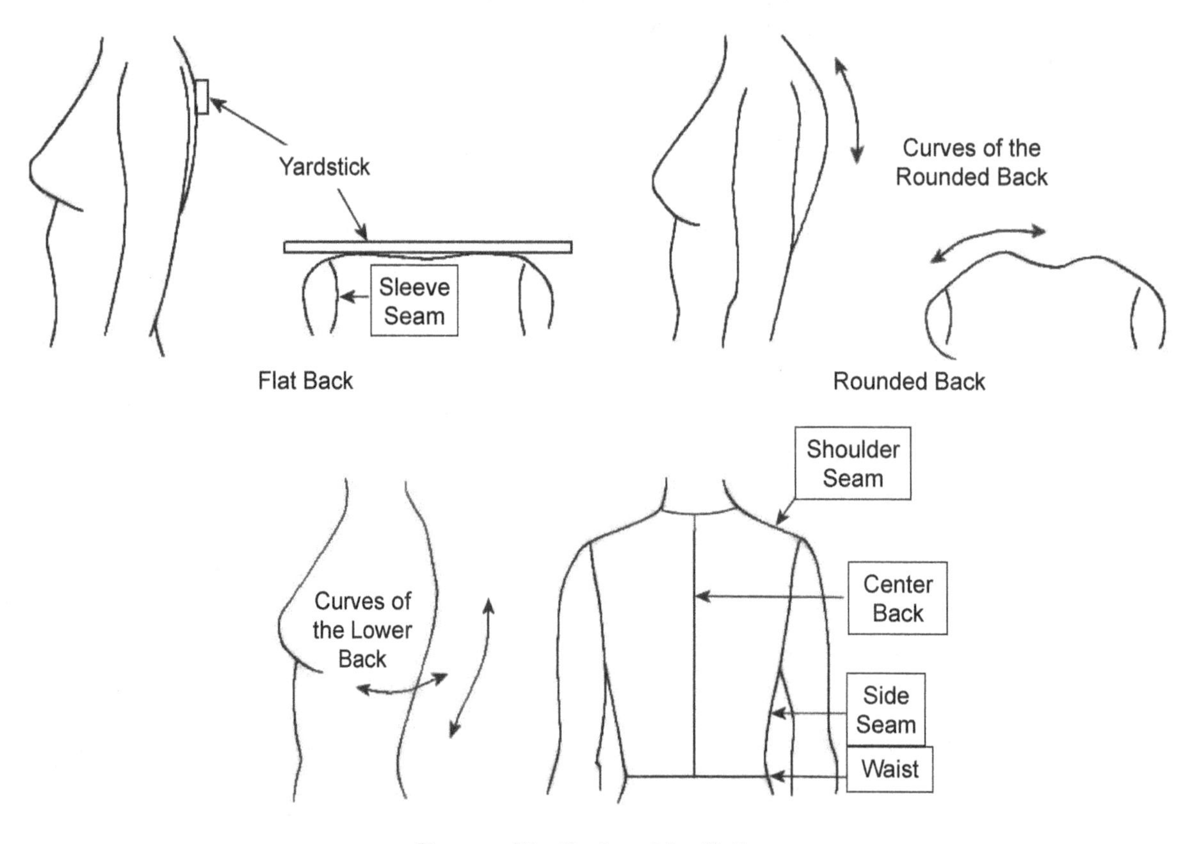

Shapes of the Back and the Pattern

2. Neck Width:		29. Center Back:	
3. Shoulder Width:		30. Side Back:	
5/6. Chest or Bust:		31. Center Back/Waist to Shoulder:	
9. Waist:		32. Armpit to Waist:	

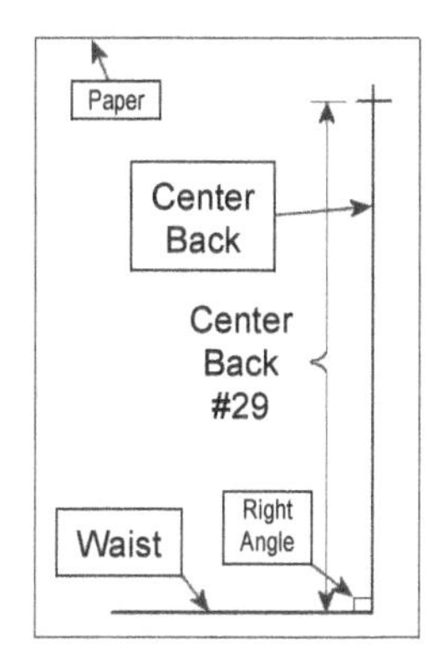

The Basic Reference Lines

Step 1. On a sheet of paper, draw a vertical line 5" (12 cm) in from the right hand side of the paper. This is the Center Back line.

Step 2. About 5" (12 cm) up from the bottom of the paper, draw a line at right angles to the Center Back line. This is the Waist line.

Step 3. Measuring up from the Waist line, mark off the Center Back measurement (#29) on the Center Back line.

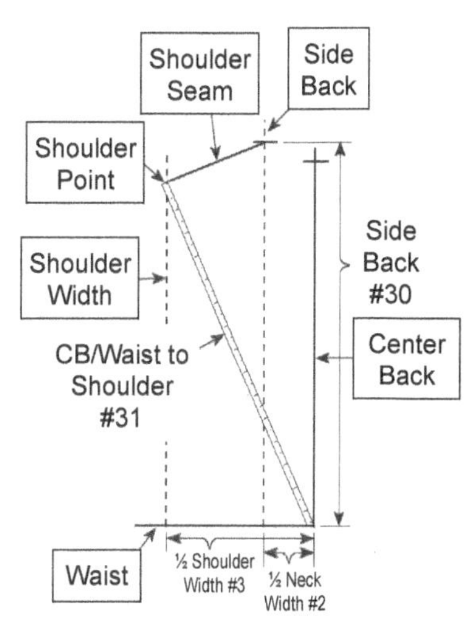

The Shoulder Seam

Step 4. On the Waist line, measure out from the Center Back line half of the Neck Width measurement (#2), then make a mark. From this point, draw a line parallel to the Center Back line. This is the Side Back line. Mark off the Side Back measurement (#30) on this line.

Step 5. On the waist line, measure out from the Center Back line half of the Shoulder Width measurement (#3), then make a mark. From this point, draw a line parallel to the Center Back line. This is the Shoulder Width line.

Step 6. To find the Shoulder Point, use the Center Back/Waist to Shoulder length (#31) to strike an arc from the Center Back at the Waist to the Shoulder Width line.

Step 7. Draw a line from the top of the Side Back length (Step 4) to the Shoulder Point to form the Shoulder Seam.

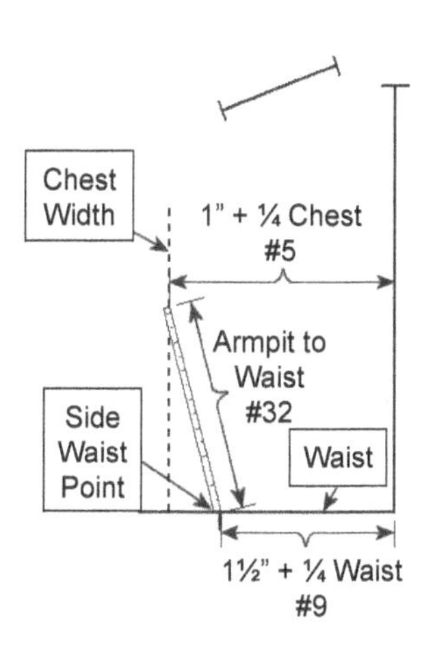

The Side Seam

Step 8. On the Waist line, measure out from the Center Back 1½" (4 cm) plus one-fourth of the Waist measurement (#9) . This is the Side Waist point.

The 1½" (4 cm) added to the Waist measurement is a dart allowance for the back dart. The back dart will be fitted according to the contours of the individual body rather than drafted in at this point.

Step 9. On the Waist line, measure out from the Center Back line 1" (2.5 cm) plus one-fourth the man's Chest measurement (#5) or the women's Bust measurement (#6), then make a mark. From this point, draw a line parallel to the Center Back line. This is the Chest Width line.

Step 10. Use the Armpit to Waist measurement (#32) to strike an arc from the Side Waist point until it intersects the Chest Width line. Mark this point and draw a line connecting it to the Side Waist point. This is the Side Seam.

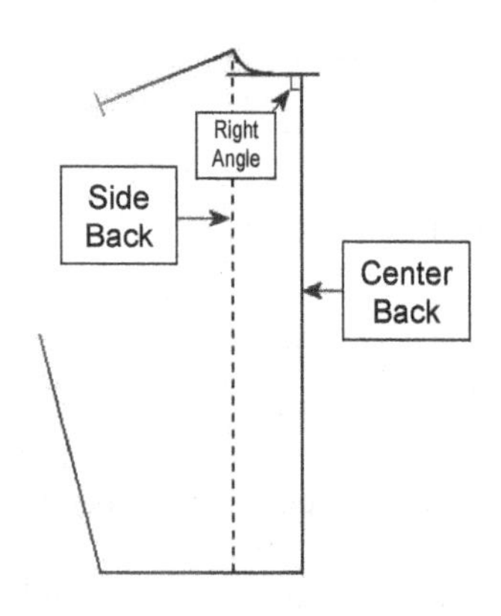

The Neck Curve

Step 11. At the top of the Center Back line, draw a line at right angles to it. Extend this line to the Side Back line. Draw in a short curve from the Shoulder Seam to this line. This is the Neck Curve.

The neck across the back is fairly flat. The back Neck Curve will therefore not dip down as much as the front Neck Curve.

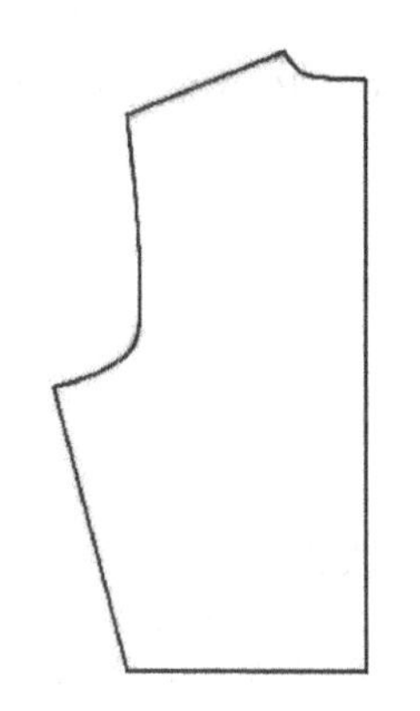

The Armscye (Armhole) Curve

Step 12. The back Armscye Curve is very shallow. It starts from the Shoulder Seam and curves slightly until it meets the Side Seam line.

Seam Allowances

Add a 1½" (4 cm) seam allowance to the Side Seam and the Shoulder Seam. Add a 1" (2.5 cm) seam allowance to the Armhole and Neck curves and add a 2" (5 cm) seam allowance at the Waist. The Center Back line is a fold line.

A Woman's Body and the Front Pattern

Women's bodies vary in the front according to the size and shape of the bust. Thus the exact shape of the bust is very important in determining how finished garments will hang.

The bust is shaped in two directions at the same time. The horizontal direction bends from the Center Front around to the Side Seam. The vertical direction slopes down from the shoulder to the Bust Apex and then bends into the Waist. These two simultaneous curves of the bust make it mandatory to include a dart or seam if the garment is to fit.

The vertical curve should be divided into two parts. The first part is for the shape of the bust from the Shoulder Seam to the Bust Apex. This is referred to as the Above the Bust shape. The second part is the shape from the Bust Apex to the Waist. This area is referred to as the Below the Bust shape.

It is necessary to make this two part distinction because while most garments must fit the Above the Bust area, not every garment fits closely Below the Bust. Each of these two shapes also affects the grain lines of a garment differently.

Important Note - While these two shapes will be referred to separately from this point onward, it is important to remember that they are both shapes for the single contour of the bust. A single dart may therefore be used to make fabric fit both shapes. And this dart may come from any seam so long as the dart points to the bust.

The Woman's Front Pattern

The woman's front pattern is drafted for one-half of the front. The Center Front and the Waist are the basic reference lines. The Bust Apex is also established as an important reference point.

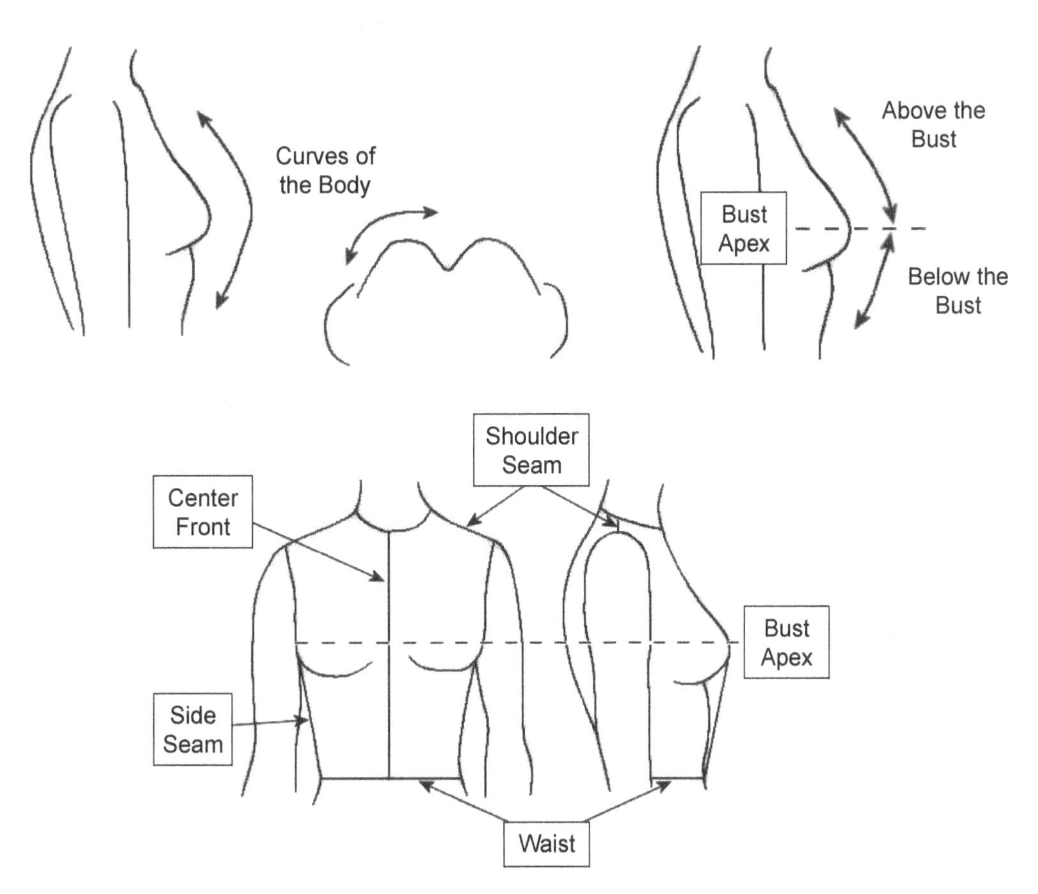

Woman's Front and the Pattern

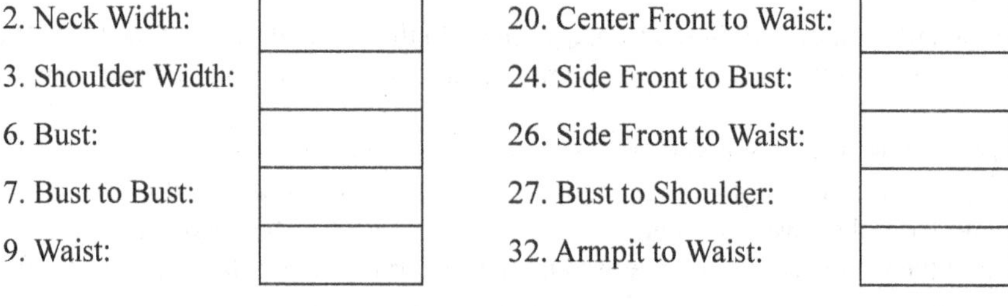

2. Neck Width:		20. Center Front to Waist:	
3. Shoulder Width:		24. Side Front to Bust:	
6. Bust:		26. Side Front to Waist:	
7. Bust to Bust:		27. Bust to Shoulder:	
9. Waist:		32. Armpit to Waist:	

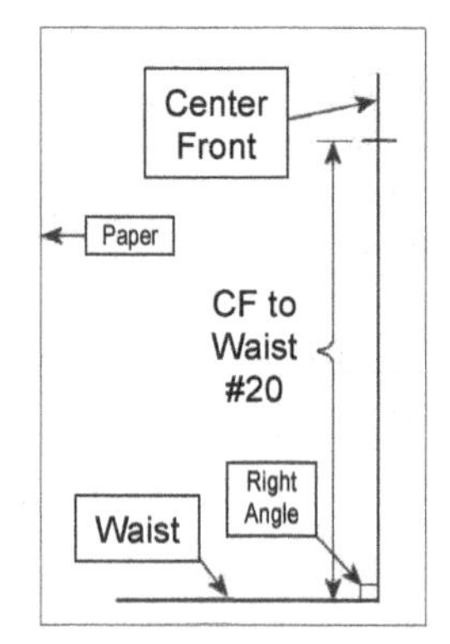

The Basic Reference Lines

Step 1. Draw a vertical line on the right side of the paper that is the Center Front to Waist length (#20). This is the Center Front line.

Step 2. At the bottom of this length, draw a line at right angles to the Center Front line. This is the Waist line.

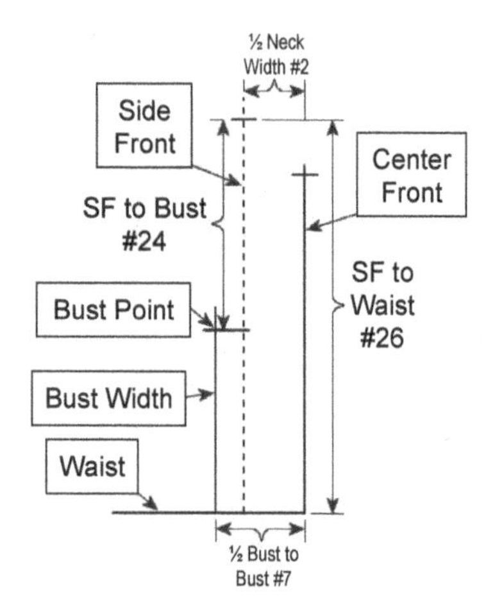

The Bust Point

Step 3. On the Waist line, measure out from the Center Front line half the Neck Width measurement (#2), then make a mark. From this point, draw a line that is parallel to the Center Front line. This is the Side Front line. Mark off the Side Front to Waist measurement (#26) on this line.

Step 4. From the top of the Side Front length, measure down the Side Front to Bust measurement (#24). Draw a short line at right angles to the Side Front line at this point. This establishes the height of the bust.

Step 5. On the Waist line, measure out from the Center Front line half the Bust to Bust measurement (#7) and make a mark. From this point, draw a line parallel to the Center Front line. This is the Bust Width line. The Bust Point is located where this line crosses the line established in Step 4.

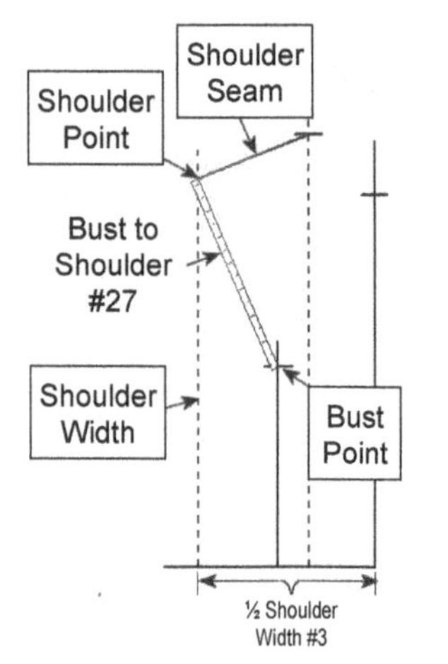

The Shoulder Seam

Step 6. On the Waist line, measure out from the Center Front line one-half the Shoulder Width measurement (#3), then make a mark. From this point, draw a line that is parallel to the Center Front line. This is the Shoulder Width line.

Step 7. To find the Shoulder Point, use the Bust to Shoulder length (#27) to strike an arc from the Bust Point to the Shoulder Width line.

Step 8. Draw a line from the Shoulder Point to the top of the Side Front length. This is the Shoulder Seam.

The Side Seam

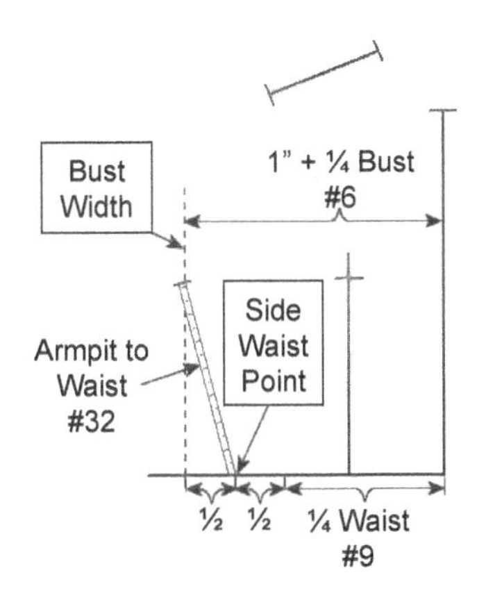

Step 9. On the Waist line, measure out from the Center Front 1" (2.5 cm) plus one-fourth the Bust measurement (#6) and make a mark.

Step 10. From this point, draw a line that is parallel to the Center Front line. This is the Bust Width line. The basic fitting Ease is 1" (2.5 cm).

Step 11. On the Waist line, measure out from the Center Front one-fourth the Waist measurement (#9) and make a mark.

Step 13. Divide the distance between the waist mark and the Bust Width line in half, then make a mark at the Waist line. This is the Side Waist Point.

Step 14. Use the Armpit to Waist length (#32) to strike an arc from the Side Waist Point to the Bust Width line. This is the top of the Side Seam. Then draw a line from this mark down to the Side Waist Point. This is the Side Seam.

The Neck Curve

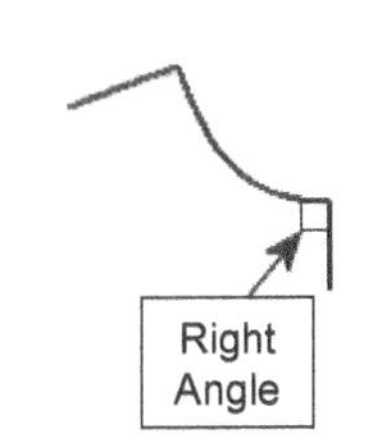

Step 15. The Neck Curve is sketched in freehand. It is almost semi-circular in shape. Be sure the intersection of the Neck Curve and the Center Front is at right angles.

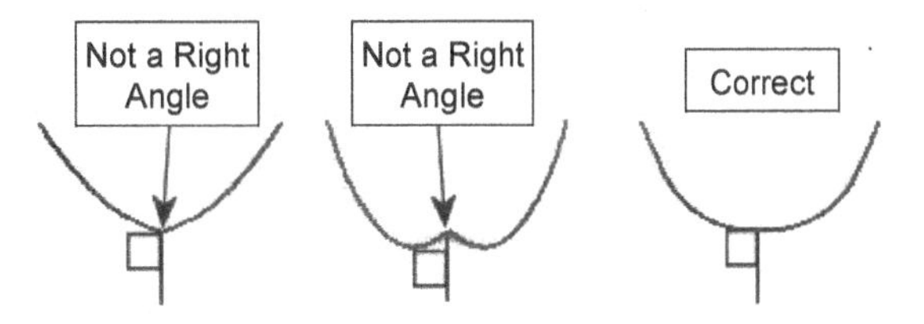

The Armscye (Armhole) Curve

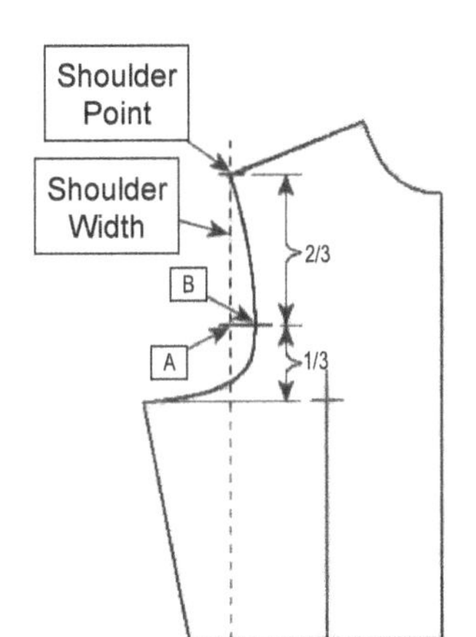

Step 16. The Armscye curve is sketched in freehand. Measure down from the Shoulder Point two-thirds of the distance from the Shoulder Point to the top of the Side Seam and mark point A on the Shoulder Width line. Measure ¾" (2 cm) in from point A toward the Center Front line and mark point B.

Step 17. Draw the Armhole Curve from the Shoulder Point to point B. Then curve it out to the top of the Side Seam. Big busts will require a more pronounced curve.

Seam Allowances

Add a 1½" (4 cm) seam allowance to the Side Seam and Shoulder Seam. Add a 1" (2.5 cm) seam allowance to the Armhole and Neck curves and 1" (2.5 cm) to the Center Front for pinning the garment closed during the fitting. Add a 2" (5 cm) seam allowance to the Waist.

Initial Fitting of the Bodice

The fitted bodice is the basis for coats, shirts, blouses, and dresses so an accurate fit is a time saver for making garments.

Start by fitting half the body with a pinning. After this fitting, baste the fitting shell together for a second fitting. If you are fitting an asymmetrical body, fit the high or larger side first and make adjustments for the other side during the second fitting.

These instructions show how to fit someone else as well as how to fit yourself without a sewing buddy. See the abbreviations DIY (Do-It-Yourself). A fitting buddy does not need to know how to sew and, with help, the process is easier. But doing it yourself yields better results than working with a careless or impatient fitting buddy.

During the initial fitting, work from the Center Front and Center Back toward the side following the sequence below:

1. Adjust the Shoulder Seam.
2. Fit the Front Darts (for women).
3. Fit the Back Darts.
4. Adjust the Side Seam.
5. Mark the Neck and Armscye Curves.
6. Mark the Waist.

Whether you are fitting yourself or someone else, you can complete all six steps in a single fitting. When fitting yourself, however, stop after the first three steps, transfer the shapes from the fitting shell to the patterns, then baste what you have already fitted before proceeding to the final three steps.

To determine the darts during a fitting, first record the dart's point with two pins indicating the vertical and horizontal positions. Once the point of a dart is established, pin the width of the dart at the armscye (armhole) for the upper part of the body and the waist for the lower part of the body. Add the dart lines when transferring the marks back to the paper pattern. Don't overwork the darts during this initial fitting.

When fitting yourself, slash the fabric of the fitting shell, overlap the darts, then tape them in place. Whereas pinning requires both hands, taping can be done with one hand so your other hand can hold the fabric in place.

Note: Taping does not require as much manual dexterity as pinning so is a good choice for a fitting buddy who does not sew.

Create a Fitting Shell

Start by creating a fitting shell out of gingham from the front and back patterns. Gingham in pastel colors in 1/4" squares works best. There is no need to sew the fitting shell until after the fit is verified. For the initial step, just pin the shoulder seams following the seam line.

Step 1. Cut two front panels with the 1" (2.5 cm) seam allowance for pinning the fitting shell closed at Center Front.

Step 2. Cut the back pattern on the fold.

Step 3. Pin the front to the back at the Shoulder Seams.

Step 4. Put the fitting shell on, then pin the Center Front closed.

Adjust the Shoulder Seam

Adjust the Shoulder Seam as necessary so the Center Front and Center Back of the fitting shell follow the Center Front and Center Back of the body. The fabric should fit smoothly on the front and back of the body.

Women with a hollow between the Bust Apex and the Shoulder Seam will not be able to smooth out this area completely. This hollow can only be fitted by placing a dart or seam between the armhole and the Bust Apex. See the section on styling the Princess Seam on page 95.

The Shoulder Seam should be on the top of the shoulder. Check for the correct placement by looking at this seam from the front and then from the back. Looking from the front, you should not be able to see any of the back pattern's fabric. Looking from the back, you should not be able to see any of the front pattern's fabric. Adjust the seam as necessary to achieve this.

Another way to verify the Shoulder Seam is on top of the shoulder is to place a book or other flat object on the shoulder and keep it parallel to the floor as seen from the side. The Shoulder Seam should be directly under the book.

Pin the Shoulder Seams carefully because garments for the upper body hang from the shoulders. If the correct slope of the shoulders is not established, then the fabric will not hang smoothly.

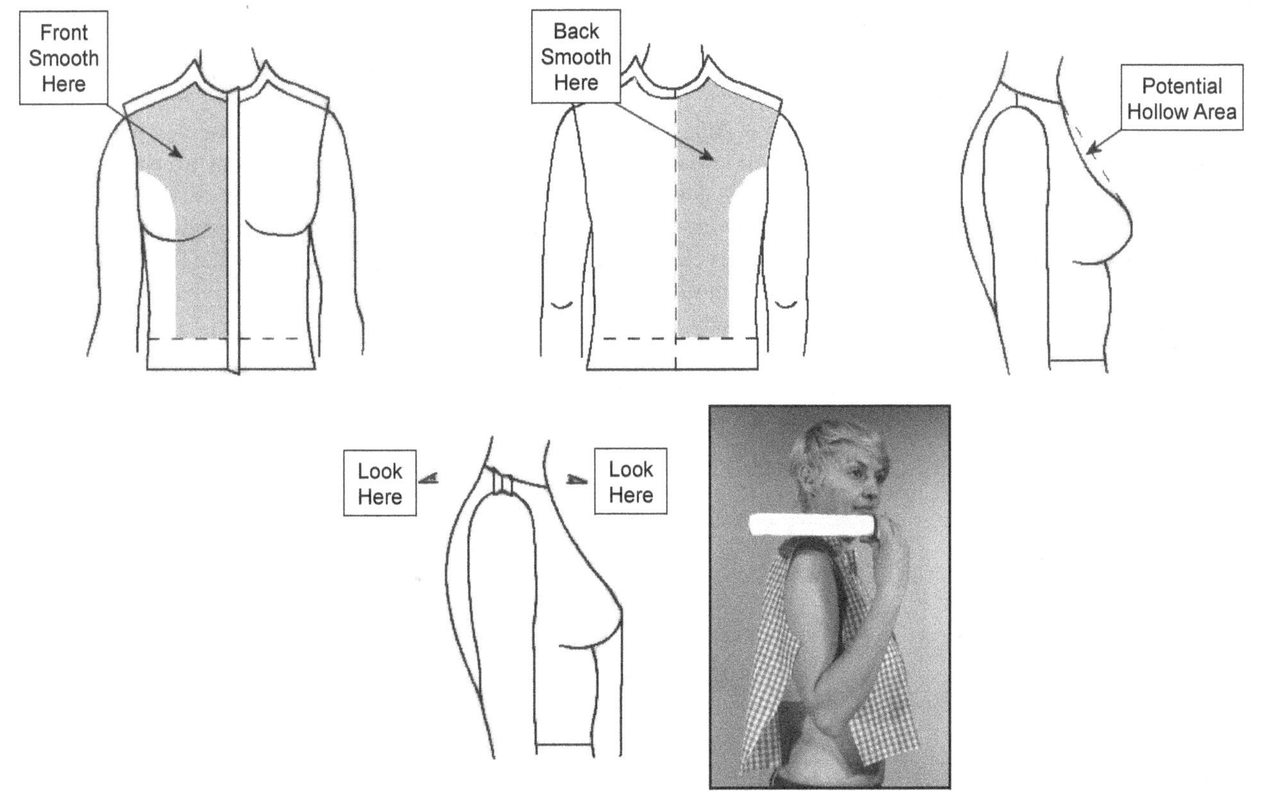

Fitting the Shoulder Seam

The Front Darts for Women

There are two front darts for women. The Above Bust Dart adjusts for where the upper chest tapers out to the Bust Apex. The Below the Bust Dart adjusts for where the Bust Apex tapers into the waist. Both darts should point to the Bust Apex. Indicate the Bust Apex with a vertical pin to indicate where the body curves toward the side. Use a horizontal pin to indicate the Full Bust level.

Note: Bras sometimes change the level of the bust. So the person being fitted should be wearing a bra that provides a standard for the garment(s) being created.

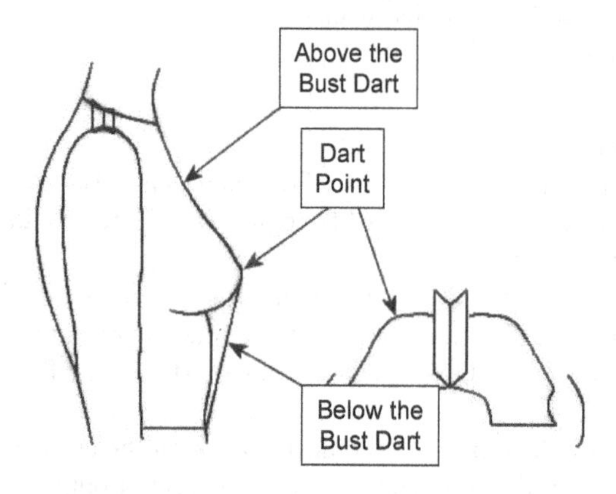

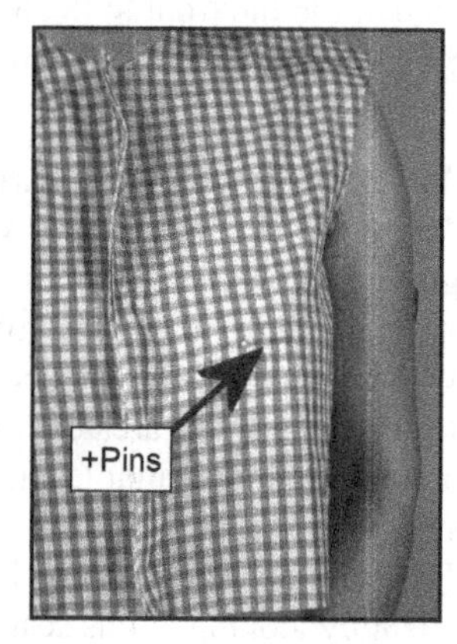

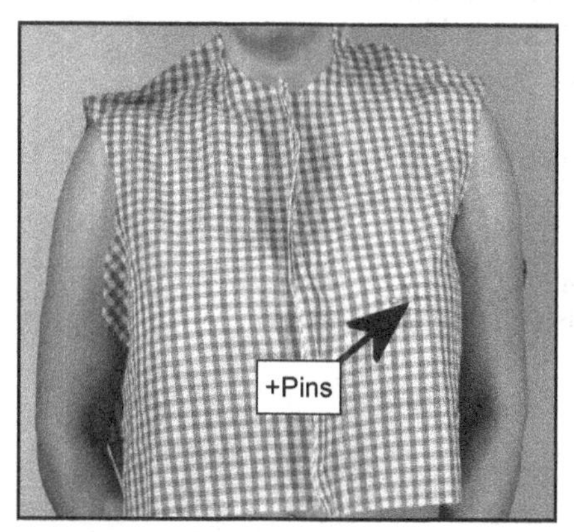

Step 1. Use a vertical pin to indicate where the bust curves around to the side of the body.

Step 2. Use a horizontal pin to indicate the location of the Bust Apex.

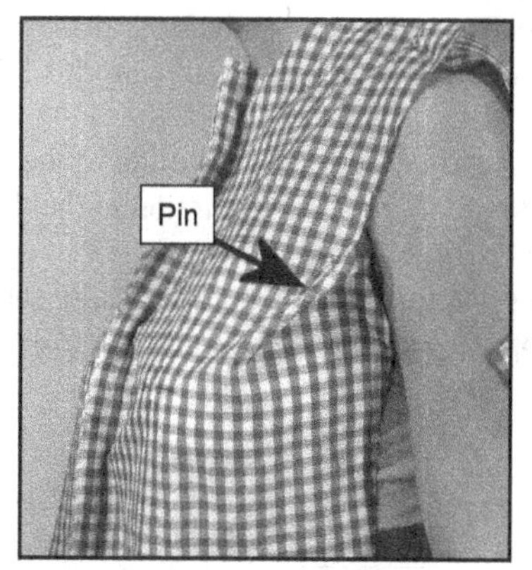

Step 3. Adjust the front side of the fitting shell so that the horizontal grain from the bust down is parallel to the floor. Pin the excess into the armscye. Put this pin as close as possible to where the arm starts going under the side of the body. Princess seams are commonly styled to this point. This is the Above the Bust Dart.

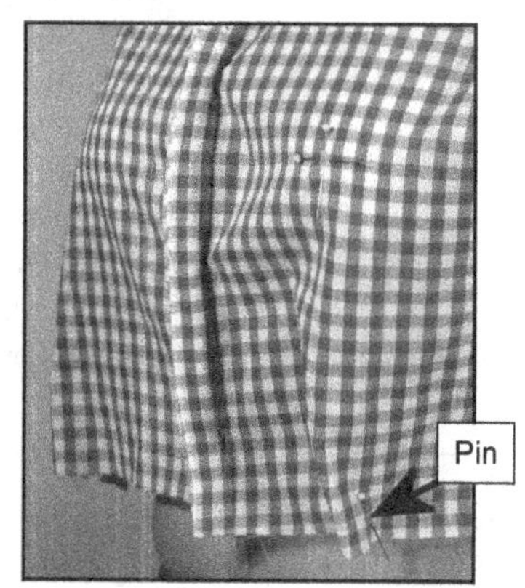

Step 4. Put a vertical pin at the waist to remove any excess fabric. Verify that the vertical grain at the side of the body is perpendicular to the floor. This is the Below the Bust Dart.

Back Darts

There are potentially two darts for the back: an Upper Back Dart and a Lower Back Dart. The Upper Back Dart adjusts for the body's contour that occurs when the shoulders are rounded. The Lower Back Dart adjusts for the contour where the shoulder blades taper into the waist.

To determine the locations for the Back Darts, stand with the back to a wall and locate the point where the body moves away from the wall.

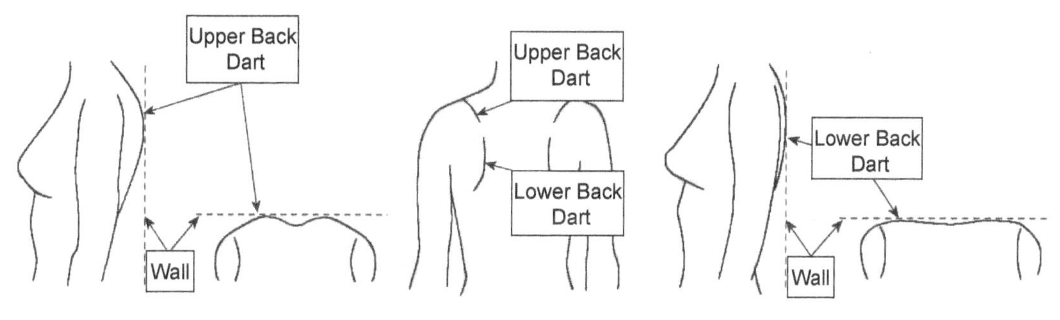

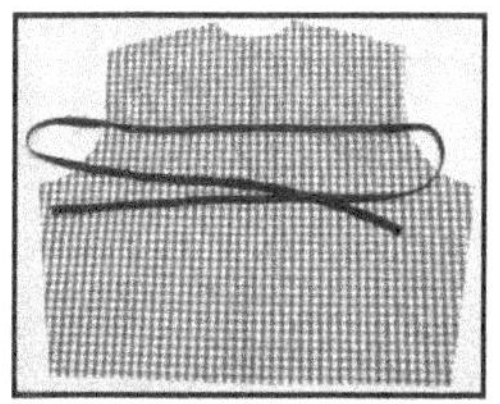
Bias Tape Sewn to Back for a DIY Fitting

If you are fitting yourself, cut a length of bias tape that is the Chest or Bust measurement plus 24" (60 cm). Then, following the horizontal grain of the fabric, zigzag the bias tape to the fitting shell at a level that is in the middle of the shoulder blades. After you have put the fitting shell on, tie the tape to hold the fabric in place.

Upper Back Dart

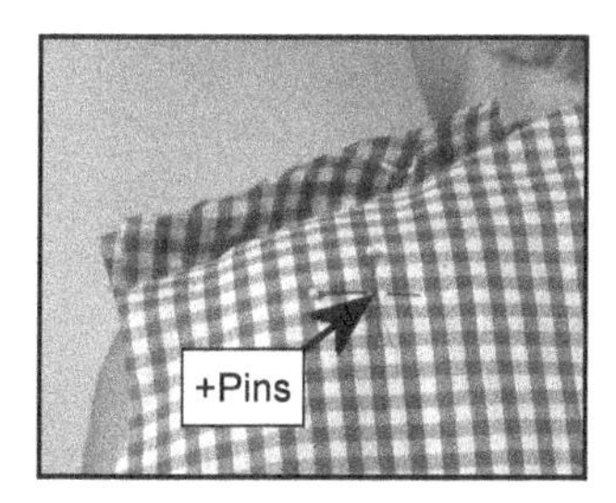

Step 1. For the dart's point, put a vertical pin where the shoulders curve away from the wall toward the arm. If you are fitting yourself, use a marking pen to indicate this position.

Step 2. Put a horizontal pin where the shoulders curve up towards the Shoulder Seam.

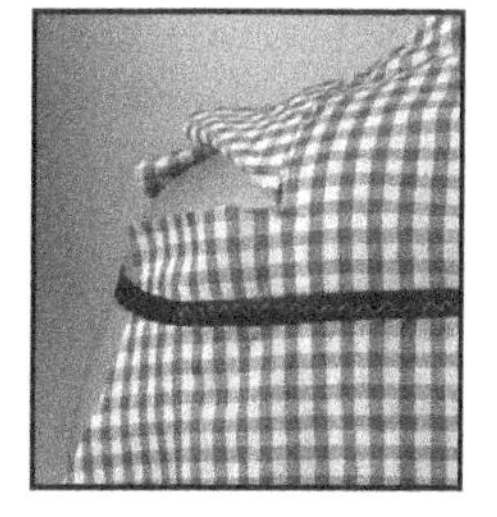

Step 3. If you are fitting yourself, remove the fitting shell. Then, following the horizontal grain of the fabric, cut from the armscye to the dart's point. Put the fitting shell back on.

Step 4. At the armscye, adjust the horizontal grain of the fabric across the shoulders so it is parallel to the floor. Pin the excess fabric in the armscye.

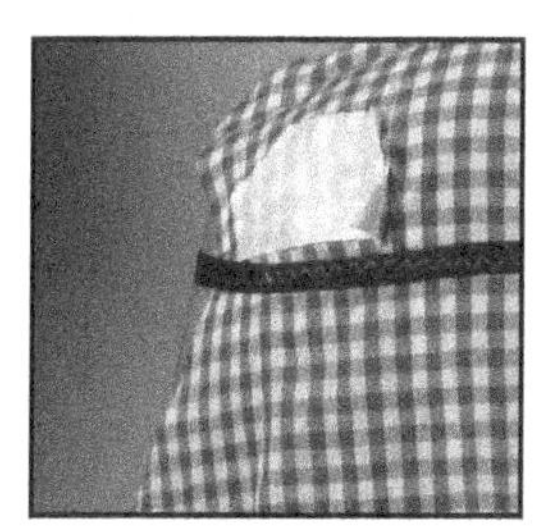

If you are fitting yourself, tape the dart closed.

Lower Back Dart

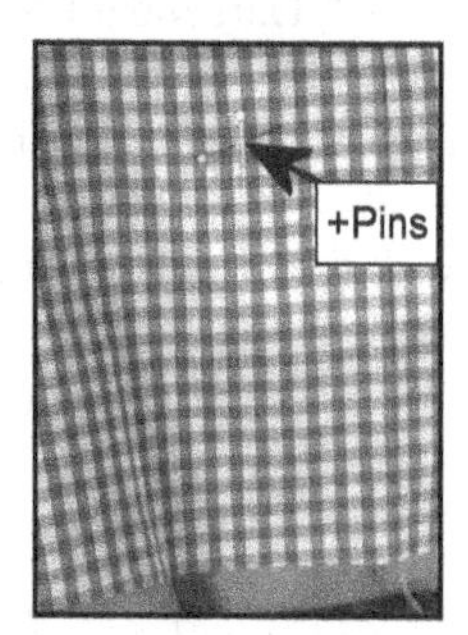

Step 1. Put a vertical pin where the shoulders curve away from the wall toward the arm. If you are fitting yourself, use a marking pen to indicate this position.

Step 2. Put a horizontal pin where the shoulders curve down towards the waist.

Step 3. If you are fitting yourself, remove the fitting shell. Then, following the horizontal grain of the fabric, cut from the armscye to the dart's point. Put the fitting shell back on.

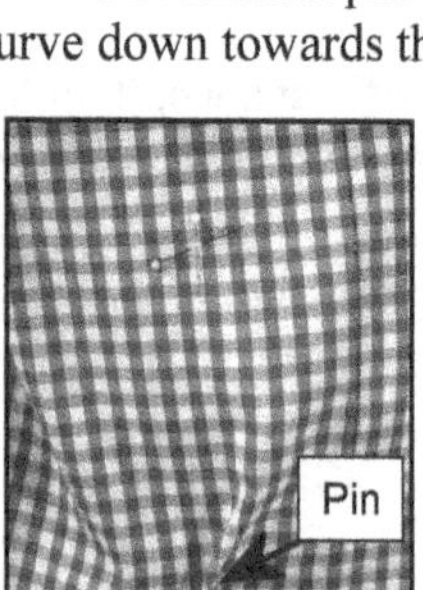

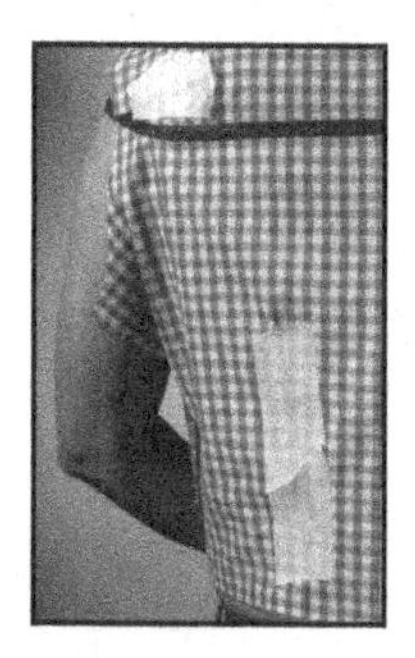

Step 4. At the waist, adjust the vertical grain of the fabric so it is perpendicular to the floor. Pin the excess fabric at the waist.

If you are fitting yourself, tape the dart closed.

The Side Seam

Adjust the paper patterns as needed, see page 72, then baste the Shoulder Seams and the darts. When fitting another person, it may be more convenient to do the entire initial fitting without this interruption.

Fit the Side Seam by smoothing the fabric from the back into the fabric from the front. It will be more accurate at this point to pin the fabric close to the body. The Ease is added back as necessary when the paper patterns are adjusted. Be careful during this step not to pull the Center Front and the Center Back out of alignment.

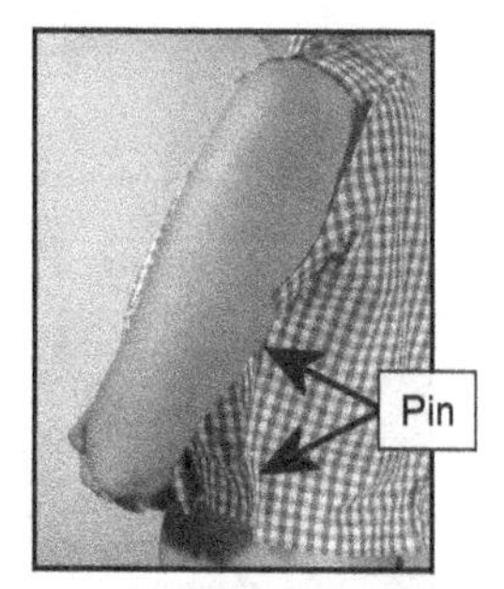

Pinned Side Seam

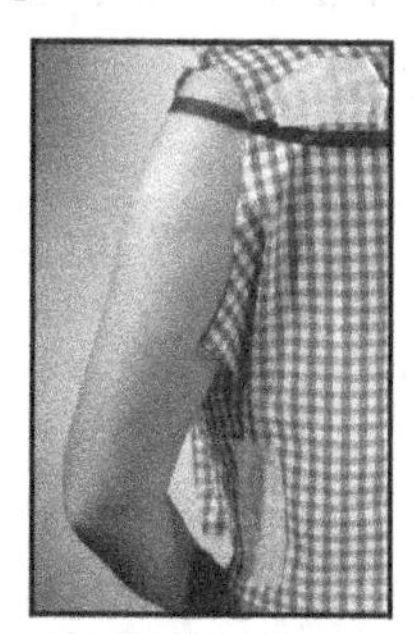

Taped Side Seam

The Waist

Correct the paper patterns and baste the seams and darts for both sides before determining the waist location.

All the Slopers should use the exact same location for the waist, see page 19. Place a string around the Waist. Make sure it is parallel to the floor around the entire body. With a marking pen, indicate the location of the string on the fitting shell.

Note for Women: The waist can be determined by placing a string around the body and tying it snugly. The string will have a tendency to find a level half way between the pelvic bone and the rib cage.

The Neck and Armscye (Armhole) Curves

Mark the Neck Curve with a marking pen. You may wish to review the correct placement for the Neck Curve as described on page 18. Make sure the point where the front Neck Curve touches the Shoulder Seam is the same point where the back Neck Curve touches the Shoulder Seam.

To draw the Armscye Curve, first establish the Shoulder Point, see page 18. Then mark where the fabric buckles between the arm and the body. Connect this mark to the Shoulder Point. Continue the curve under the arm. Repeat this procedure for the back.

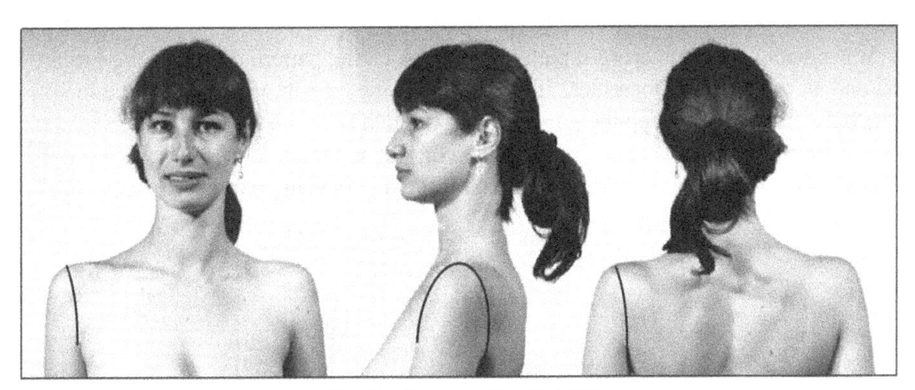

Location for Armscye (Armhole) Seam

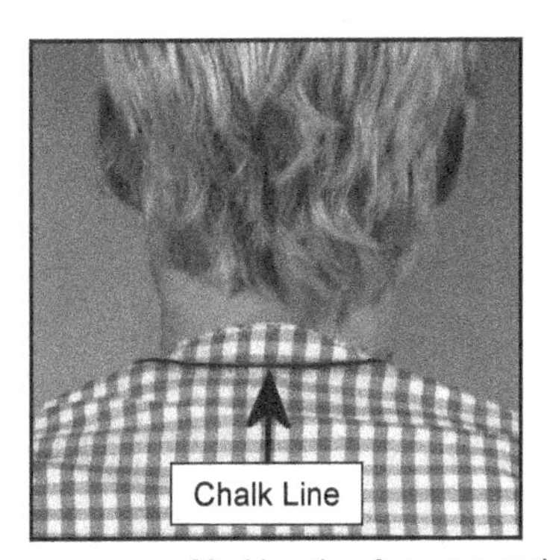

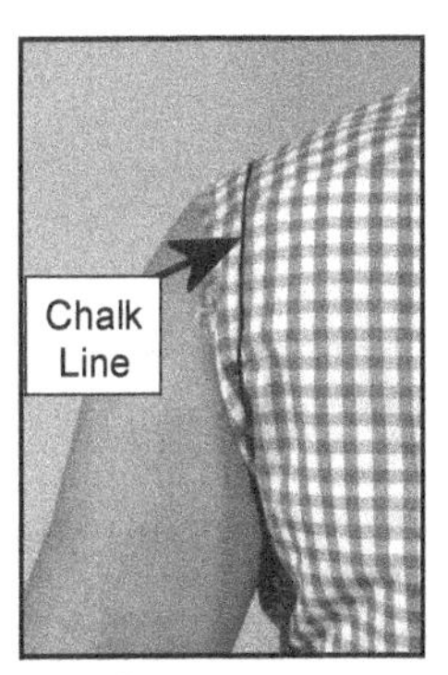

Marking the Armscye and Neck Seams
for DIY Applications

Adjust the Patterns for the Darts

During fittings, the locations of the darts and seams can be adjusted. Always record the results from the fittings on the paper patterns. During this process, you can further optimize darts and seam locations as well as verify the patterns have the correct amount of Ease.

You can adjust the patterns as you proceed thorough each stage of the fitting, thus simplifying the DIY process. Or, you can make adjustments after completing the initial fitting.

> **Important Note** – Immediately after you remove the fitting shell, it is extremely important to mark the location of all the pins used during the fittings.
>
> When you are marking the pins that indicate the dart widths, mark both sides of the dart. When you are marking seams, be sure to do the following:
>
> 1. Put a pin at right angles to the seam line through the middle of the seam. This will serve as a sewing notch.
> 2. Mark the pins where they appear on the front of the fitting shell.
> 3. Mark the pins where they appear on the back of the fitting shell.
> 4. Remove the pins.

When using semi-transparent pattern paper, place the pattern on top of the fitting shell and mark the fitting locations. If you have left the pins in, you can feel the location of the pins. Be sure you keep the paper pattern aligned with the fitting shell.

If your pattern paper is not semi-transparent, put sewing tracing paper between the fitting shell and the paper pattern, then transfer the marks using a tracing wheel.

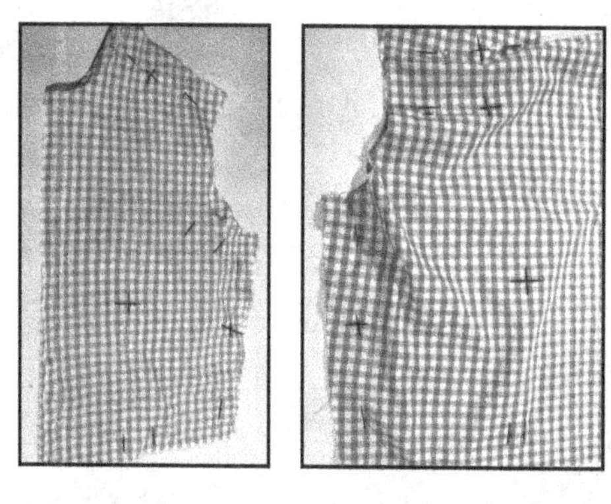

Record the Shoulder Seam

Maintain an accurate location of the sewing notch in the middle of the Shoulder Seam. This will expedite and simplify all your fitting issues.

Step 1. Transfer the location of the Shoulder Seam from the fitting shell to the front and back paper patterns.

Step 2. Draw a straight line for the Shoulder Seam on the front and back patterns.

Step 3. Transfer the sewing notch from the fitting shell to the paper pattern.

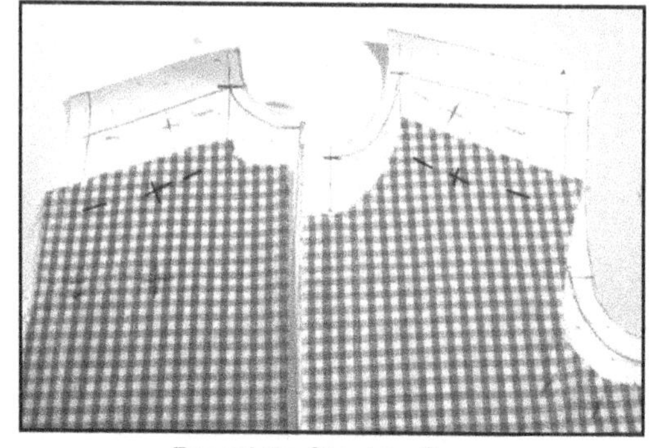

Record the Shoulder Seam

Record the Upper Back Dart

The centerline of the Upper Back Dart should be kept at right angles to the Center Back.

Step 1. Transfer the location of the Upper Back Dart's point from the fitting shell to the paper pattern.

Step 2. Draw a line at right angles to Center Back that starts at the dart's point and extends to the Armscye. This is the dart centerline.

Step 3. Measure the width of the Upper Back Dart at the Armscye and mark half this width on each side of the dart's centerline.

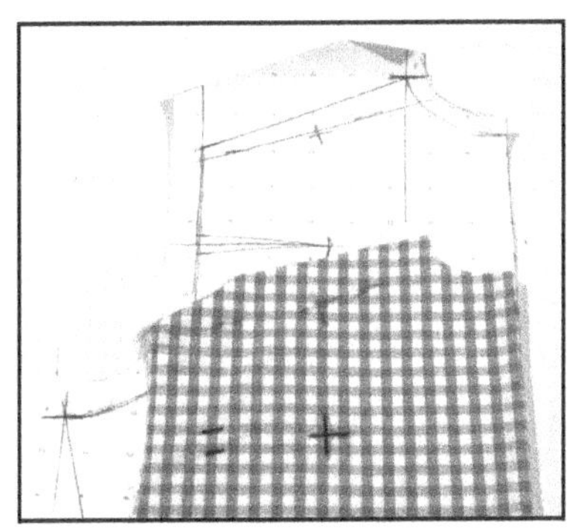

Record the Upper Back Dart

Record the Lower Back Dart

The centerline of the Lower Back Dart should be parallel to the Center Back.

Step 1. Transfer the location of the Lower Back Dart's point from the fitting shell to the paper pattern.

Step 2. Draw a line parallel to the Center Back, going from the dart's point down to the waist. This is the dart centerline.

Step 3. Measure the width of the Lower Back Dart at the waist and mark half this width on each side of the dart centerline.

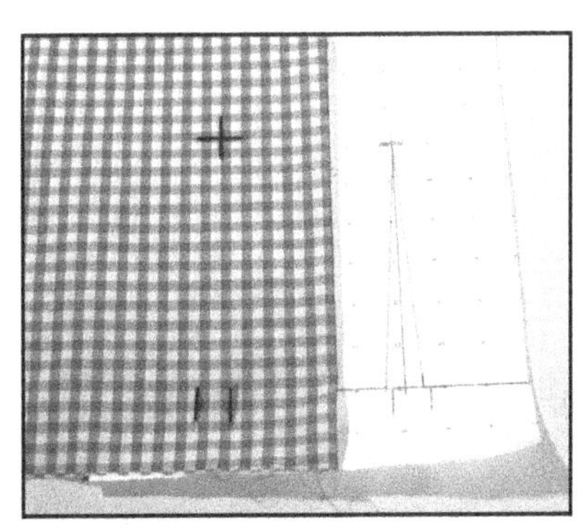

Record the Lower Back Dart

Record the Front Bust Darts for Women

The two front darts for women control the shaping of the bust's contours. These two darts should shape the fabric toward the Bust Apex.

> **Important Note:**
> When these darts are used to create a design, the patterns need to be pivoted at the Bust Apex.
> When the darts are sewn, the points of the darts should not converge right at the apex, but be set back. Use a Bust Circle to record how far back these dart points should be located.

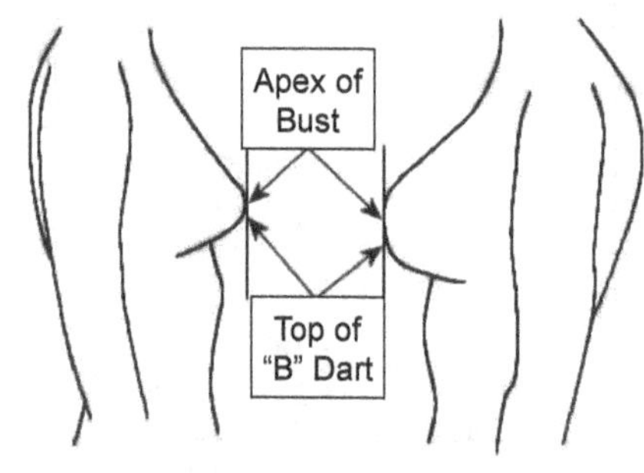

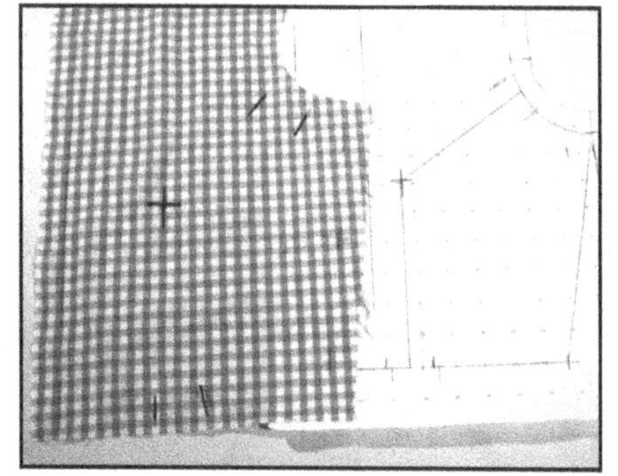

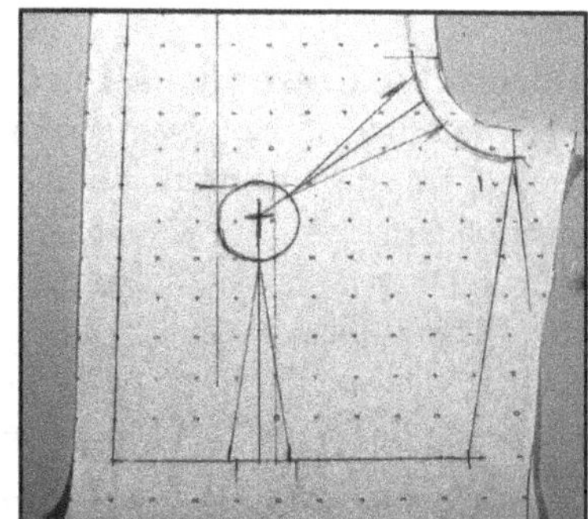

Step 1. Transfer the location of the Bust Apex from the fitting shell to the paper pattern.

Step 2. Draw a line parallel to Center Front from the Bust Apex down to the waist.

Step 3. Measure the width of the Below the Bust Dart at the waist then mark half this width on each side of the dart centerline.

Step 4. Transfer the dart width of the Above the Bust Dart to the pattern at the Armscye.

Step 5. On the paper pattern, divide the width of the Upper Bust Dart in half, then draw a line from this mark to the Bust Apex.

Step 6. Subtract the Above Bust measurement (#4) from the Bust measurement (#6). Then use the chart below to determine the radius of the Bust Circle.

Step 7. Draw a Bust Circle around the Bust Apex.

Step 8. To prepare the fitting shell for the next fitting, draw the dart legs from the dart widths at the waist and armscye to the edge of the Bust Circle.

Bust Circle				
Bust - Above Bust	1" (2.5 cm)	2" (5 cm)	3" (7.5 cm)	4" (10 cm)
Radius of Bust Circle	1" (2.5 cm)	1½" (3.8 cm)	2" (5 cm)	2½" (6.3 cm)

Adjust the Patterns for the Side Seam

When fitting slopers, you may have to change the Ease that was originally drafted into the Side Seam. Use the steps below to verify that the correct Ease is still in the Sloper patterns.

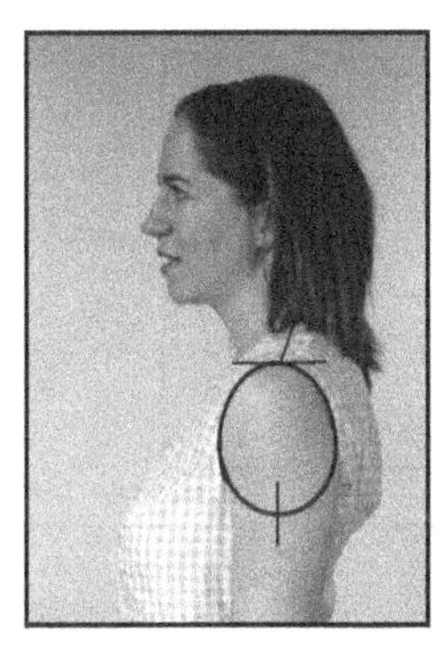

1. Position the top of the Side Seam in the middle of the armscye seam.
2. Adjust the patterns for the Ease at the bust/chest.
3. Adjust the angle of the Side Seam to provide Ease at the waist.

Position the Side Seam

Position the top of the Side Seam half way around the armscye seam so that the Side Seam will coincide with the shape of the Sleeve Cap.

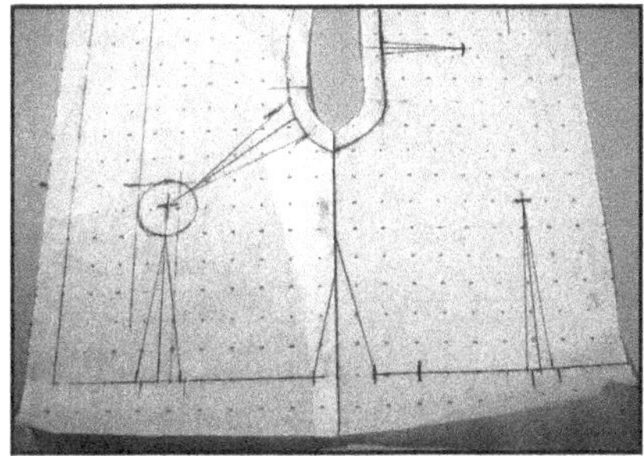

Step 1. On the front pattern, from the top of the Side Seam, draw a line straight down to the waist. This line should be parallel to the Center Front line.

Step 2. On the back pattern, from the top of the Side Seam, draw a line straight down to the waist. This line should be parallel to the Center Back line.

Step 3. Matching the lines drawn in Steps 1 and 2, tape the front pattern to the back pattern.

Step 4. Measure around the armscye from the front shoulder seam to the back shoulder seam. Skip over the dart widths. This is the length of the Armscye seam.

Step 5. Divide the length of the Armscye seam in half.

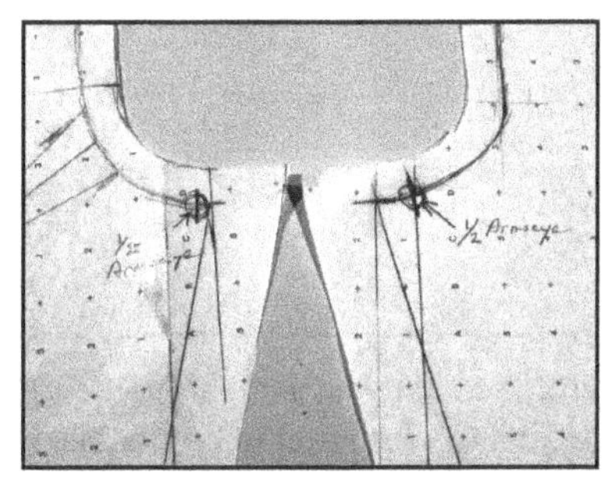

Step 6. On the front pattern, measure down the Armscye from the shoulder seam, skipping the Above the Bust dart, and mark off half the length of the Armscye seam. This is the top of the front Side Seam.

Step 7. On the back pattern, measure down the Armscye from the shoulder seam, skipping the Upper Back Dart, and mark off half the length of the Armscye seam. This is the top of the back Side Seam.

This is the new location for the Side Seam that is used to adjust for Ease.

Adjust the Ease at the Bust/Chest

Use the chart below to determine the Ease for half the Bust Measurement for women (#6) or half the Chest measurement for men (#5). This needs to be the distance from the Center Front to the Center Back lines.

Enter the Bust (#6) or Chest (#4) measurement: (a)	
Divide by 2: (b)	
Add 2" (5 cm) of Ease: (c)	

Adjust the patterns so the distance between Center Front and Center Back equals the measurement in (c).

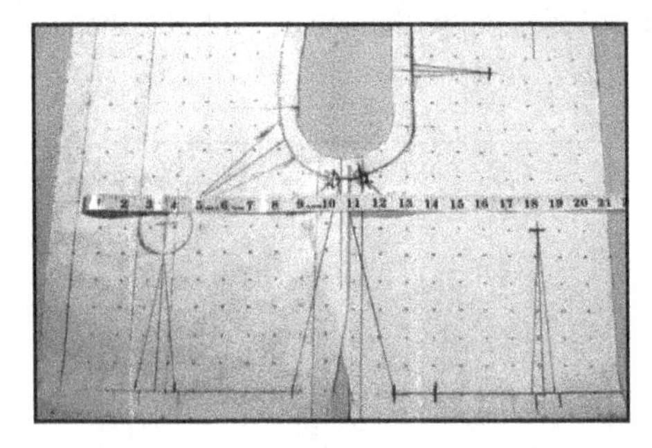

Step 1. Separate the patterns so the distance from Center Front to Center Back equals (c) in the chart. Keep the Center Front and Center Back lines parallel to each other, then tape them in place.

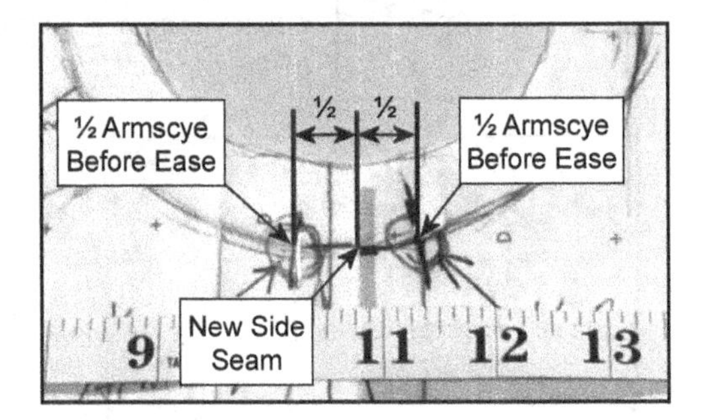

Step 2. Measure the distance between the top of the front Side Seam and the top of the back Side Seam established on page 75. Divide this measurement in half and mark off half this distance on both the front and back patterns. This is now the top of the Side Seams adjusted for Ease.

Step 3. Verify that the Side Seams are still halfway around the Armscye seam.

Adjust the Ease at the Waist

The waist of the paper patterns needs to be adjusted to retain the angle of the Side Seam while preserving appropriate Ease.

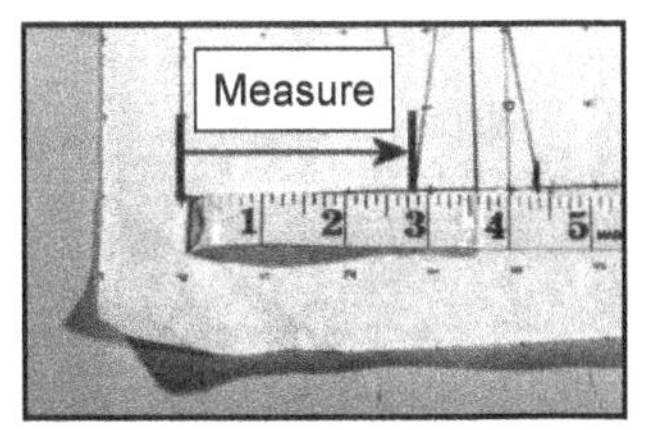

Measure CF to Front Dart

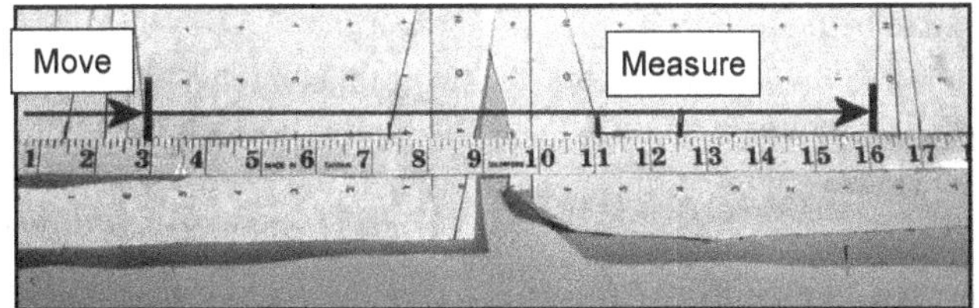

Measure from Front Dart to Back Dart

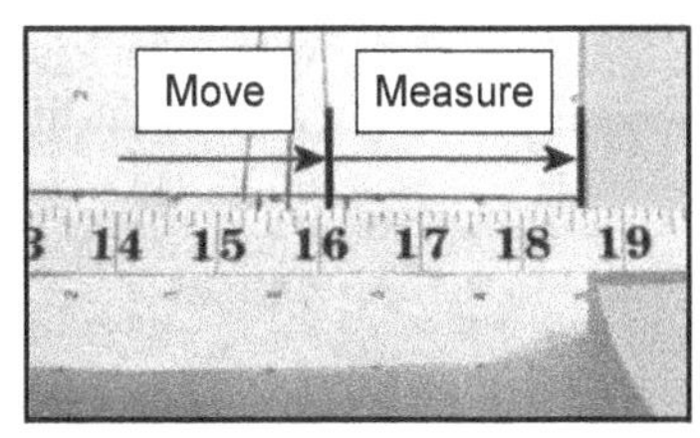

Measure from Back Dart to CB

Step 1. At the waist, measure the patterns from Center Front to Center Back, skipping over the darts. Record the measurement in (a)

Step 2. Find the Waist measurement (#9) on the measurement chart and record it in (b).

Step 3. Divide the Waist measurement by two and record it in (c).

Step 4. Add 1" (2.5 cm) of Ease to (c) and record it in (d).

Step 5. Subtract (d) from (a) and record it in (e).

Step 6. Divide (e) by 2 and record it in (f).

Center Front to Center Back at Waist on pattern: (a)	
Enter the Waist measurement (#9): (b)	
Divide (b) by 2: (c)	
Add 1" (2.5 cm) of Ease to (c): (d)	
Subtract (d) from (a) = (e)	
Divide (e) by 2: (f)	

Use (f) to change the front and back Side Seams at the waist.

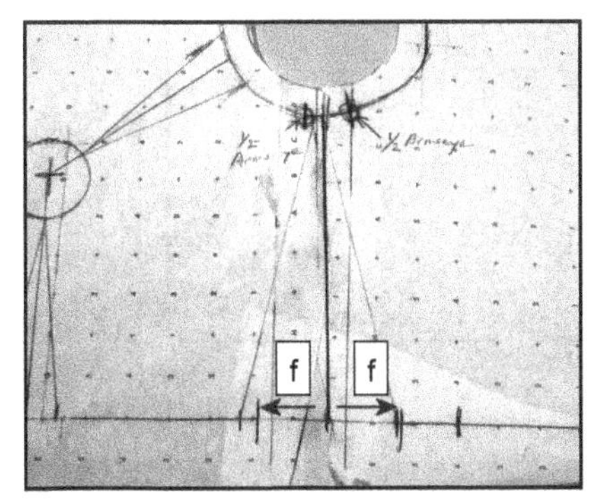

Step 7. On the front pattern's waist line, measure out from the Side Seam line the distance (f) and make a mark.

Step 8. On the back pattern's waist line, measure out from the Side Seam line the distance (f) and make a mark.

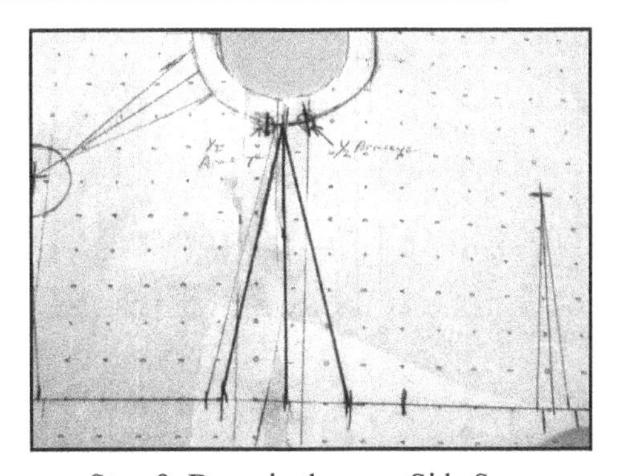

Step 9. Draw in the new Side Seam lines on the front and back patterns.

Prepare the fitting shell for another fitting by adjusting the dart and seam lines, then basting it together.

Verify the Sloper with a Second Fitting

For the second fitting, sew the darts and Side Seams on both sides of the fitting shell. Use a medium stitch length such as 4 mm. This allows the removal of stitching if and when changes need to be made.

Put the fitting shell on and with the horizontal grain at the bust/chest parallel to the floor, use a weighted chain to verify the key vertical grain lines are at right angles to the floor, see the photos below.

Using Photos to Verify Fit of the Bodice

You can use photographs to make accurate determinations of how much your patterns may need to be adjusted. The camera should be located at the full bust level. The photographs need to be taken from the angles shown below. The drawings below each photo outline the body as viewed from above.

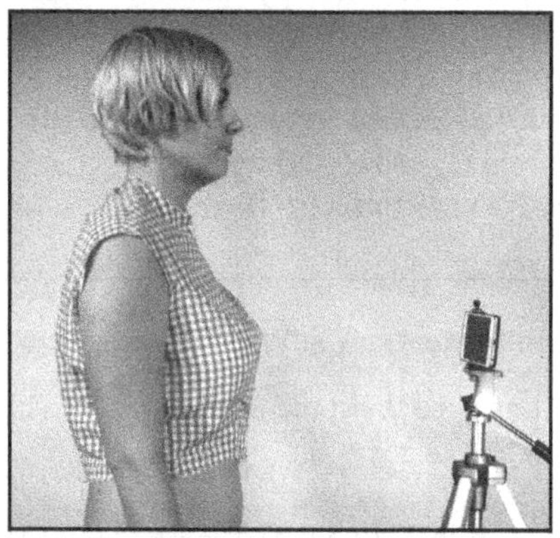

Camera at Full Bust Level

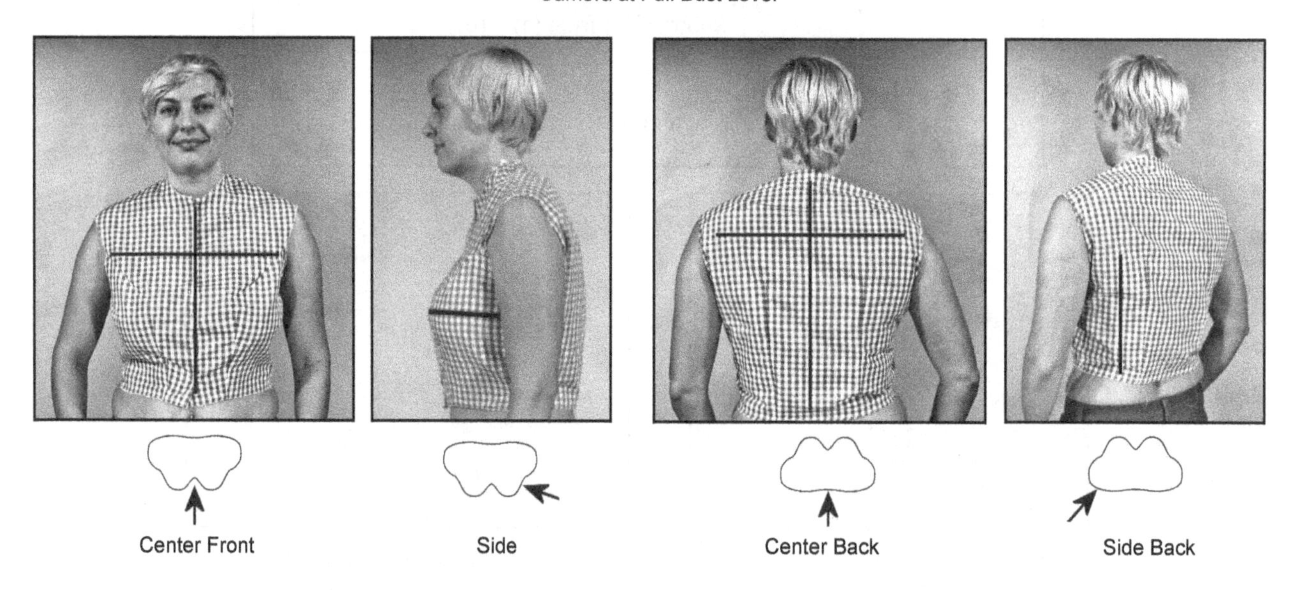

The Sleeve Sloper

The sleeve presented here is a fairly simple pattern that will require little if any fitting. There are two versions of the basic sleeve. First, the fundamental shape of the sleeve will be drafted. The second version includes a dart at the elbow for closely fitted sleeves.

The Body and the Sleeve

For pattern drafting purposes, the arm can be divided into three parts. The upper part is where the arm joins the body. The portion of the pattern which covers this part of the arm is called the Sleeve Cap. Next is the upper arm, which is basically a cylindrical shape. The last part is the lower arm, from the elbow to the wrist, which is also cylindrical in shape.

The upper arm and the lower arm are joined together by the elbow. Notice that the lower arm bends forward slightly at the elbow as the arm hangs naturally at the side.

This bend at the elbow has two important effects on sleeve patterns. First, the back of the arm will be longer than the front. Secondly, a tightly fitted sleeve must have a dart at the elbow to compensate for the bend. The fabric must bend horizontally around the arm and vertically from the upper arm to the lower arm. Loose fitting sleeves do not require a dart, and the arm, in this case, may be treated as one continuous cylinder.

The arm and the resulting sleeve pattern may also be divided vertically into a front, outside, back, and inside. These vertical divisions will be important later when diverse sleeve designs are created.

The Sleeve Pattern

There are two basic reference lines for the sleeve. The first is a straight line down the outside of the arm. This line starts at the Shoulder Point and is called the Sleeve Centerline. The second basic reference line divides the pattern into a Sleeve Cap portion and an Arm portion. This line is at right angles to the Sleeve Centerline and is called the Biceps line.

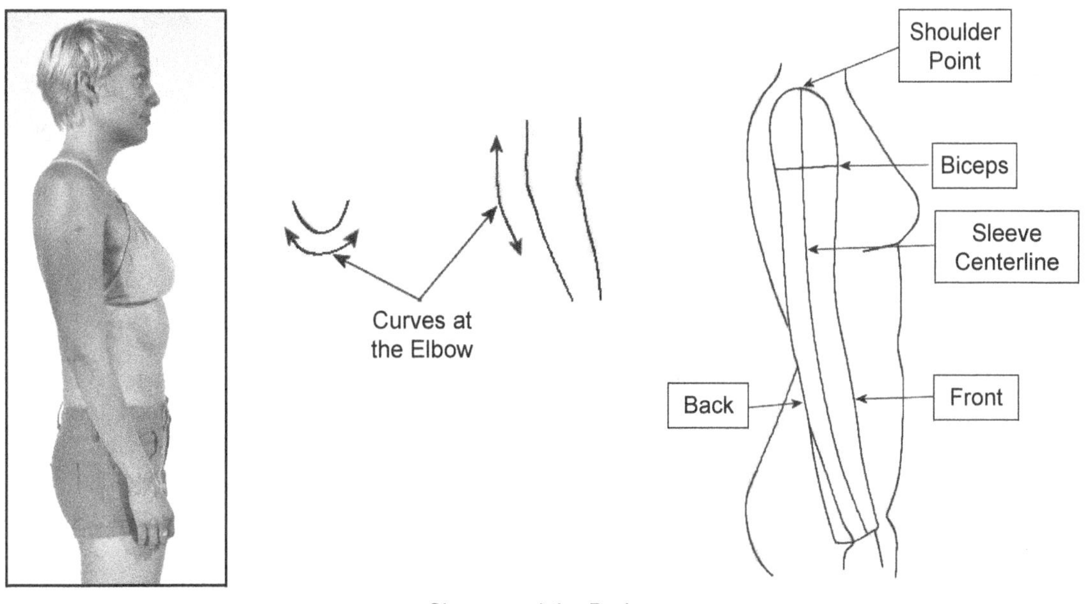

Sleeve and the Body

10. Biceps:		33. Arm Length:	
12. Palm:		34. Shoulder to Elbow:	
		35. Sleeve Cap:	

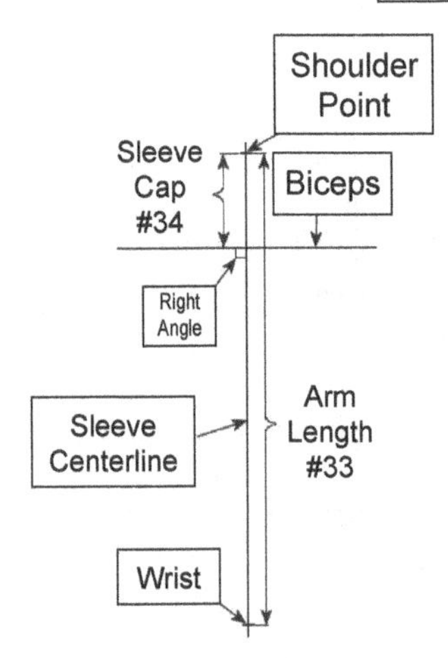

The Basic Reference Lines

Step 1. In the middle of a sheet of paper, draw a vertical line and mark off the Arm Length measurement (#33). This is the Sleeve Centerline. The top of this length is the Shoulder Point; the bottom is the Wrist.

Step 2. On the Sleeve Centerline, measure down the Sleeve Cap length (#35). From this point, draw a line at right angles to the Sleeve Centerline. This is the Biceps line.

> **Note** - The Sleeve Cap length is usually between 5" and 6" (12 and 15 cm). If your measurement differs, recheck it carefully.

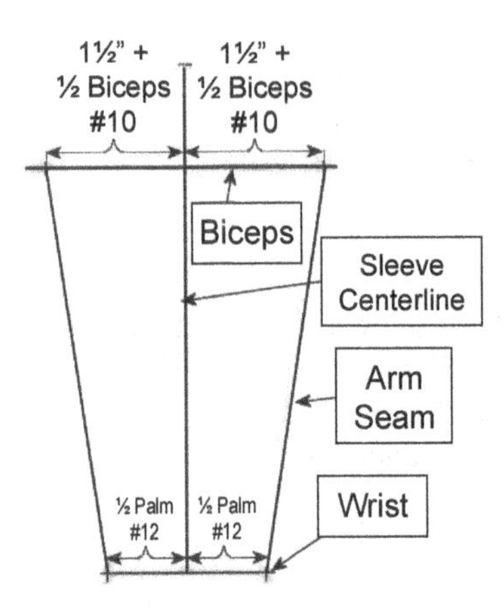

The Arm Portion

Step 3. On the Biceps line, mark off 1½" (4 cm) plus half the Biceps measurement (#10) on each side of the Sleeve Centerline.

The Sleeve Centerline will divide the pattern in half. The 1½" (4 cm) on each side of the Sleeve Centerline is the Ease.

Step 4. At the bottom of the Arm Length measurement, draw a line at right angles to the Sleeve Centerline. This is the Wrist line. On the Wrist line mark off half of the Palm measurement (#12) on each side of the Sleeve Centerline.

The Palm measurement is used at the Wrist line to indicate how big the pattern must be for the hand to get through the sleeve.

Step 5. Connect the marks on the Biceps line to the marks on the Wrist line to establish the sleeve's Arm Seam.

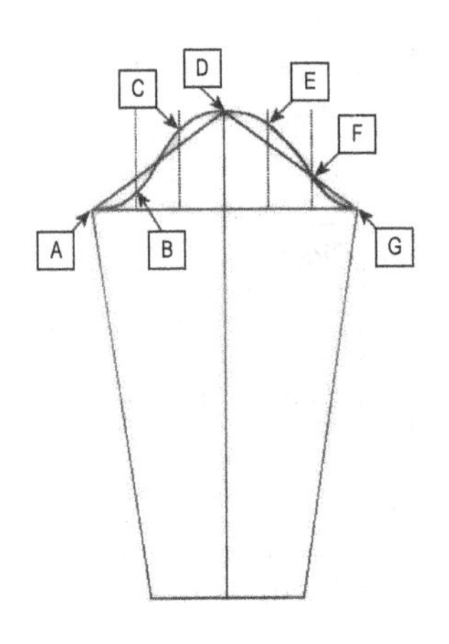

The Sleeve Cap

The line of the Sleeve Cap seam is a standard geometric shape and drafting it using the following technique works very well for most people without any fitting.

Step 6. Divide the Biceps line into six equal parts. Draw lines at right angles to the Biceps line from each of these points.

Step 7. Draw two diagonal lines from the Shoulder Point to the end of each side of the Biceps line.

Step 8. Mark points A, B, C, D, E, F, and G as indicated. Point A is at the end of the Biceps line. Point B is ¾" (2 cm) below the diagonal line. Point C is ¾" (2 cm) above the diagonal line. Point D is at the Shoulder Point. Point E is 1" (2.5 cm) above the diagonal line. Point F is on the diagonal line. And point G is at the end of the Biceps line.

Step 9. Draw in the Sleeve Cap line by connecting these points. Notice that the Sleeve Cap has a front side and a back side. Mark your pattern accordingly.

The front curve of the Sleeve Cap is more pronounced from point C to point A than the back curve between point E and point G. This is because the curve of the body is more pronounced in the front than in the back.

The Sleeve Cap Length

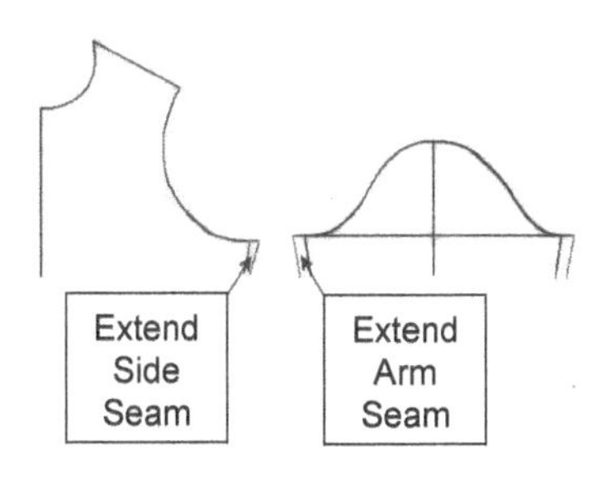

Step 10. On the front bodice pattern, measure the length of the Armscye Curve and note this length.

Step 11. On the Sleeve Pattern, measure the length of the front Sleeve Cap Curve from the Shoulder Point to the Biceps line. This curve should be ⅜" (9 mm) longer than the front Armscye Curve.

If the Sleeve Cap is shorter than it should be, extend out the Arm seam. If the Sleeve Cap is longer than it should be, let out the Bodice's Side Seam.

The bodice is expanded rather than making the sleeve smaller because the Ease must be maintained around the arm.

Step 12. Using the same measurements, repeat these same procedures for the back Bodice pattern and the back of the Sleeve Cap.

Sleeve Cap Ease

The Sleeve Cap line is made larger than the Armscye so the sleeve may be eased into the body of the garment. This allows the sleeve's fabric at the top of the arm to shape over the curve of the shoulder.

Sleeve Cut from Paper

Cut six ⅛" darts in the sleeve cap to simulate the effect of sewing ease.

"Ease" Darts Taped Closed

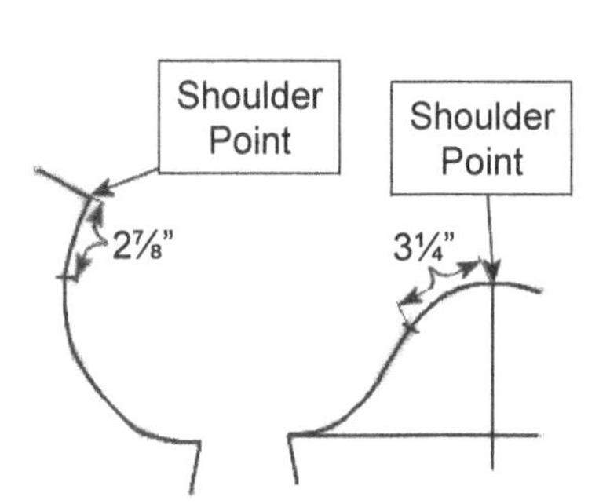

The following procedure will place the Ease in the proper part of the sleeve.

Step 13. On the front Armhole Curve of the bodice, measure 2⅞" (7.3 cm) from the Shoulder Point and make a mark.

Step 14. On the front portion of the Sleeve Cap curve, measure 3¼" (8.2 cm) from the Shoulder Point and make a mark.

These two points will be lined up during the sewing procedure, as will the Shoulder Points, to create ⅜" (9 mm) in the front Sleeve Seam.

Step 15. Using the same measurements, repeat Steps 13 and 14 for the back.

Note: The backs of the sleeve and the bodice are commonly marked with two notches each to indicate the back. The front commonly has one notch. This keeps the left sleeve from being put into the right armhole.

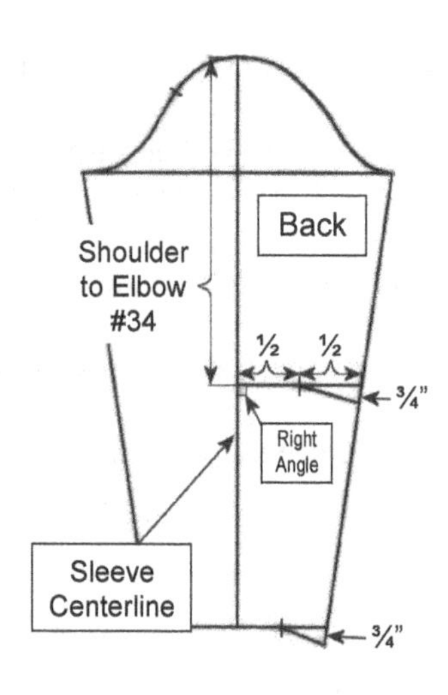

The Elbow Dart

Step 16. On the Sleeve Centerline, measure down the Shoulder to Elbow length (#34) and make a mark. From this point, draw a line at right angles to the Sleeve Centerline towards the back of the sleeve. This is the Elbow line.

Step 17. On the Elbow line, divide the sleeve in half between the Sleeve Centerline and the Arm Seam, then make a mark. This establishes the point of the elbow dart.

Step 18. On the Arm Seam, measure down ¾" (2 cm) from the Elbow line. Connect this mark to the dart's point.

The dart, as it is now drawn, removes fabric from the Arm Seam. Fabric must be added back to the length of the seam below the Wrist line to keep the two Arm Seams the same length.

Step 19. Extend the Arm Seam down ¾" (2 cm) and mark the new length.

Step 20. To establish the back of the arm on the Wrist line, divide the Wrist measurement in half between the Sleeve Centerline and the Arm Seam. Curve the Wrist line from this point to the new extended Arm Seam length.

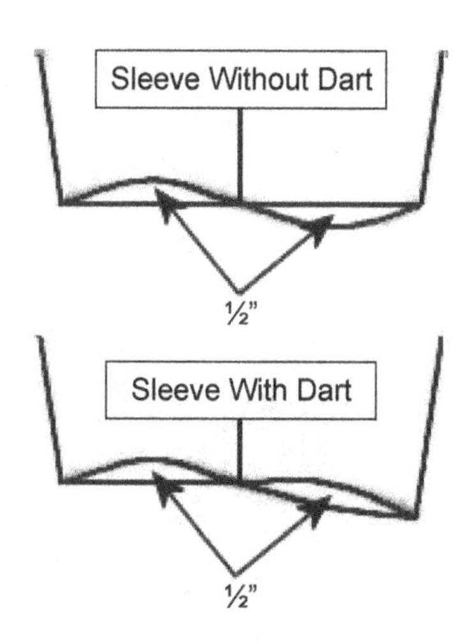

Curving The Wrist Line

Wrap a piece of elastic around the biceps so that it is parallel to the floor. Now measure down the front of the arm, then down the back. Notice the front is 1" (2.5 cm) shorter than the back.

The Wrist line may be shaped to correspond to this difference. This curved shape may be added to either a sleeve pattern that has an elbow dart or one without.

Step 21. Divide the Wrist line into four equal parts and mark the front and the back. Make the front wrist ½" (12 mm) shorter than the existing Wrist line and the back wrist ½" (12 mm) longer. Curve the Wrist line to blend these points together.

Seam Allowances

Add a 1½" (4 cm) seam allowance to the Underarm Seam. Add a 1" (2.5 cm) seam allowance to the Sleeve Cap curve.

Fitting the Sleeve

There should be little adjustment required for the Sleeve Cap.

The best way to fit the sleeve is to baste it into the armhole. Put the fitting shell on and check the fit. If the sleeve does not hang smoothly down the arm, pull the Sleeve Cap up at the seam line until it does. Pin the excess fabric out.

Take the fitting shell off. Take the basting out. Correct the Sleeve Cap line. Baste and check the fit again.

If the process above does not resolve your issues, use the following steps to adjust the fit of the sleeve into the body of the fitting shell. This process allows you to adjust the Ease of the body and the sleeve to optimize the way they work together.

1. Before you sew the sleeve's Underarm Seam or the bodice's Side Seam, sew just the Shoulder Seam.
2. Sew the sleeve into the body of the garment.
3. Baste the Side Seam and Underarm Seam as one continuous seam.
4. Adjust the basting until you achieve the desired fit.

As you are following this process, keep checking the fit to include the range of motion necessary to move the arm.

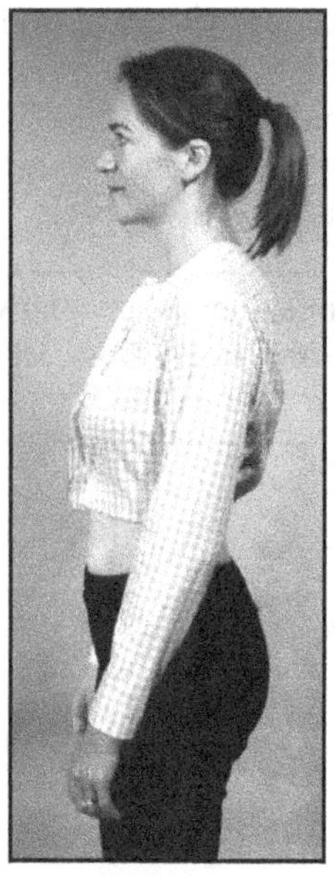

Verifying the Fit

Pattern Alteration Techniques

Alex

Slopers, after they have been fitted, show the shape of the wearer's body. The examples in this section demonstrate the principles using designs for standard garments. The principles used to achieve these patterns may be modified and applied to create original designs.

Patterns can be altered in two ways. The position of the seam lines or the dart lines can be changed. Or patterns can be expanded to add more fullness to certain areas of the body. Most designs will use both these changes.

The process is simple. Draw lines on a copy of the Sloper for the new dart and seam locations. Then trace the Sloper onto a new sheet of pattern paper to create the new designs. Always keep the Sloper with the design lines for future reference.

To practice these pattern alteration techniques, use quarter scale patterns. These can then be used as a reference to create full sized patterns. The quarter scale patterns illustrated here were created from the Slopers made for my model Alex. Use these or reduce your own fitted patterns to quarter scale, see page 178. You can then make prototype garments that can be tested on a Mini-Me Dress Form, see page 179.

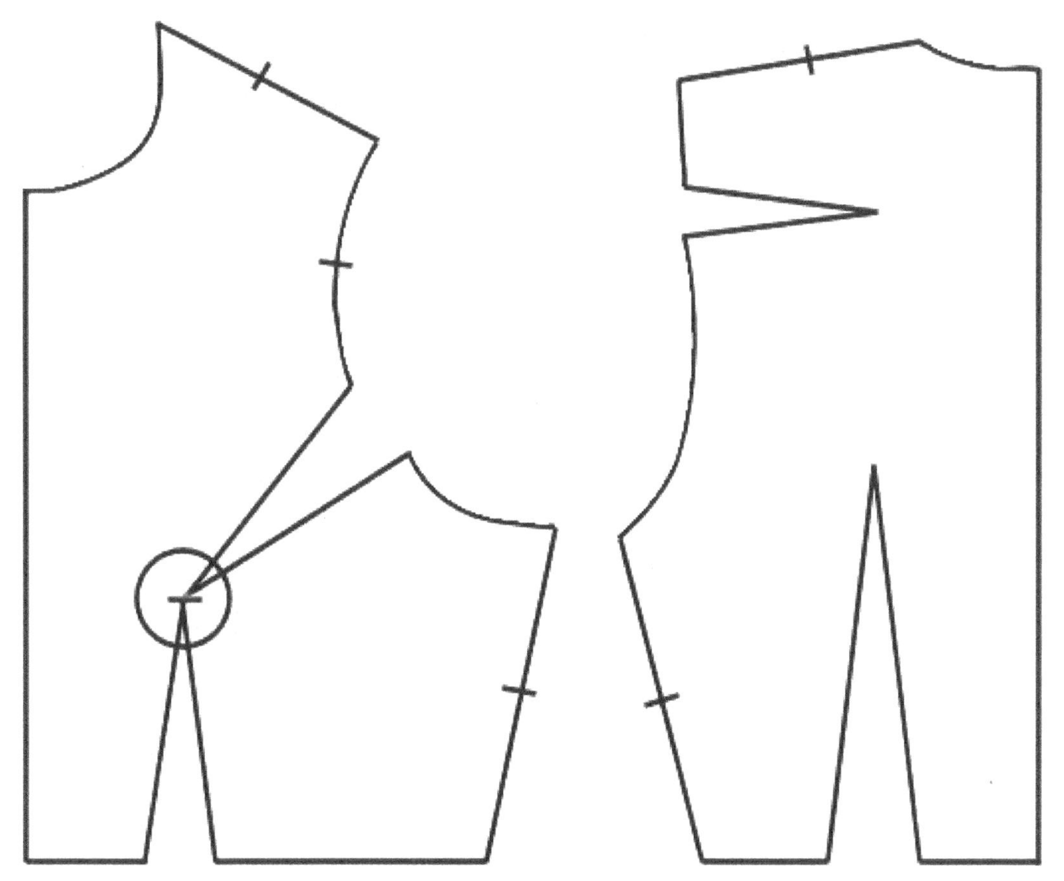
Quarter Scale Patterns (Created for model: Alex)

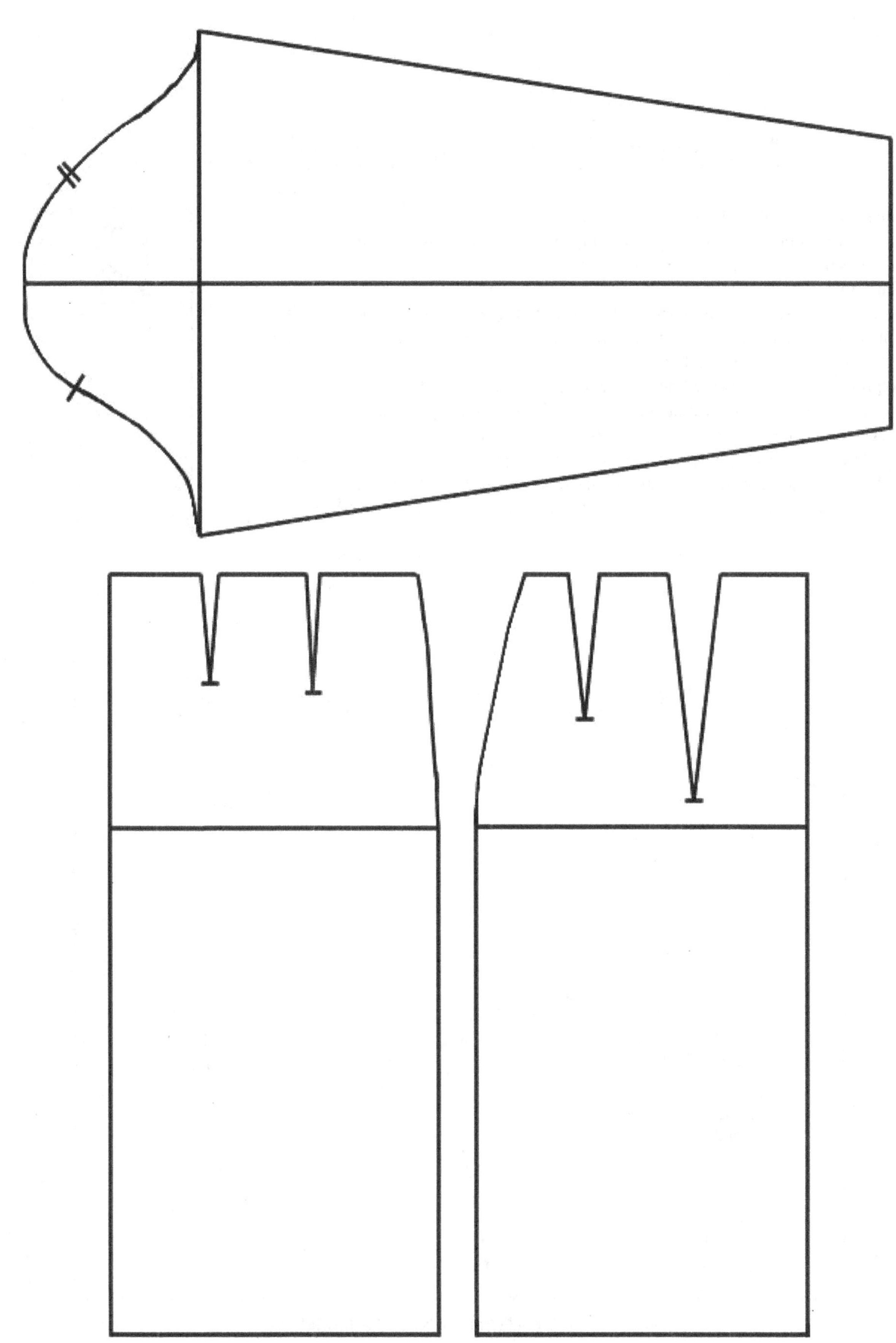

Quarter Scale Patterns (Created for model: Alex)

Changing Seam Locations

Seam lines can be changed to different positions without affecting the fit of the Slopers. There are two basic types of seam lines: external lines and internal lines.

External lines define the edge of the garment. Raising or lowering a hem line on a dress or skirt changes a garment's external line. Necklines are also external lines. Changing external lines does not affect a garment's fit.

Internal lines are the seam lines inside a garment's shape. These lines may or may not affect the fit. For instance, a yoke on a man's shirt does not change the fit. It only changes a garment's appearance by adding additional lines. The Princess Seam, on the other hand, usually not only adds new visual lines to the body, but changes how closely a garment follows the body.

Changing External Lines

Variations of necklines are shown on page 86. These variations may be achieved by simply drawing in a neckline's desired shape on the pattern.

The neckline shown below illustrates how a Sloper may be changed. Measure the body, apply these measurements to the pattern, then draw in the desired neckline.

The Procedure

Step 1. Measure down the body at Center Front to determine the neckline's desired depth. Mark this length on the Center Front of a copy of the Sloper.

Step 2. Measure on the shoulder how far out the neckline is to be. Mark this length on the Sloper's Shoulder Seam.

Step 3. Draw in the shape of the desired neckline.

Step 4. Place a piece of pattern paper over the Sloper. Trace the Sloper following the line of the new neckline.

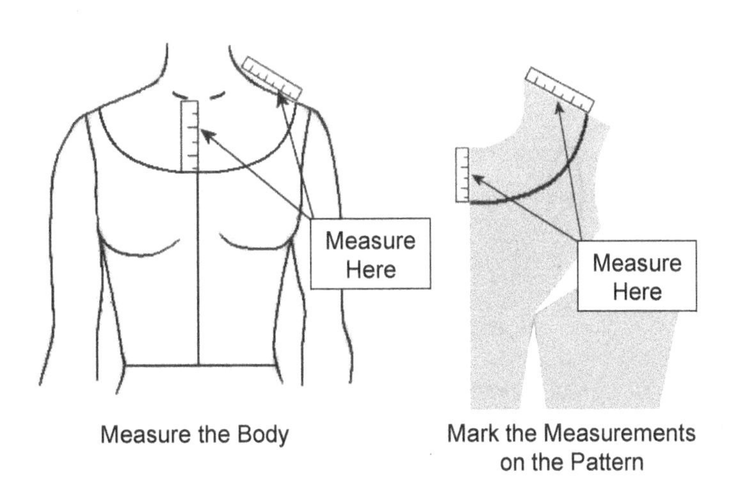

Measure the Body

Mark the Measurements on the Pattern

Neckline Variations

These neckline variations can be created by following the same procedure. Measure the body for the neckline's location, then mark the pattern accordingly.

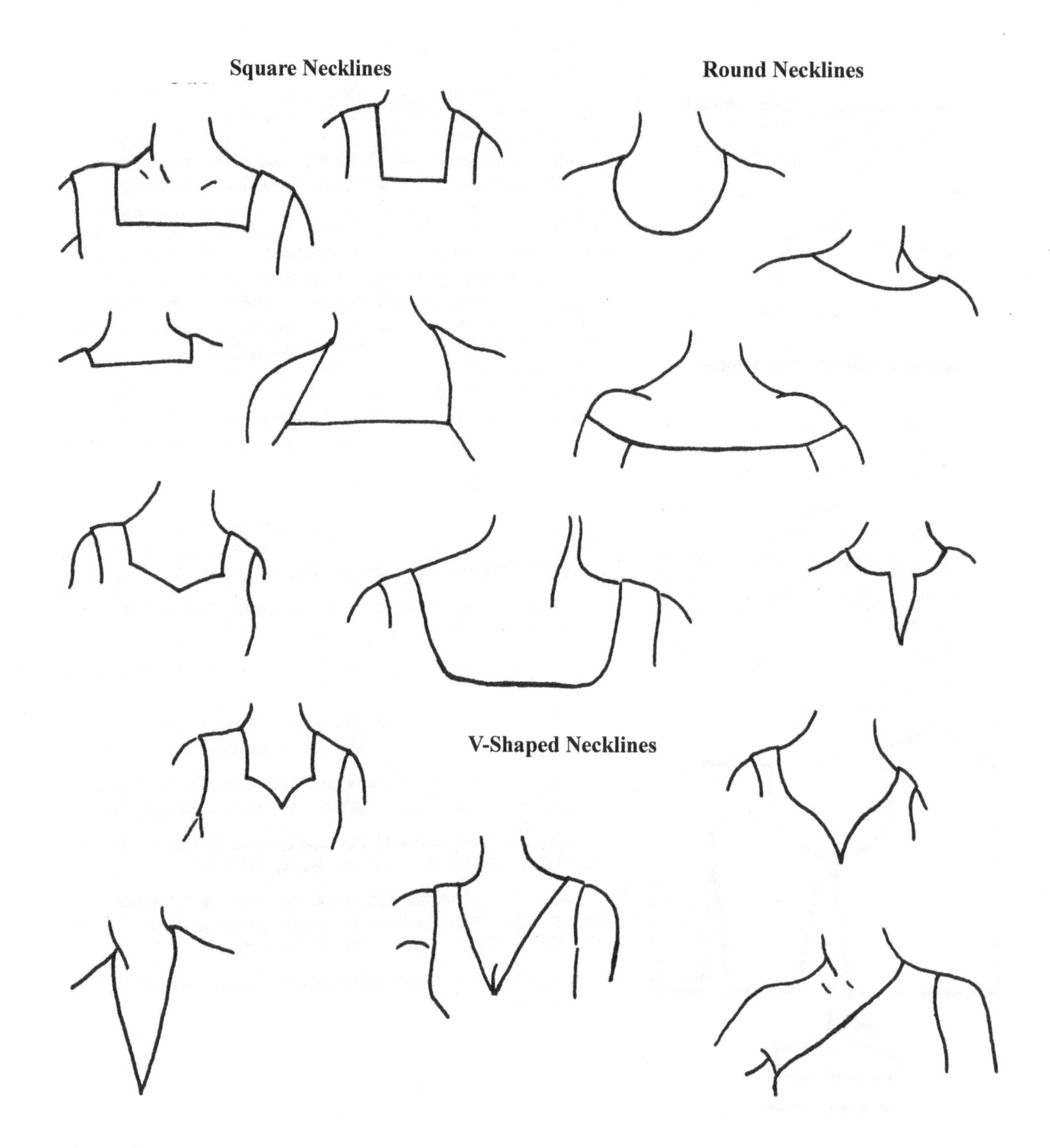

Changing Internal Lines

Altering internal seam lines which do not affect fit is a process of adding new seam lines and removing unwanted seams. Many variations in the appearance of garments are possible by adding this type of internal seam line to the design. These internal seam lines may be left as plain seams or their decorative value may be enhanced by making them flat-felled or corded seams. They may also be used to join contrasting fabric together.

There are two basic approaches to changing seams. One is cutting and taping. The other is tracing the patterns. For both approaches, follow the sewing lines of the pattern and not the seam allowance lines. The following instructions show how to use both approaches to add a yoke to a man's shirt.

Creating Designs by Cutting and Taping

Cutting and Taping is perhaps the easiest to understand because you cut new seam lines and tape together unwanted seam lines. This process, however, does require the pattern to be copied twice, once for the design and a second for adding the necessary seam allowances.

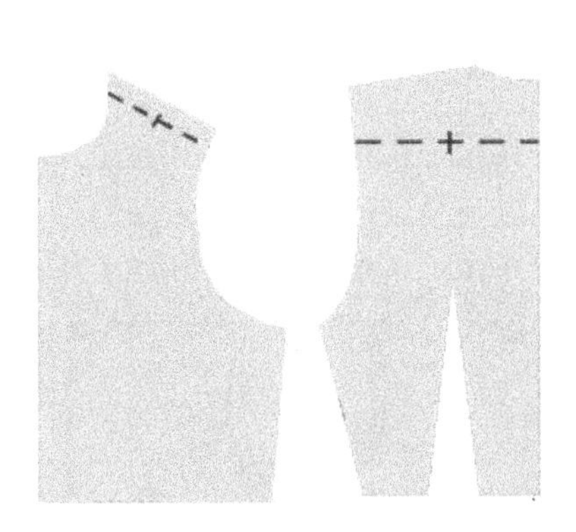

Step 1. Determine the new seam lines by measuring the body. A conventional man's shirt yoke will drop the front shoulder seam by 1" (2.5 cm) and add a back seam straight across the shoulders 1½" (4 cm) down from Center Back.

Step 2. Draw the new seam lines on a copy of the Sloper and include sewing notches.

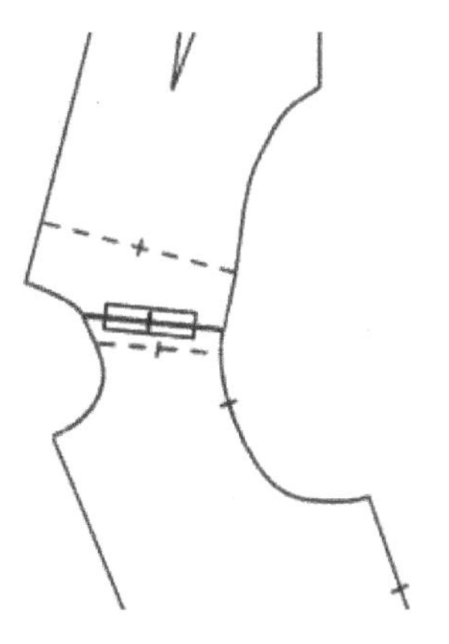

Step 3. Tape the back pattern to the front pattern at the shoulder seam being careful to align the seams using the sewing notch.

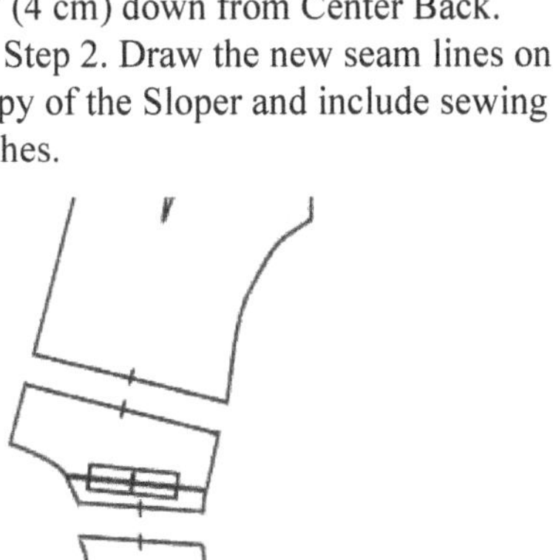

Step 4. Cut the pattern apart along the new seam line.

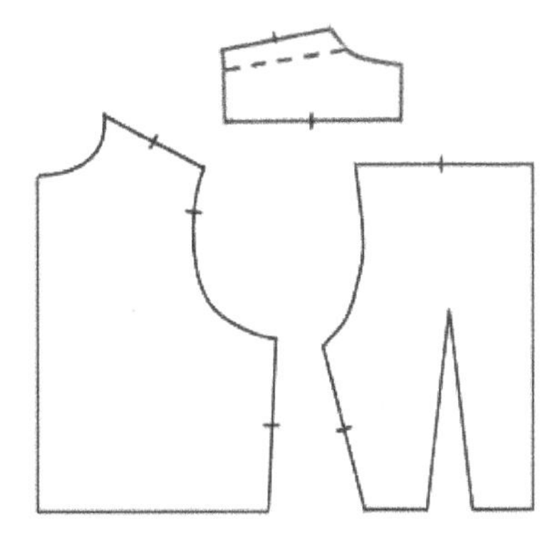

Step 5. Trace the separate pattern pieces onto new sheets of pattern paper so that seam allowances may be added.

Creating Designs by Tracing

Tracing simplifies the process of creating new designs and is the basis for the instructions for the rest of this book.

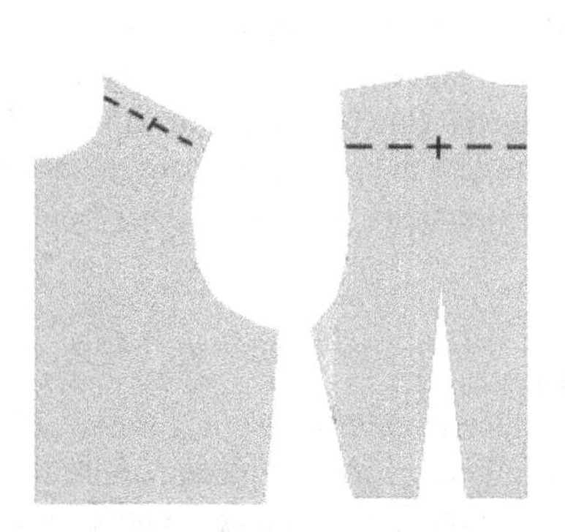

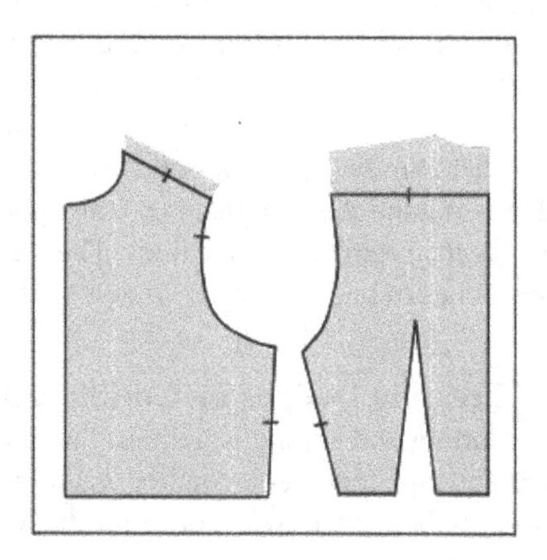

Step 1. On a copy of the Slopers, draw in the design lines desired for the yoke.

Step 2. Place the Slopers so there is adequate room between them to allow for seam allowances.

Step 3. Place a new sheet of pattern paper on top of the Slopers and, excluding the yoke, trace the seam lines for the body of the shirt.

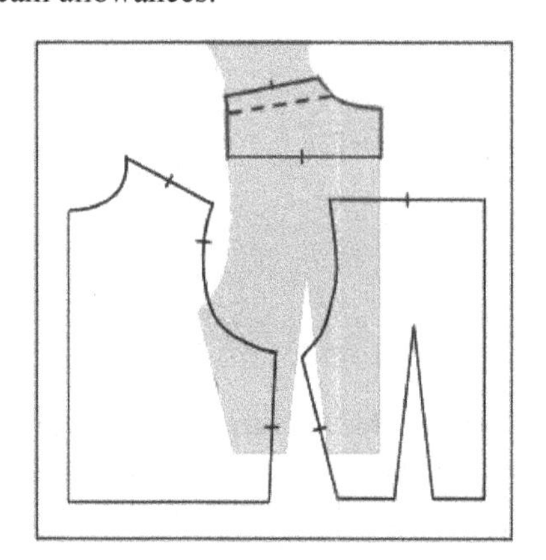

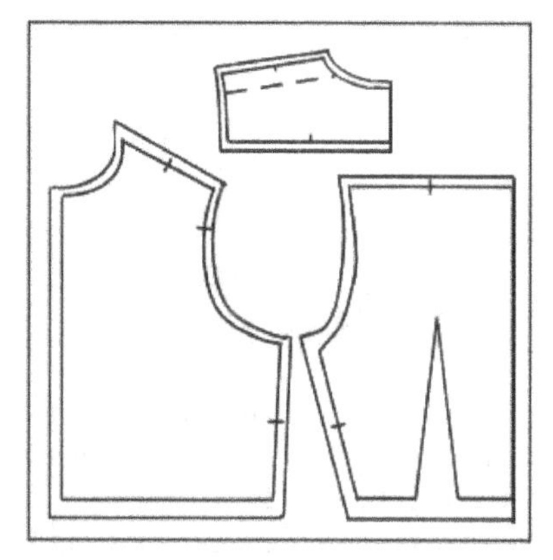

Step 4. Adjust the Slopers so the Shoulder Seams match, then move the pattern paper to allow adequate room for seam allowances around all the patterns.

Step 5. Trace the shape of the yoke pattern.

Step 6. Add seam allowances to all the pattern pieces. When you are testing a new design, it is a good idea to allow for some adjustment during fitting by using seam allowances such as 1½" (4 cm) on the Side Seams.

Men's Shirt Yokes

These are variations of men's shirts that can be created using the procedures shown on the previous two pages. To determine the seam locations desired, measure the body, then apply these measurements to the Slopers. For more about shirts, see page 141.

Changing Dart Locations

The following instructions illustrate how a woman's bust darts can be shifted to various locations. There are two bust darts on the Sloper: the Above the Bust Dart and the Below the Bust Dart. Because both darts are for the single contour of the bust, they may be shaped at any location.

When the location of the Bust Dart is changed, the alteration must be made at the Bust Point. After the new dart is created, the legs of the darts must be adjusted to the edge of the Bust Circle. The Below the Bust Dart may either be left as fullness in the garment, or it may be included in the new dart.

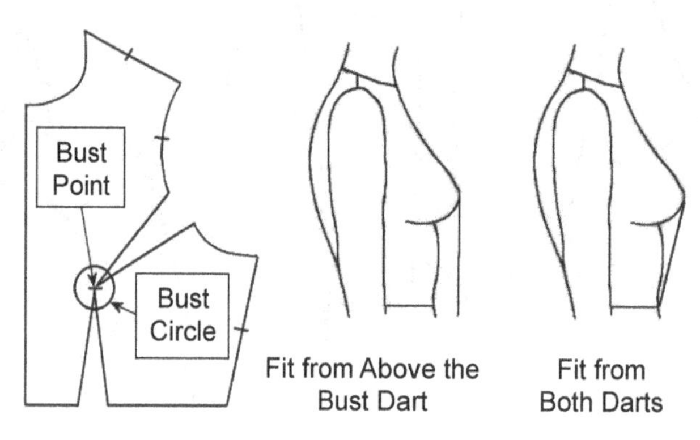

Side Seam Bust Dart

A common dart changes the shape of the Above the Bust Dart to the Side Seam.

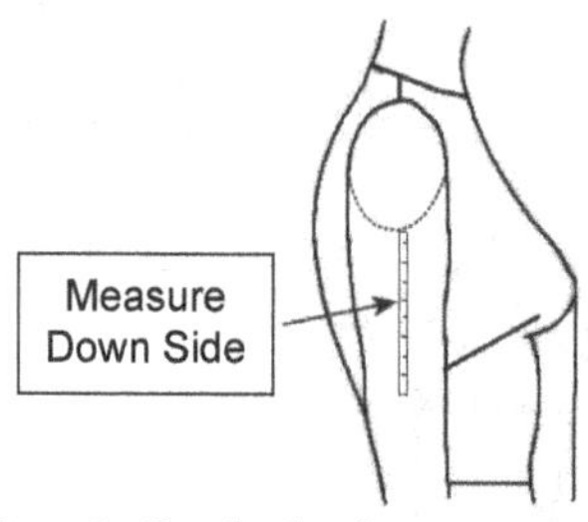

Step 1. On the body, measure down the Side Seam to the desired location for the end of the dart.

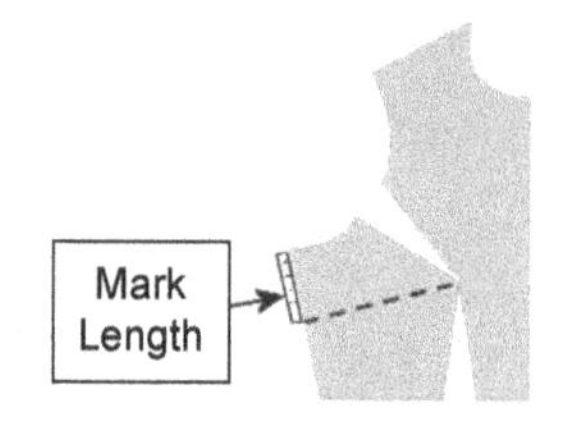

Step 2. On a copy of the Sloper, measure down the Side Seam to the new location of the dart and draw the design line from the Side Seam to the Bust Point.

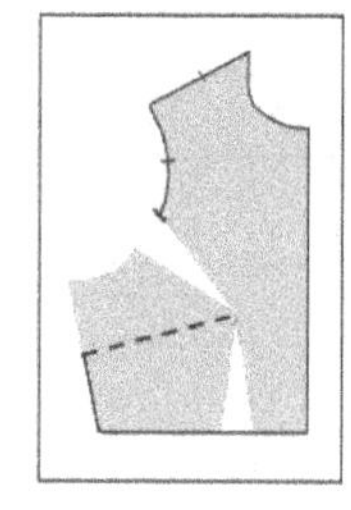

Step 3. Place a piece of pattern paper on top of the Sloper.

Step 4. Trace from the top of the Above the Bust Dart around the pattern to the new dart design line.

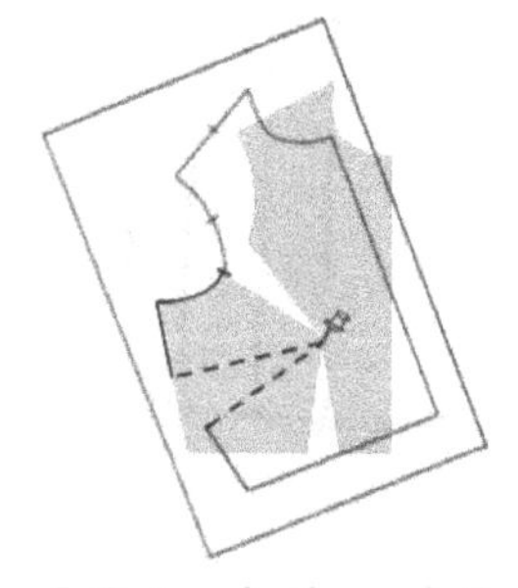

Step 5. Put a pin through the Bust Point, then pivot the pattern paper to close out the Above the Bust Dart.

Step 6. Trace from the closed dart down to the new dart design line on the Sloper.

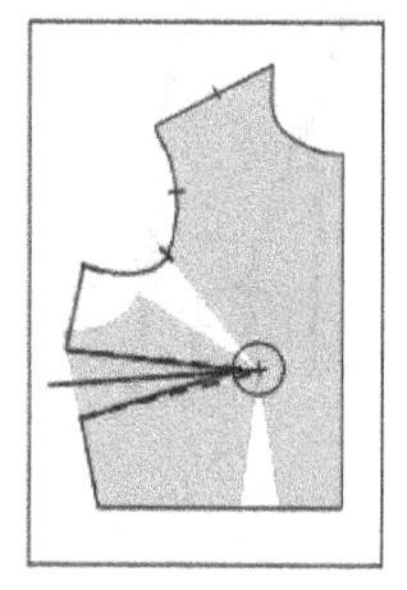

Step 7. At the Side Seam, measure the dart width and draw a dart centerline halfway between the two dart legs.

Step 8. Redraw the dart legs to the edge of the Bust Circle.

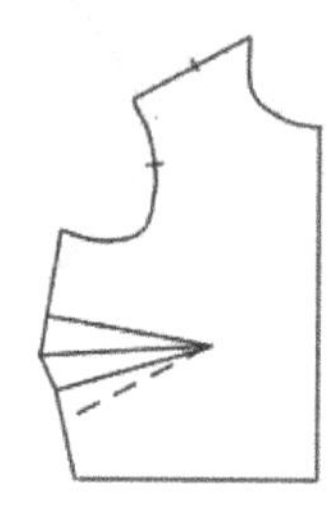

Step 9. Draw a temporary line that is half the dart width down from the bottom leg of the dart.

Step 10. Measure the length of the line from Step 9 and apply it to the dart centerline, then draw in the dart point.

Including The Below the Bust Dart

The shape of the Below the Bust dart can be included in a new dart to create a garment that is fitted at the waist. However, when this type of design includes a hem that extends below the waist, you may need a seam at the waist to maintain an appropriate fit.

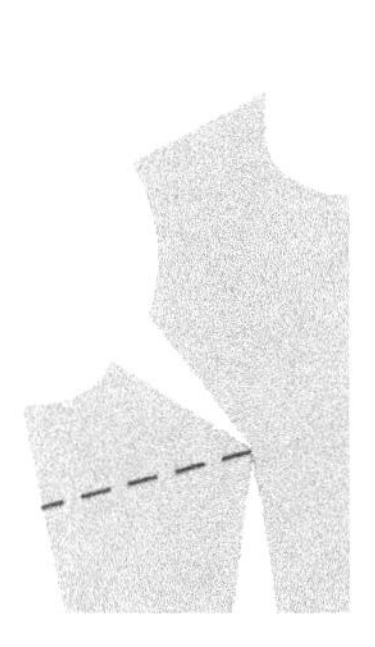

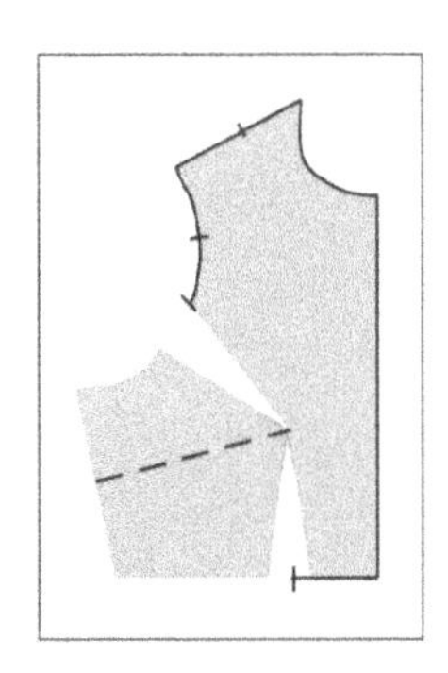

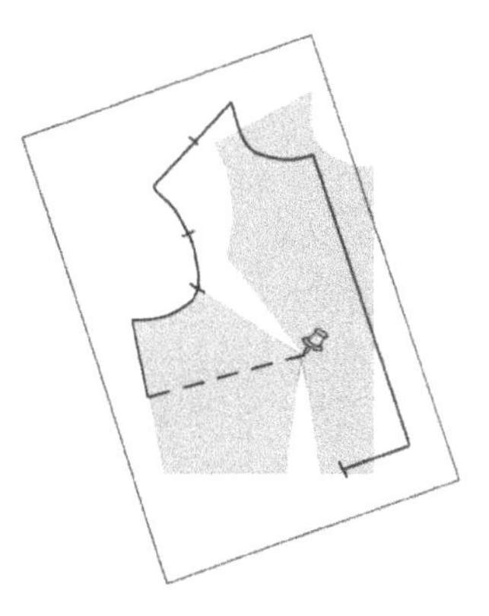

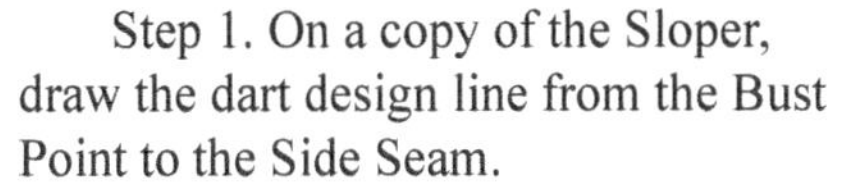

Step 1. On a copy of the Sloper, draw the dart design line from the Bust Point to the Side Seam.

Step 2. Place a piece of pattern paper on top of the Sloper.

Step 3. Trace from the top of the Above the Bust Dart around the pattern to the Below the Bust Dart.

In this example, only half the Below the Bust Dart width is going to be used.

Step 4. Put a pin through the Bust Point, then pivot the pattern paper to close out the Above the Bust Dart.

Step 5. Trace from the closed dart down to the new dart design line on the Sloper.

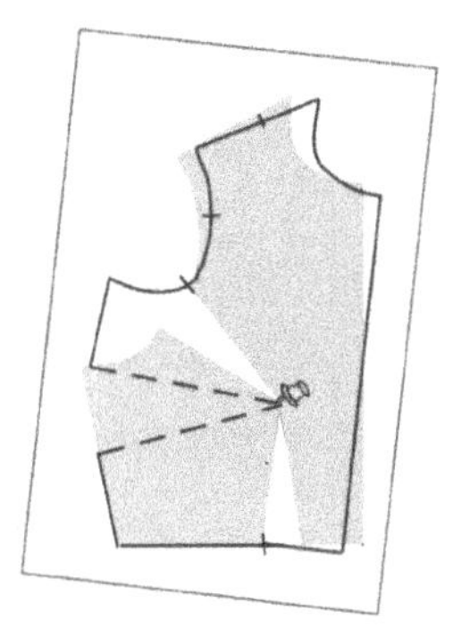

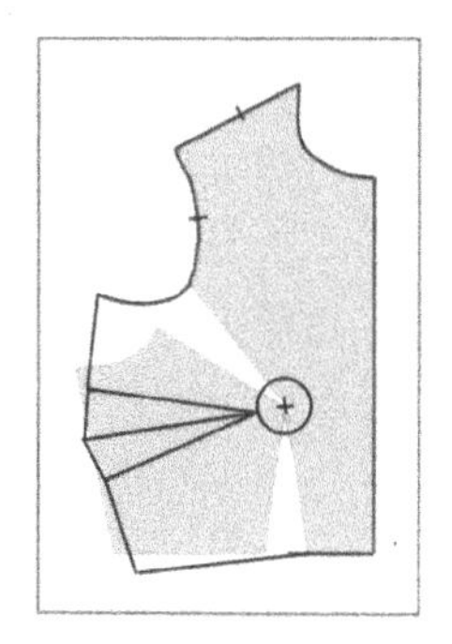

Step 6. Pivot the pattern paper to close out the remainder of the Below the Bust Dart on the Sloper.

Step 7. Trace from the closed dart up to the new dart design line.

Step 8. Draw in the shape of the dart as shown on page 90.

Note: The slight downward curve of the new waist is an indication that this variation will need a horizontal seam near the waist to maintain the same quality of fit as the Sloper.

Center Front Dart

The dart to the Center Front seam is rarely if ever used as illustrated below. However, this pattern will be the basis for the cowl neckline described on page 147.

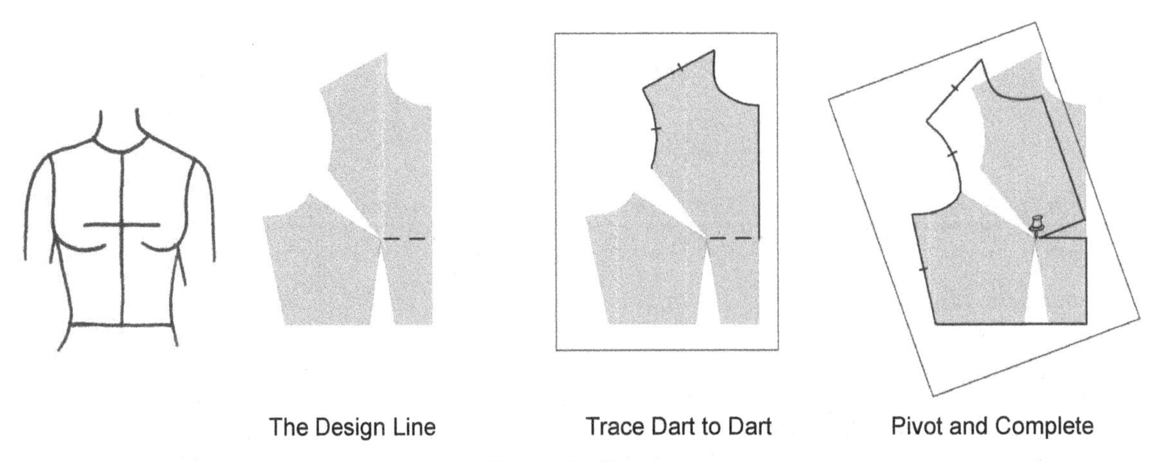

French Dart

The French Dart extends down to the waist or to just below it. The design Ease for the Side Seam must be established to draft this dart.

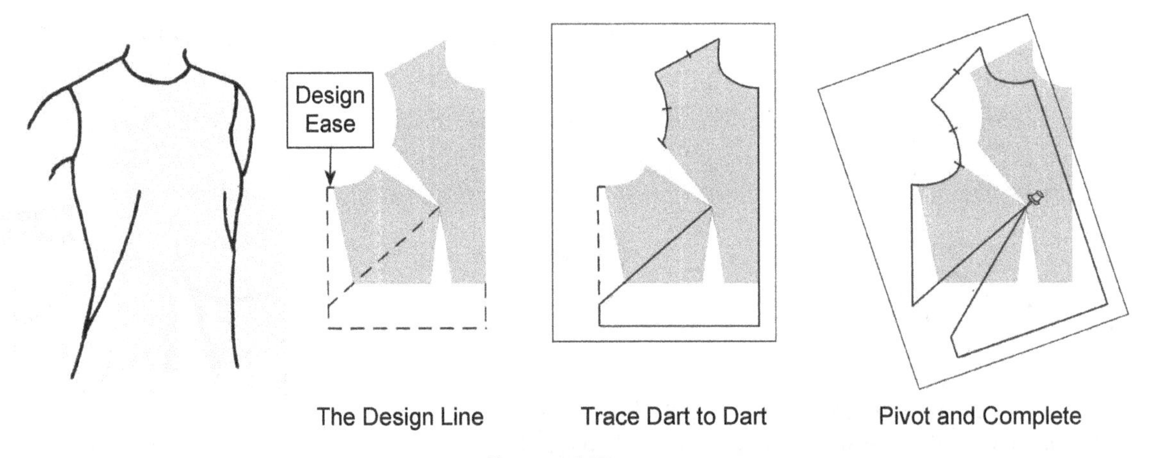

Curved Dart

Darts do not need to be limited to straight lines. However, this type of curved dart may not be appropriate for some fabrics. Test carefully before committing to this design.

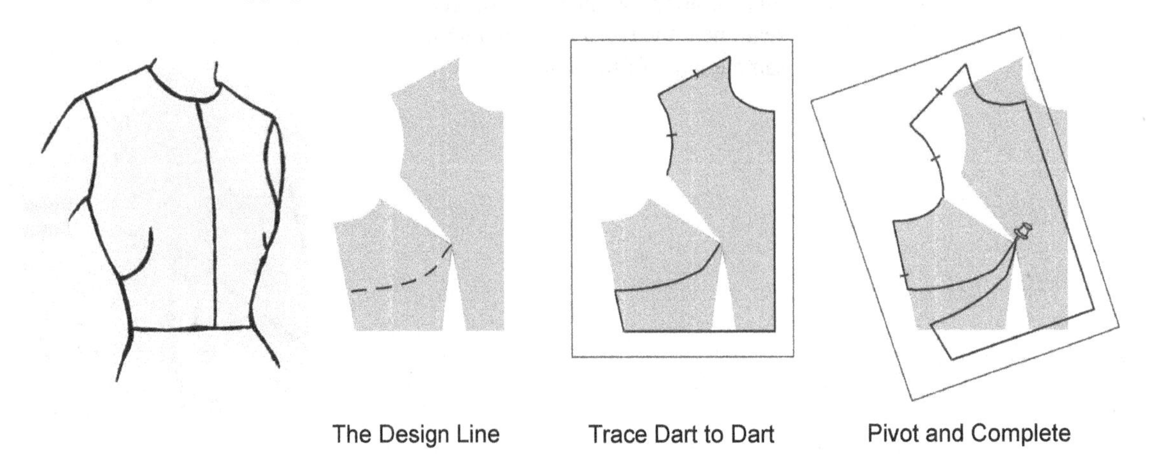

Shoulder Darts

The dart of the Sloper may be changed to multiple darts. To prepare the Sloper, draw in the desired dart lines, then divide the Above the Bust Dart width into as many dart widths as there are new darts. In the example below, three darts are created.

In addition to adding multiple darts, the pattern shown here also has the Shoulder Seam lowered in front. The portion of the pattern taken off the front is added to the back pattern as shown on page 87.

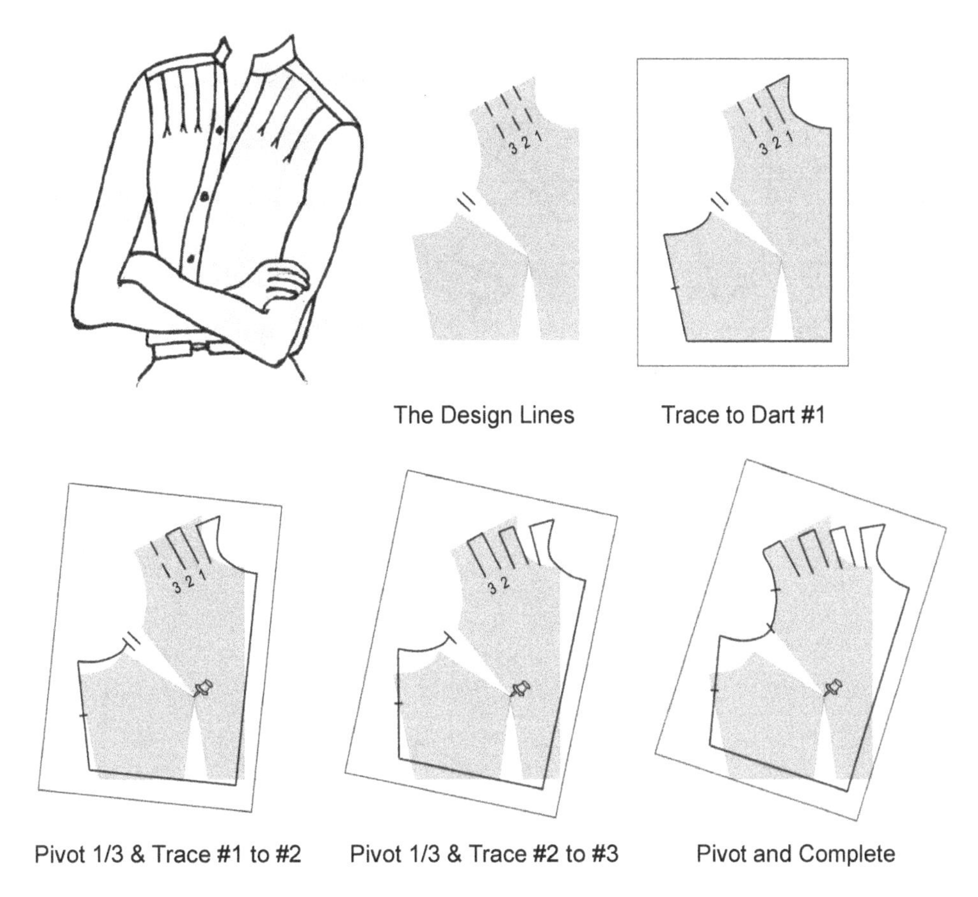

The Design Lines | Trace to Dart #1

Pivot 1/3 & Trace #1 to #2 | Pivot 1/3 & Trace #2 to #3 | Pivot and Complete

Shoulder Gathers

Darts may be sewn as gathers, smocking, or shirring. The following shows the Shoulder Seam dropped on the front pattern. Then the Above the Bust dart is changed to the new Shoulder Seam. The top of the dart is shaped with an arc.

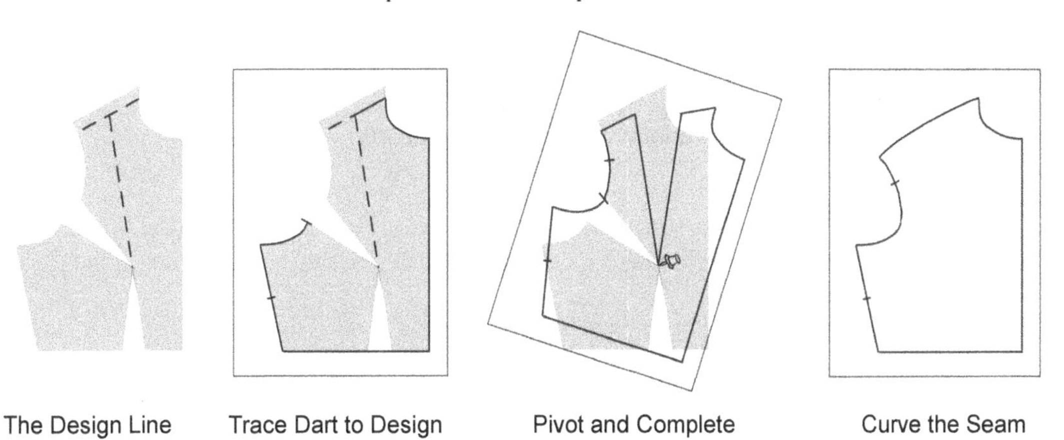

The Design Line | Trace Dart to Design | Pivot and Complete | Curve the Seam

Variations For Shoulder Gathers

The designs shown here can all be made using the pattern alteration procedure described on the preceding page. The variations are achieved by changing the height of the Shoulder Seam, using different openings for the garments, and/or adding different sleeve and collar styles.

Variations of Shoulder Gathers

Changing Darts To Seams

Bust Darts may be changed to seams so long as the seam passes through or very close to the Bust Point.

Princess Seams

The classic seam line that illustrates changing darts to seams is the Princess Seam. This seam follows the contours of the body resulting in garments that can be very flattering to the body. The following examples show variations of the Princess Seam.

Princess Seam to the Armscye

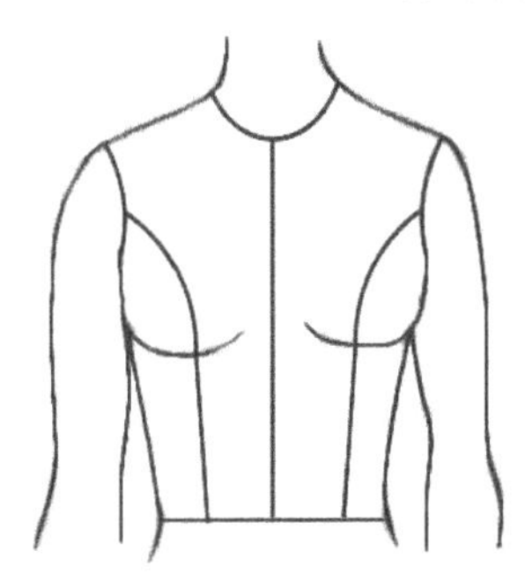

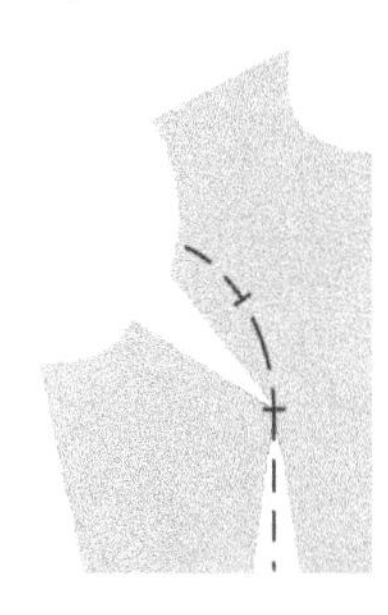

Step 1. On a copy of the Sloper, draw in the desired Princess Seam line following straight down the Below the Bust Dart centerline. Include sewing notches.

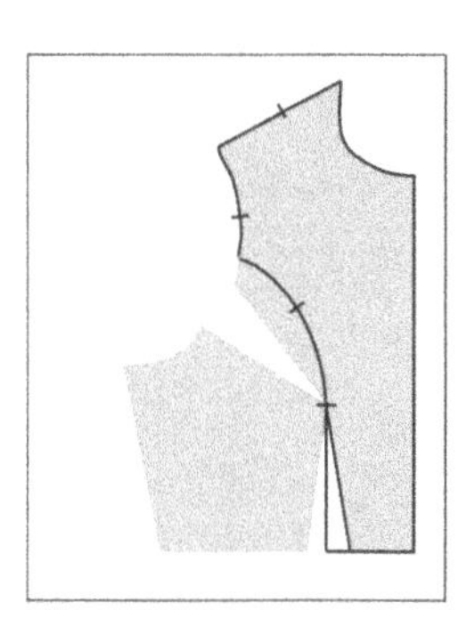

Step 2. Place a piece of pattern paper on top of the Sloper.

Step 3. Trace the front section from Center Front to the Princess Seam. Include the inside leg of the Below the Bust dart.

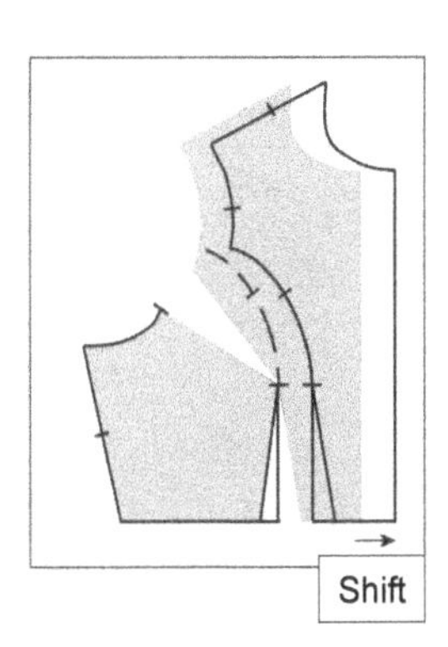

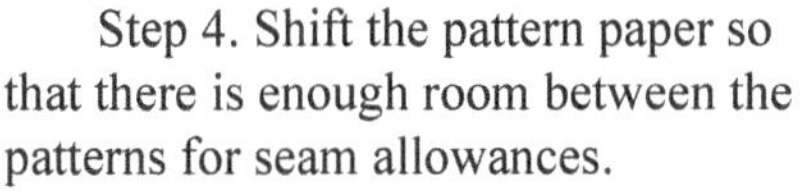

Step 4. Shift the pattern paper so that there is enough room between the patterns for seam allowances.

Step 5. Trace the side section from the Princess Seam up to the bottom of the Above the Bust Dart. Include the outside leg of the Below the Bust dart.

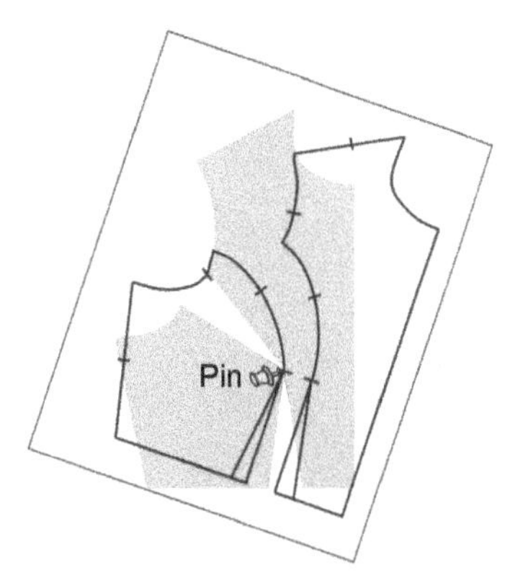

Step 6. Put a pin in the Bust Point and pivot the pattern paper to close out the Above the Bust Dart.

Step 7. Complete the side panel by tracing the curve of the Princess Seam.

Princess Seam to the Shoulder

Another variation of the Princess Seam carries the seam lines up to the shoulders instead of curving them out to the armscye.

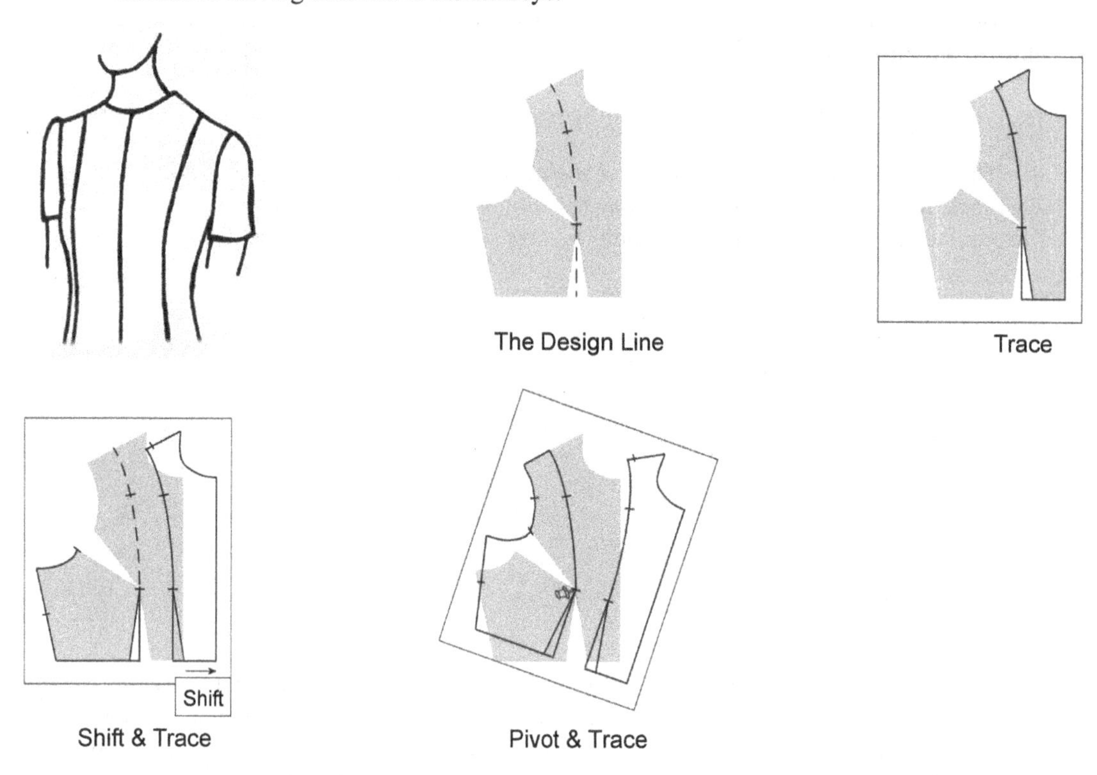

Princess Seam with a Dart

This variation of the Princess Seam shows what happens when the seam lines do not go over the Bust Point. Additional shaping must be achieved with a small side dart. To create the Side Seam dart, see page 90.

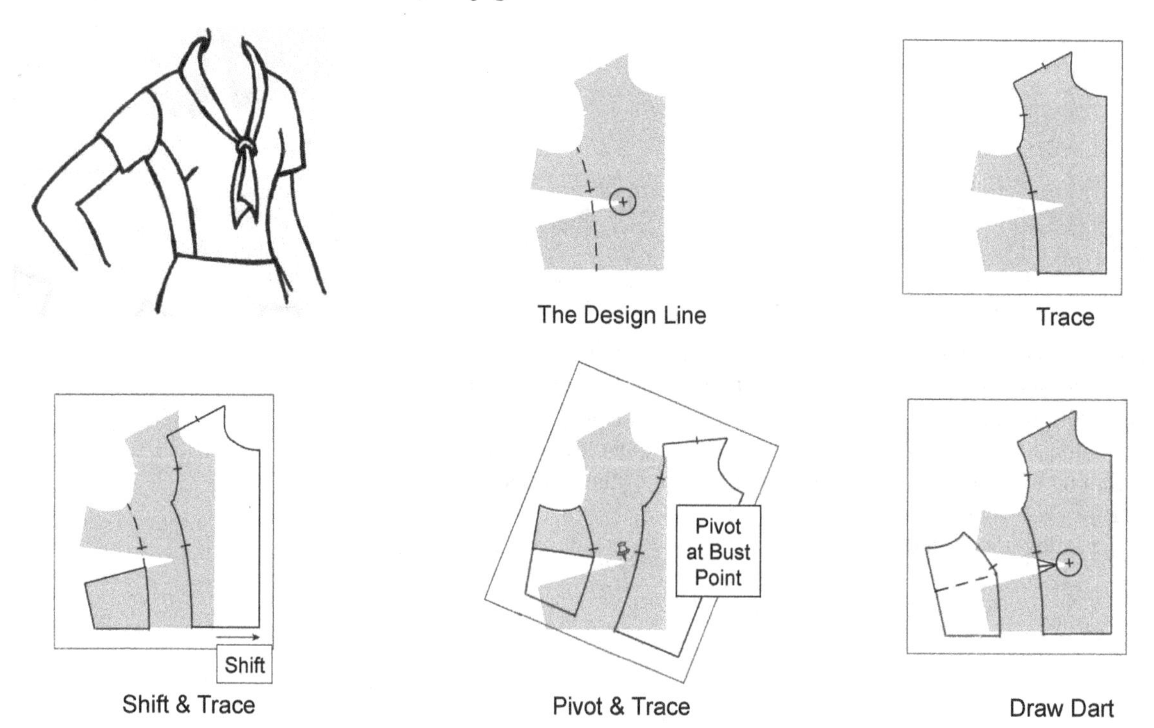

Princess Seam Variations

The illustrations below show some of the different designs that may be created using the Princess Seam line.

Front Yoke

Darts can be changed to a variety of different seam lines as long as these lines cross over the Bust Point.

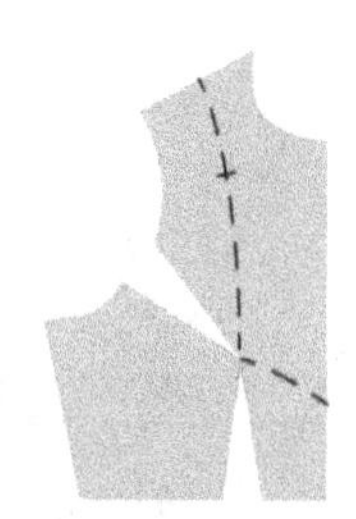

The Design Lines

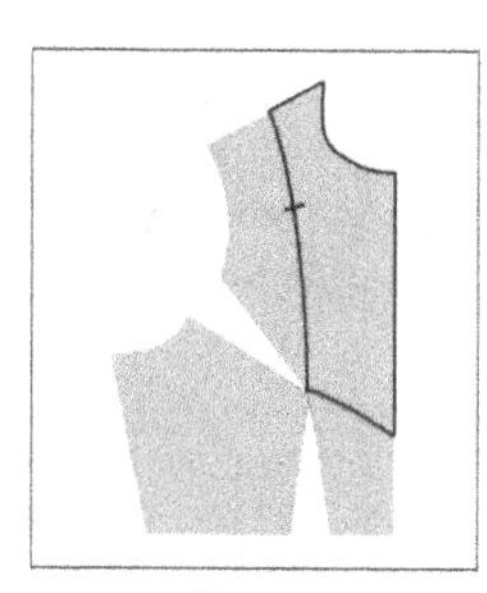

Trace

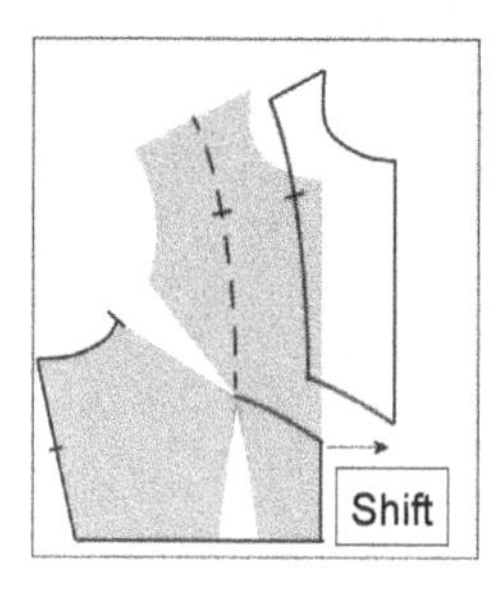

Shift & Trace

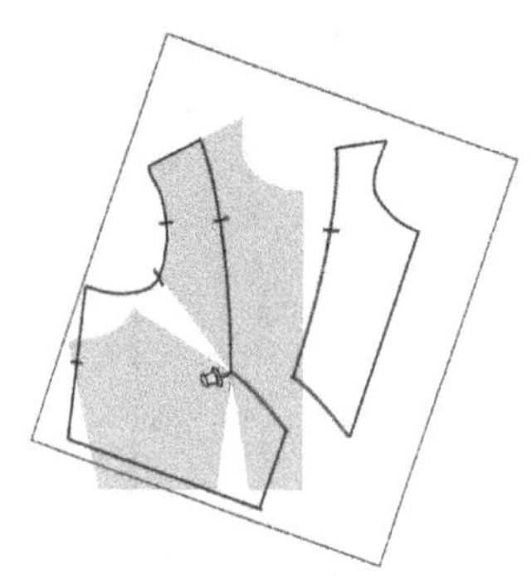

Pivot & Complete

Front Seam Variations

To create original designs, relate the lines of the design to the body. Measure as necessary and draw the lines on a copy of the Sloper.

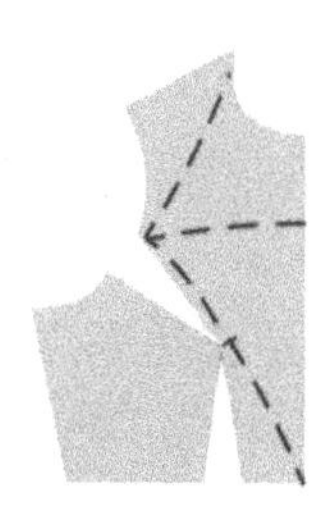

The Design Lines

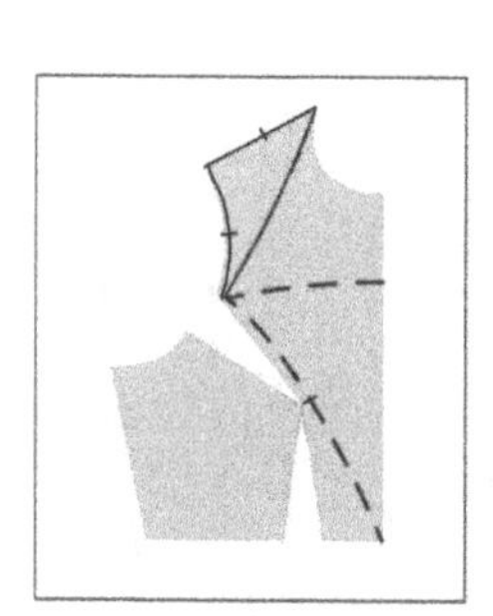

Trace

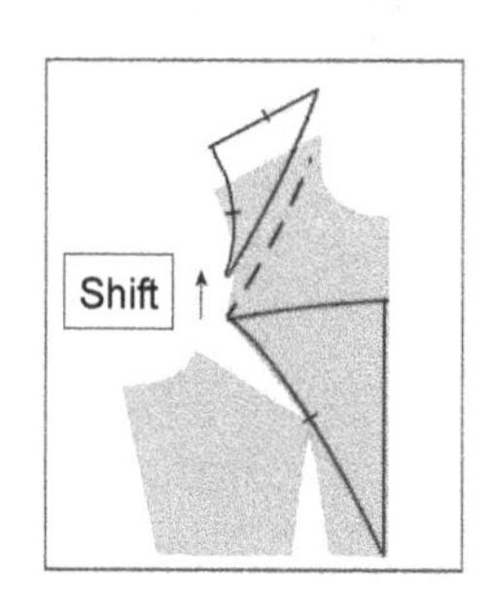

Shift & Trace

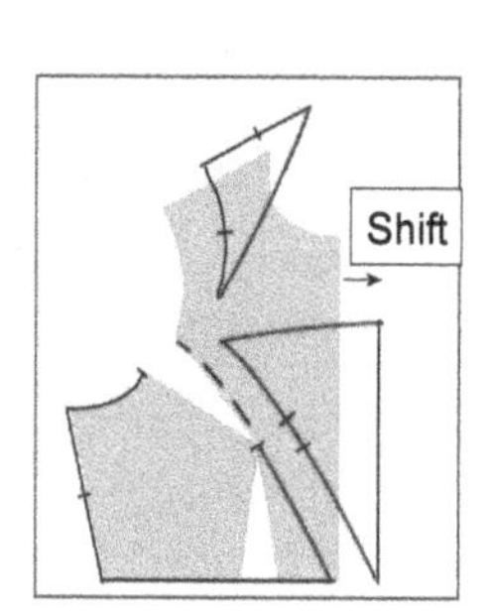

Shift & Trace

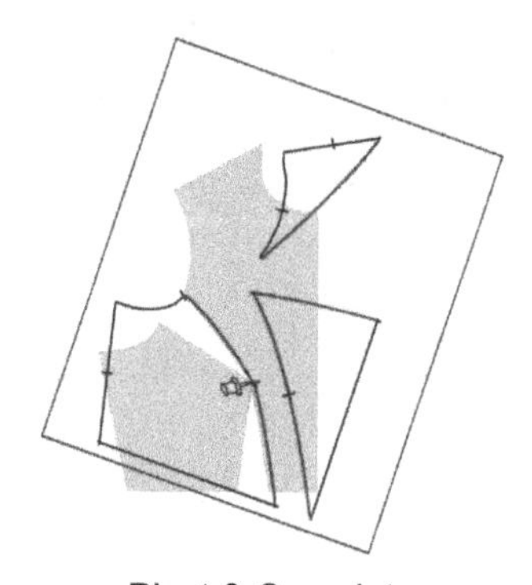

Pivot & Complete

The Bust Seam Line

A design may use a seam line straight around the bust, remaining parallel to the floor. This seam line can be located at any level within the Bust Circle without requiring additional fitting.

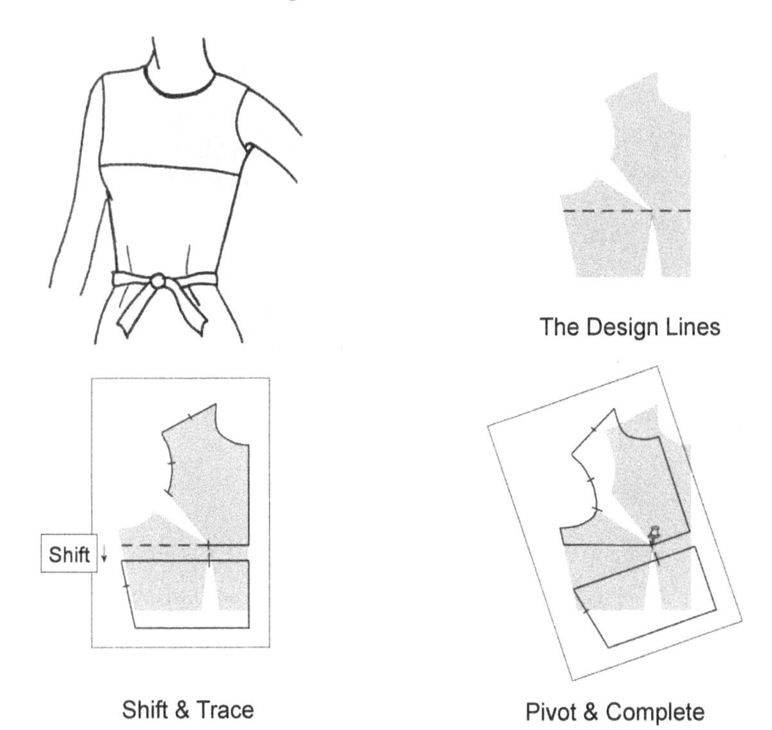

The Design Lines

Trace

Shift & Trace

Pivot & Complete

Changing Back Darts to Seams

The same principle of changing darts to seams can be applied to Back Darts. When the Sloper has an Upper Back Dart, it indicates a rounded back. To create a yoke for this type of contour, start by altering the Upper Back Dart to the Shoulder Seam.

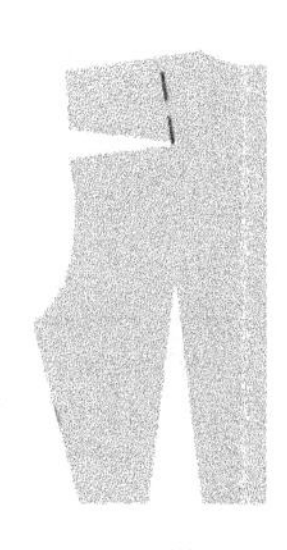

The Design Line

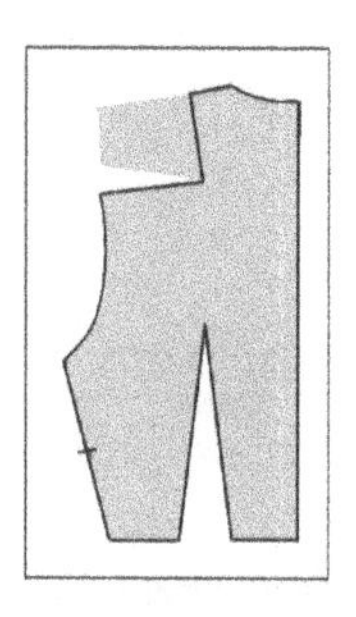

Trace

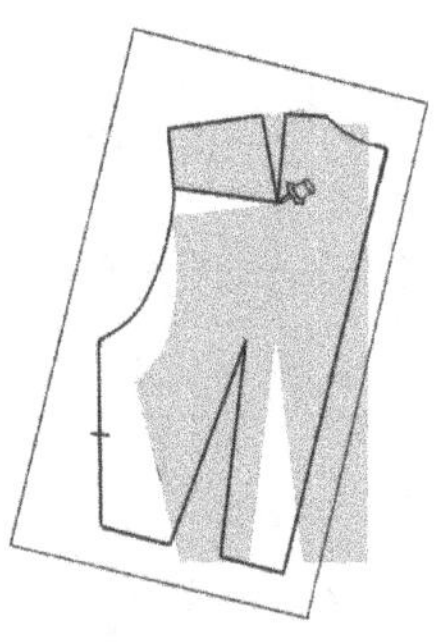

Pivot & Complete

Shirt Yoke

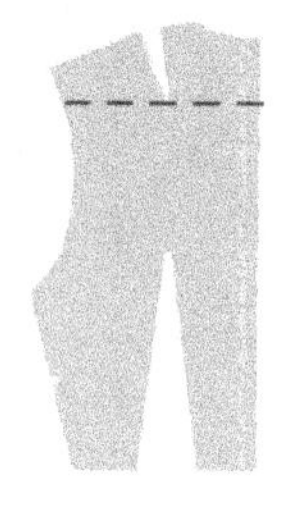

The Design Lines

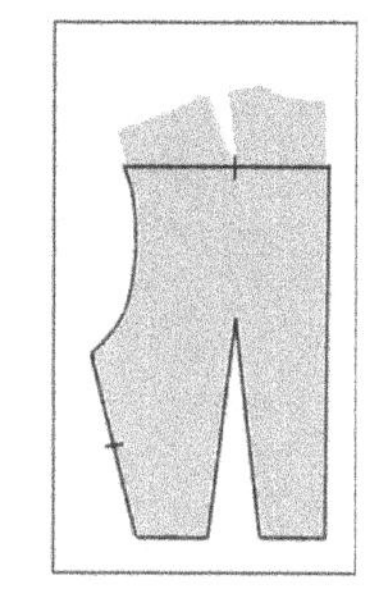

Trace

Shift

Shift & Trace

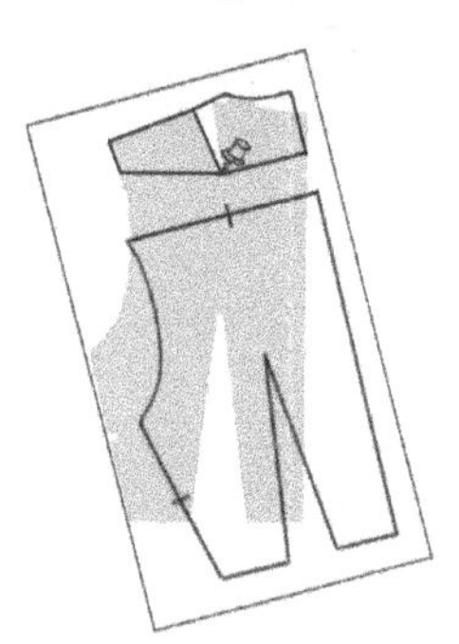

Pivot & Complete

Principles of Adding Fullness

Fitted patterns follow the lines of the body. If a design is for a garment that does not follow the body, the pattern must be expanded accordingly. The illustrations below show the difference between a fitted skirt and a full skirt.

Location Of Fullness

Fullness will be located in a garment where the Slopers are expanded. If the Side Seam is expanded, then the fullness will appear on the side of the body. If the pattern is expanded in the middle, then there will be fullness in that portion of the body.

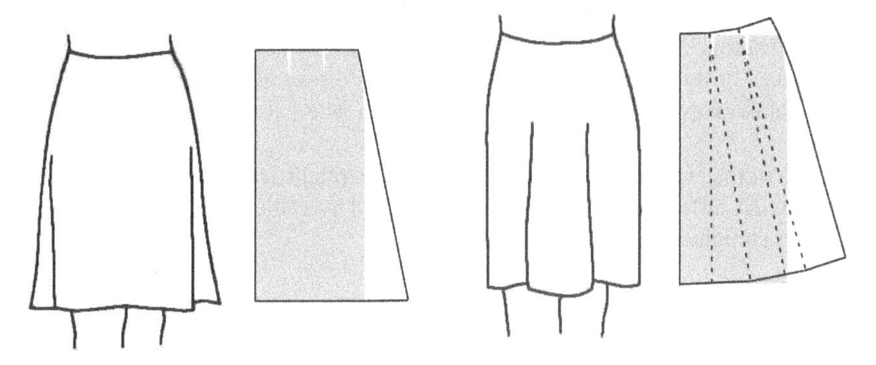

Changing Darts To Fullness

Darts may be changed to fullness by cutting through the center of the dart and down to the hem. The dart is then taped closed. The wedge of the dart now appears below the Hip line instead of above it. The fullness will appear only in the skirt where it appears in the pattern, below the Hip line. The waist-to-hip area will still be fitted.

Another dart shaped wedge can be created by taping together the Side Seams of the front and the back patterns. This eliminates the Side Seam and creates fullness on the side of the body.

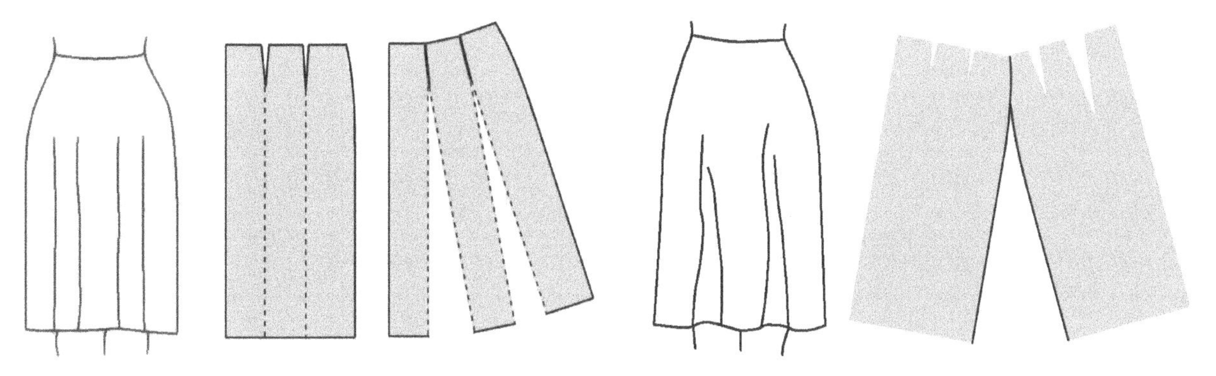

Adding Fullness

To add fullness to the waist-to-hip area, the pattern must be cut in a number of sections and spread apart. Fullness will appear in the garment wherever the patterns are spread.

The pattern may be spread only at the hem with the waist remaining fitted, only at the waist with the hem remaining fitted, or the pattern may be expanded at both the waist and the hem.

Notice how the seam lines curve when fullness is added to one seam and not the other. If both seams are expanded, then the seam lines remain straight.

When the waist is expanded, the fabric must be gathered into a waistband.

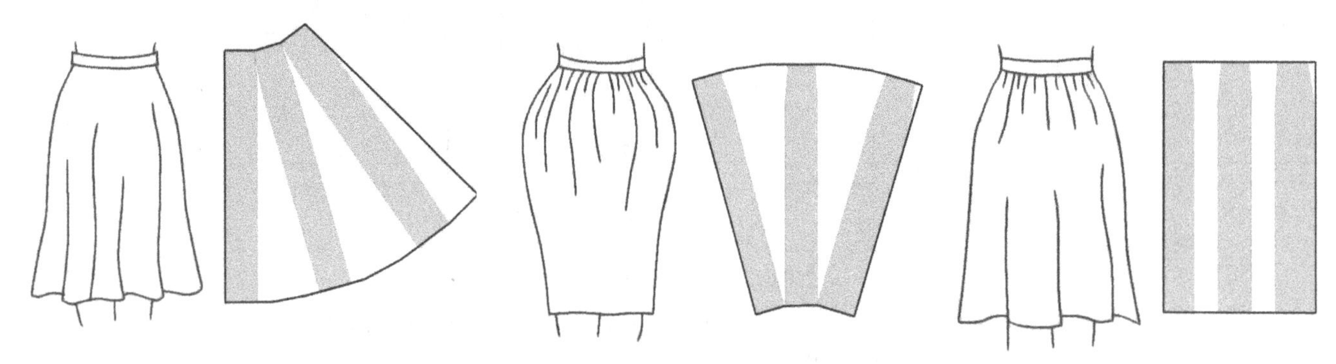

Transition from Fitted to Full

If a single pattern piece is to go from fitted to full, the changes in the pattern pieces cannot be too abrupt. To create a strong contrast from a fitted shape to a full shape, one of two things must be done. Either divide the garment into several pattern pieces so that no one piece makes an extreme change. Or, place a seam where the transition from fitted to full occurs.

Notice that the curved seam fits smoothly into a straight seam of the same length to create fullness. A different kind of fullness is achieved by gathering a long straight seam into a shorter straight seam.

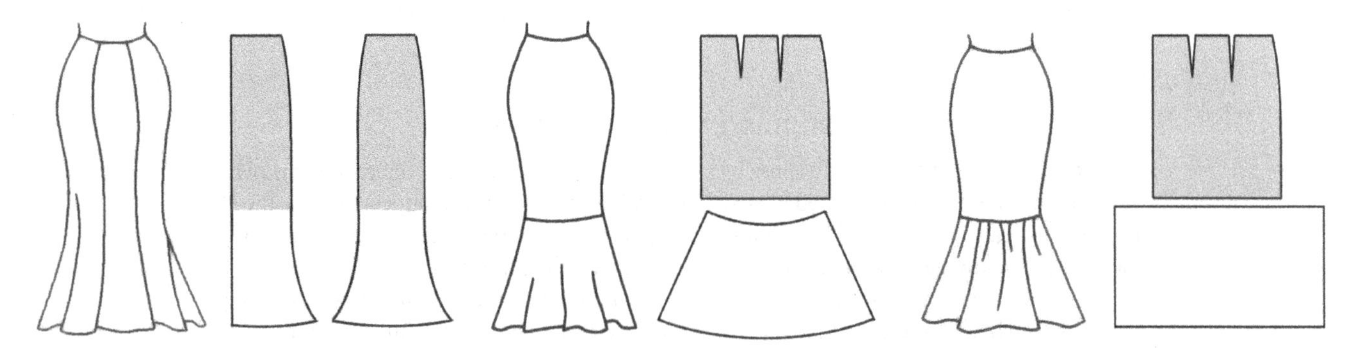

Determining Fullness

The amount of fullness to use depends on both the desired design and the nature of the fabric. Fullness added to stiff and/or heavy fabrics has a tendency to make the garment stand away from the body. Light weight and/or supple fabric will drape into the body in graceful folds.

Taking the nature of the fabric into consideration, use the following guidelines for fullness.

Slight Fullness - Expand the fitted patterns so that they are half again larger than their fitted size. For example, a seam that is 12" (30 cm) long would be expanded to 18" (45 cm). This is usually the minimum amount of fullness that must be added to a pattern to be visually effective.

Medium Fullness - Expand the fitted patterns to twice their original size. For example, the 12" (30 cm) seam becomes 24" (60 cm).

Considerable Fullness - Expand the fitted patterns to three times their original size. The 12" (30 cm) seam would be 36" (90 cm). This is normally the maximum amount of fullness that can be added to a pattern without the garment becoming cumbersome.

Another way of approximating the desired amount of fullness is to lay out a tape measure to the desired size of the design. Shape the tape measure to include the fullness.

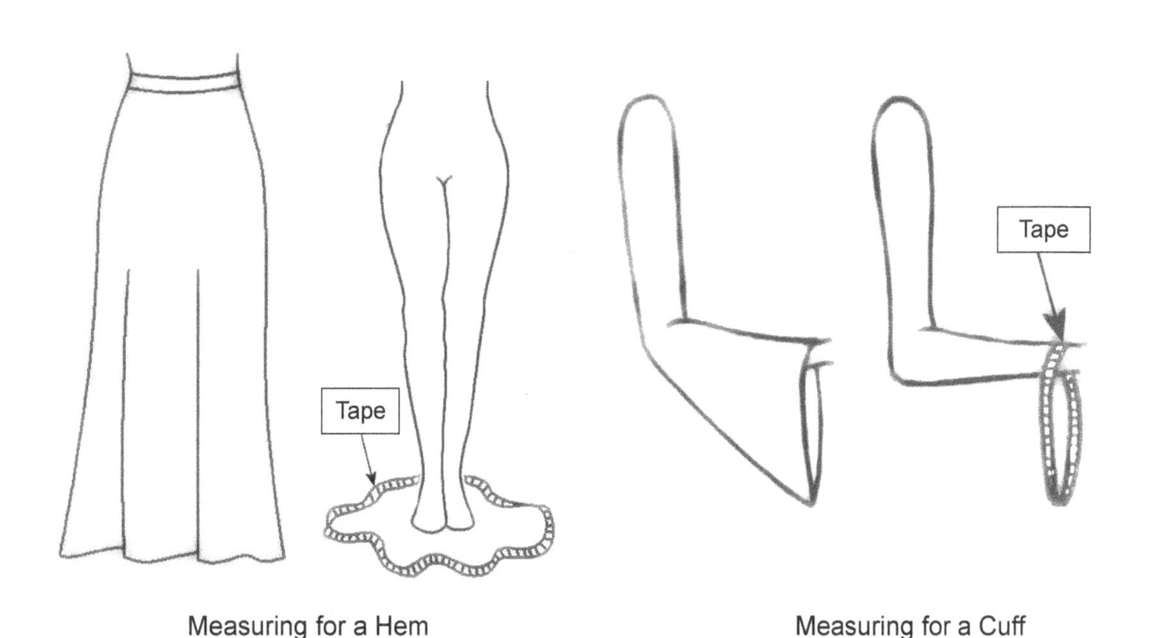

Measuring for a Hem

Measuring for a Cuff

Fullness in Princess Seams

Three variations of the Princess Seam are shown here to illustrate control of fullness. The patterns for these designs only show the changes to the Princess Seam and the Side Seam.

Straight Side Front

The first Princess Seam line shows the Side Front seam being drawn straight down from the Bust Point. No fullness is added to the pattern at this point. Fullness is added to the Side Seam to allow for comfort of movement. This pattern would be appropriate for a coat.

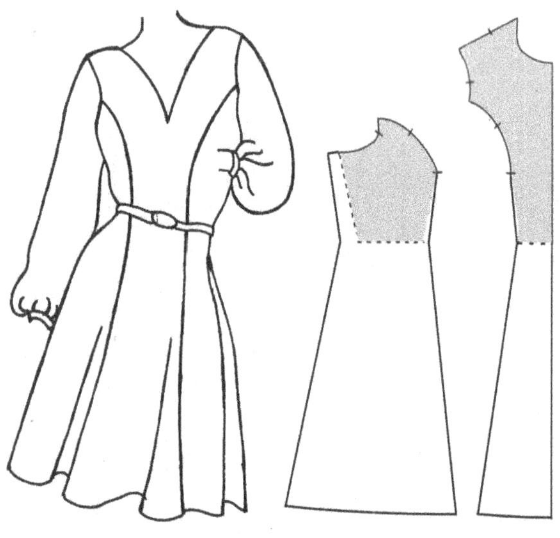

Flared Side Front

The second Princess Seam has fullness added to both sides of the Side Front line and to the Side Seam. This pattern would be appropriate for a dress that calls for fullness at the body's Side Front location.

Notice that the Side Front line is shaped in to include part of the "B" dart. This will make the garment fit at the waist.

Decorative Side Front

In this final variation of the Princess Seam, the Side Front line of the front pattern is shaped out to the side. The Side Front line on the side pattern is shaped in by the exact same amount. No fullness is added to the Side Front. Instead the Side Front shapes into the waist and then back out at the hem, creating a visual hourglass effect.

The Procedures for Adding Fullness

Adding fullness is the process of making a pattern larger than the Sloper. The expansion shapes fabric from one side of the garment to another. For example, the fullness in an A-line skirt can have a fitted waist that flares to a wide hem.

The following instructions illustrate how to add fullness to a woman's blouse that has a seam at the full bust level. This is the same seam described on page 99. The lower portion of the blouse can have fullness just at the full bust level, an even amount of fullness from the bust seam to the hem, or mixed fullness with some at the bust and more at the hem.

Cut and Spread

One way to envision this would be to take a copy of the Sloper pattern and cut it into strips which can be manually spread out, then copied onto another sheet of paper as illustrated below.

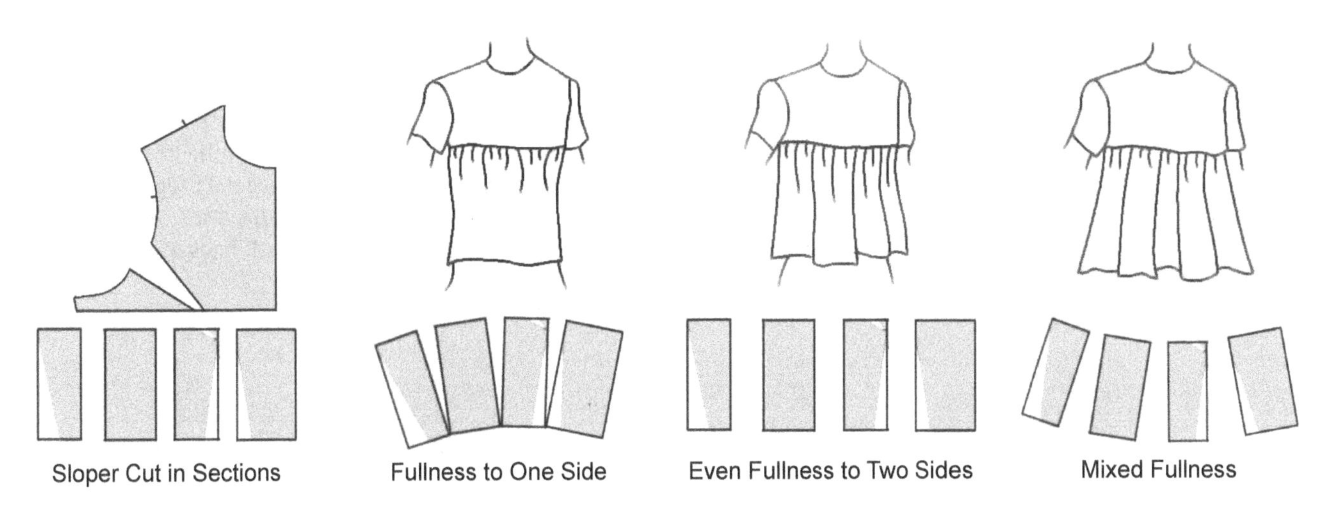

Sloper Cut in Sections | Fullness to One Side | Even Fullness to Two Sides | Mixed Fullness

Pivot and Shift

The cut and spread technique makes it easy to visualize what is happening to the pattern. However, keeping the pieces in an appropriate arrangement to create the pattern can be tricky. The instructions shown here use the Pivot and Shift technique as it allows more control over the results. The illustrations show how the pattern paper needs to be placed over the Slopers. Pivot and Shift can be used to add fullness to any design.

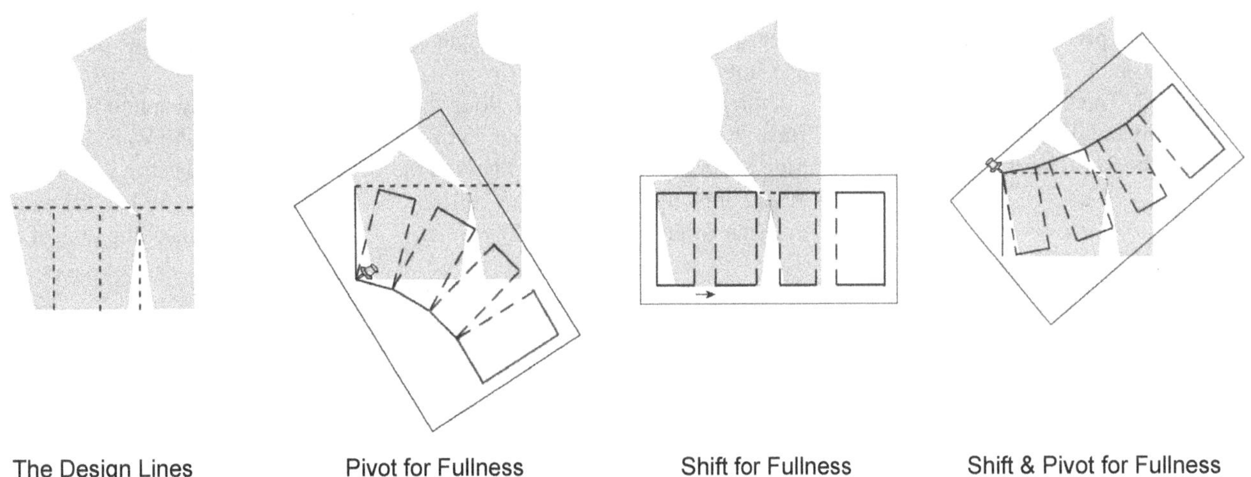

The Design Lines | Pivot for Fullness | Shift for Fullness | Shift & Pivot for Fullness

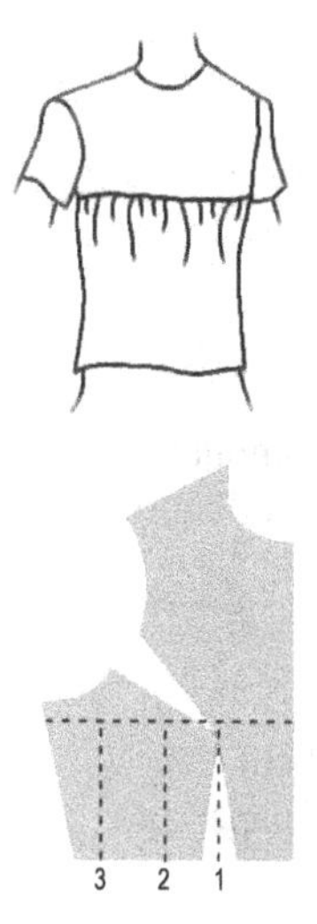

Adding Fullness to One Side

This design adds fullness to the seam at the bust while leaving the length at the waist unchanged. For the shape of the pattern from the bust up, see page 99.

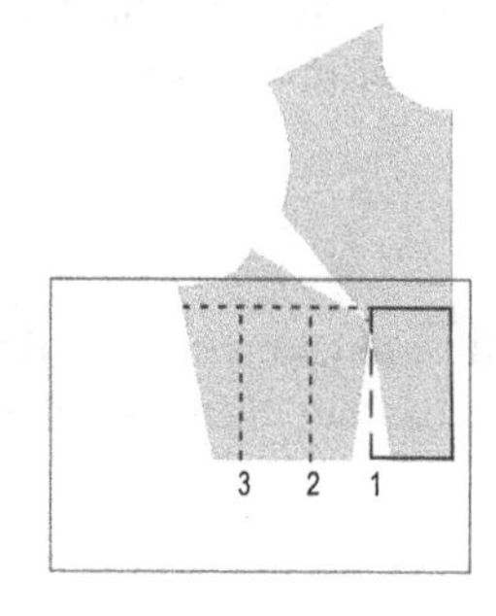

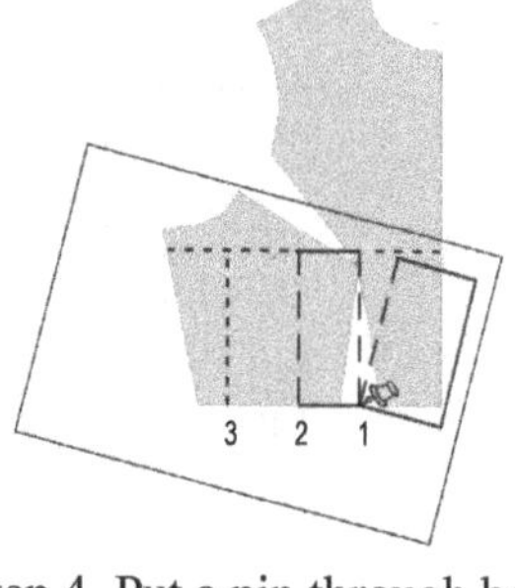

Step 1. On the Sloper, draw a dotted line to indicate where the bust seam is to be located.

Step 2. On the Sloper, draw dotted Slash lines to indicate where fullness is to be added. These Slash lines should be spaced frequently enough to ensure a smooth curve in the final pattern. Number these lines.

Step 3. Place a sheet of pattern paper over the Sloper. Trace the Sloper from the Bust Seam, down the Center Front, then along the Waist to Slash #1. Indicate the location of the Slash line with a series of dashes.

Step 4. Put a pin through both patterns at the bottom of Slash #1 and pivot the pattern paper to add the desired amount of fullness.

Step 5. Trace the Sloper along the Bust Seam and the Waist from #1 to #2. Indicate the Slash lines with dashes.

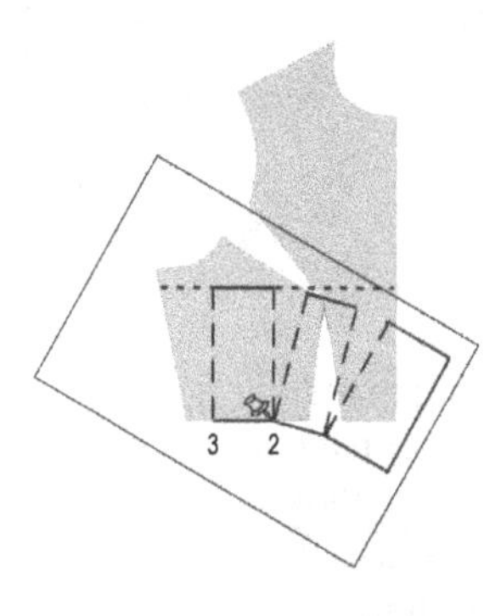

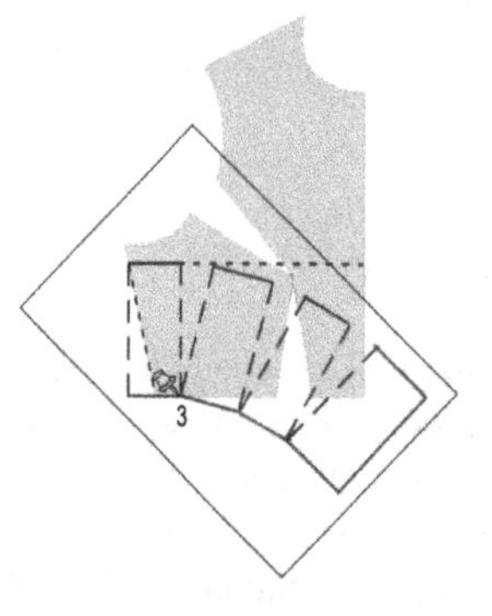

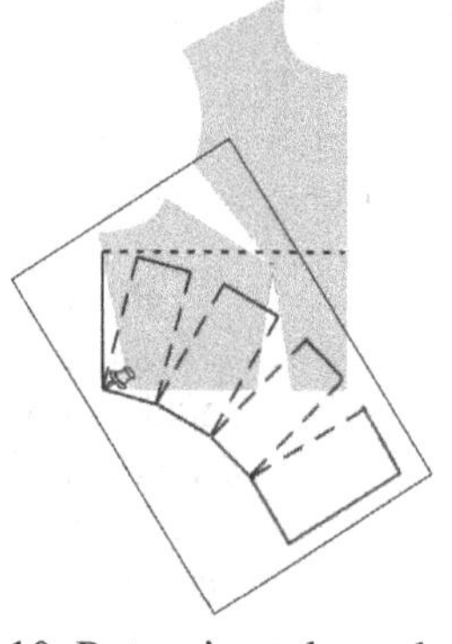

Step 6. Put a pin at the bottom of Slash #2 and pivot the pattern paper to add fullness.

Step 7. Trace the Sloper along the Bust Seam and the Waist from #2 to #3. Indicate the Slash lines with dashes.

Step 8. Put a pin at the bottom of Slash #3 and pivot the pattern paper to add fullness.

Step 9. Trace the Sloper along the Bust Seam and the Waist from #3 to the Side Seam. To add a little fullness at the Waist, draw a line straight down from the Side Seam at the bust to the waist.

Step 10. Put a pin at the end of the new Waist and pivot the pattern to add fullness.

Step 11. Draw a line for the new Side Seam from the Waist to the Bust Seam line at the bust.

Step 12. To complete the pattern, draw lines to connect the tops of the Slash lines.

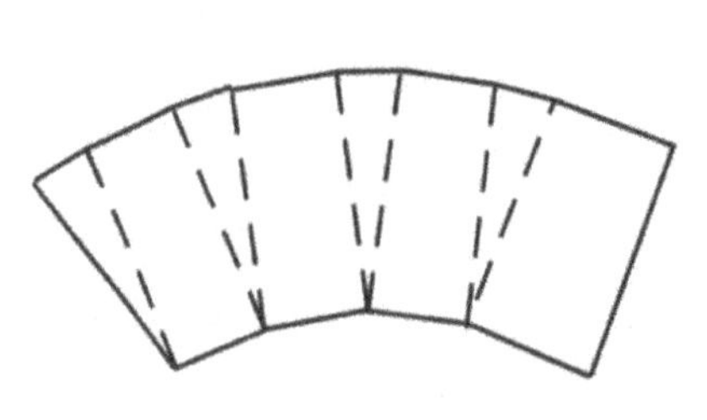

The Finished Pattern

Adding Fullness to Two Sides

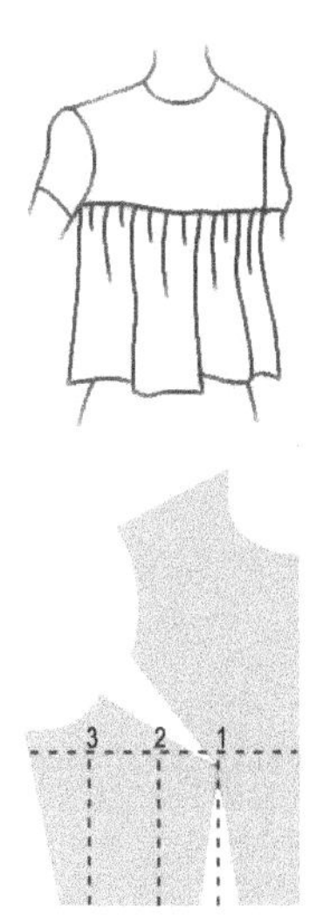

The procedure described here adds an equal amount of fullness to two sides of the pattern by tracing and shifting the pattern.

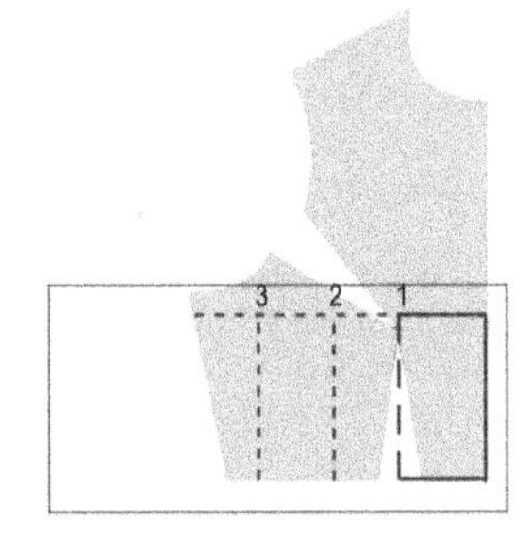

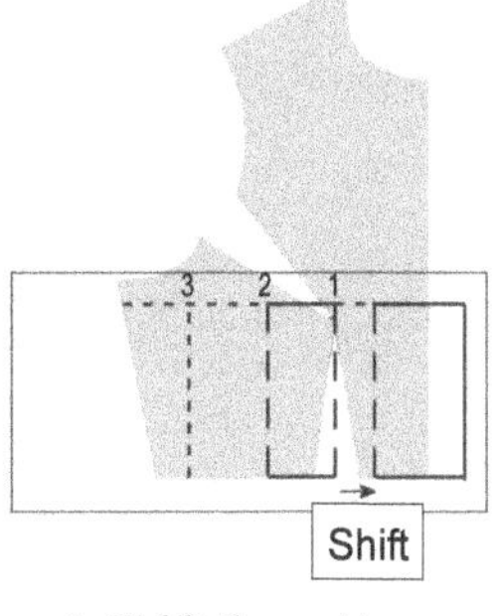

Step 1. On the Sloper, draw a dotted line to indicate where the bust seam is to be located.

Step 2. On the Sloper, draw dotted Slash lines to indicate where the fullness is to be added.

Step 3. Place a sheet of pattern paper over the Sloper. Trace the Sloper from the Bust Seam, down the Center Front, then along the Waist to Slash #1. Indicate the location of the Slash line with a series of dashes.

Step 4. Shift the pattern paper to add the desired amount of fullness.

Step 5. Trace the Sloper along the Bust Seam and the Waist from #1 to #2. Indicate the Slash lines with dashes.

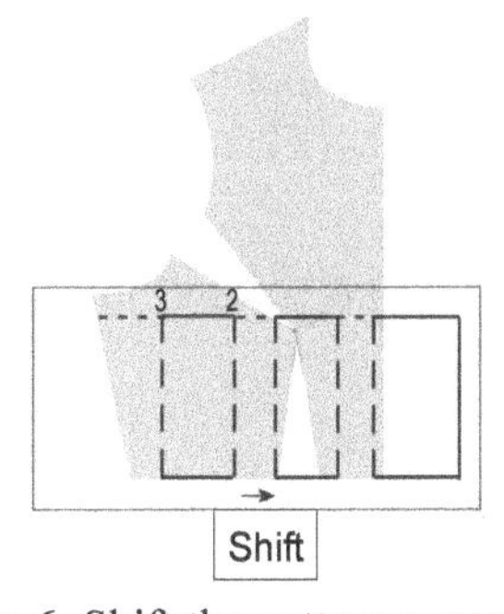

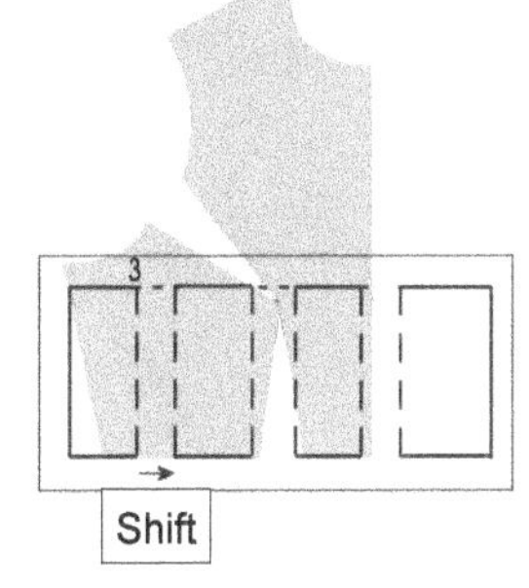

Step 6. Shift the pattern paper to add fullness.

Step 7. Trace the Sloper along the Bust Seam and the Waist from #2 to #3. Indicate the Slash lines with dashes.

Step 8. Shift the pattern paper to add fullness.

Step 9. Trace the Sloper along the Bust Seam and the Waist from #3 to the Side Seam.

Step 10. To add a little fullness at the Waist, draw a line straight down from the Side Seam at the bust to the waist.

Step 11. To complete the pattern, draw lines to connect the tops of the Slash lines.

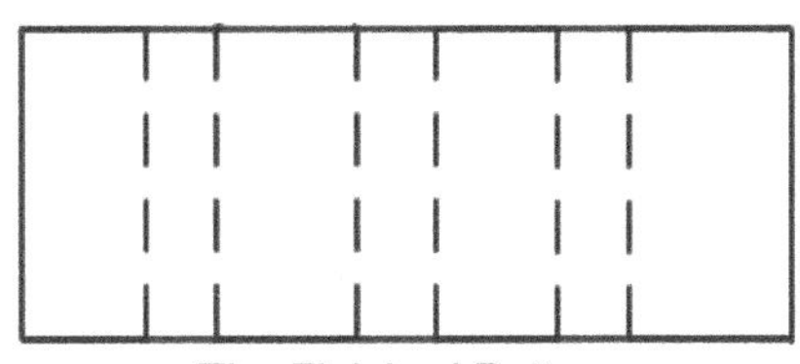

The Finished Pattern

Adding Mixed Fullness

In some cases, a design may require some fullness be added to one side of a pattern, more fullness added to the opposite side. The following procedure combines the two previous techniques.

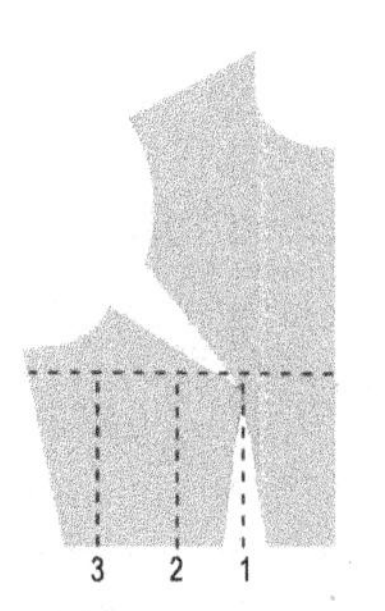

The Design Line

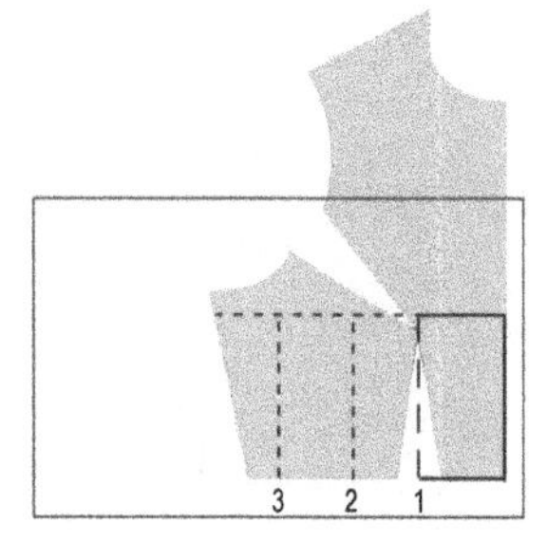

Trace CF to #1

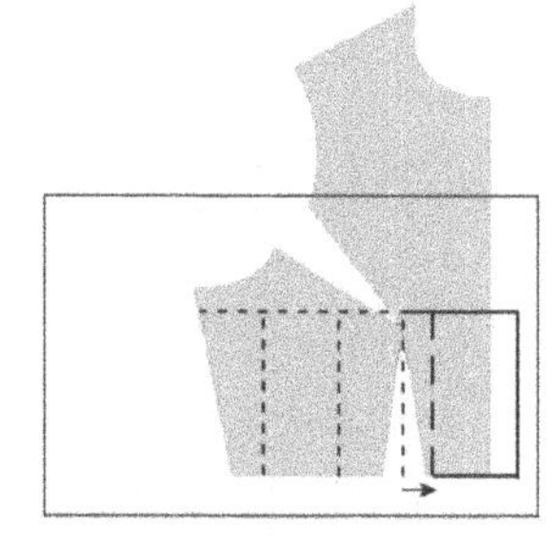

Shift

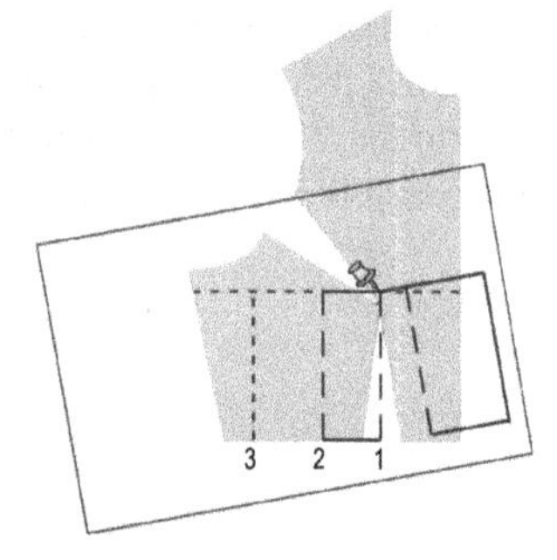

Pivot & Trace #1 to #2

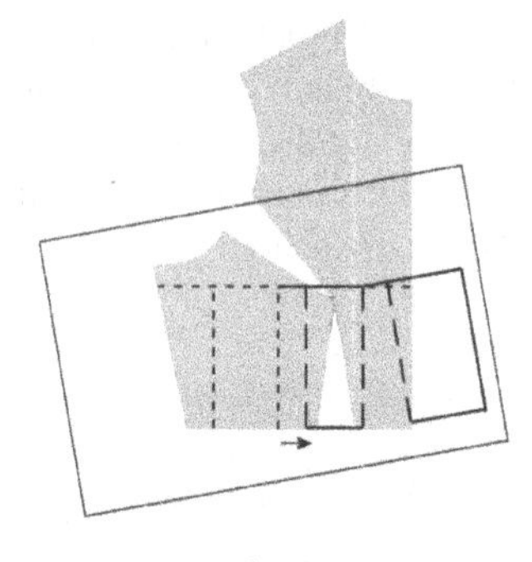

Shift

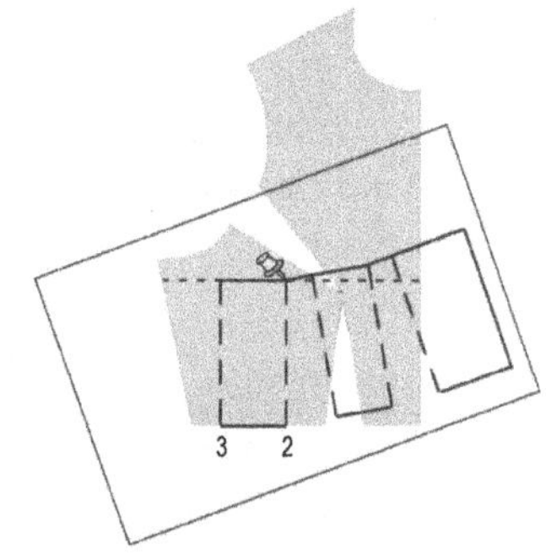

Pivot & Trace #2 to #3

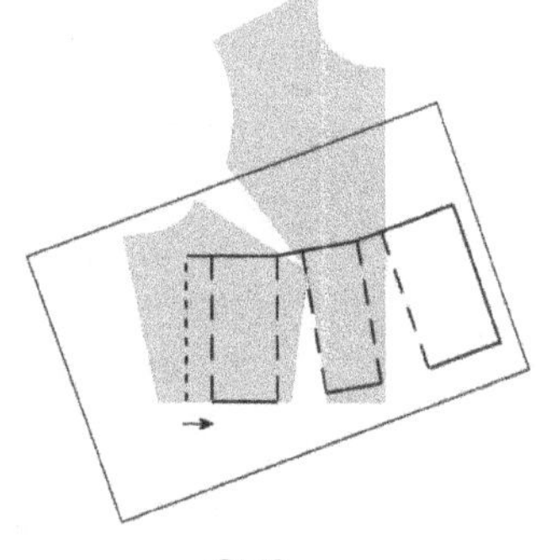

Shift

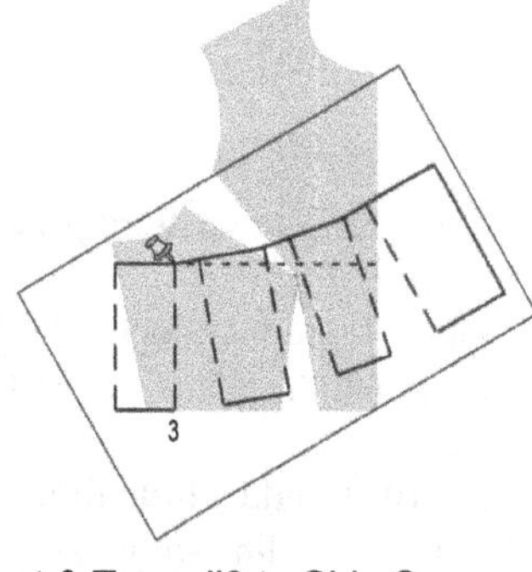

Pivot & Trace #3 to Side Seam

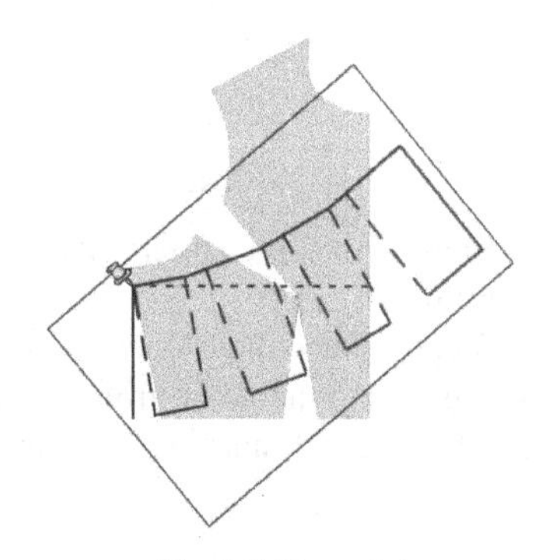

Pivot & Complete

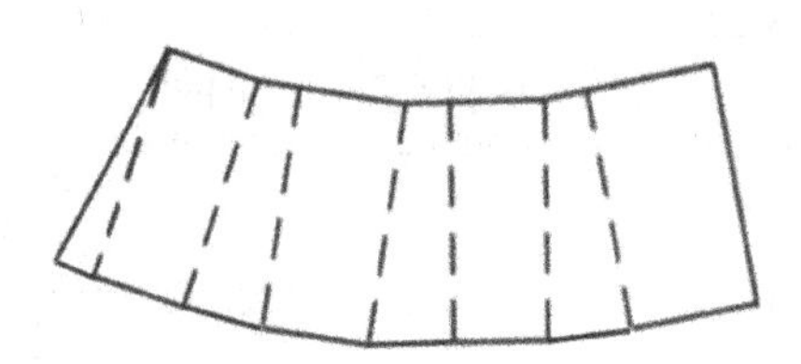

The Finished Pattern

Gathers From The Dart

The fullness for this design is created by shifting the shape of the dart to above the bust. The extra fabric from the shape of the dart is gathered into the yoke. No additional fullness needs to be added to the Slopers.

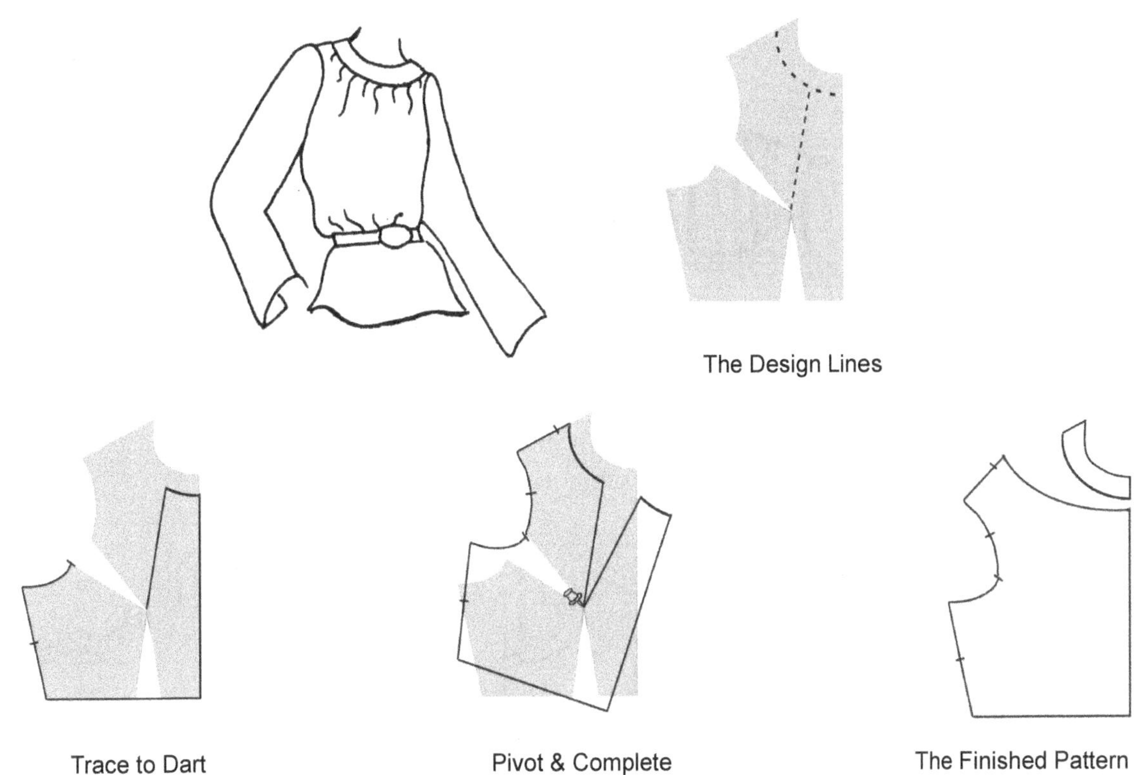

The Design Lines

Trace to Dart

Pivot & Complete

The Finished Pattern

This design converts the Above the Bust Dart to fullness but does not expand the pattern at the full bust level. If you want additional fullness in this area, you need to expand the pattern some more as shown below.

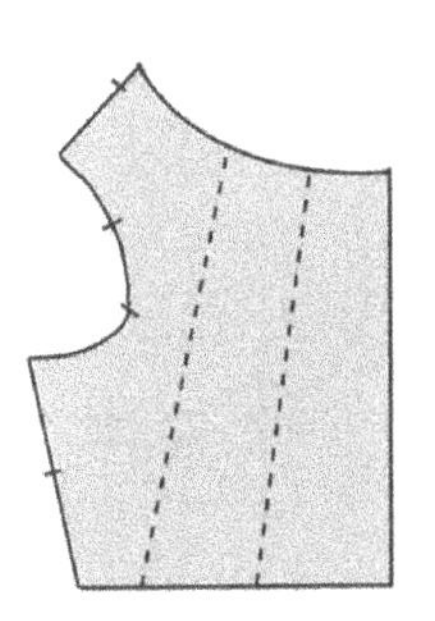

The Design Lines

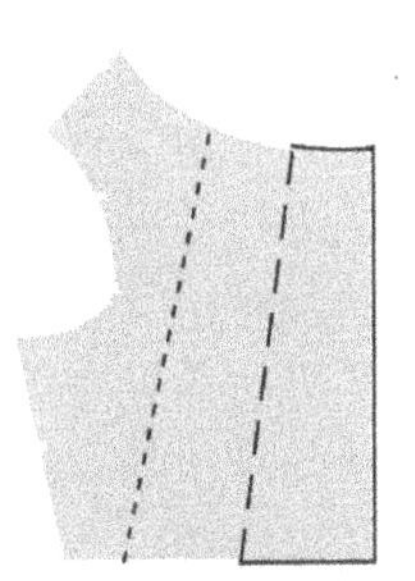

Trace to #1

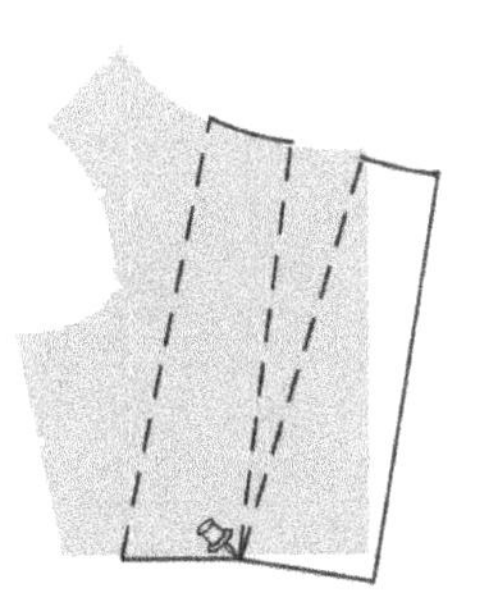

Pivot & Trace to #2

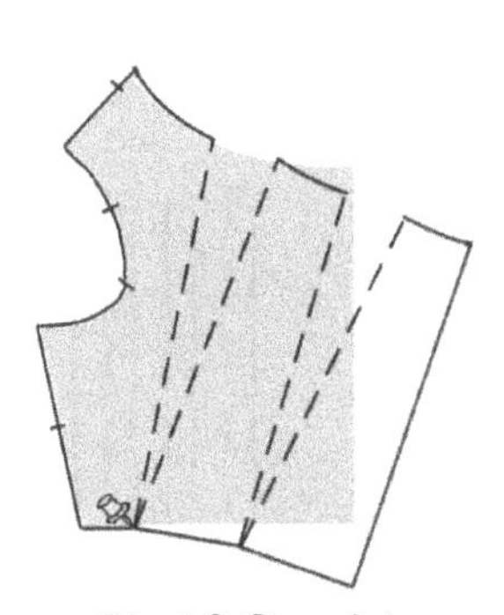

Pivot & Complete

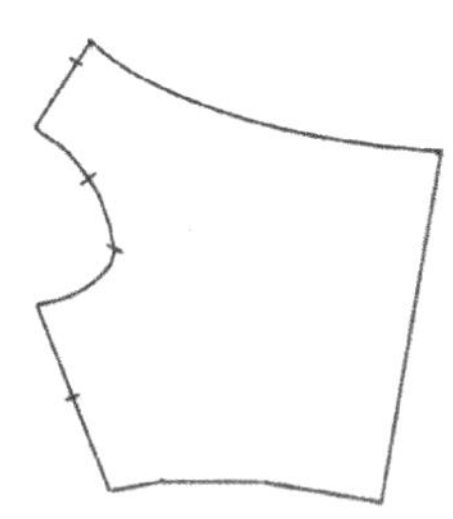

The Finished Pattern

Pleats

Pleats are a specialized type of fullness. The best procedure for creating patterns for pleats is to take a piece of pattern paper and fold it exactly the way the pleats are to appear. Transfer the portion of the pattern that is to be pleated to the folded paper. Add a ½" (12 mm) sewing allowance and cut the folded paper on this seam allowance line. Unfold the paper for the shape of the pattern. Mark the location of the folds clearly.

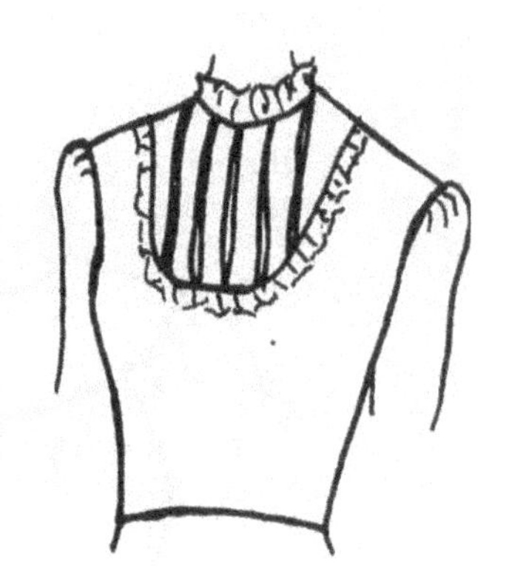

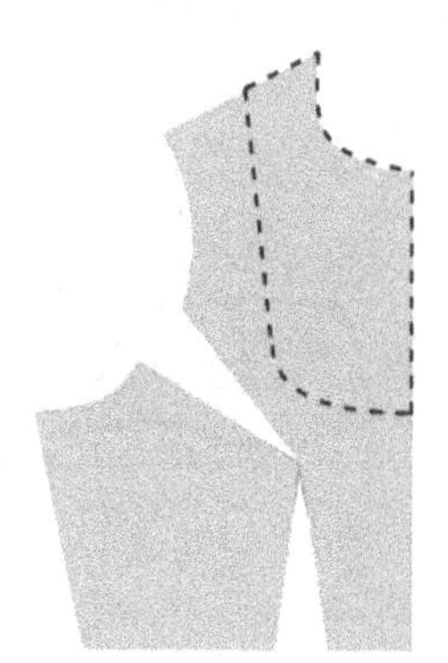

The Design Lines

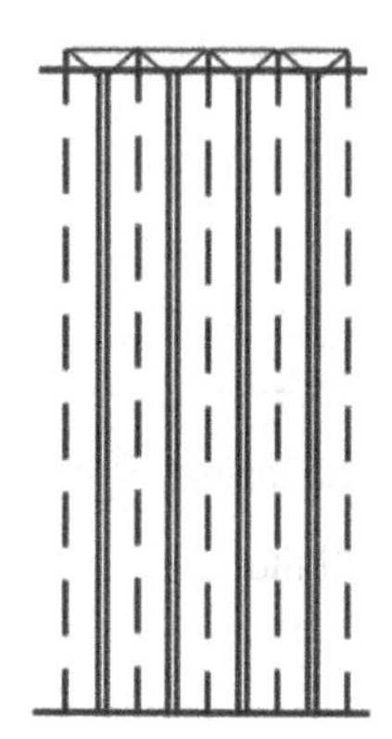

Paper Folded for Box Pleats

Pattern on Top of Folded Paper

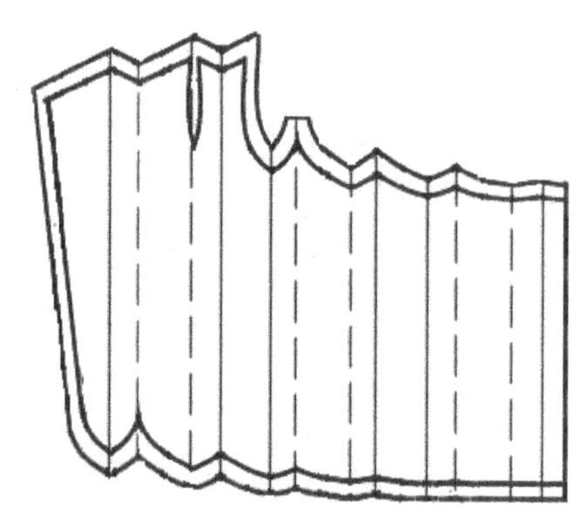

The Unfolded Pattern

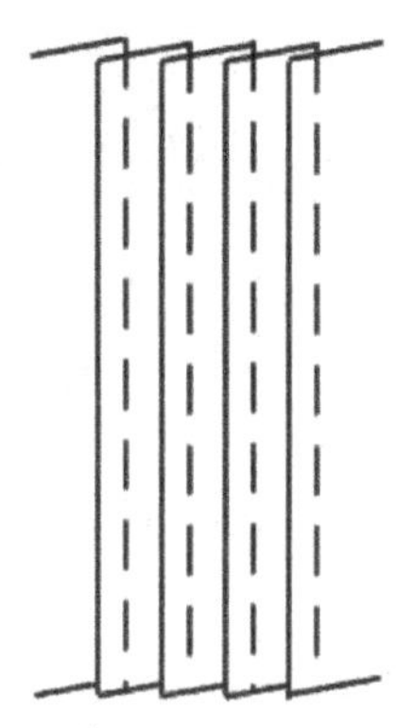

Paper Folded for Knife Pleats

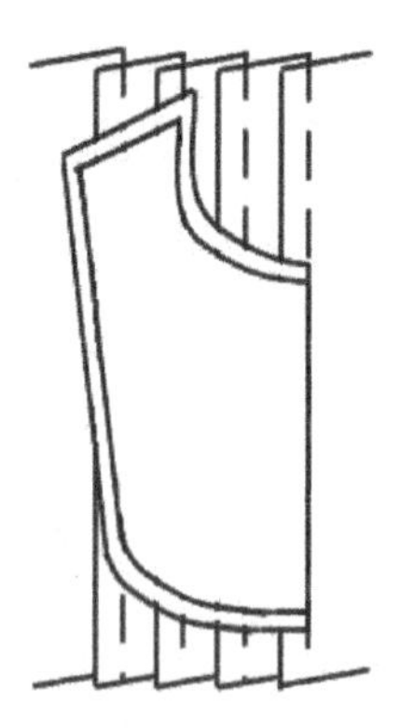

Pattern on Top of Folded Paper

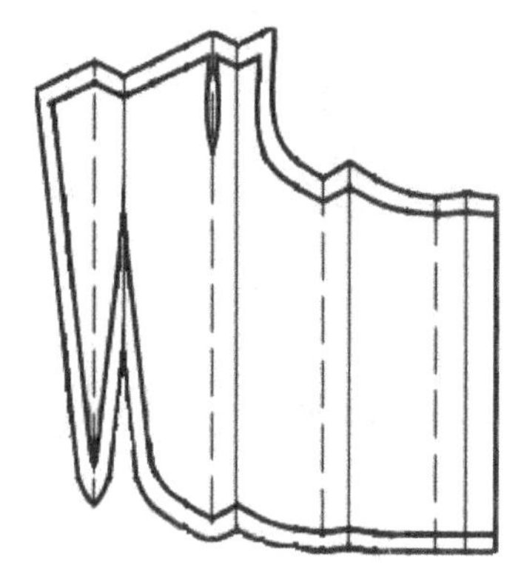

The Unfolded Pattern

Sleeve Variations

Many different types of sleeves can be created by changing the location of the seam lines, adding fullness to the patterns, or using both techniques.

Adding Fullness To The Arm Seam

The sleeves in these illustration are created by changing the shape of the arm seam. The top of the sleeve remains fairly fitted. Fullness is added from the elbow down.

Important Note - To design the pattern for the gathered sleeve, the length of the pattern must be expanded as well as the width. If a cuff is to be added, subtract the length of the cuff from the sleeve length.

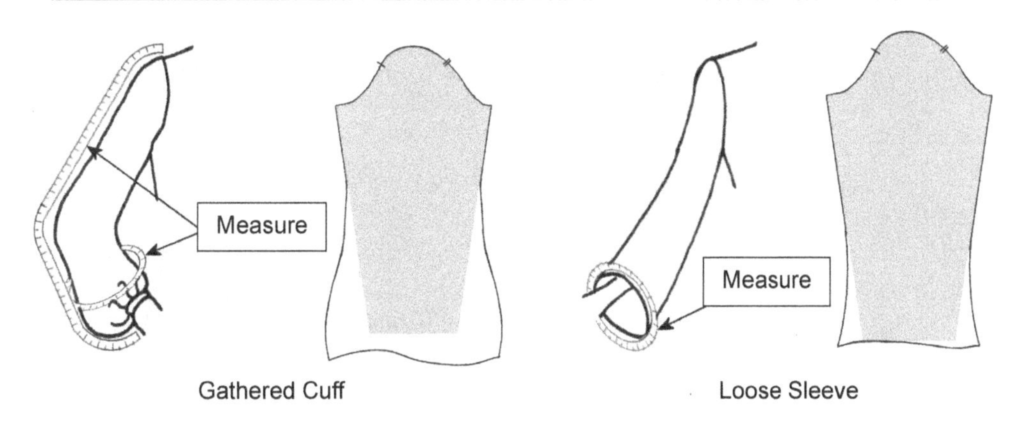

Gathered Cuff   Loose Sleeve

Changing The Arm Seam

Occasionally, designs require very full, loose sleeves as in choir robes. If the fullness is added to the Underarm Seam of the Sleeve Sloper, the sleeves will hang gracefully only when the arms are held out to the side of the body. When the arms are forward, the sleeve will twist. To prevent the sleeves from twisting, the Underarm Seam must be changed to the back of the arm.

To change the location of the Underarm Seam, mark the new seam on the Sleeve Cap. The back of the arm is halfway between the Sleeve Centerline and the Underarm Seam. Lay a piece of pattern paper over the Sloper and trace the Sleeve Cap from the left side to the Back of Arm seam location. Shift the pattern paper so that the traced left end of the Sleeve Cap touches the right end of the Sleeve Cap. Trace to the new seam location. The fullness for the sleeve may now be added to the Back of Arm seam.

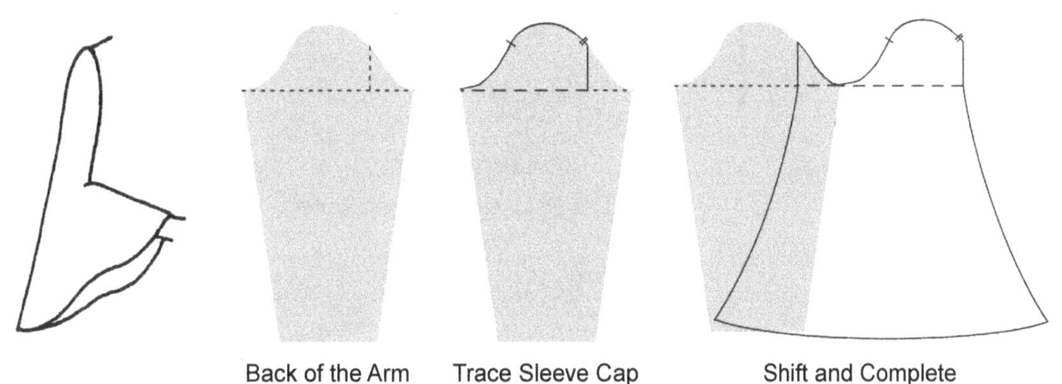
Back of the Arm   Trace Sleeve Cap   Shift and Complete

Flounced Sleeve

This design for a Flounced Sleeves has the upper arm fitted and the lower arm full. To achieve this effect, a seam must be added where the sleeve makes a transition from fitted to full. The upper portion is traced directly from the Sloper.

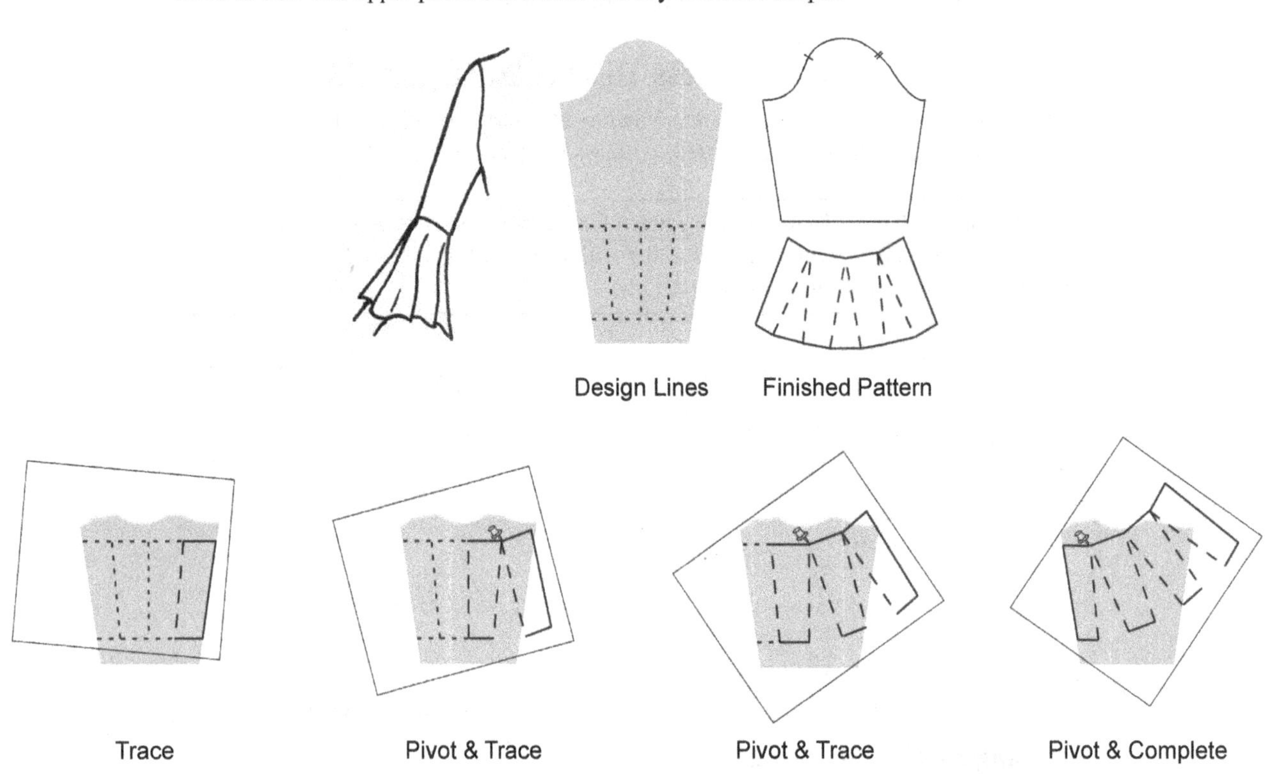

Gathered Sleeve Top

To create gathers in the Sleeve Cap, draw dotted lines on a copy of the Sleeve Sloper where the fullness is to be located. Trace the pattern, adding the desired fullness. If the arm portion of the sleeve is to remain fitted, pivot the pattern paper at the Biceps line. Add the bottom fitted portion of the sleeve as the last step. Notice that the height of the sleeve is increased as well as the length of the Sleeve Cap seam.

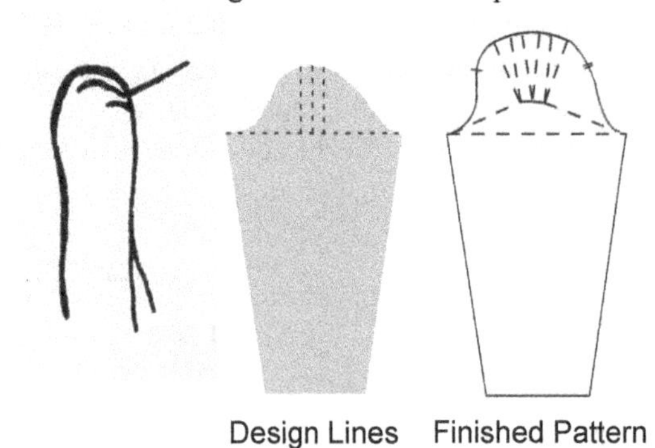

Trace

Pivot & Trace

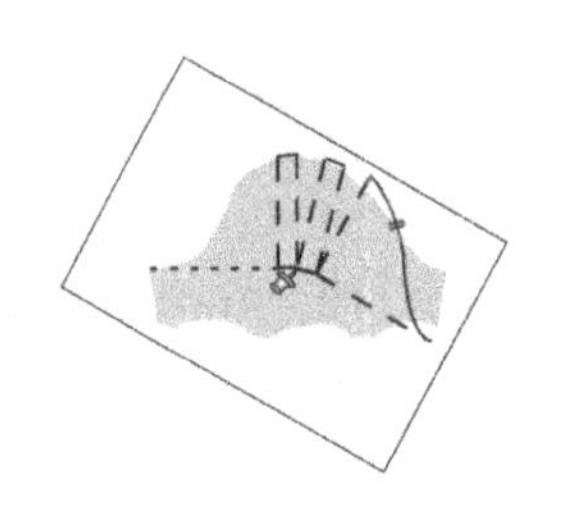

Pivot & Trace

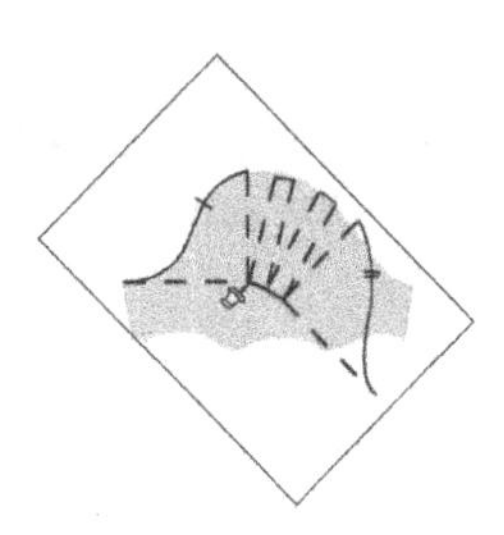

Pivot & Complete

Gathered Sleeve Cap

The fullness of the sleeve on page 112 will be gathered into the top of the garment. If the fullness is to be gathered into more than just the top, the pattern must be expanded across a larger portion of the Sleeve Cap.

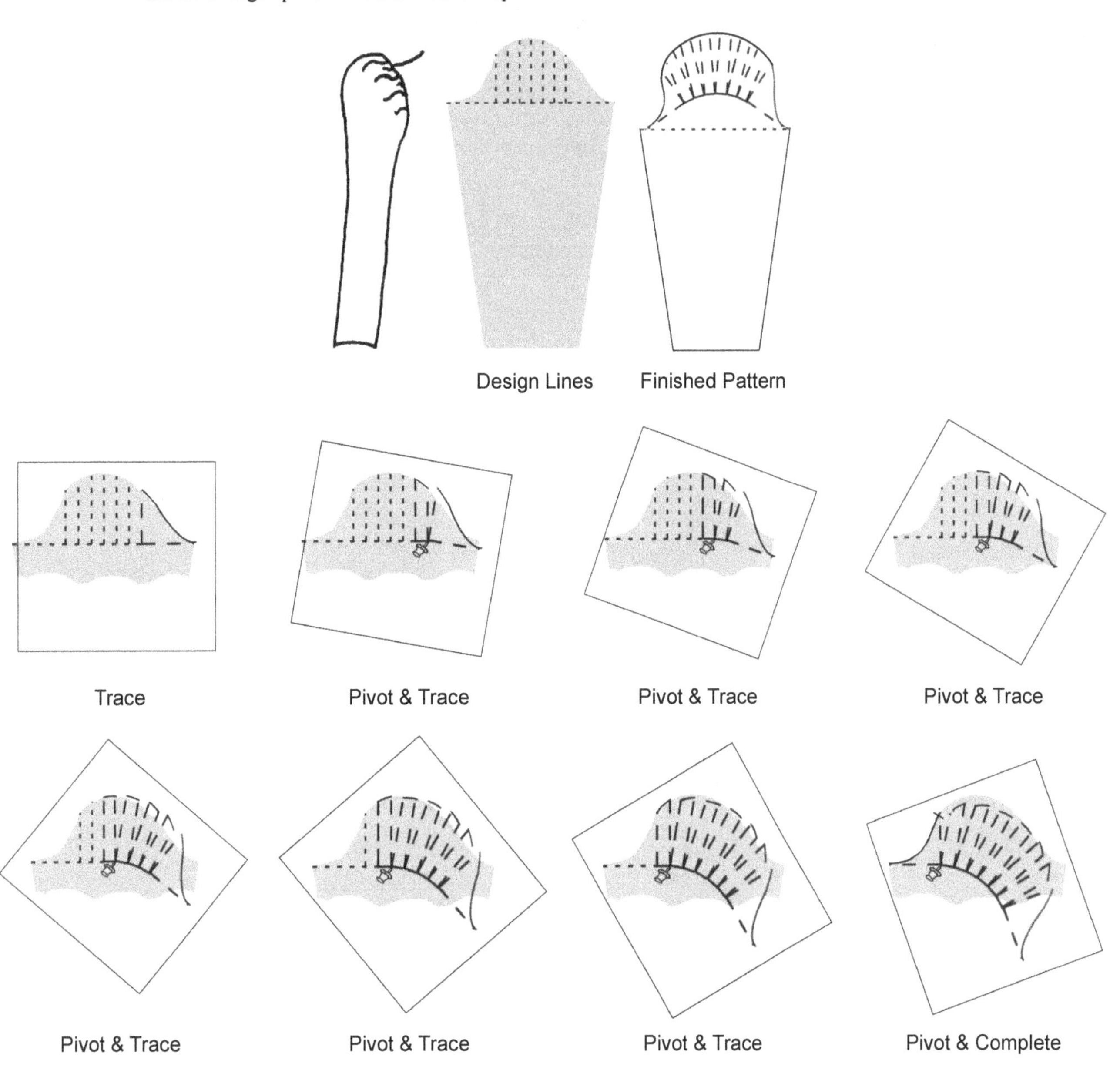

Leg-Of-Mutton Sleeve

The Leg-of-Mutton sleeve has fullness in both the Sleeve Cap and the upper portion of the arm. The lower portion of the arm is fitted. Establish a line on the Sloper to indicate how far down the fullness is to be located. Add dotted vertical lines to the pattern and place pattern paper over it. The pattern paper will be pivoted at the horizontal line that indicates the length of the fullness. Add the fitted portion of the lower arm as the last step.

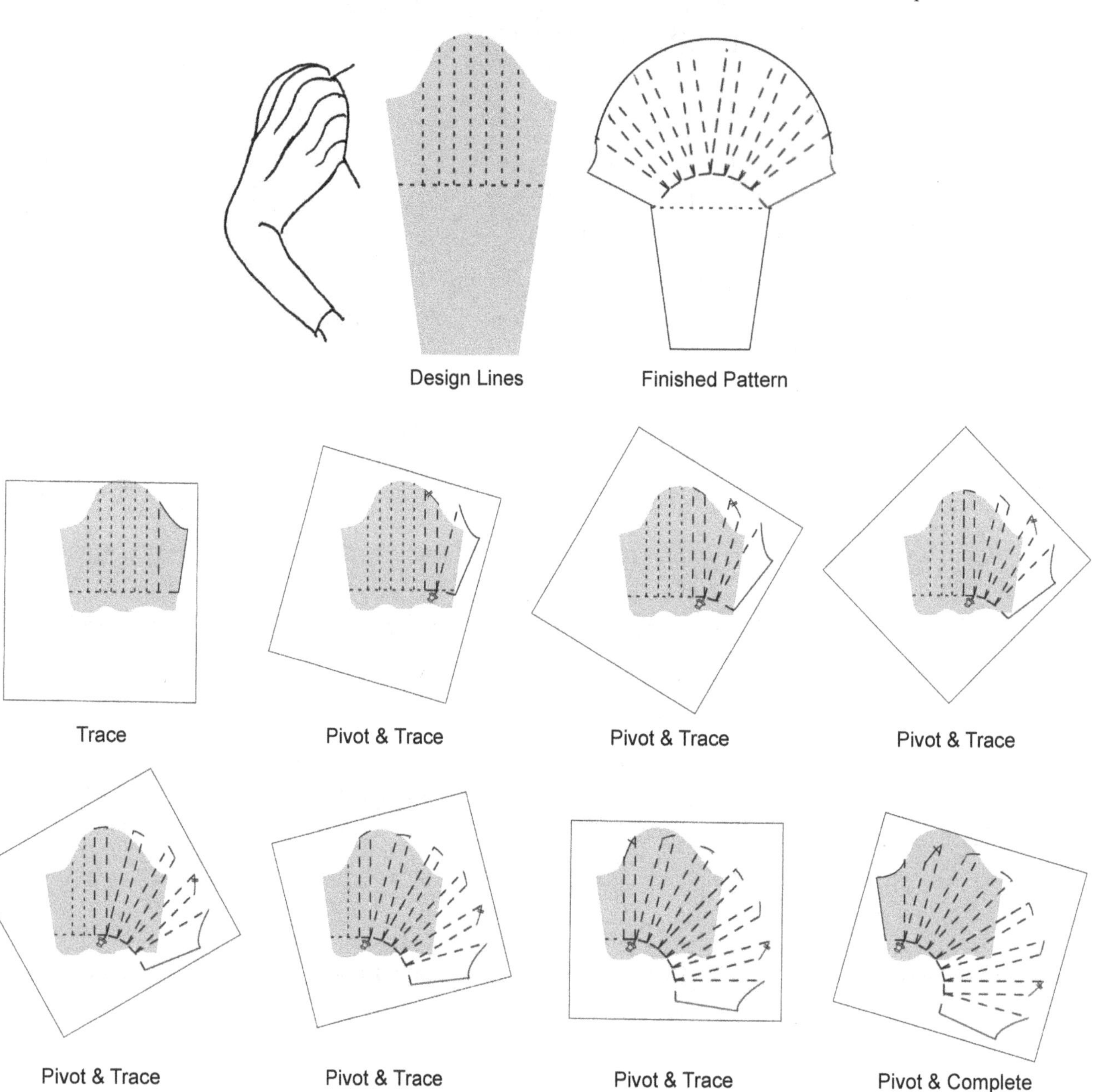

Puffed Sleeve

The Puffed Sleeve pattern has more fullness added to the top and the bottom seams than it has added to the width of the pattern. To achieve this effect, divide the pattern into an upper and lower portion at the Biceps line. Next, use the Shift and Pivot techniques, see page 105. Then combine the new upper portion of the pattern to the new lower portion.

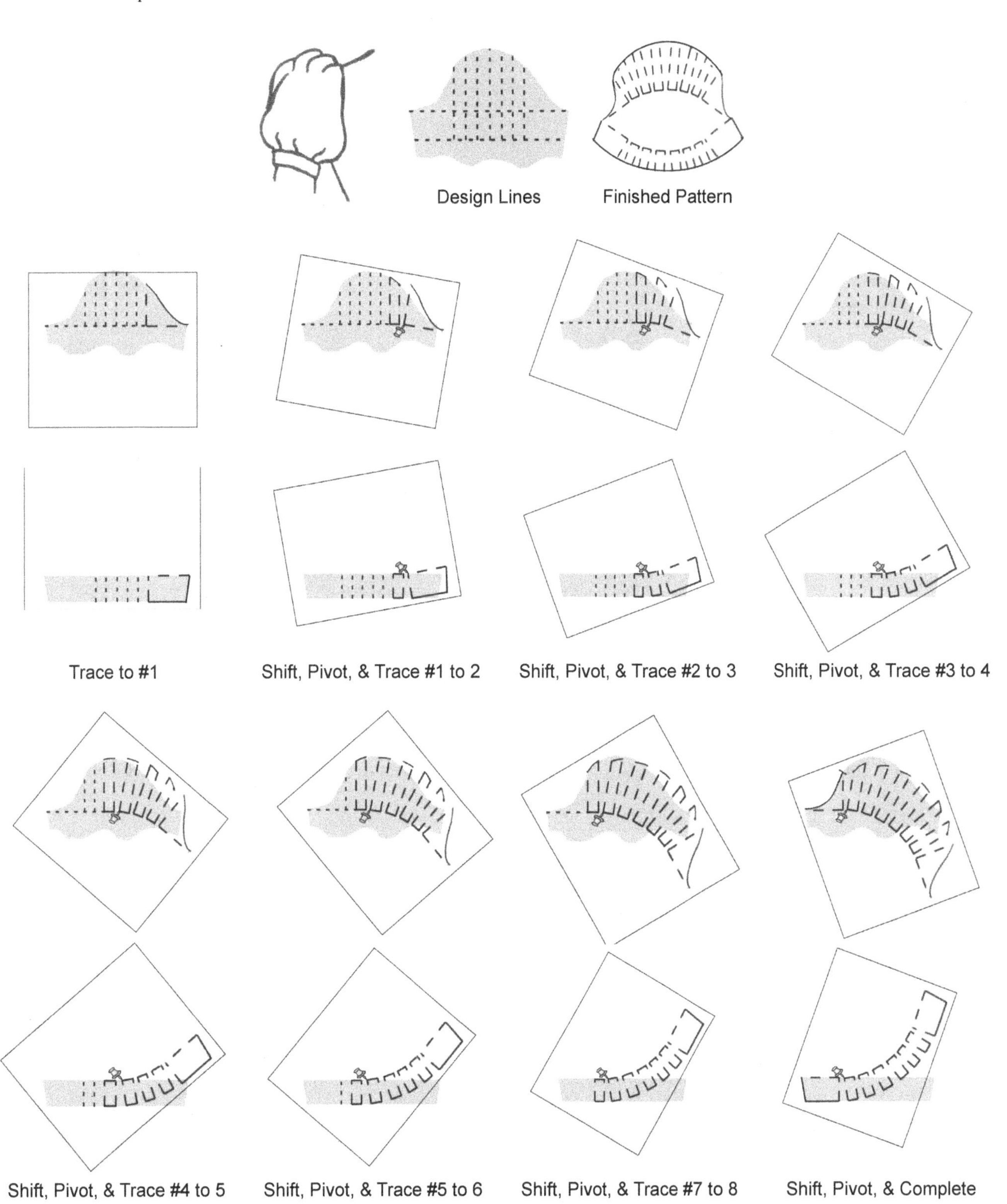

Bell Sleeve

The design for the Bell Sleeve calls for the sleeve to hang away from the outside of the arm. This shape is used for men's short sleeve shirts. To achieve this effect, the shape of the Sleeve Cap line must be changed. Notice how the final pattern has a shorter sleeve cap height than the Sloper.

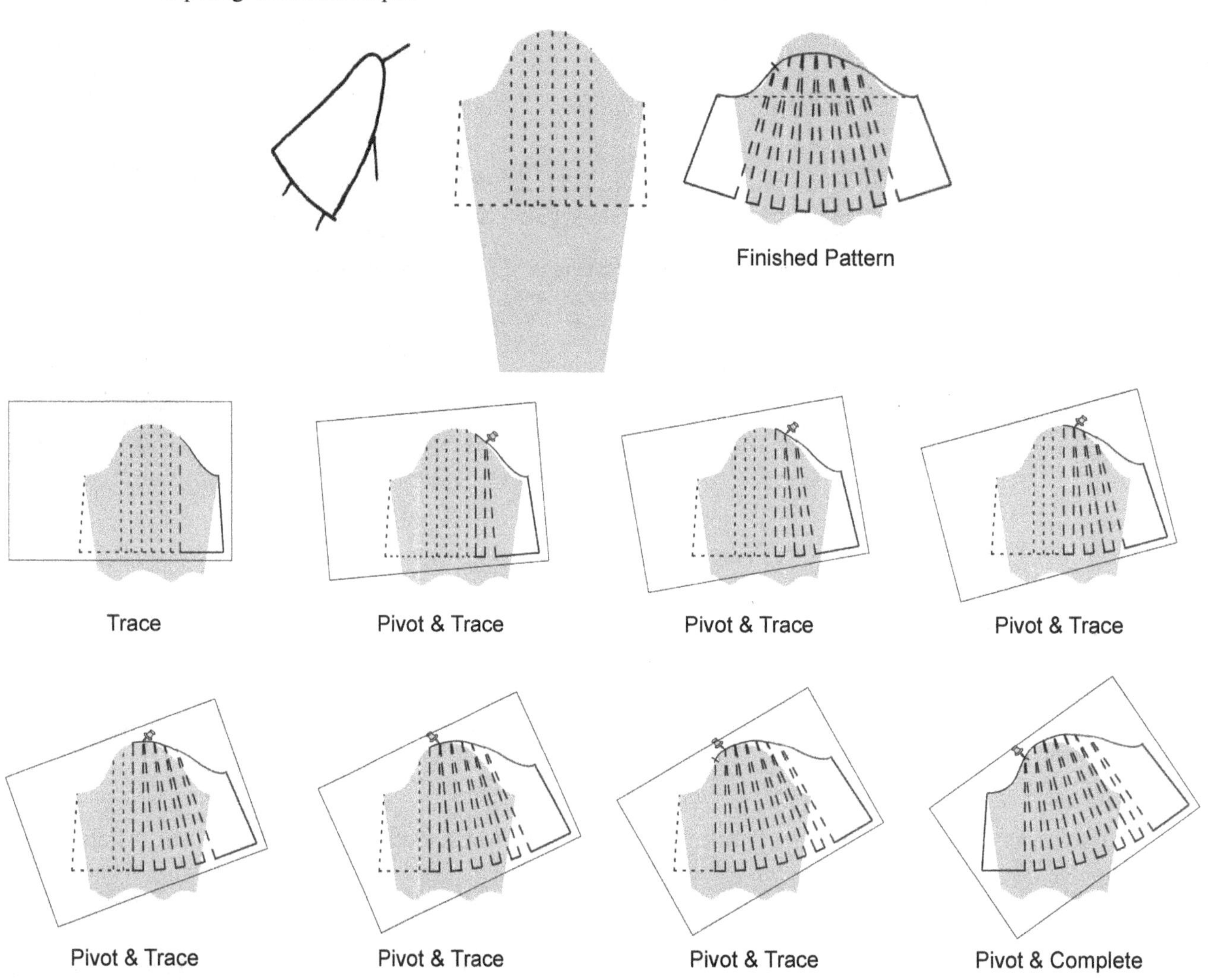

Cape Sleeve

The Cape Sleeve is drafted the same way the Bell Sleeve is created except more fullness is added. There are no gathers in the design of the Sleeve Cap. The extreme curve of the final Sleeve Cap line is what creates the sleeve's draped effect. Notice no fullness is added under the arm.

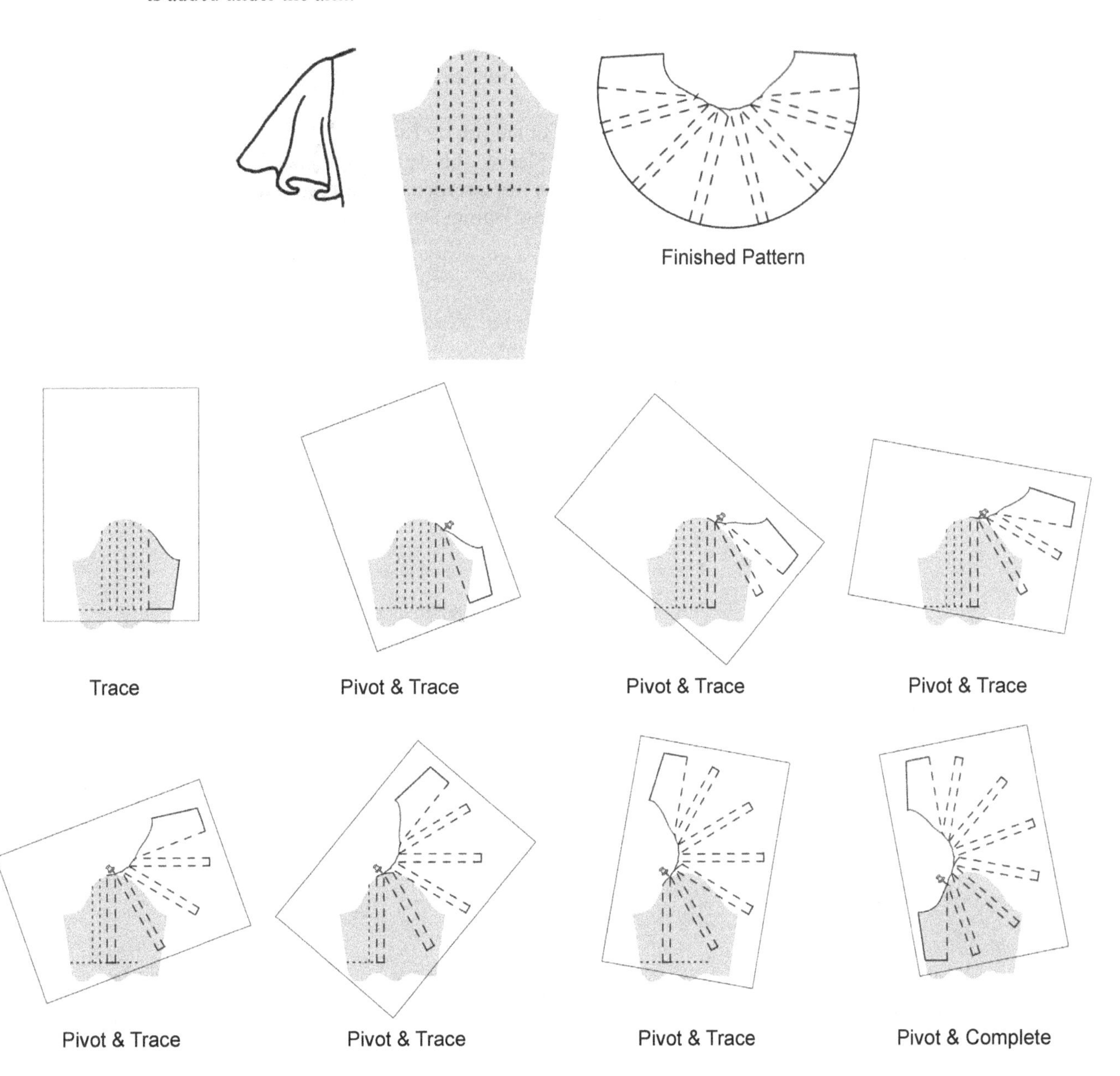

Raglan Sleeve

The Raglan Sleeve follows the principle of changing the seam line location. Draw in the desired shape of the Raglan Seam on the front and back Slopers for the body of the garment. Indicate alignment notches.

Trace the sleeve pattern. Place the Shoulder Point of the traced sleeve pattern on top of the front Sloper's Shoulder Point. Put a pin through both patterns at this point. Pivot the traced sleeve pattern until the Sleeve Cap line touches the Armhole Curve at the new Raglan Seam line. Trace the upper portion of the Raglan Sleeve from the basic front pattern.

Follow the same procedure for the back of the sleeve, The traced Shoulder Seams from the Slopers form the dart of the Raglan Sleeve. This dart compensates for the shape of the body at the shoulder. The body bends in two directions at this point. One bend is from the shoulder down the arm. The other bend is from the front of the body to the back.

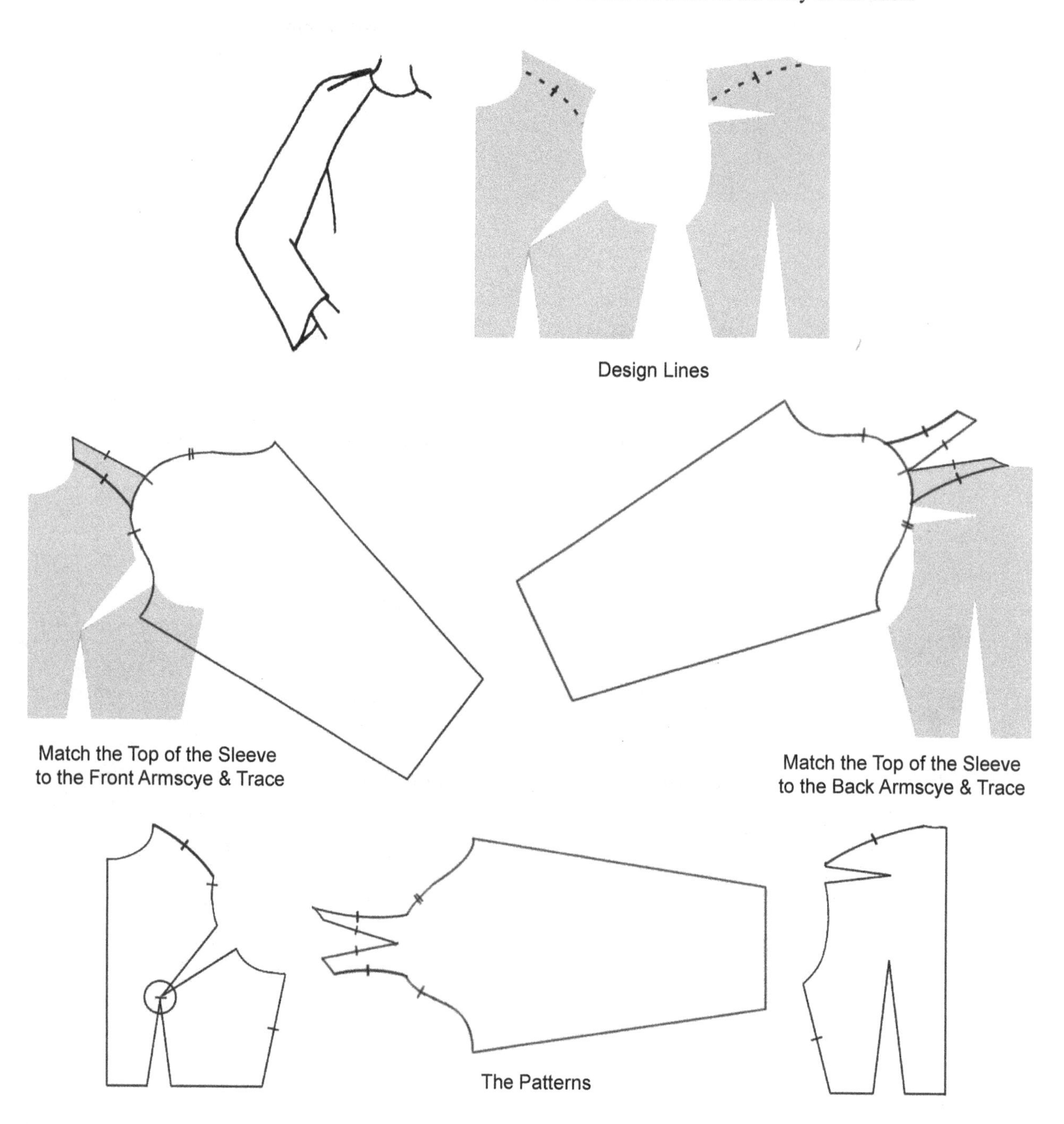

Square Armscye Seam

The same principle used to create the Raglan Sleeve may be applied to other designs. A portion of the body is added to the sleeve. However, the new seam lines on the body must intersect with the Armscye before this curve goes under the arm.

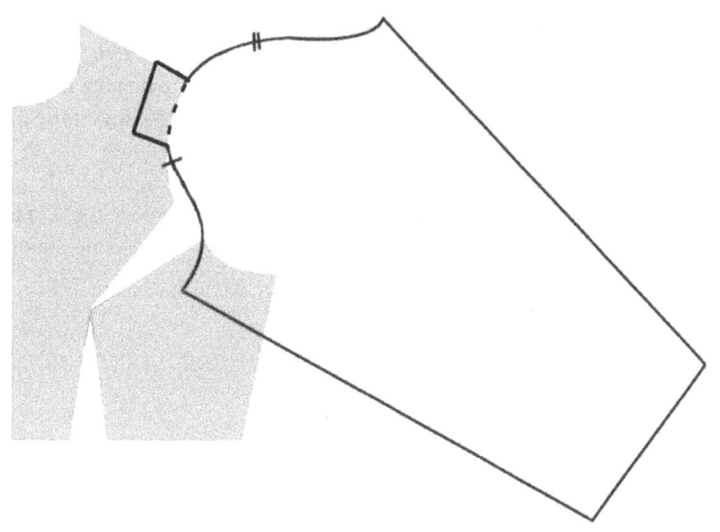

Part of the Bodice added to Sleeve

Dropped Shoulder

To create the Dropped Shoulder design, add a portion of the sleeve to the body.

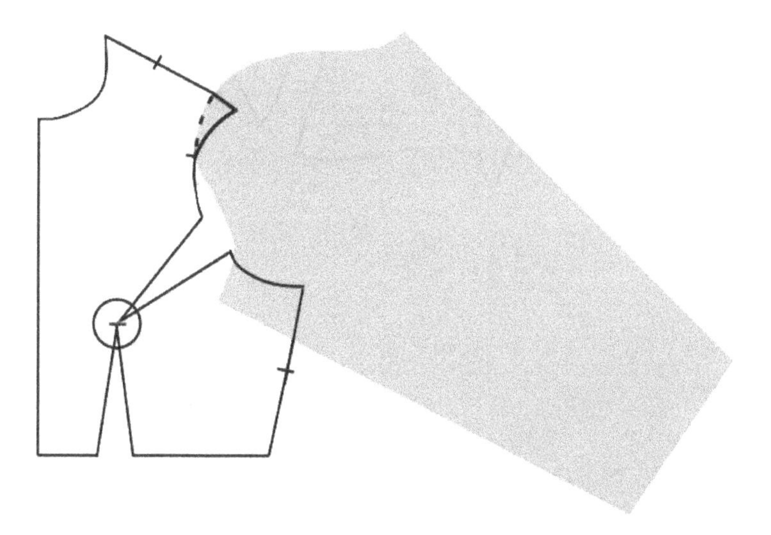

Top of the Sleeve added to Bodice

Tunic Sleeve

The Tunic Sleeve is historically the original sleeve pattern. The sleeve and the body of the garment are one continuous piece of fabric and is not meant to be fitted where the arm joins the body.

A common problem with this style is that the top tends to shift back making the fit around the neck uncomfortable. This will not happen if a pattern is created from the Slopers by extending the Shoulder Seam then adding half the Sleeve Sloper as shown below. The difference in the slope of the Shoulder Seam compensates for differences in posture. The combined underarm/Side Seam of the front should match the underarm/Side Seam of the back.

Seam lines may be added to this pattern in any manner to simulate designs such as the Fitted Sleeve look or the Raglan Sleeve look. As long as the sleeve and the body of the garment lie flat on a table, however, it is a tunic sleeve. There is no shaping to fit under the arm.

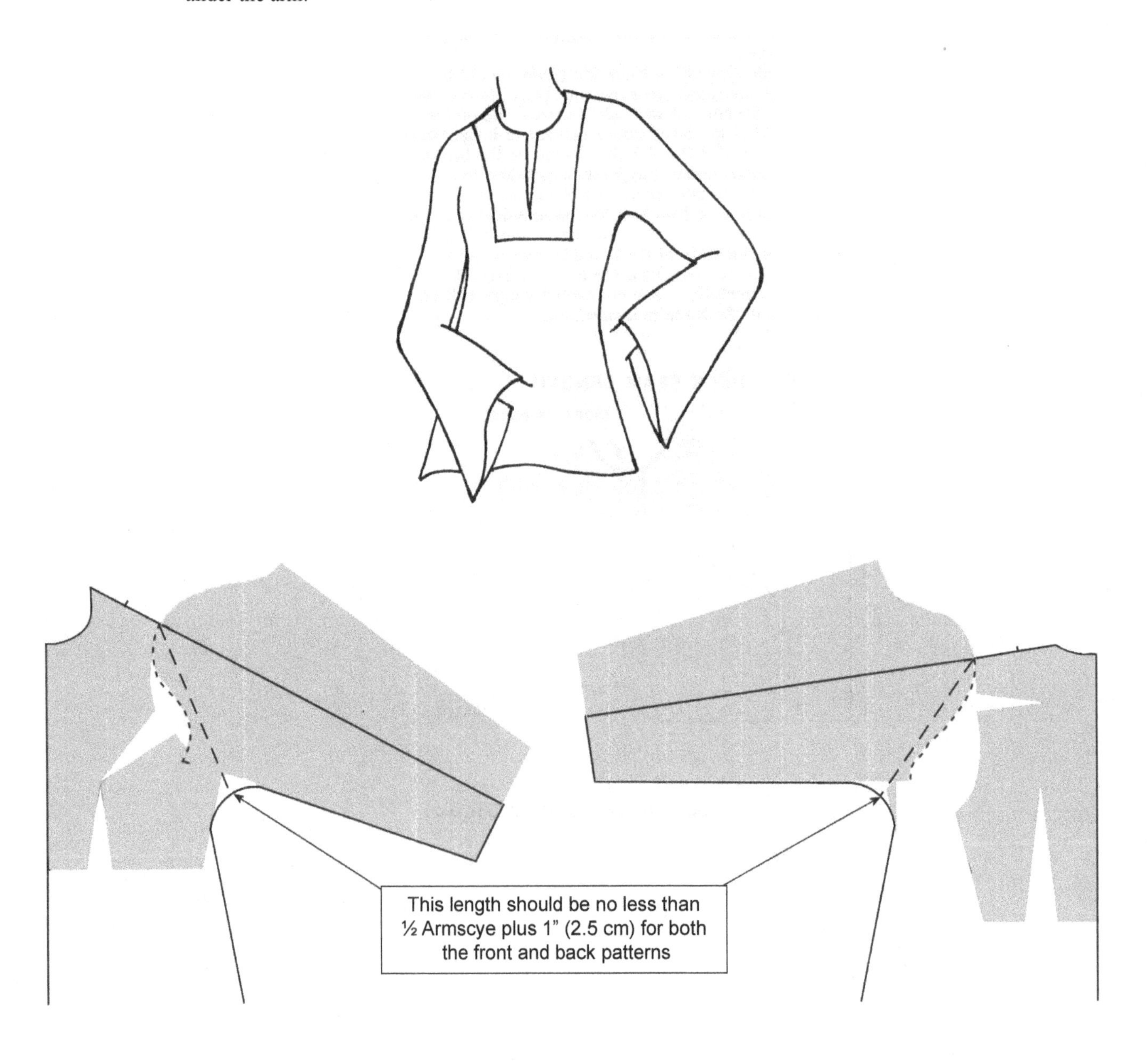
This length should be no less than ½ Armscye plus 1" (2.5 cm) for both the front and back patterns

Collars

Three different collar shapes can be created using the specialized pattern alteration techniques described here. The Mandarin Collar follows the contours of the neck. The Shirt Collar follows the neck and then rolls over and falls back down. The Flat Collar follows the shape of the body instead of the shape of the neck. The direction that the Flat Collar travels is controlled by the shape of the collar seam that joins the collar to the body of the garment. This seam is referred to as the Collar Neck Seam.

The first step in drafting collars is to determine the length of the Collar Neck Seam. Place the front and back basic bodice patterns together at the Shoulder Seam. Measure the distance from Center Front to the Center Back following the curve of the Neckline seam.

The length around the Neckline seam should be equal to half the Neck measurement (#1). Remember the Neck measurement was taken around the entire neck. If half of the Neck measurement is longer than the distance around the Neckline seam on the bodice, the Neck measurement may have been taken too loosely. If the length around the Neckline seam of the bodice is longer than half the Neck measurement, then the Neck measurement may have been taken too tight, or the Neckline of the fitted bodice may have been drawn too far out from the neck. Check the dimensions carefully.

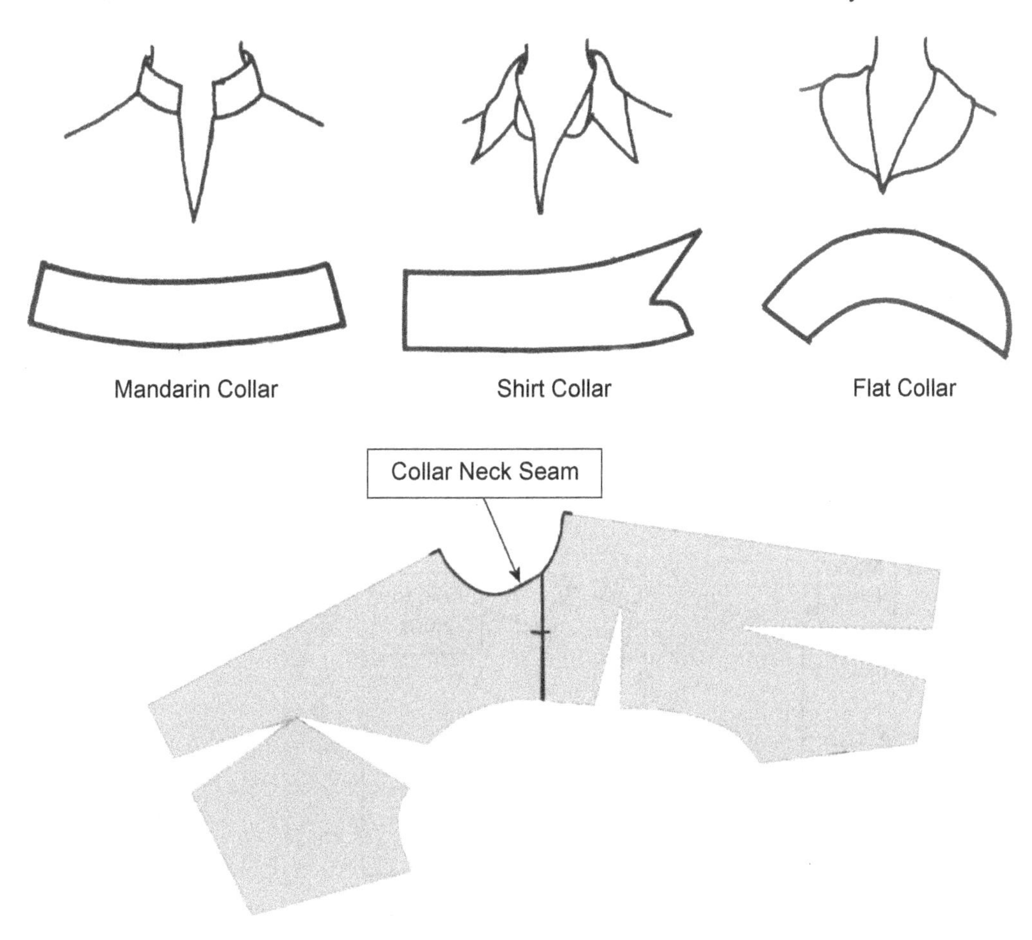

Mandarin Collar

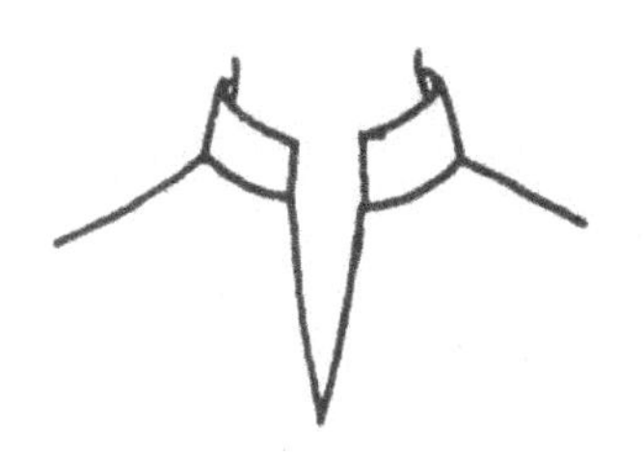

The Mandarin Collar is designed to follow the shape of the neck. The neck tapers from large to small as the neck gets closer to the head. The Mandarin Collar must therefore taper from a long Collar Neck Seam to a shorter Collar Top seam. These two seams must then be curved to keep them following the taper of the neck evenly around the body.

The procedure used to curve the Collar Top Seam and the Collar Neck Seam may also be used to curve the seam lines of other patterns such as shaping full skirts or long tapered cuffs on sleeves.

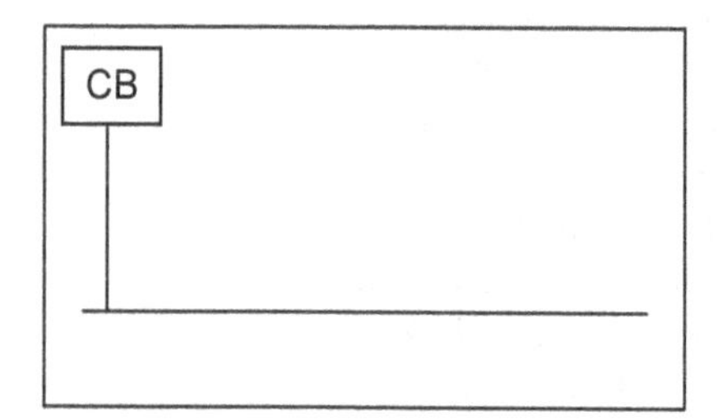

Step 1. At a distance of 1" in from the left hand edge of a piece of 8½" x 11" (A4) paper, draw a vertical line. This is the Center Back Fold line.

Step 2. At a distance of 2" (5 cm) from the bottom of the paper, draw a line at right angles to the Center Back Fold line. This is the Collar Baseline. Extend the Collar Baseline ½" to the left of the Center Back Fold line.

Step 3. On the Center Back Fold line, measure up from the Collar Baseline the height desired for the collar. In this example, the collar will be 1½" (4 cm) high. From this point, draw a line at right angles to the Center Back Fold line. This is the Collar Top line. Extend the Collar Top line a half an inch to the left of the Center Back Fold line.

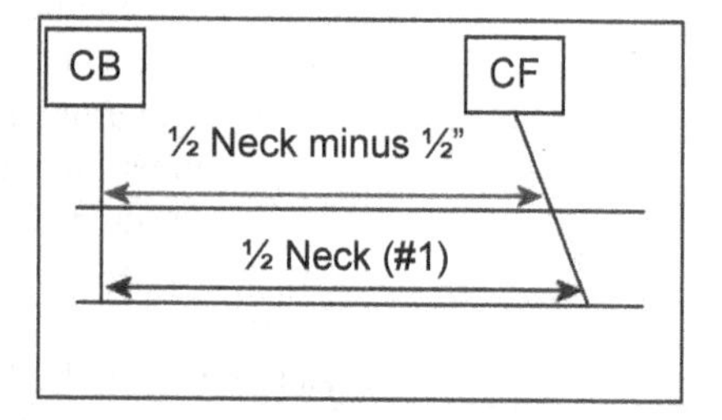

Step 4. Mark off one-half the Neck measurement (#1) on the Collar Baseline starting from the Center Back Fold line and measuring to the right. This is the Center Front point.

Step 5. Subtract ½" (12 mm) from half the Neck measurement. Mark this length on the Collar Top line measuring to the right from the Center Back Fold line. This is the Center Front point on the Collar Top line.

Step 6. Draw a line from the Center Front point on the Collar Baseline through the Center Front point on the Collar Top line. Extend this line above the Collar Top line.

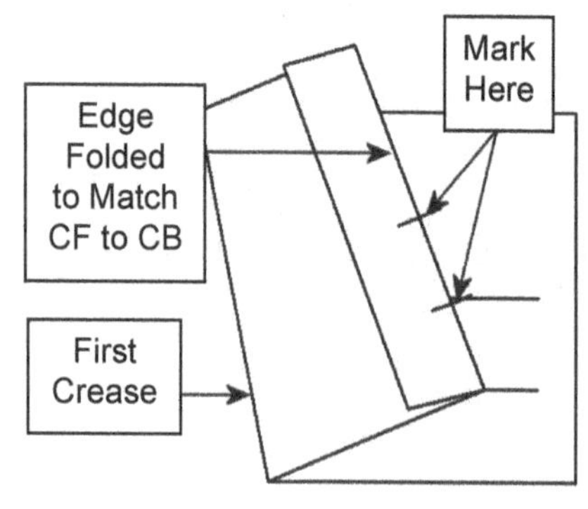

Step 7. Turn the left hand edge of the paper pattern under at the Center Back Fold line.

Step 8. Now fold the pattern to the right so that the Center Back Fold line coincides with the Center Front line for its full length. Notice that this is a diagonal fold. Crease this fold.

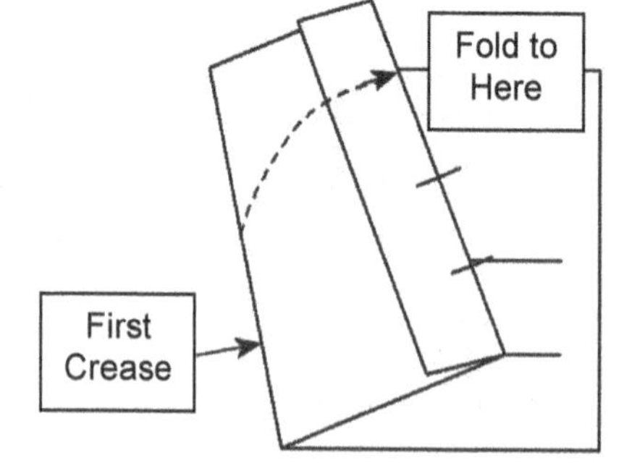

Step 9. Keep the paper folded in this manner. The Collar Baseline and the Collar Top line, from the left side of the Center Back Fold, appear on the back flap of the paper. Mark these points from the Center Back Fold line onto the Center Front line.

Step 10. Without opening the folded paper, fold it a second time so that the crease on the left side will coincide with the Center Front line. Crease the new fold.

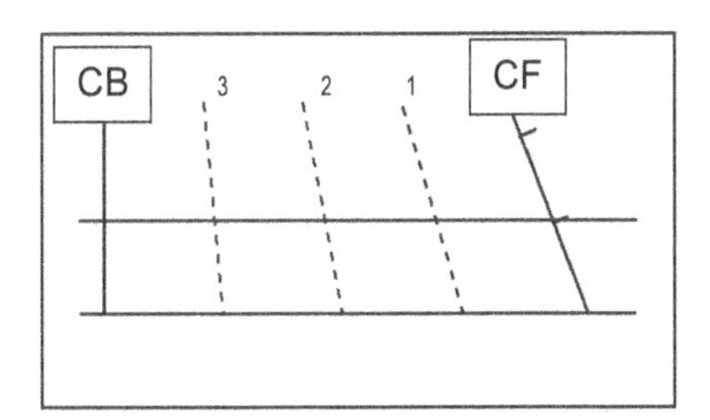

Step 11. Unfold the pattern. There should now be three creases in the pattern dividing the collar equally into fourths. Mark the creases with dotted lines and number them as illustrated.

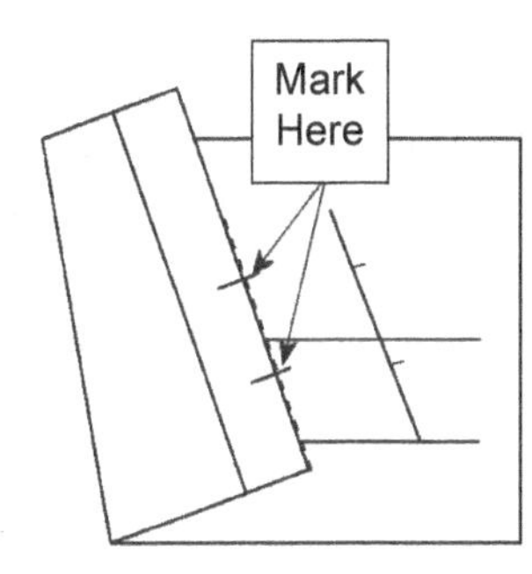

Step 12. Fold the pattern back from left to right again. This time the Center Back Fold line will be placed on the first dotted line.

Mark the points where the Collar Top and the Collar Baseline from the Center Back Fold line land on this dotted line.

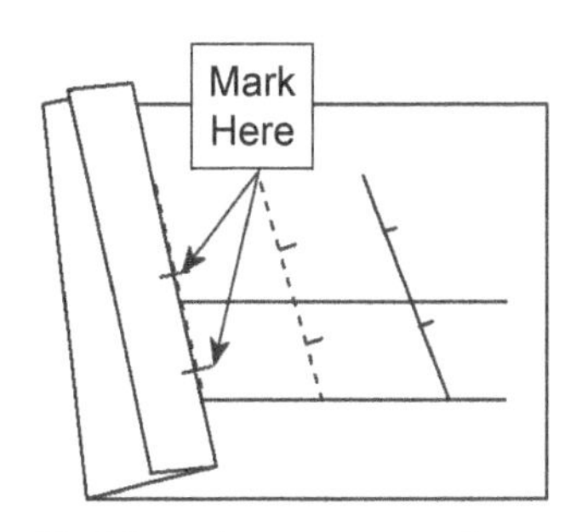

Step 13. Move the pattern so that the Center Back Fold line coincides with the second dotted line.

Mark the points from the Collar Top and the Collar Baseline at the Center Back Fold line onto the second dotted line.

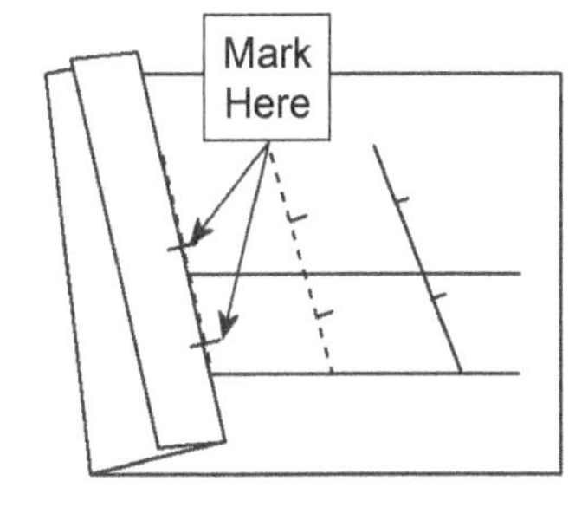

Step 14. Move the pattern so that the Center Back Fold line coincides with the third dotted line. Mark the points from the Collar Top and the Collar Baseline at the Center Back Fold line onto the third dotted line.

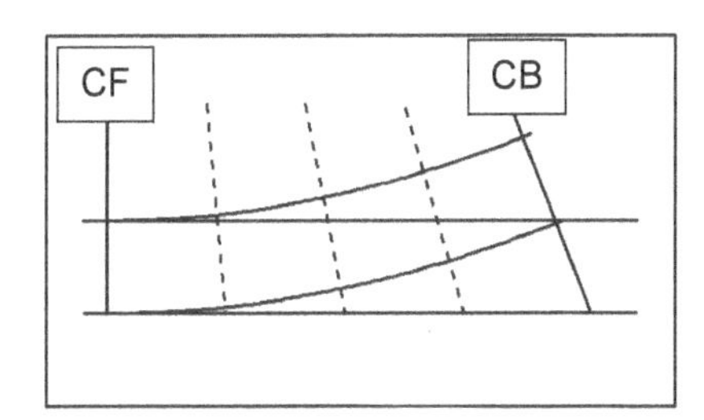

Step 15. Unfold the pattern and connect the points on the dotted lines as illustrated. The lower curved line of this pattern is the Collar Neck Seam.

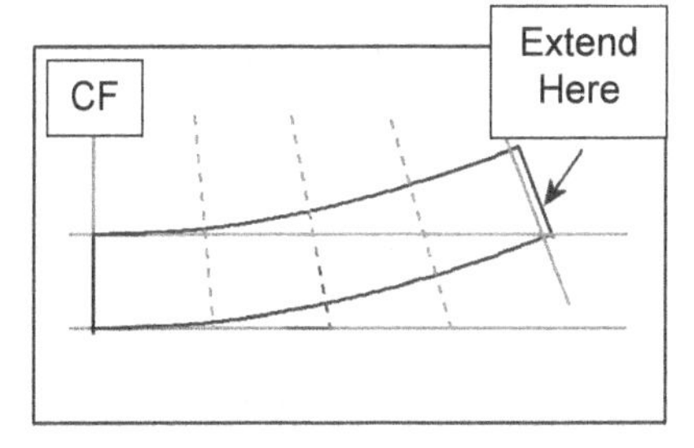

Step 16. This procedure for curving the seam lines will shorten them slightly. To correct this, measure the straight Collar Baseline and extend the curved Collar Neck Seam to this length. Do the same with the Collar Top line.

Step 17. Connect the extended Collar Top line to the extended Collar Neck Seam to form the front of the collar.

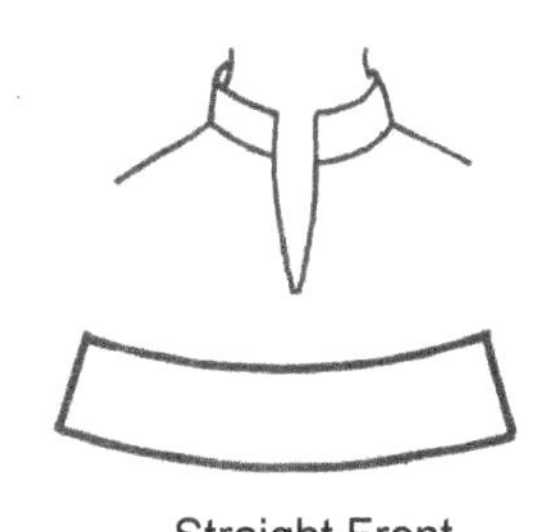

Straight Front

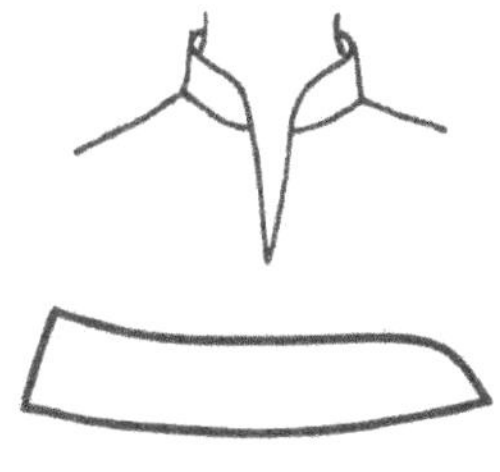

Curved Front

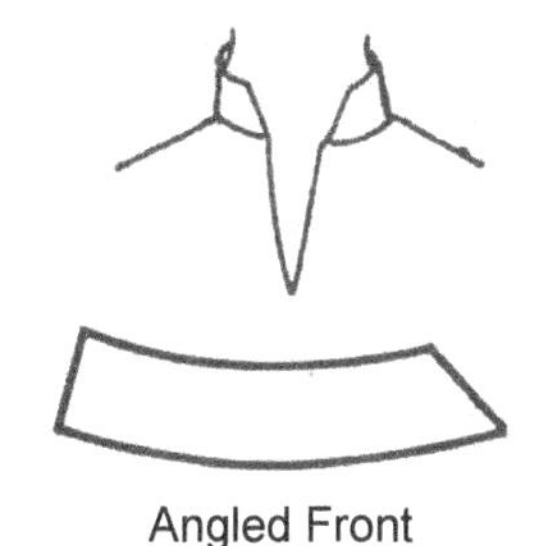

Angled Front

As shown above, the front of the collar may be shaped for any design desired. These designs will not affect the fit of the collar.

The Mandarin Collar as drafted follows the contour of the neck. To create a Mandarin Collar that stands out slightly from the neck, the pattern must be flatter. To achieve this effect, during Step 5, subtract ¼" (6 mm) from the Neck measurement, instead of ½" (12 mm) .

Top = Neck (#1) less ½"

Top = Neck (#1) less ¼"

Shirt Collar I

The Shirt Collar is most commonly used on men's shirts and some women's blouses. It stands up next to the neck then rolls over and falls away.

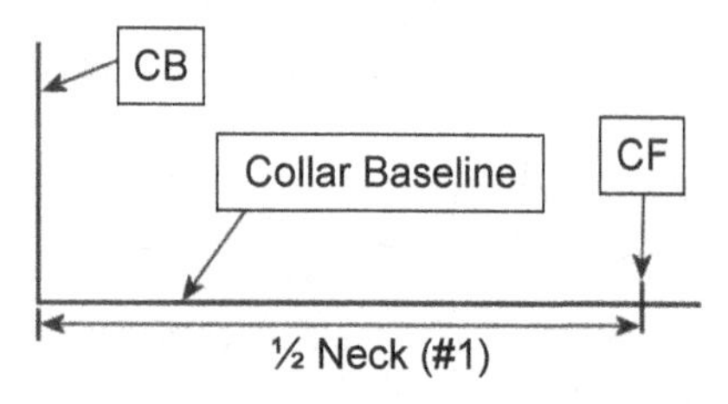

Step 1. Draw a baseline for the collar. Mark off half of the Neck measurement (#1) on this line. This establishes the Center Back, CB, and the Center Front, CF, of the collar.

Step 2. At the Center Back point, draw a line at right angles to the Collar Baseline. This is the Center Back Fold line.

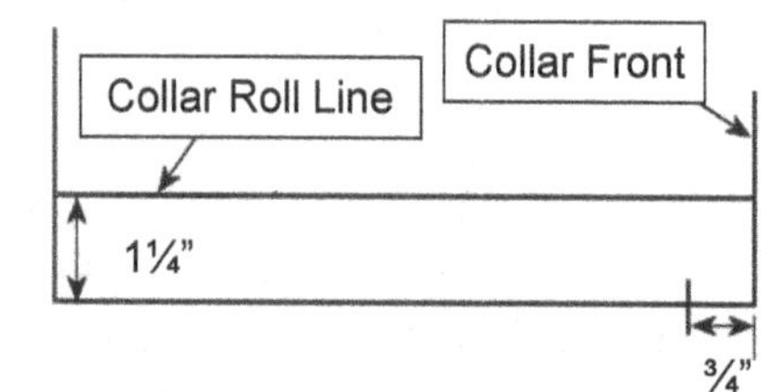

Step 3. Mark a point ¾" (2 cm) out from the Center Front mark. From this point, draw a line at right angles to the Collar Baseline. This is the Collar Front.

The ¾" (2 cm) added to the Center Front is for the Button Overlap of the shirt or blouse.

Step 4. On the Center Back Fold line, measure up 1¼" (3 cm). From this point, draw a line parallel to the Collar Baseline. This is the Collar Roll line.

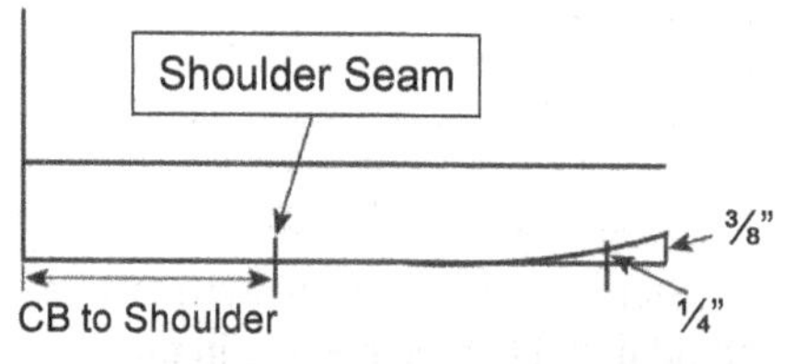

Step 5. Measure the Neckline seam of the back bodice from the Center Back to the Shoulder Seam. Measuring out from the Center Back Fold line, mark this length on the Collar Baseline. This is the Shoulder Seam mark.

Step 6. Mark a point ¼" (6 mm) above the Collar Baseline at the Center Front mark.

Step 7. Mark a second point ⅜" (9 mm) above the Collar Baseline on the Collar Front line.

Step 8. Curve the Collar Neck Seam from the Shoulder Seam mark to the points established in Steps 6 and 7.

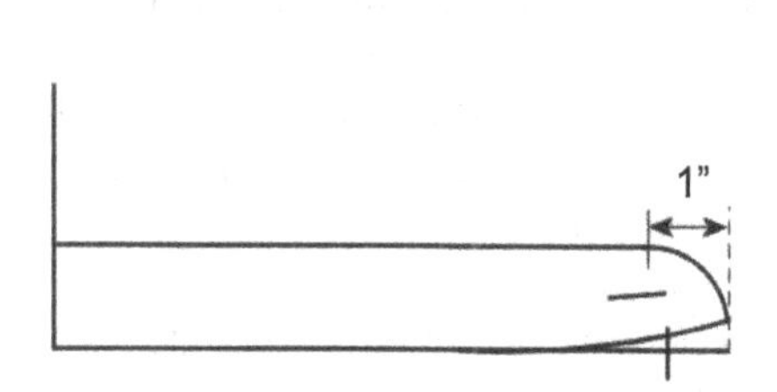

Step 9. On the Collar Roll line, mark a point 1" (25 mm) in from the Collar Front. This is the Collar Shaping Point.

Step 10. Curve the front of the collar from the Collar Shaping Point to the Collar Front line. This curve is strictly for appearance and does not affect the fit of the garment.

Step 11. If a button is to be used, mark the buttonhole starting from the Center Front. The buttonhole should be half way between the Collar Roll line and the Collar Neck Seam.

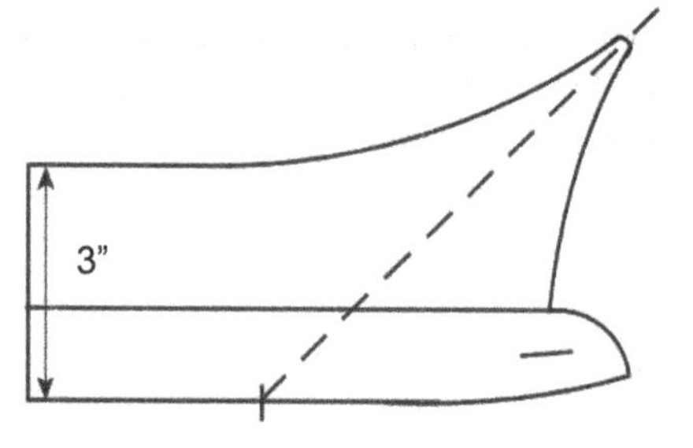

Step 12. Draw a line from the Shoulder Seam mark at a forty-five degree angle to the Collar Baseline. This is the Collar Point line.

Step 13. Mark a point on the Center Back Fold line 3" (7.6 cm) above the Collar Baseline. This will be the top of the collar.

Step 14. Starting from the point established in Step 13, shape in the desired design for the top of the collar.

The top of the collar should be kept parallel to the Collar Baseline until it passes the Shoulder Seam mark. If the collar is made too wide in this area, or if the top of the collar is not kept parallel to the bottom, the collar will not sit properly at the back of the neck.

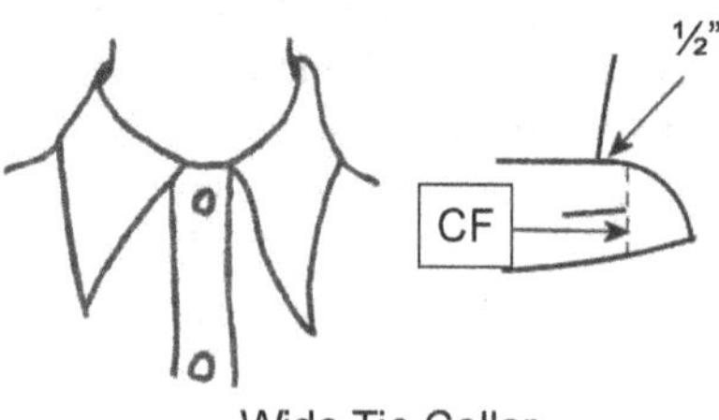

Wide Tie Collar

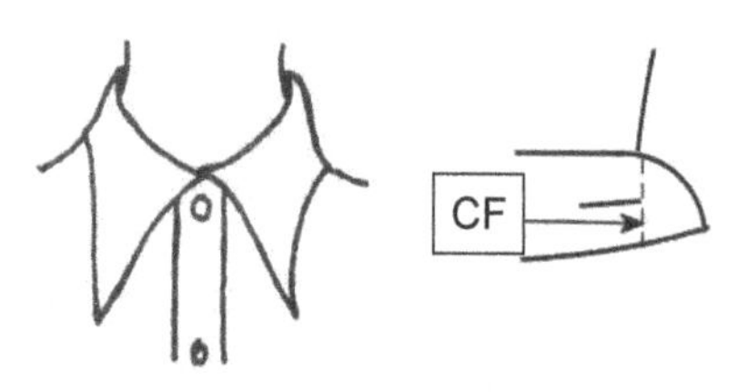

Narrow Tie Collar

The front of the collar can be adjusted for different tie widths. For wide ties, the collar should be shaped 1/2" (12 mm) to the side of Center Front. For narrow and string ties, the collar can be shaped closer to the Center Front line.

Shirt Collar II

A second type of Shirt Collar may be designed to stand up closer to the neck even when left unbuttoned. This collar will be cut in two separate pieces. The lower piece will be based on the Mandarin Collar and the upper piece will fall down from this.

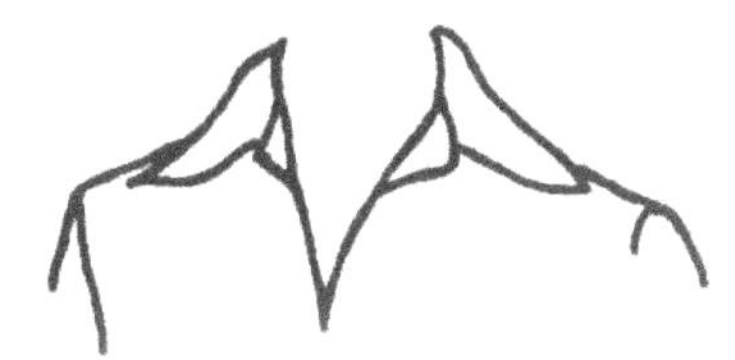

Shirt Collar I

Shirt Collar II

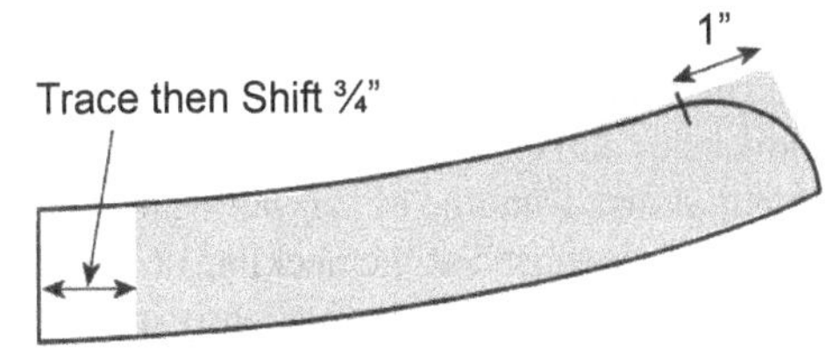

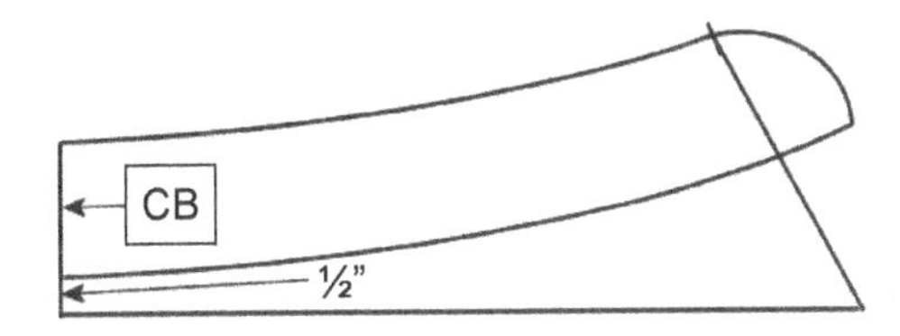

Step 1. Trace the Mandarin Collar from Center Back to Center Front. Shift the pattern to the side and add an additional ¾" (18 mm) to the front of the pattern. This is the Button Overlap.

Step 2. To establish the Collar Shaping Point, measure in 1" (25 mm) from the Center Front.

Step 3. Starting at the Collar Shaping Point, curve the front of the collar. This completes the standing portion of this shirt collar.

Step 4. Place another piece of pattern paper over the Standing Portion of the collar.

Step 5. Trace the Center Back Fold line and extend it down ½" (12 mm) below the Collar Neck Seam.

Step 6. Trace the top of the pattern to the Collar Shaping Point.

Step 7. Draw in the desired shape of the collar. A line drawn at right angles to the bottom of the Center Back Fold line usually creates a good shape for the top of the collar.

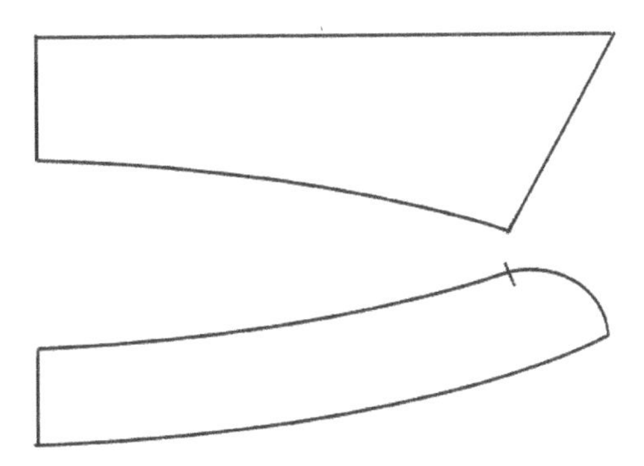

The Finished Pattern

Flat Collars

Once the initial shaping of the Collar Neck Seam is determined, Flat Collars may be designed in many different ways.

This collar's versatility is based on the fact that it is designed to shape to the body rather than the neck. Therefore, this collar may be used with any shape neckline. Nor is there any restriction on shaping the backs of these collars.

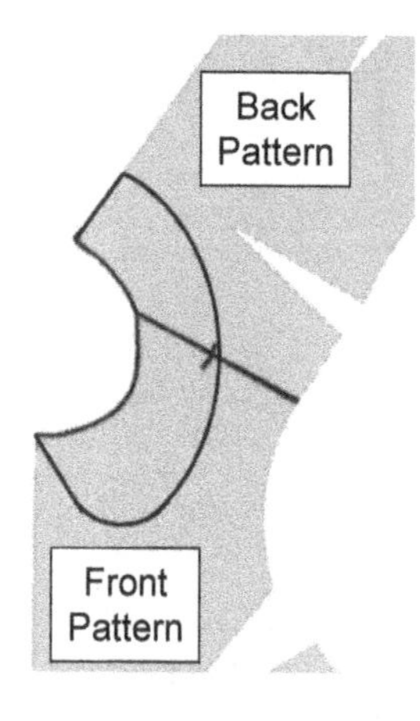

The Basic Flat Collar

The basic flat collar is designed to lie perfectly flat on the body of the garment.

Step 1. Lay out the front and the back Slopers as if the Shoulder Seams were sewn together.

Step 2. Place a piece of pattern paper over the Slopers and trace the Center Back line and the Neck Curve.

Step 3. Draw in the desired shape of the collar.

Step 4. Add seam allowances and cut out the pattern.

This pattern has a potential disadvantage in that the seam which joins the collar to the body can be exposed at the neckline. To eliminate this problem, the collar must be designed to roll up slightly on the neck.

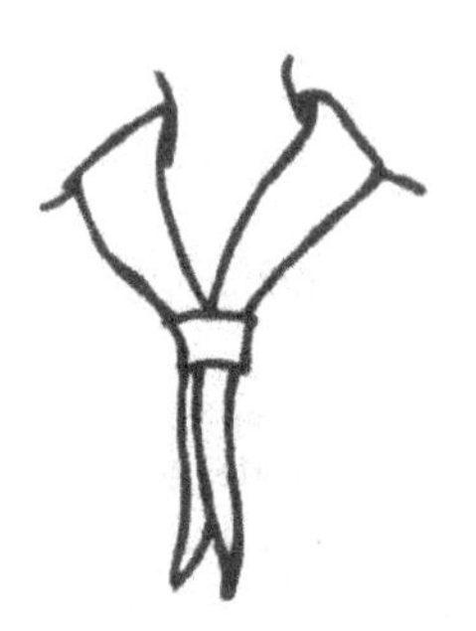

Rolling The Flat Collar

Step 1. Place the front and back basic bodice patterns together as before. Put a pin through both patterns where the Shoulder Seam meets the Neck Seam.

Step 2. Pivot the front pattern over the back pattern so there is one inch between the Shoulder Points.

Step 3. Trace the Center Back and the Neck Curve as before and draw in the desired collar design.

Some designs may require the flat collar stand higher next to the neck. To achieve this effect, increase the amount that the front Shoulder Seam is pivoted over the back.

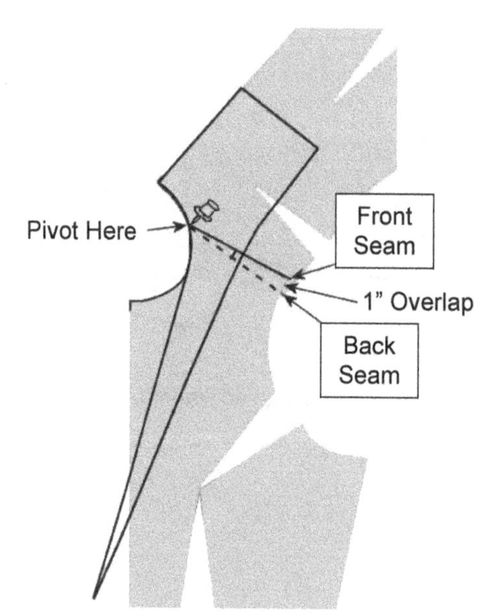

Adjusting The Flat Collar

If the Slopers are pivoted at the Shoulder Seam so the Neck Curve for the collar is no longer a smooth curve, adjust as shown below.

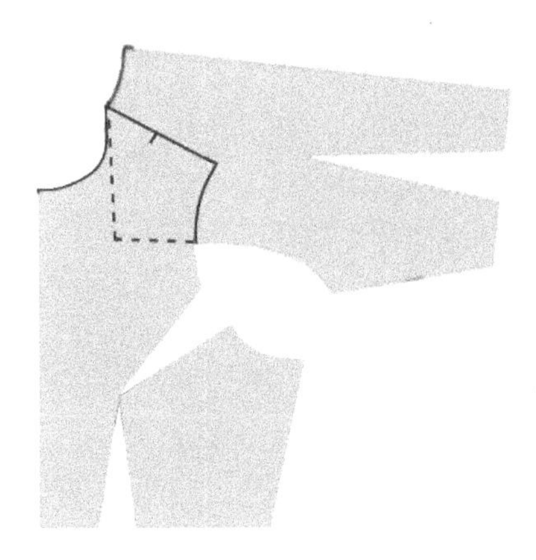

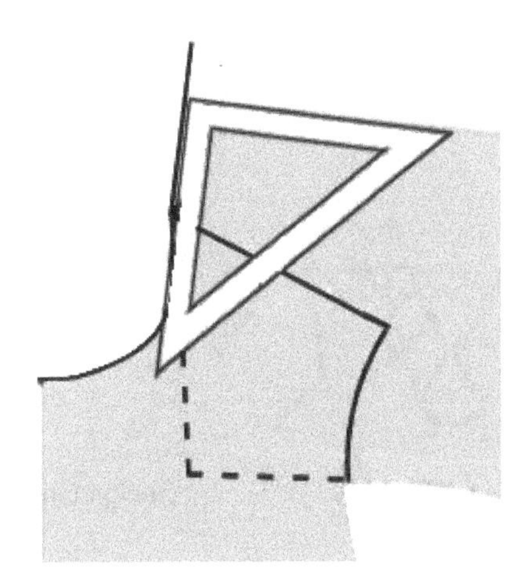

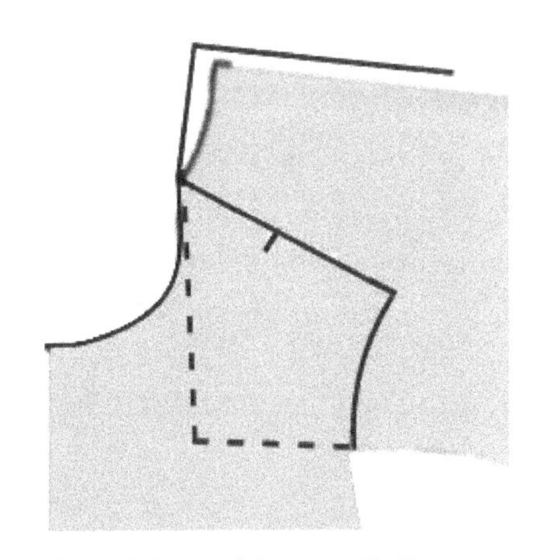

Step 1. Pivot the Slopers as indicated, then place a sheet of pattern paper over them.

Step 2. Place a right angle ruler on the Center Back line (the square corner of a piece of paper may be used).

Move the right angle ruler along the Center Back line until the other leg of the right angle touches the Neck Curve at the Shoulder Seam.

Step 3. Draw a line along the edge of the ruler. This is the back portion of the new Collar Neck Seam.

Step 4. Extend the new Collar Neck Seam past the Sloper for the back.

Step 5. Measure the bodice pattern from the Center Back to the Shoulder Seam following the Neck Curve.

Step 6. Measuring out from the Shoulder Seam, mark this length on the new Collar Neck Seam.

Step 7. Draw the new Center Back seam at right angles to the new Collar Neck Seam. This is the Center Back line of the collar.

The Flat Collar Chart

To create flat collars for a variety of designs, it is not necessary to pivot the patterns at the Shoulder Seam for each design. Instead, you can make a single Flat Collar Chart of the various Collar Neck Seams and Center Back lines for different degrees of pivot.

First, pivot the Slopers so that there is 1" (2.5 cm) between the Shoulder Points. Lay a sheet of pattern paper on top of this and trace the front Shoulder Seam, the back Neck Curve, and the Center Back line. Continue this process with different degrees of pivot, adjusting the Collar Neck Seam for a smooth curve when necessary.

To use this chart, place the Flat Collar Chart on the Shoulder Seam of the front Sloper, then draw in the shape of the collar design.

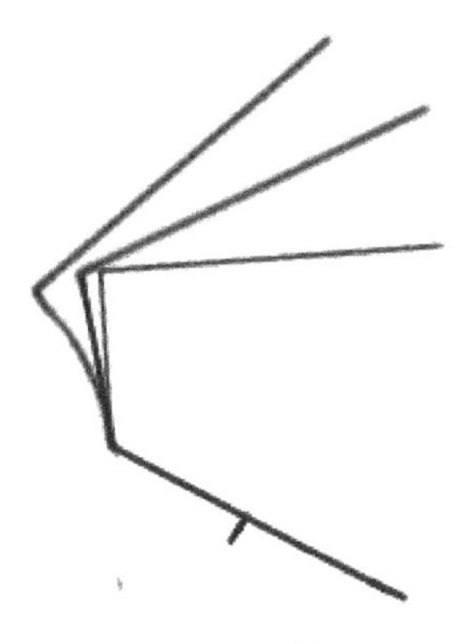

Flat Collar Chart

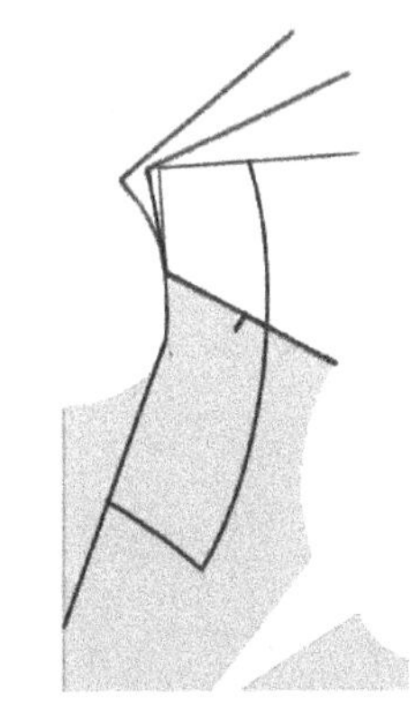

Flat Chart on a Sloper

Adding Fullness to Collars

Fullness can be added to collars by drawing the basic collar shape first. Then, on the pattern, make dotted lines where the fullness is to be added. Pivot and trace this pattern as described on page 105.

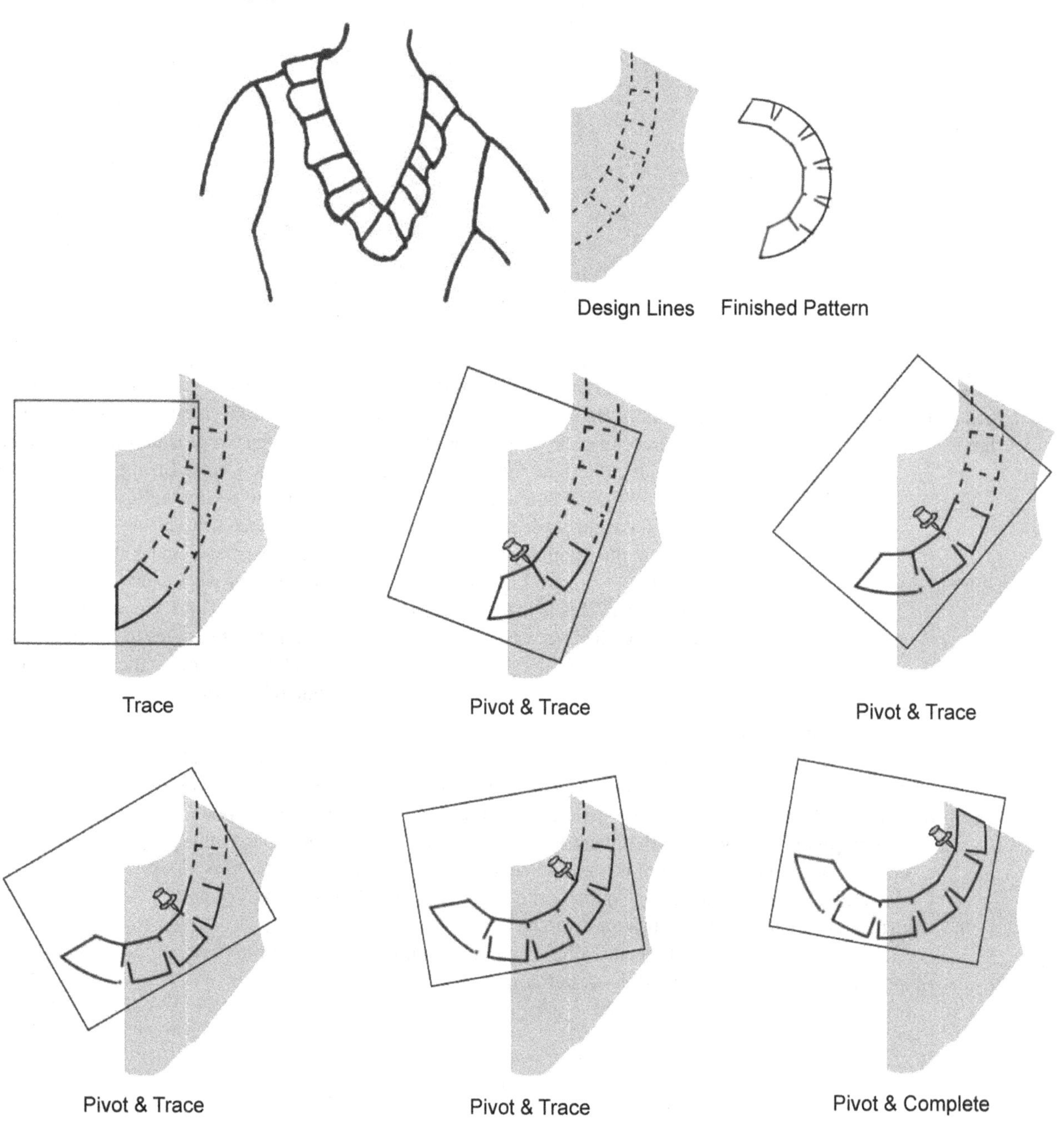

Designing Garments

Designing garments is primarily a matter of selecting diverse elements. It is best to coordinate your choices with a sketch. This sketch can be made by drawing the desired design on top of a body silhouette such as the ones shown below. These simple sketches are sometimes referred to as croquis. Body silhouettes can be found on the internet, copied from magazines, or created by tracing photographs of the person who is to wear the garment. Tracing photographs helps to ensure that the garment's proportions are appropriate for the proportions of the individual's figure.

After determining the garment's basic shape, you can establish the design details. These details can include: how the garment is to be fastened (buttons, zippers, or a wrap around); the size, type, and location of the waistband; and the size, type, and location of the pockets.

The final design decisions are how much Ease to add to various parts of the body and the exact amount of fullness to give to the patterns.

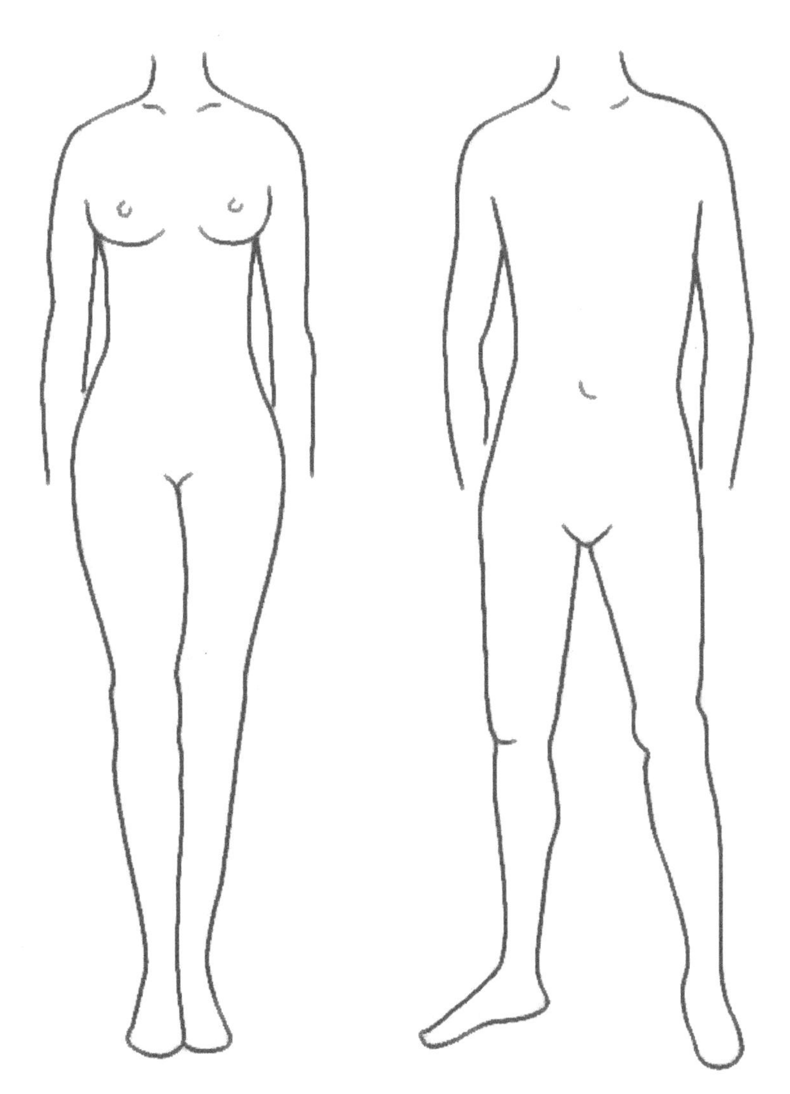

Skirts

Skirts hang from the waist-to-hip region. They vary in design primarily by changing the amount of fullness and the manner by which this fullness is controlled.

Skirt Waistbands

The top of the skirt can be established by a waistband. The waistband can be either at the natural waist or hang lower on the body. If it is lower than the natural waist, the size of the body at the waistband must be smaller than the hip dimension.

Waistbands at the natural waist can be cut from a straight piece of fabric as wide as 2" (5 cm). For the body of the skirt, the waist on the Skirt Sloper should be lowered by half the width of the waistband.

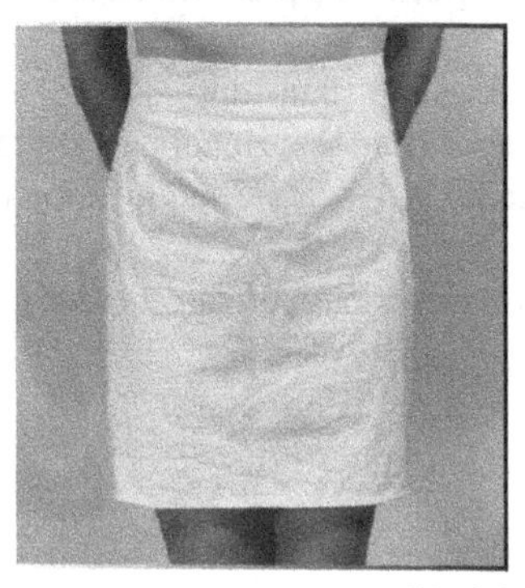

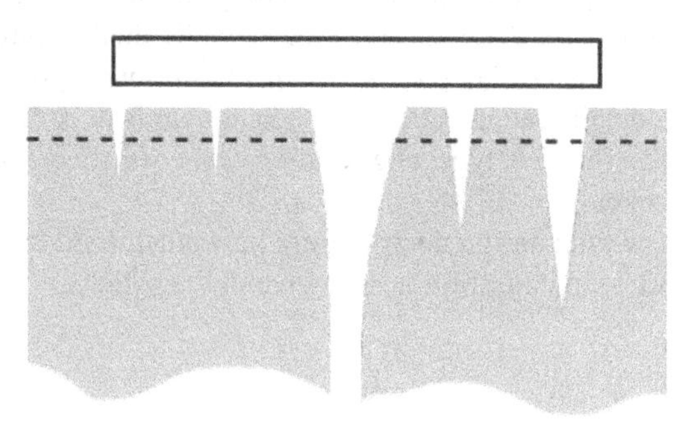

Straight Waistband at Natural Waist

When the skirt starts below the natural waist, the waistband either needs to be small, such as ¾" (2 cm), or shaped to the contour of the body. A straight waistband on a lowered waist will stand out from the body. To create a contoured waistband, draw in the desired design lines and, pivoting from the dart's point, trace the Skirt Sloper. This process is shown below for a back pattern.

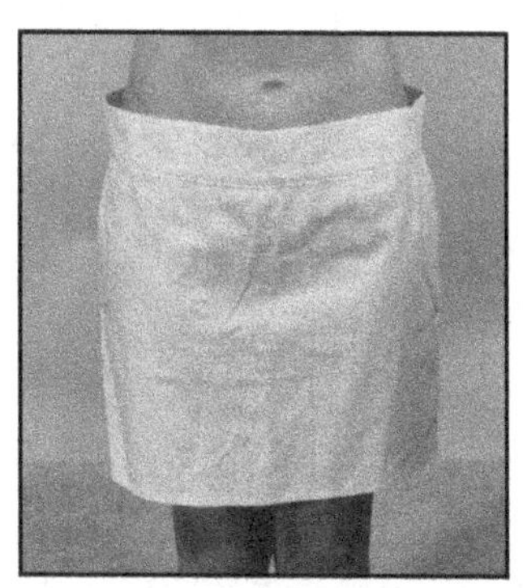

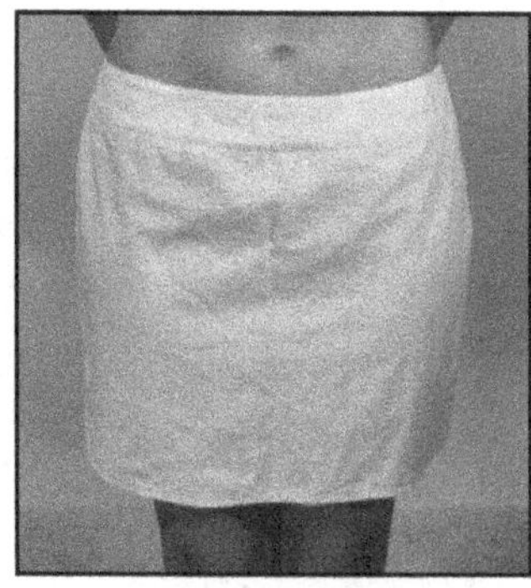

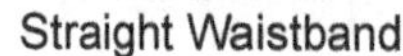

Straight Waistband

Contoured Waistband

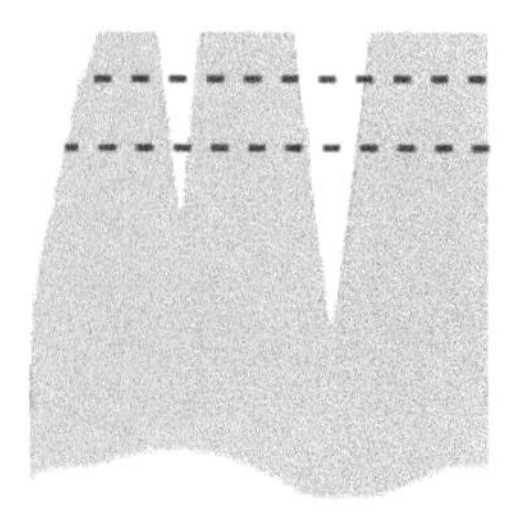

The Design Lines

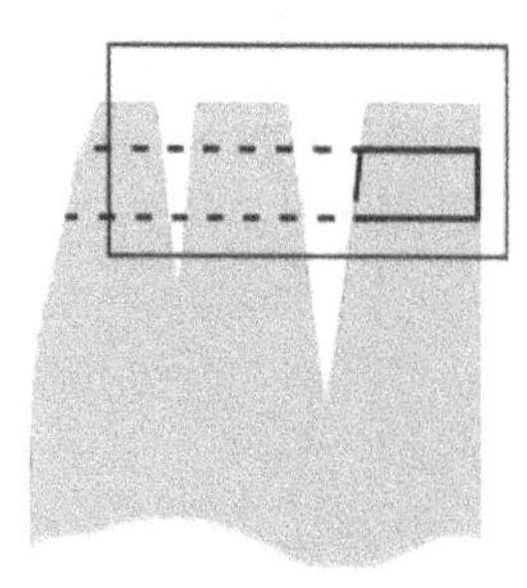

Trace CB to Dart

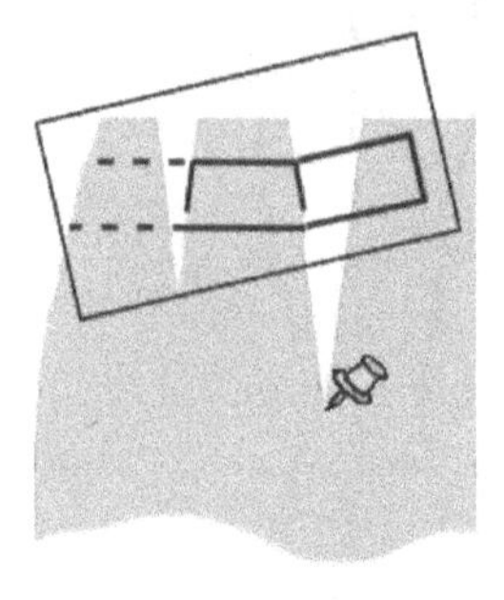

Pivot Dart & Trace

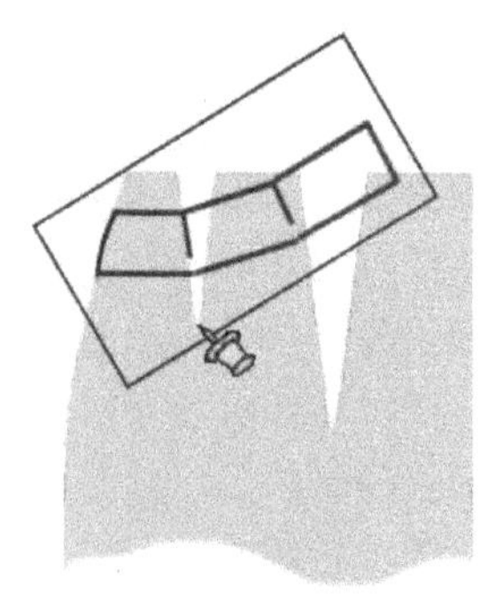

Pivot Dart & Trace

Fitted Pencil Skirt

Fitted skirts can be created directly from the Skirt Sloper. It is the closest possible fit in a skirt. All other skirt designs have more Ease and/or fullness added to the Skirt Sloper.

The Pencil Skirt is a variation of the fitted skirt that tapers from the hips to the hem. The desired hem circumference can be calculated by simulating the dimension with a tape measure.

One factor that should be taken into account is the stride of the person who is to wear the skirt. The Pencil Skirt described here modifies the pattern to provide more room for the movement of the legs by adding a Kick Pleat in the Center Back seam.

The Kick Pleat allows the bottom of the Center Back Seam to remain open. The Kick Pleat is between 1½" and 2" (4 to 5 cm) wide and at least 6" (15 cm) high. One side of the Kick Pleat is turned under along the Center Back line. The other side is folded in half to provide an extension behind the Center Back seam.

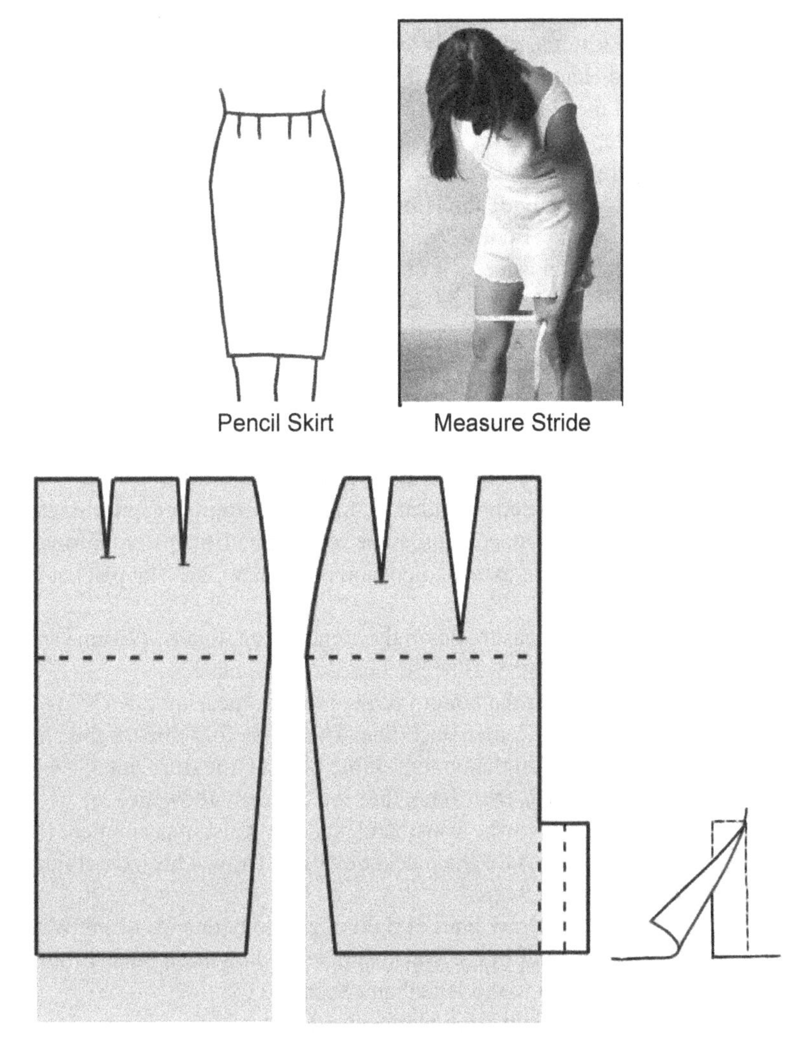

Pencil Skirt

Measure Stride

Sloper Traced with Tapered Side Seams & Kick Pleat

Kick Pleat

Full Skirt

Full Skirts with fitted waists can be created by altering the fitted skirt patterns as described starting on page 101. The Full Skirt may also be created as follows.

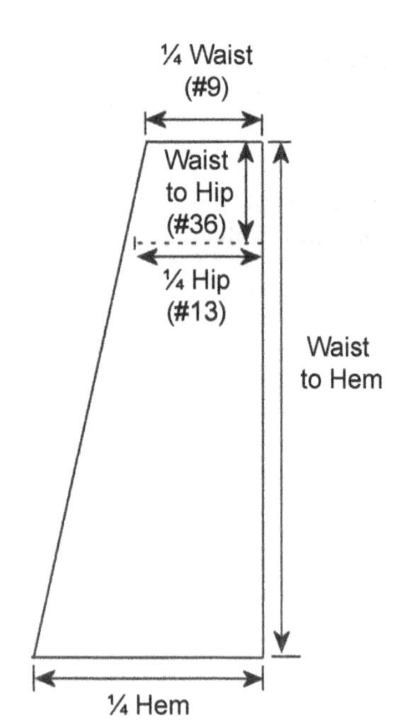

The Full Skirt Pattern

Step 1. Draw a line that is the Waist to Hem length. This will be the Center Front/Center Back line.

Step 2. Draw a line at right angles to the top of the Center Front/Center Back line. This will be the Waist line.

Step 3. Determine how many sections the skirt is to have. These sections are called gores. The skirt may have four, six, eight gores or more. Divide the Waist measurement (#9) by the number of gores and mark this length on the Waist line. A four gore skirt is illustrated here.

Step 4. Draw a line at right angles to the bottom of the Center Front/Center Back line. This is the Hem line. Divide the desired Hem measurement by the number of gores in the skirt and mark this length on the Hem line. The procedure for estimating the desired Hem measurement is described on page 103. Connect the side of the Waist to the side of the Hem.

Step 5. Measure down the Center Front/Center Back line the Waist to Hip measurement (#36) and draw a line at right angles. This is the Hip line.

Step 6. Divide the Hip measurement (#13) by the number of gores and mark this length on the Hip line.

This step is a check on the pattern to make sure that the taper of the skirt from the Waist to the Hem has allowed enough room for the Hips. Adjust the Side Seam as necessary.

Step 7. Curve the skirt pattern using the technique described for curving the seams of the Mandarin Collar starting on page 122.

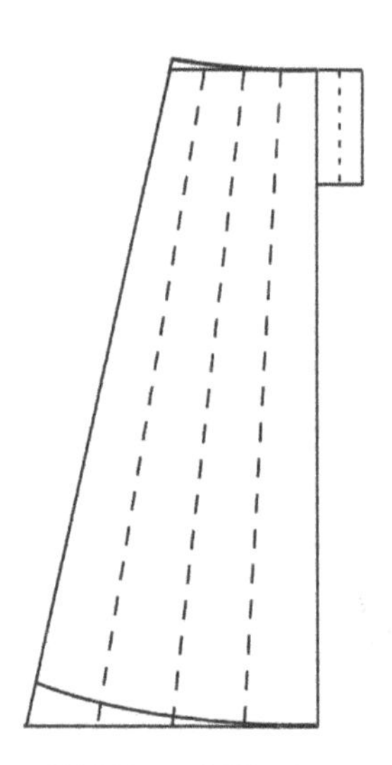

Skirt Gore & Placket

The Skirt Placket & Waistband

A placket can be added to this skirt pattern at Center Back. The placket creates an opening in the skirt that may be secured with snaps or buttons. The right side of the skirt will lap over an extended portion of the left side. The placket will need to be used with a waistband.

Step 8. Measure down the Center Back line 8" (20 cm) and draw a line at right angles to it. This will be the bottom of the placket.

Step 9. On the bottom of the placket, measure out 1½" (4 cm) and draw a dotted line parallel to the Center Back line. This is the fold line for the placket extension.

Step 10. On the bottom of the placket, measure out 3" (7.6 cm) and draw a line parallel to the Center Back line. Add a seam allowance.

Step 11. For the Waistband, add the Waist measurement (#9), ½" (12 mm) of Ease, and 1½" (4 cm) for the placket overlap. Draw a horizontal line that is this length. This is the Waistband Seam.

Step 12. Draw lines at right angles to both ends of the Waistband Seam. Mark off twice the height of the Waistband desired on these lines. From these marks, draw a line that is parallel to the Waistband Seam.

Step 13. Add seam allowances to all patterns.

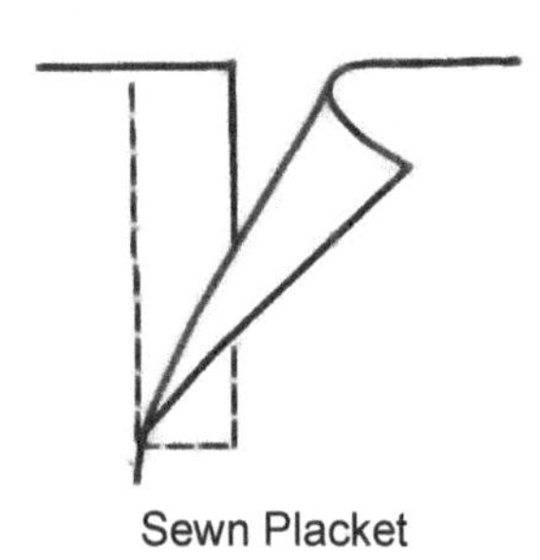

Sewn Placket

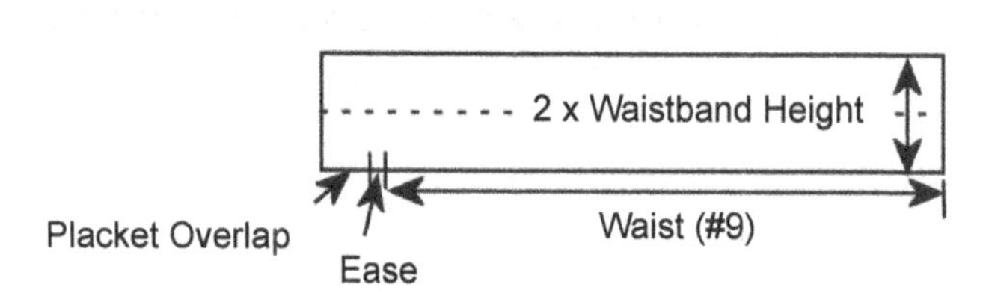

Wrap Around Skirt

A Wrap Around Skirt can be created by making the full skirt pattern described on page 132 larger by one-fourth the Waist size and one-fourth the Hem size. This additional fourth is the lap over portion of the skirt.

Leave the placket off this skirt. Make the Waistband at least three to four times the Waist measurement. This allows the Waistband to go around once with the skirt, a second time for the wrap around, and the remainder will be the tie of the skirt.

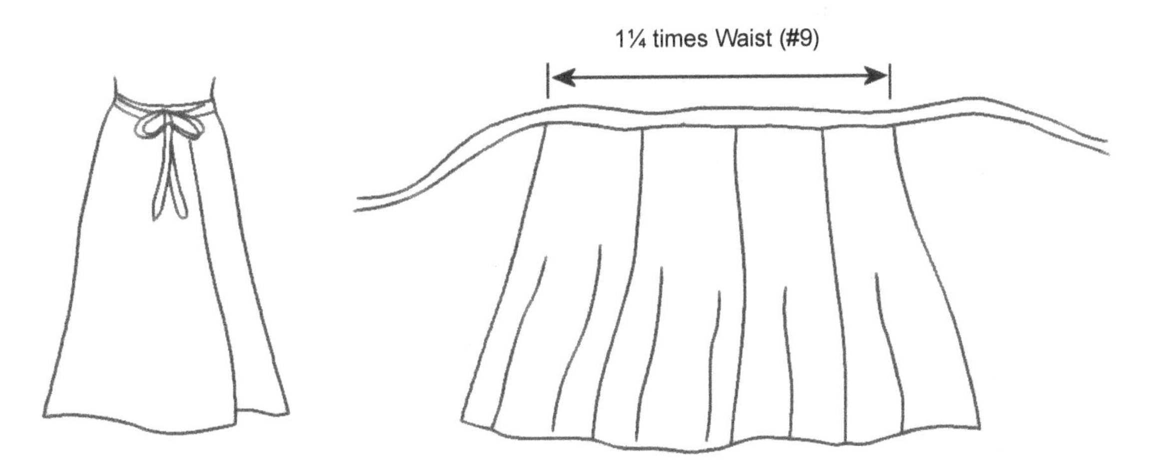

Dirndl Skirt

The Dirndl Skirt is historically one of the earliest skirt patterns. It is a rectangular piece of fabric that is gathered at the waist. If this skirt is cut out of light weight fabric, the top edge can be turned over to form a casing for elastic.

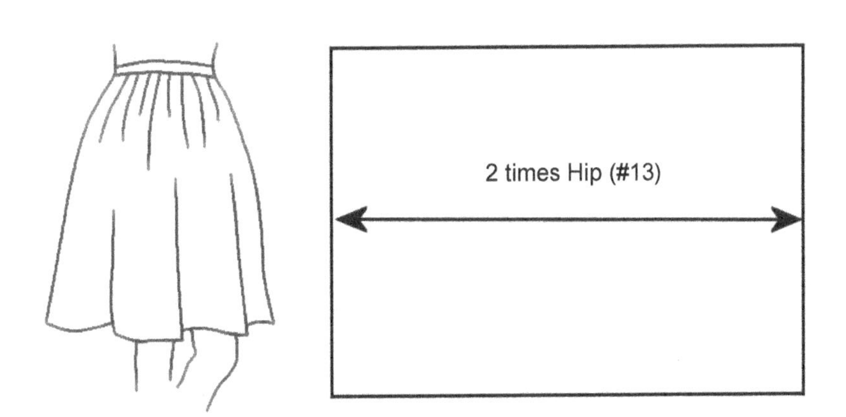

Skirt Variations

Other variations of the skirt are shown here. Pleated Skirts can be created by folding the paper as was described on page 110. Ruffles can be added by shaping the patterns as described on page 105.

Skirts can also be varied by changing the size of the Waistband and by changing the opening from zippers to buttons or the wrap around style.

Pockets can also add interest to skirt designs. These will usually be patch pockets which will be top-stitched in place. They may be designed to any shape desired.

Pants

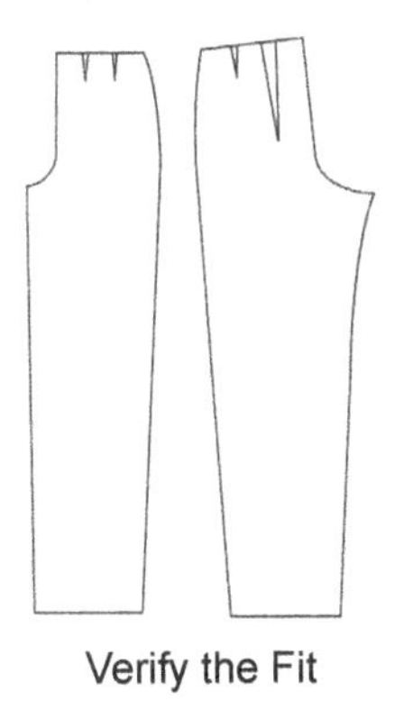
Verify the Fit

Variations in the styling of pants were given starting on page 53. The remaining considerations in designing pants patterns are how to create waistbands, plackets, pockets, and cuffs.

Important Note: Once pants legs are cut for details, their overall fit cannot be adjusted by changing the Side Seams. So when you are styling pants, always verify their fit in the fabric for the finished garment before cutting the details for pockets, waistband, and/or a yoke.

Cut the legs from waist to hem. Then baste the Inseam, Side Seam, and Crotch Curve. Try it on and verify the fit.

Pants Waistbands

There are two basic types of waistbands: the Straight Waistband and the Contoured Waistband. The first step in designing either waistband is to determine the height of the pants pattern and the width of the waistband.

For Men - Men's pants are usually not cut to the natural waist. They are 2" to 3" (5 to 7.5 cm) lower than this. The desired height for the pants should be determined during the fitting (page 51, Step 9).

The pants pattern must be lowered by the width of the waistband. This distance should be the same as the width of the belt that is to be worn with the pants, but not less than 1" (2.5 cm) wide.

For Women - The tops of women's pants are commonly at the natural waist. This height is determined during the fitting. A waistband at this point can be about 1" (2.5 cm) wide. The middle of the waistband should coincide with the top of the fitted pants pattern. Therefore, the pants pattern must be dropped by half the waistband width.

Pants may also be styled lower on the body. To achieve this design, determine the desired height of the pants during a fitting. Subtract the width of the waistband to get the correct height for the pants pattern. Some Ease may need to be removed at the Side Seams for the waistband.

For Men and Women - To determine the length of the waistband, measure the pants pattern at the new seam line that will join the pants to the waistband. Measure this distance from Center Front to Center Back skipping over any darts. For the distance around the entire body, multiply this length by two. This is the Waistband Length.

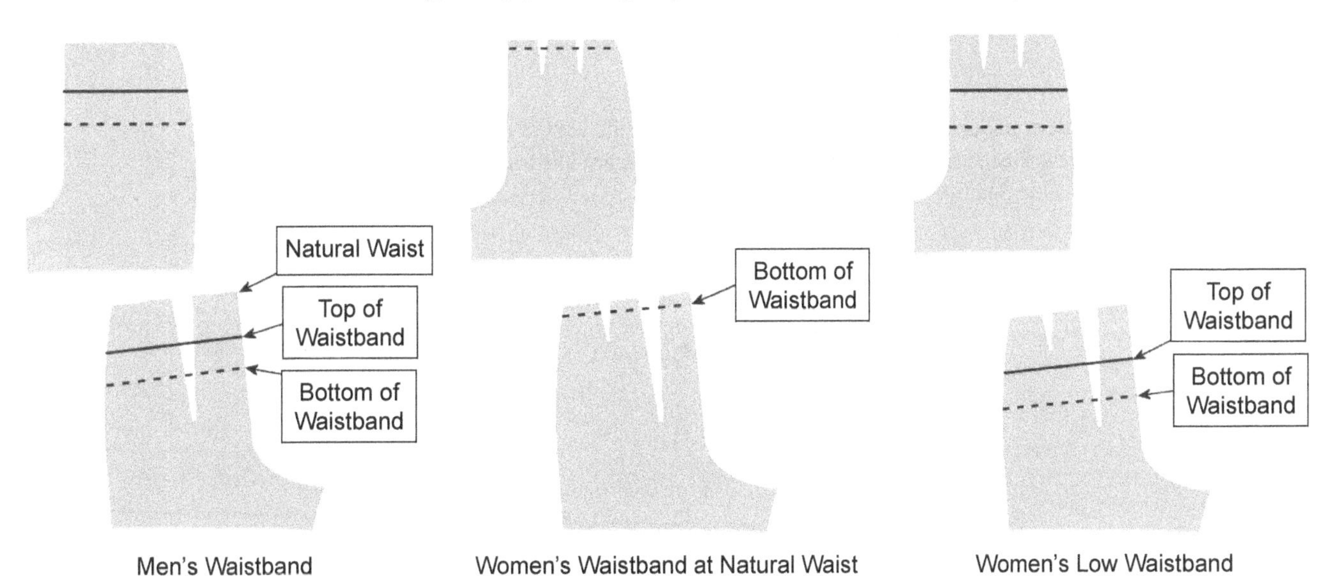

Men's Waistband   Women's Waistband at Natural Waist   Women's Low Waistband

The Straight Waistband

Step 1. Draw a line and mark off the Waistband Length. Add the width of the placket at one end of this line. This will usually be 1½" (4 cm). This line is the Waistband Seam.

Step 2. Draw lines at right angles to both ends of the Waistband Seam. Mark off twice the height of the desired waistband on these lines. From these marks, draw a line that is parallel to the Waistband Seam.

Step 3. Add seam allowances to the pattern and cut.

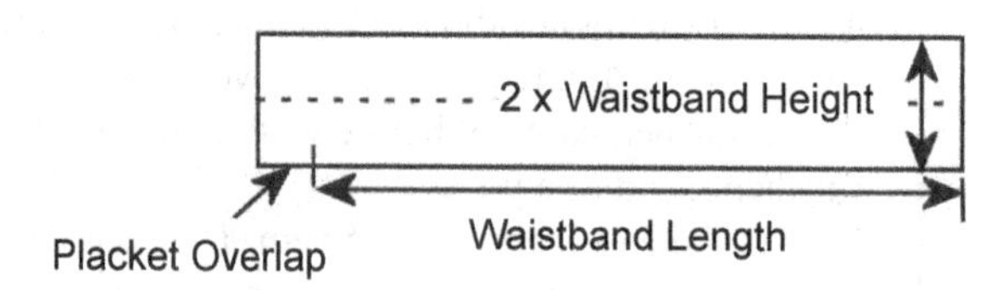

The Contoured Waistband

The Contoured Waistband is designed to follow the shape of the body. The description below shows how to create a Contoured Waistband for women's pants. The same procedure may be followed to create a Contoured Waistband for men.

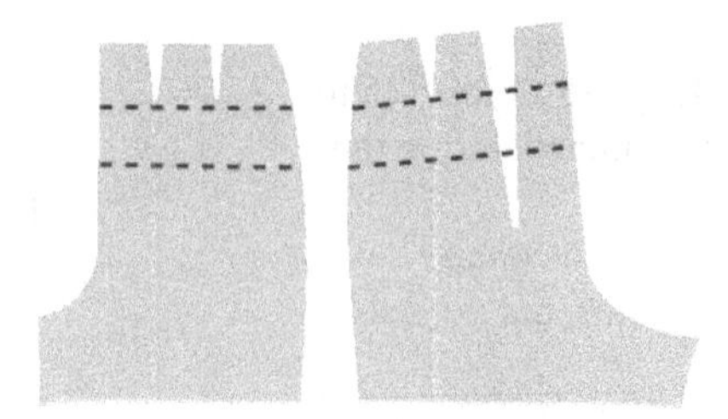

Step 1. On a copy of the Pants Sloper, draw in the desired top for the pants on the Sloper. Then draw in the height of the waistband.

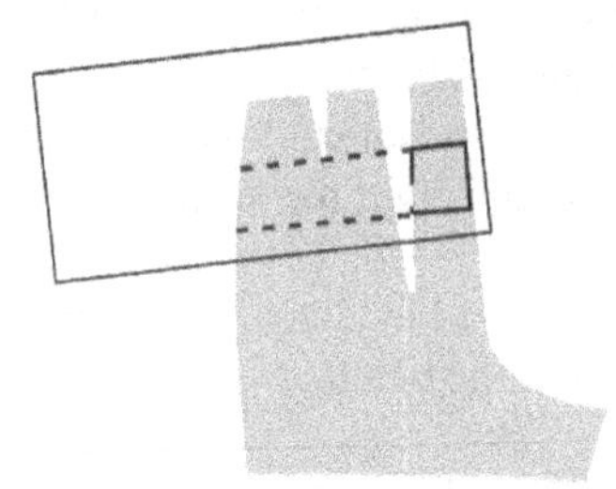

Step 2. Place a piece of pattern paper over the Sloper and trace from the Center Back to the Hip Dart. Draw a dotted line to indicate the closest leg of the Hip Dart.

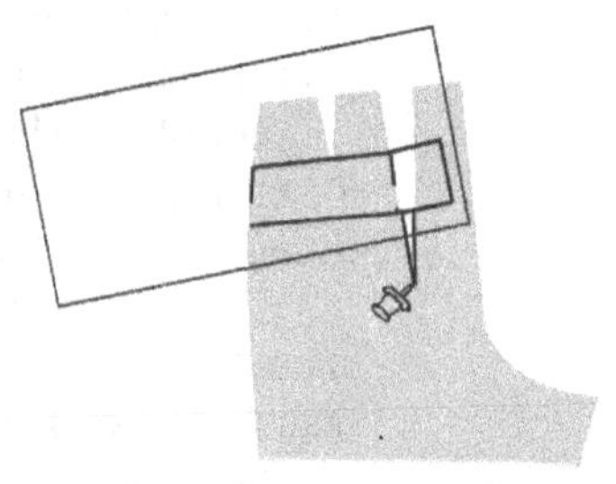

Step 3. Pivot the pattern paper from the point of the Hip Dart. Trace to the Side Seam and draw in a dotted line at the Side Seam.

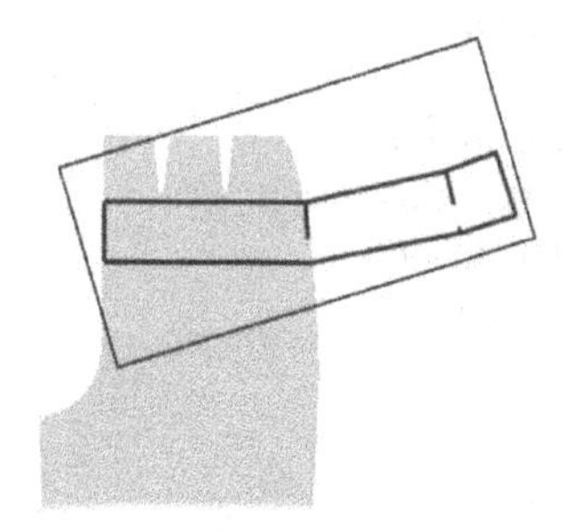

Step 4. Shift the pattern paper so the dotted line from the back Side Seam coincides with the front Side Seam. Trace to Center Front.

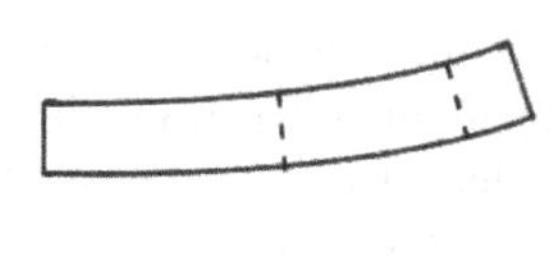

Step 5. Smooth out the curves of the Waistband and add seam allowances to all the patterns.

Plackets

Plackets are a means of reinforcing garments where an opening is to occur. On one side, the placket is a facing. On the other, the placket extends behind the faced side. The Placket is usually 1½" (4 cm) wide and 7" (18 cm) long. If the Waistband is low, the length of the Placket may need to be shortened.

For Men - The left side conventionally laps over the right side. Therefore, the left side is the faced side and the right side is the extension.

For Women - The right side laps over the left side. The right side is the faced side and the left side is extended.

> **Important Note:** Do not extend the placket below the straight portion of the Center Front line. The garment is designed to curve under the body at this point.

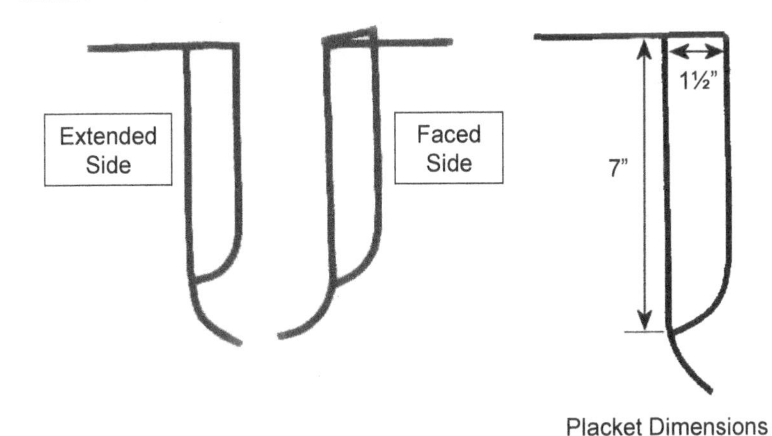

Placket Dimensions

Pockets

There are four basic types of pockets for pants: the Patch Pocket, the Welt Pocket, the Seam Pocket, and the Slashed Pocket.

The Patch Pocket is sewn to the outside of the garment. It may be drawn to any desired shape and top-stitched in place.

The Welt Pocket is created by cutting a slit into the fabric and sewing a pocket on the inside. This is an exercise in sewing rather than in drafting so it is not described here.

If these two pockets are placed in the back of the pants, they should be kept on the side of the hip. This will prevent anything in the pockets from being sat on.

The Inseam Pocket and the Slashed Pocket are created by changing the patterns.

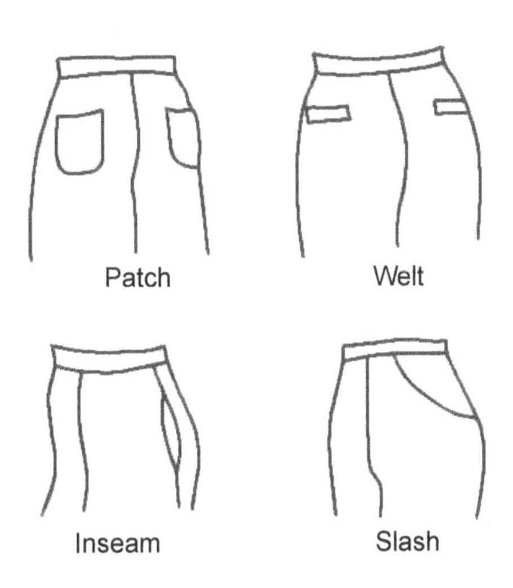

Slashed Pockets

Slashed pockets are sewn into the shape of the front pants leg. The following procedure creates a jeans style pocket that is secured to both the waistband and the Side Seam to ensure the integrity of the pant's shape. A full size pattern is included on page 139.

This pocket consists of a lining folded in half and sewn along the bottom and into the Side Seam to create the pocket. For jeans, the pocket lining is usually a lighter weight material than the body of the pants. To maintain a consistent look for the leg, use a facing of the jeans material for the inside of the pocket.

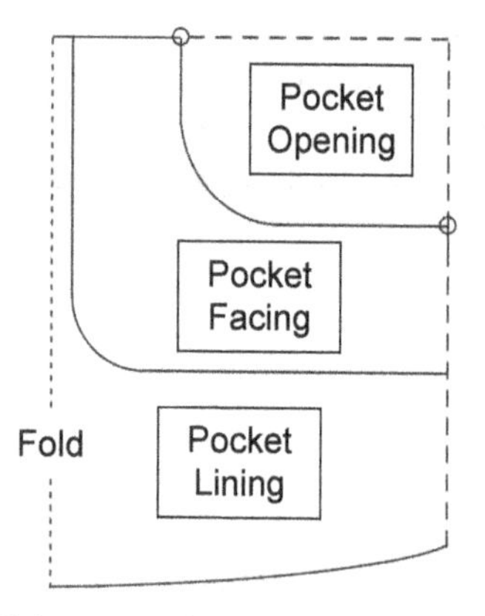

This pattern includes a circle at the waist and a circle at the Side Seam for aligning the pocket to the Pants Sloper.

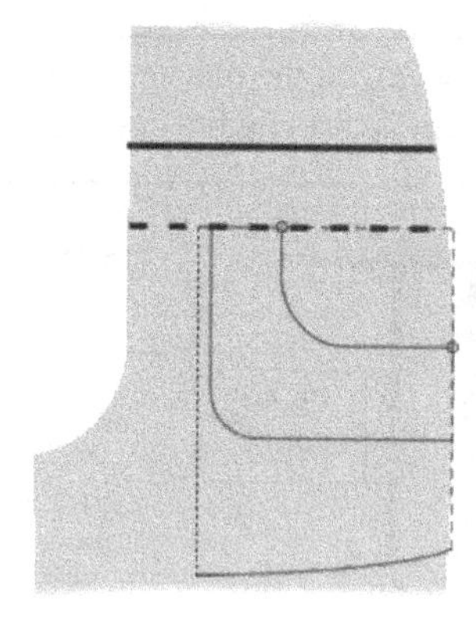

Step 1. Place the pocket pattern on top of the Pants Sloper aligning the circle at the waist to the waistband seam. Then slide the pattern so the circle at the Side Seam matches the Side Seam of the Sloper.

Step 2. Trace the shape of the Sloper Side Seam to the pocket pattern.

Step 3. Trace the shape of the waistband seam to the pocket pattern.

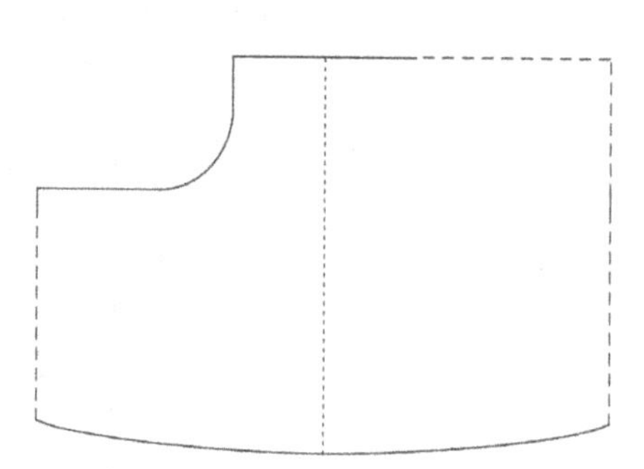

Step 4. Make a copy of the pocket pattern as shown above.

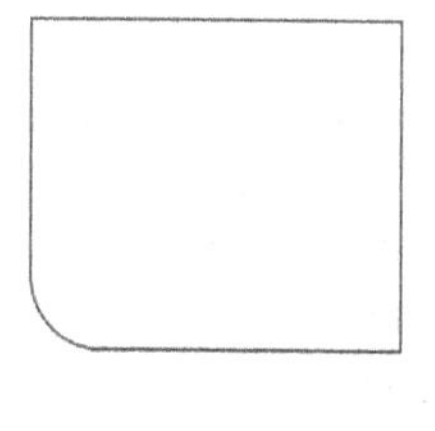

Step 5. Make a copy of the facing pattern. The facing pattern does not require any seam allowances as the edges of the facing will all be concealed inside the pocket.

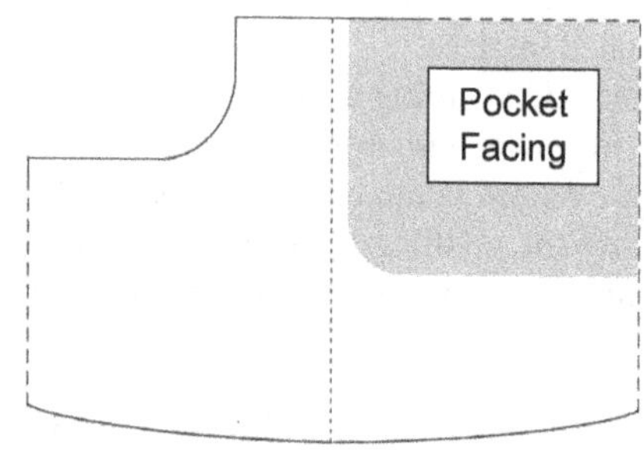

The first step in sewing this pocket is to attach the facing to the pocket lining as shown above.

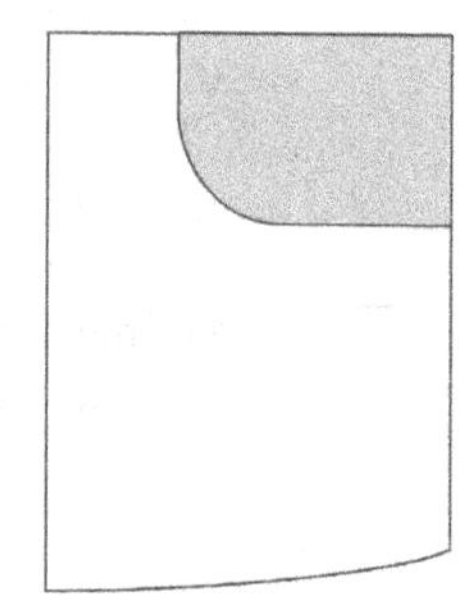

After the facing is attached, the pocket is folded and attached to the leg.

Jeans Pocket Pattern

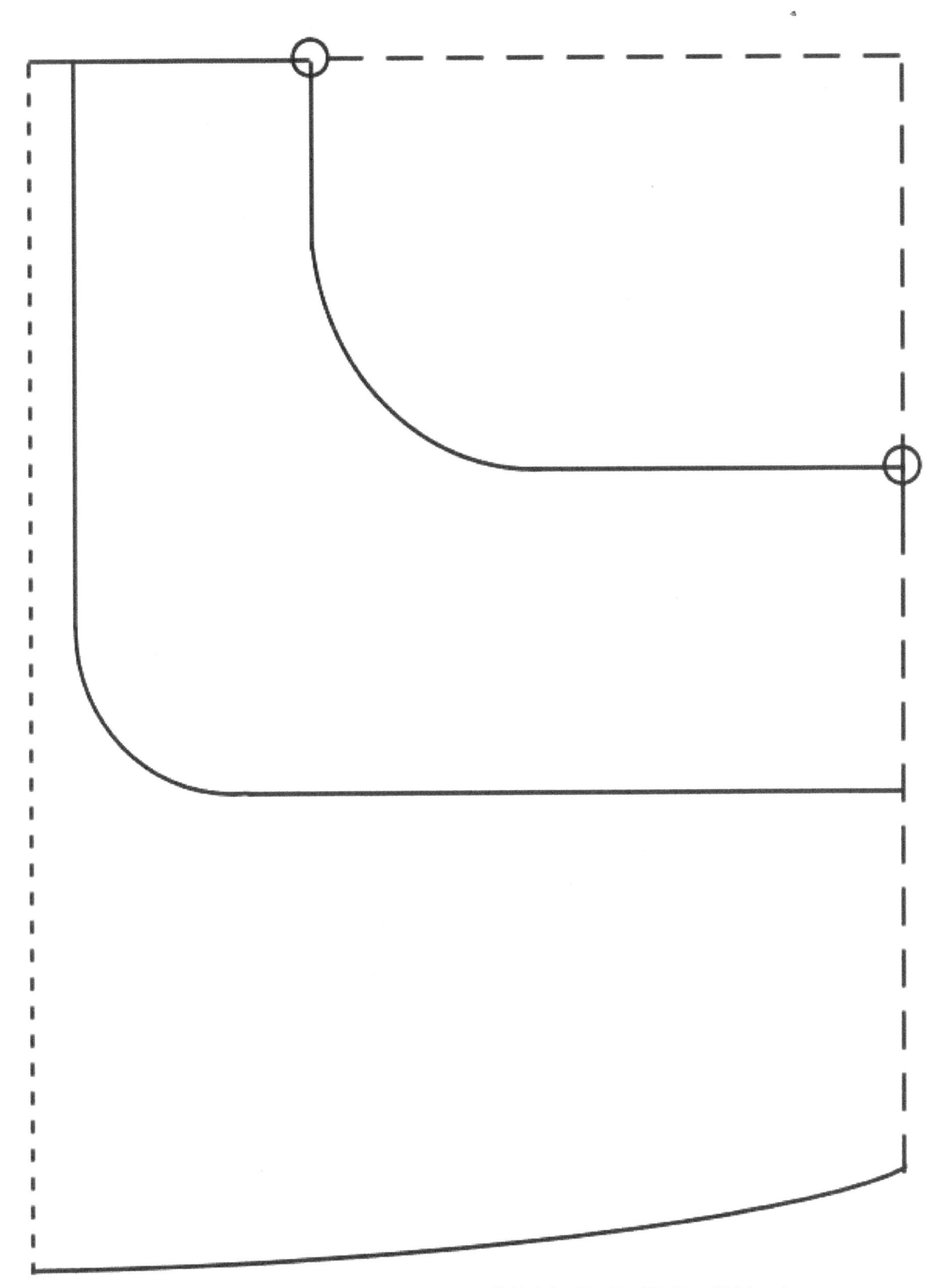

Full Size Jeans Pocket Pattern measuring 8" high by 6" wide (20.32 x 15.24 cm)

Cuffs

Cuffs may be added to any pants pattern.

Step 1. Fold a piece of pattern paper in the desired shape of the cuff. The first fold establishes the inside of the cuff. The second fold is for the outside of the cuff. The third fold will be the hem inside the pants leg.

Step 2. Place the tracing paper over the pants pattern and trace the desired shape of the leg. Make the top of the cuff ⅛" (3 mm) larger than the pants leg. This will keep the cuff from interfering with the fall of the fabric.

Step 3. Unfold the pattern and transfer all of the marks to the front side of the pattern.

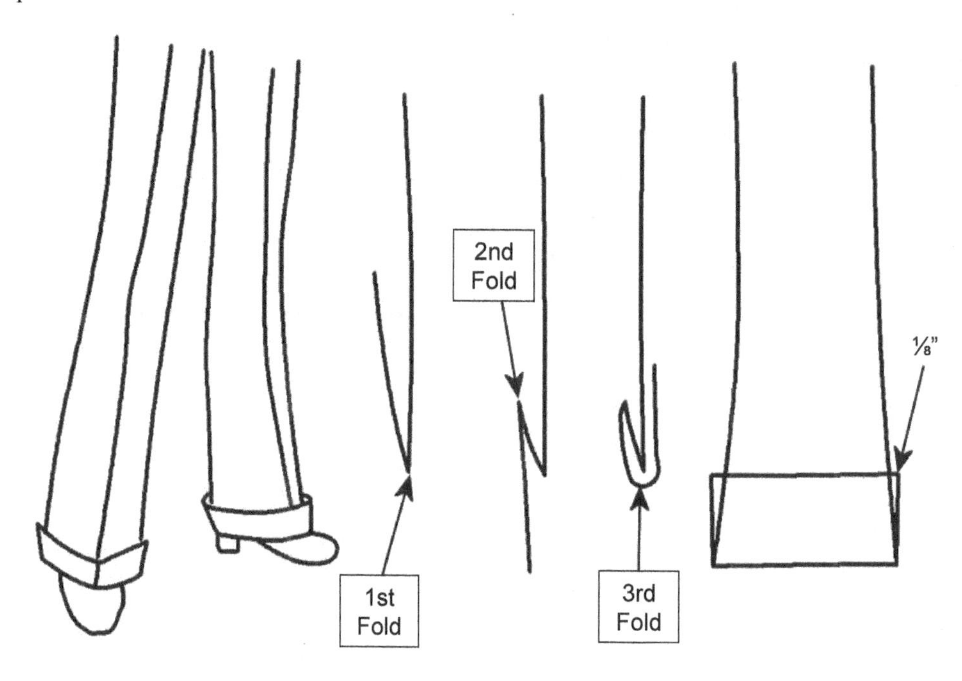

Shirts and Blouses

Men's shirts are styled in a conventional fashion. This shape is described here. Many women's blouses are an imitation of this styling except a dart is usually added to the Side Seam. The location of this dart may be changed to create different designs.

The Body of the Shirt

To create the shirt pattern, change the Bodice Sloper as follows.

1"
Waist to Hips #36
2"
2"
¼ Hips #13

The Shirt Length

Step 1. Extend the Center Front line down from the Waist line. Mark off the Waist to Hip length (#36) on this extension.

Step 2. Draw a line at right angles to the Center Front line from the Hip length. This will be the Hem line.

Step 3. Mark off one-fourth the Hip measurement (#13) on the Hem line.

The Side Seam

A total of 2" (5 cm) of Ease is added to the body dimensions on the front and back patterns to create a comfortable fit. This adds 4" (10 cm) to each side of the body for a total of 8" (20 cm) of Ease around the entire body.

Step 4. Add 1" (2.5 cm) of Ease to the Side Seam at the Chest. Remember the basic pattern already has 1" (2.5 cm) of Ease here.

Step 5. Add 2" (5 cm) of Ease to the side of the Waist and the Hip marks.

Step 6. Using the Ease marks described above as guides, draw in the new Side Seam.

Step 7. Trace the Neck Curve, Shoulder Seam, and the Armhole Curve. Extend the Armhole Curve straight out to the new Side Seam.

This Side Seam may be styled in other ways. For instance, a casual shirt that is designed to hang outside the pants may have a seam straight from the Chest to the Hip line.

Shaping the Shirt Bottom

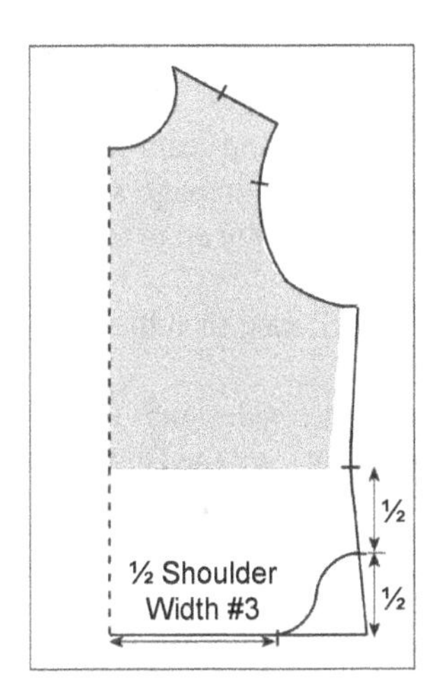

For shirts that are to be tucked into pants, the bottom of the shirt should be shaped on the side. This will prevent the shirt from riding up the side as the body moves.

Step 8. Mark off half the Shoulder Width (#3) on the Hip line. This measurement indicates the width of the front of the body.

Step 9. Divide the distance from the Waist to the Hips in half at the Side Seam.

Step 10. Draw a curved line between these two points as illustrated.

Button Location

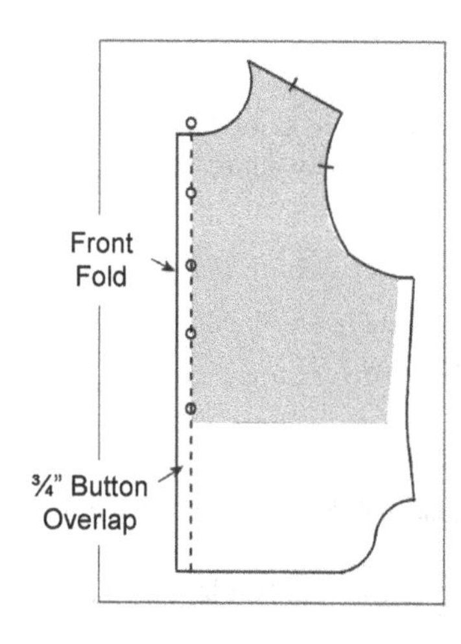

Shirts are conventionally buttoned down the Center Front line of the body.

Step 11. Locate the first button one inch above the Waist line.

Step 12. The top button will be in the collar. Make a mark ½" (12 mm) above the neck line.

Step 13. To position the middle button, divide the distance between these two buttons in half.

Step 14. To position another button, divide the distance between the bottom and middle buttons in half.

Step 15. To position the final button, divide the distance between the top and middle buttons in half.

Button Overlap

The fabric for the shirt will have to extend beyond the Center Front to provide a means of fastening the buttons. This distance is normally ¾" (18 mm).

Step 16. Measure out ¾" (18 mm) from the Center Front line and draw a line parallel to the Center Front line. This is the Front Fold of the shirt.

> **Note:** Buttons larger than ¾" (18 mm) in diameter require a larger Button Overlap. The Button Overlap should be the diameter of the button being used.

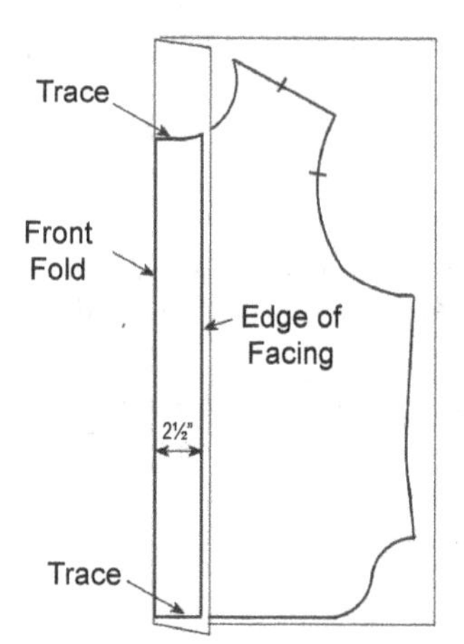

The Facing

Step 17. To create a facing, fold the pattern on the Front Fold line.

Step 18. Trace the Neck Seam and the Hem of the shirt onto the facing.

Step 19. Measure 2½" (6 cm) in from the Front Fold line and draw a line parallel to it. This is the inside edge of the facing.

The facing is styled 2½" (6 cm) in on the garment so the edge of the facing will not be exposed when the garment is left unbuttoned at the collar.

The straight edge of the facing should be placed on the selvedge of the fabric when the shirt is cut out.

The Back Pattern

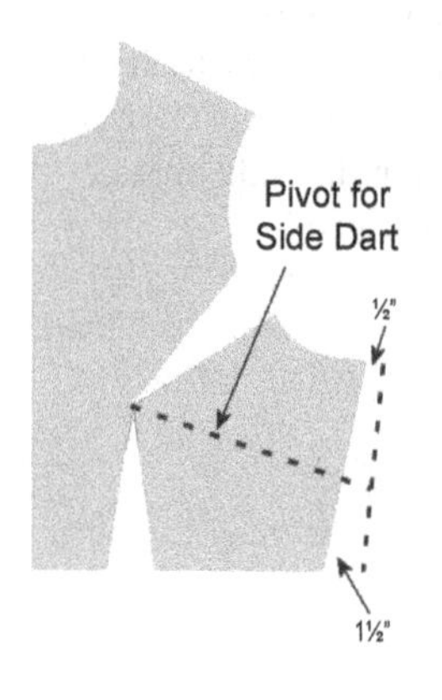

The back pattern can be styled the same way the front pattern was created except that the Center Back will be a fold line. When the Center Back is placed on the fold of the fabric and cut out, it will create a single piece for the back.

This completes the patterns for the body of the shirt. Other yokes and seam lines may be added to the basic shirt pattern by following the instructions starting on page 87.

For Women - With two exceptions, the same procedure may be followed to create blouses for women.

First, the Side Seam should be extended on the Front Bodice Sloper, then the Above the Bust Dart should be pivoted to the Side Seam, see page 90.

Second, 6" (15 cm) of total Ease is usually sufficient for women's designs. This means that the Waist and the Hip should be extended out 1½" (4 cm) and the Bust should be expanded by ½ (12 mm).

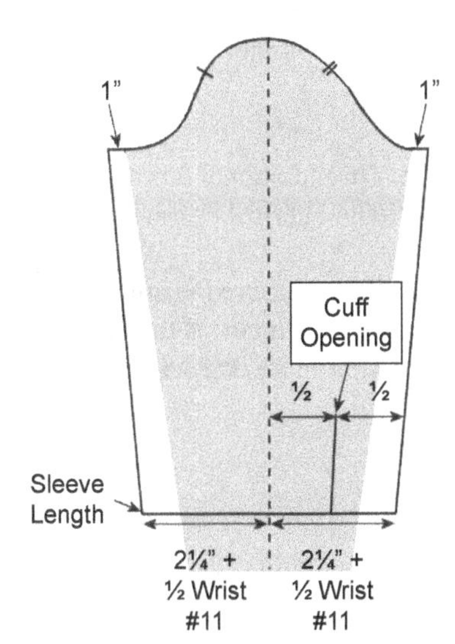

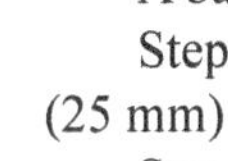

The Shirt Sleeve

Men's shirt sleeves also have a conventional style.

Step 1. The sleeve pattern must be shortened by the width of the cuff that is to be added. On the Sleeve Sloper, draw a line 2½" (6 cm) above the bottom of the sleeve. This is the Sleeve Length line. This shortens.

Step 2. Add 2¼" (5.7 cm) to half the Wrist measurement (#11). Mark this length on the new Sleeve Length line measuring out from either side of the Sleeve Centerline. This establishes the width of the bottom of the sleeve.

Step 3. Extend the Sleeve Cap line straight out by the same amount of Ease that was added to the body of the design. This was 1" (25 mm) for men and ½" (12 mm) for women.

Step 4. Draw in the new Arm Seam from the expanded Sleeve Cap line to the new Sleeve Length line.

Step 5. The cuff of shirt sleeves open at the back of the arm instead of in the Underarm Seam. Draw a line for this opening that is half way between the Sleeve Centerline and the new Underarm Seam. This line should be 4" to 5" (10 to 15 cm) long.

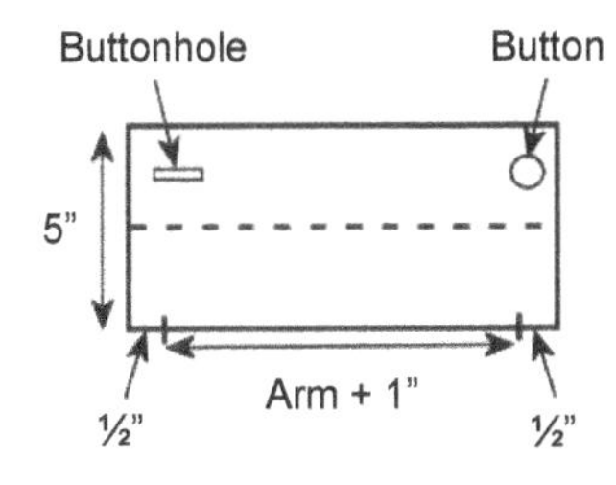

The Cuff

A basic height for a straight cuff is 2½" (6 cm) and it can be drafted as follows:

Step 1. Measure the circumference of the arm 2½" (6 cm) above the wrist. Add 1" (25 mm) of Ease to this dimension.

Step 2. Draw a horizontal line on a piece of paper and mark off the length determined in Step 1. This is the Cuff Seam. The length of this line at this point is the distance from the button to the buttonhole.

Step 3. Add a ½" (12 mm) to either side of the Cuff Seam to create a Button Overlap. Draw two lines at right angles to the Cuff Seam from these points.

Step 4. Measure up 5" (15 cm) from the Cuff Seam and draw a line parallel to the Cuff Seam from this point. To determine the Wrist line of the Cuff (the dotted line), fold the pattern in half.

Step 5. Mark the location of the buttons and buttonholes on the pattern. Add seam allowances and cut out the pattern.

The width of the cuff will be shorter than the width of the sleeve. The difference between these two lengths will be taken up in pleats in the sleeve. These pleats will be located on the outside portion of the arm.

Full Sleeves and Tapered Cuffs

Full sleeves and tapered cuffs present two additional options for pattern drafting.

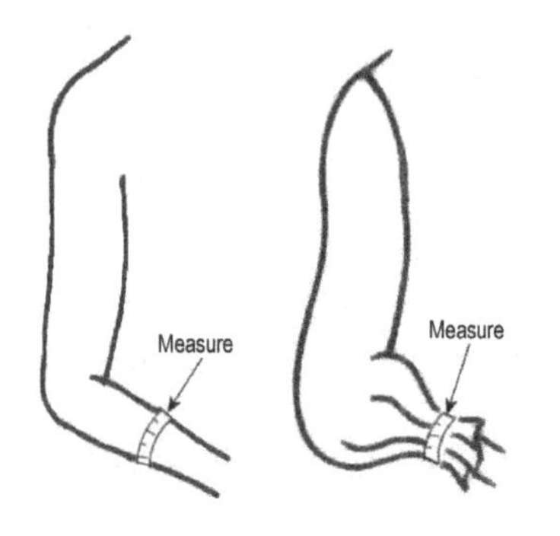

Measure the Arm then with Fabric

Full Sleeves

A full sleeve will add additional fabric around the arm. This additional fabric shrinks the effective size of cuffs. To correct this problem, an additional Fabric Allowance must be added to the dimensions of the cuff when it is drafted.

Measure the bare arm at the desired height of the cuff. Then measure the arm around the fullness of the fabric. The difference between these two measurements is the Fabric Allowance. This measurement may be as much as 1" (2.5 cm) or more depending on the amount of fullness and the weight of the fabric.

The Tapered Cuff

The cuff pattern must be drafted for half the cuff first. This will then be changed to a full cuff. Draft a tapered cuff as follows:

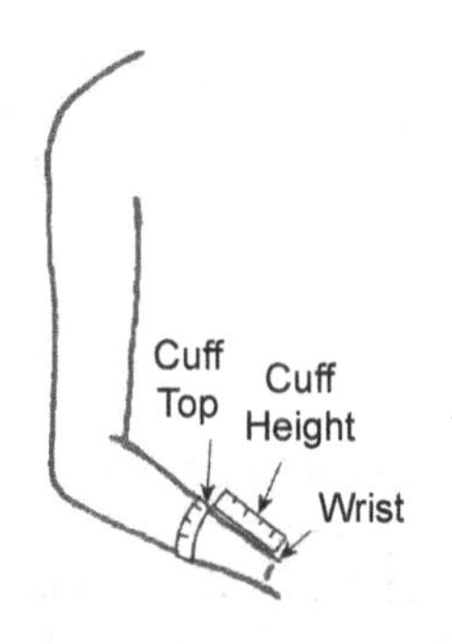

Step 1. Measure the arm where the top of the cuff is to be located. This is the Cuff Top Length. Measure the desired Cuff Height.

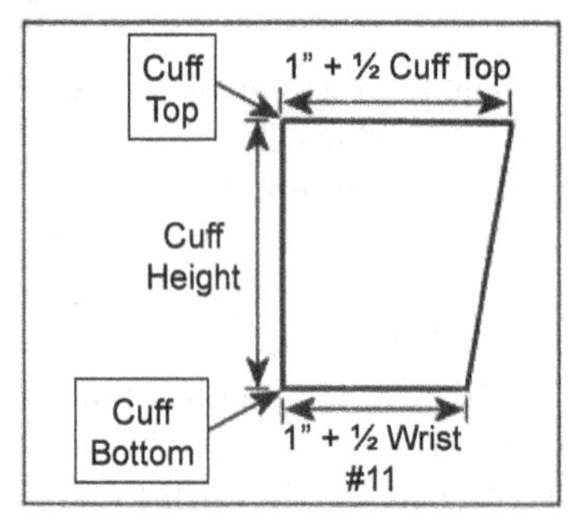

Step 2. On a piece of paper draw a vertical line that is the Cuff Height. Draw lines at right angles to both ends of this line. This establishes the Cuff Top and the Cuff Bottom.

Step 3. On the Cuff Bottom mark off 1" (2.5 cm) plus half the Wrist measurement (#11). For Ease and a Button Overlap, add 1" (2.5 cm) to the Wrist measurement.

Step 4. On the Cuff Top line, mark off 1" (2.5 cm) plus half the Fabric Allowance plus half the Cuff Top Length (Step 1).

Step 5. To form the edge of the cuff, connect the mark on the Cuff Top to the mark on the Cuff Bottom line.

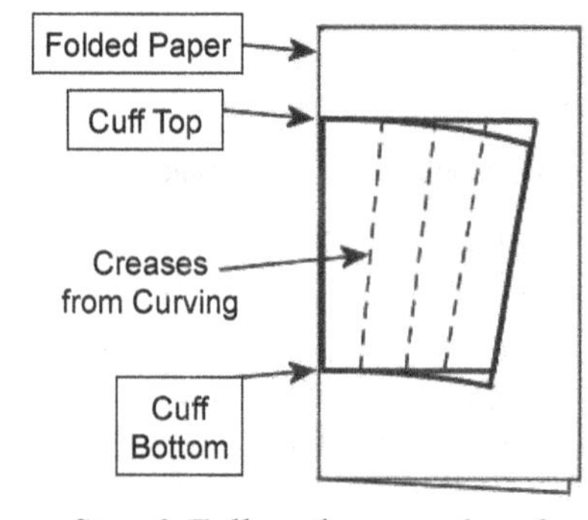

Step 6. Follow the procedure for curving the seams as described starting on page 122.

Step 7. Fold the paper of this pattern along the Cuff Height line and trace the curved half of the pattern. When the paper is unfolded, it will be the shape of the full cuff.

Step 8. Draw in the button and buttonhole locations a ½" (12 mm) in from the edge of the pattern. Add seam allowances and cut out the pattern.

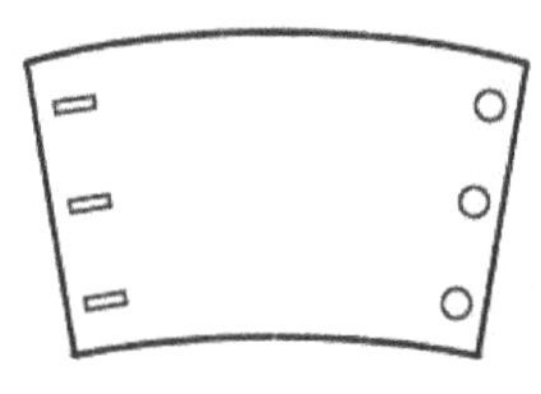

Tapered Cuff Pattern

Dresses and Tops

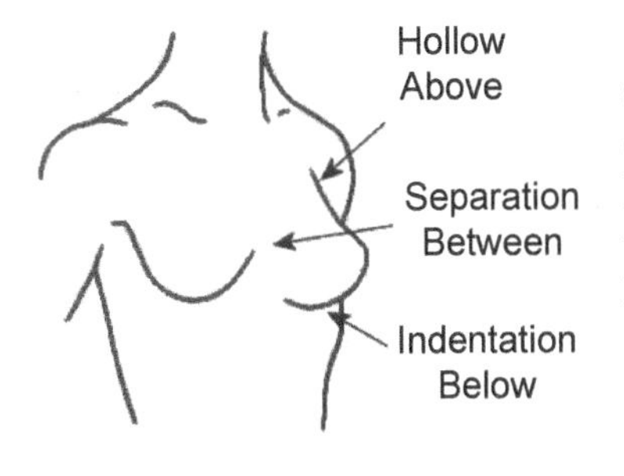

Dresses and Tops present an infinite variety of styling possibilities. A Peasant Top is created from measurements taken as illustrated below rather than from a Sloper. Other designs can be created from the Slopers using the alteration techniques already described. But high waistlines, low necklines, and wrap around styles require special consideration when they follow contours of the bust that are not reflected in the Bodice Sloper such as a hollow above the bust, shaping below the bust, and the separation between the breasts.

Peasant Top

Measure the Sleeve Top from the normal Shoulder Seam location to the desired top of the blouse. This measurement and the Blouse Top measurement will be doubled on the pattern to create double fullness. The Underarm Length should be measured up from the normal Side Seam location.

Fold the patterns along the Sleeve Top and the Blouse Top lines to create a casing for an elastic or a draw string.

The sleeves will be sewn to the garment's body along the Underarm Seams. Sew the casing closed next. Then sew the Sleeve Seams and Side Seams.

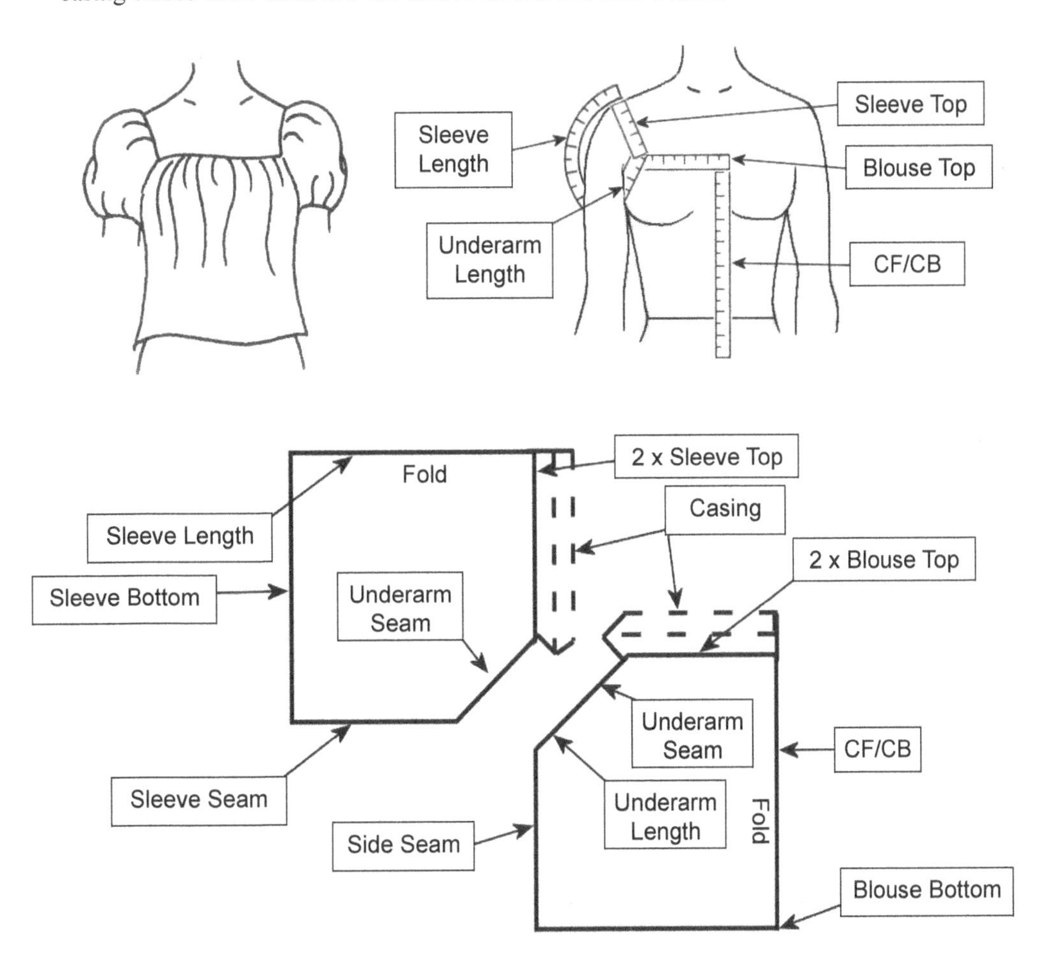

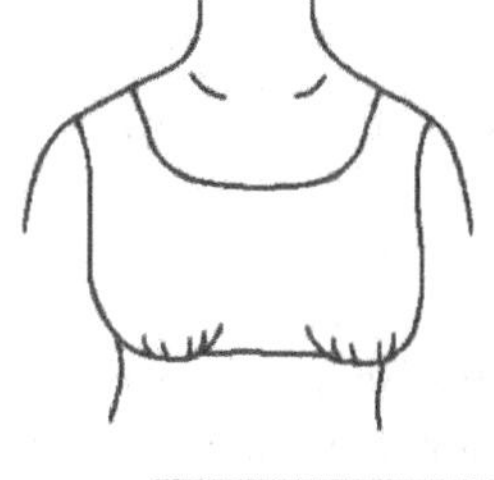

High Waistlines

The High Waistline is designed to fit closely under the bust. It can be created as follows.

> **Note:** If the new waistline is to be parallel to the floor, as in this illustration, draw the new waistline parallel to the waistline of the Sloper.

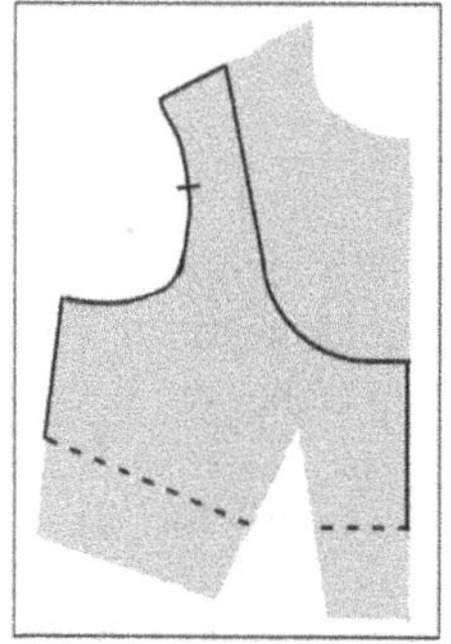

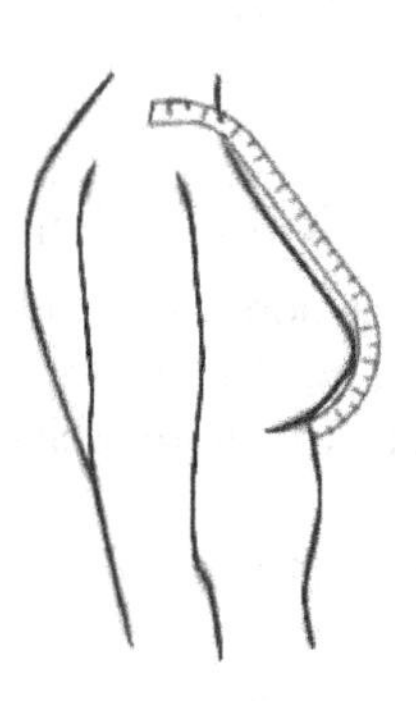

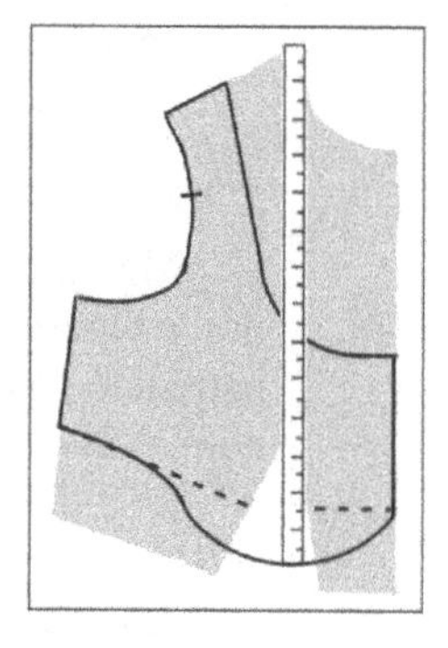

Step 1. Place a sheet of pattern paper over a copy of the front Bodice Sloper that has both dart shapes below the bust.

Step 2. Draw in the new waistline. Then draw in the neckline and trace the Sloper down to the new waistline.

Step 3. On the body, measure the length of the Side Front from the shoulder to the rib cage distance.

Step 4. Mark this length on the pattern, then redraw the high waistline.

This curve on the pattern will appear as a straight waistline in the finished garment.

If the garment is going to be fitted with a dart, the size of the dart should be verified in a fitting.

Low Necklines

A Low Neckline cut from the Bodice Sloper may not fit closely to the body because of the hollow above the bust. To correct this problem, cut a fitting shell from scrap fabric to verify the fit of the desired design. This example uses the same design as shown for the high waistline.

To prevent the garment from sliding off the shoulders, a low neckline in front should be accompanied by a high neckline in back.

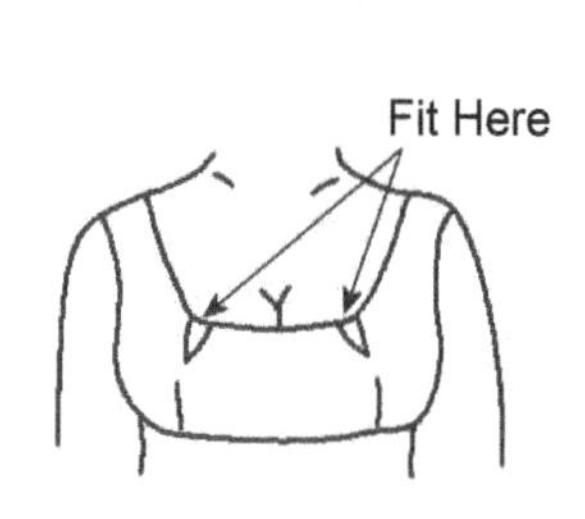

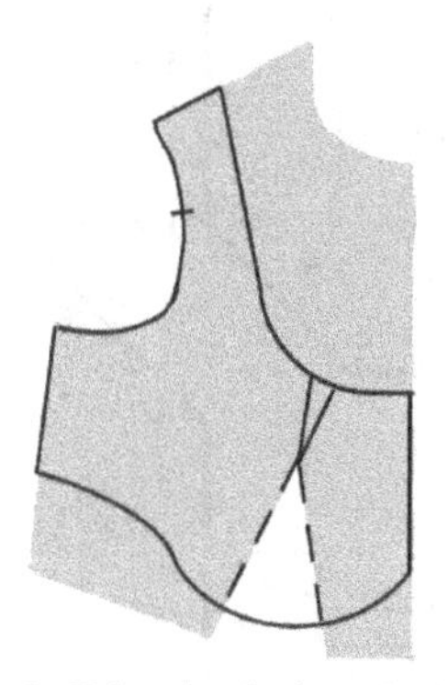

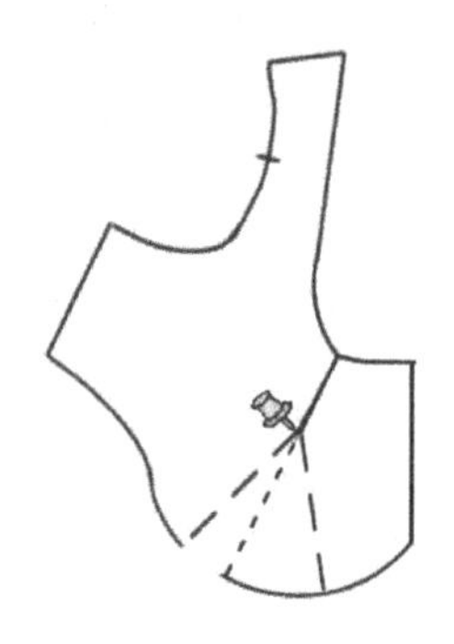

Step 1. Cut a fitting shell using the high waistline pattern.

Step 2. Put the fitting shell on and fit a dart into the neckline so that the fabric follows the body smoothly.

Step 3. Take the fitting shell off and transfer the neckline dart to the high waistline pattern.

Step 4. On a new sheet of pattern paper, trace the original high waistline pattern, pivoting the neckline dart to the Below the Bust Dart location.

Cowl Necklines

Cowl Necklines are a variation of the low neckline that can be drafted by using the specialized pattern alteration technique described here. To eliminate any possible embarrassment when bending over, a garment with a low Cowl Neckline should include a fitted top under the cowl.

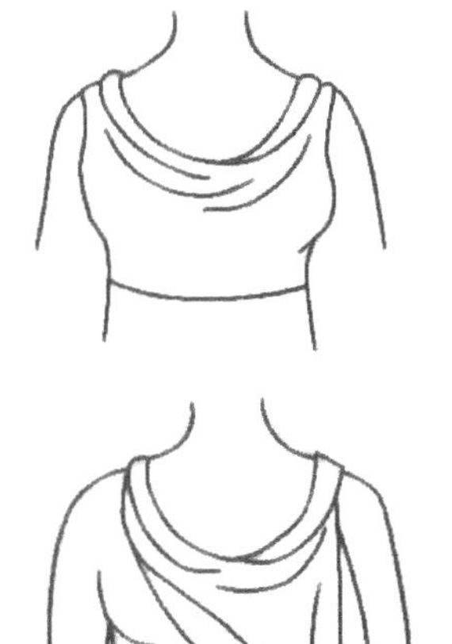

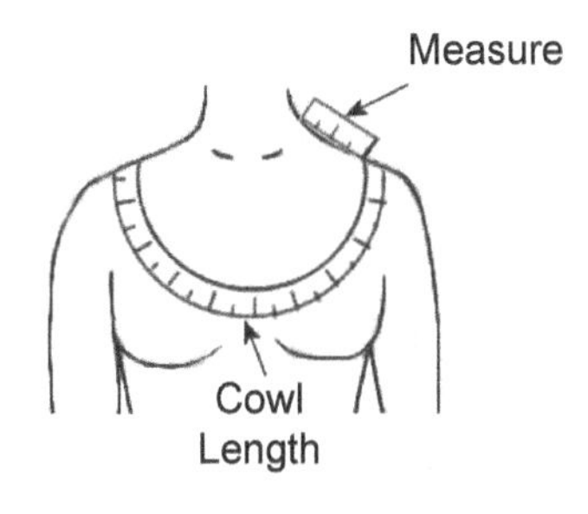

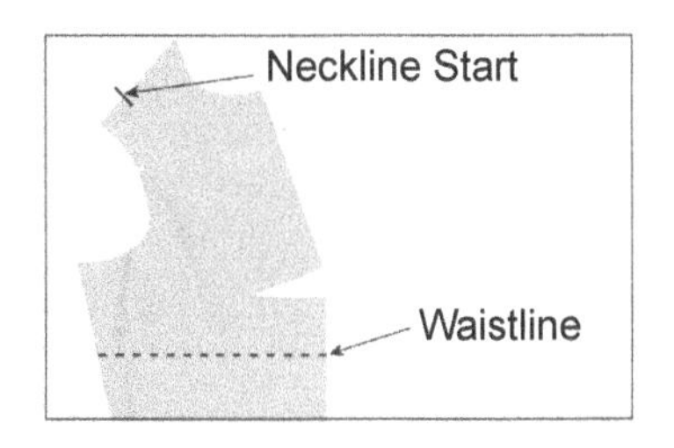

Step 1. Take the fabric that is to be used for the Cowl Neckline and fold it on the true bias (this is a forty-five degree angle to the grain of the fabric). Hold it in the shape of the desired neckline. See if it falls in graceful folds or breaks in unattractive creases. Adjust the fabric for the best appearance. Take note of the shape of the top of the neckline.

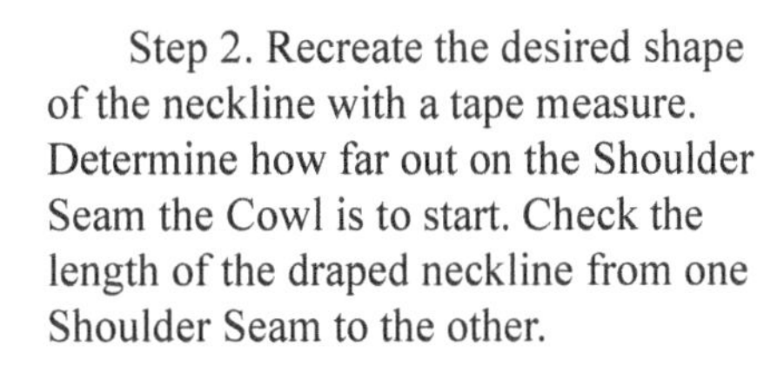

Step 2. Recreate the desired shape of the neckline with a tape measure. Determine how far out on the Shoulder Seam the Cowl is to start. Check the length of the draped neckline from one Shoulder Seam to the other.

Step 3. Place a sheet of pattern paper over a copy of the front Bodice Sloper that has the dart shape pivoted to Center Front, see page 92.

Step 4. Mark on the Shoulder Seam the point from which the Cowl Neckline is to drape. This is the Neckline Starting Point. Draw in a dotted line to indicate the Waistline.

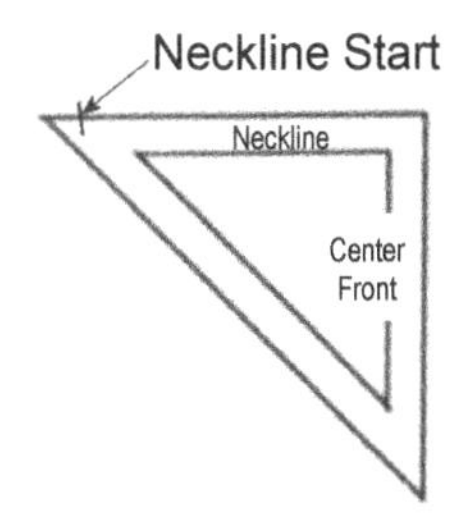

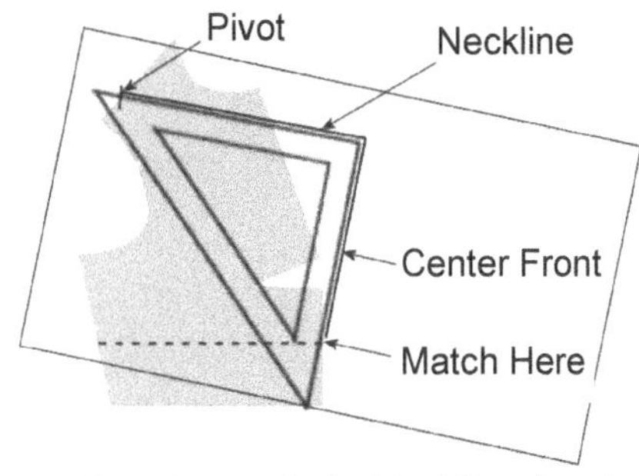

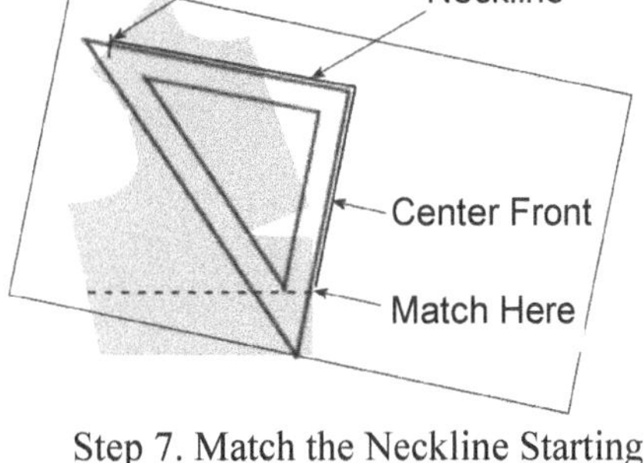

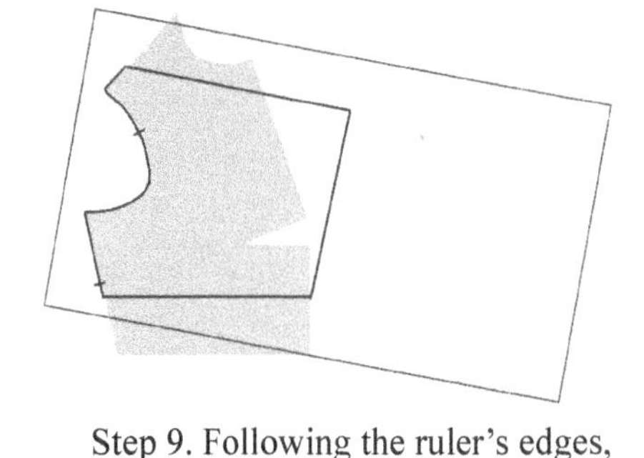

Step 5. Take a large right angle ruler (or a sheet of paper with a square corner). Mark one of the sides as the Neckline. Mark the other right angle side as the Center Front line.

Step 6. On the Neckline edge of the ruler, measure out from the right angle half the length of the desired Cowl Neckline and make a mark. This is the Neckline Starting Point.

Step 7. Match the Neckline Starting Point on the ruler to the Neckline Starting Point of the bodice. This will be the pivot point for the ruler.

Step 8. Pivot the ruler until the Center Front line on the ruler coincides with the Center Front on the bodice at the new Waist line as indicated by the dotted lines.

Step 9. Following the ruler's edges, draw in the Neckline and the Center Front for the Cowl.

Step 10. Trace the rest of the cowl pattern from the Sloper. The Center Front line will be a fold line.

Step 11. Add a 2" to 3" (5 to 7.5 cm) Facing to the Neckline and round off the waistline at Center Front.

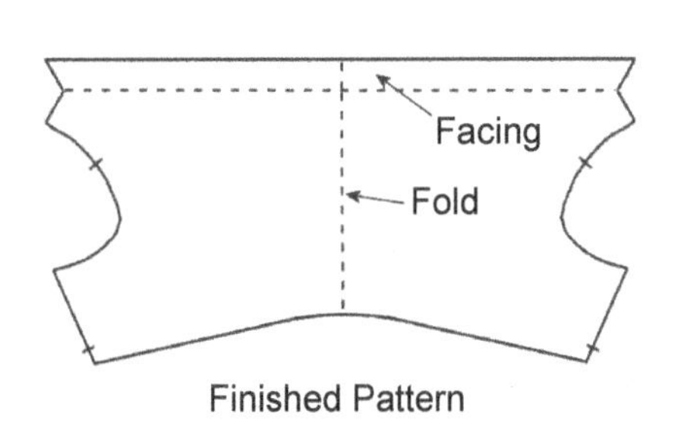

Finished Pattern

Wrap Around Closings

The Wrap Around closing for a dress or top can be created by drawing the desired design directly onto the Bodice Sloper.

The Wrap Around Seam will fit between the breasts instead of riding over the top. The length of this seam must be shortened. Cut the design out of scrap fabric for a trial fitting. Adjust the garment at the Shoulder Seam and at the Waist so that the grain of the fabric at the bust remains parallel to the floor.

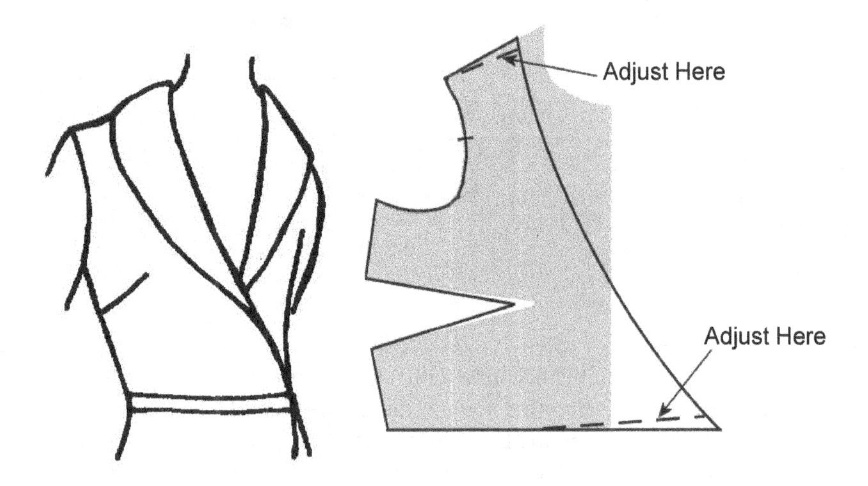

Working with Knits

The primary difference between knits and woven fabric is that knits can assume a three-dimensional shape without darts and seams. You can see this in action if you take a knit fabric and stretch it over your fist. The fabric will remain smooth as it changes to a three-dimensional shape. The degree it will remain smooth depends on the qualities of the specific fabric.

The ability of knits to stretch also means that many designs do not require opening devices. The knit garment can simply be pulled over the head or up over the hips.

Handkerchief & Circular Skirts

A handkerchief or circular skirt is a good example of a knit garment that eliminates seams and can be pulled on without any additional closing device. This type of skirt is made by folding a single piece of fabric widthwise, then lengthwise, then cutting a waist circle in the center as shown below.

The waist circle should be reinforced with elastic. To determine the length of the elastic, wrap the elastic around the body at the desired waist line and pull until it is the length required.

To draw circles, use a tape measure with a hole in one end. Pin the tape measure to the corner that is to be the center of the circle. Then use a pencil inserted through the hole to draw the circle.

Step 1. Fold the fabric lengthwise, then widthwise. The corner where the folds meet is the center of the waist circle.

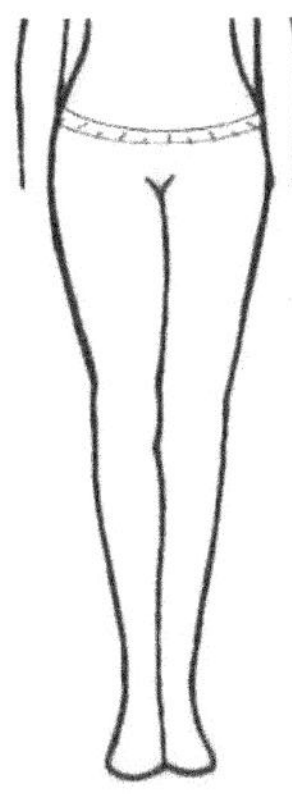

Step 2. Measure the circumference of the body at the desired location for the waist.

Step 3. Find the measurement for waist circle from the "Circumference of a Circle" on the Patternmaking Ruler, see page 169.

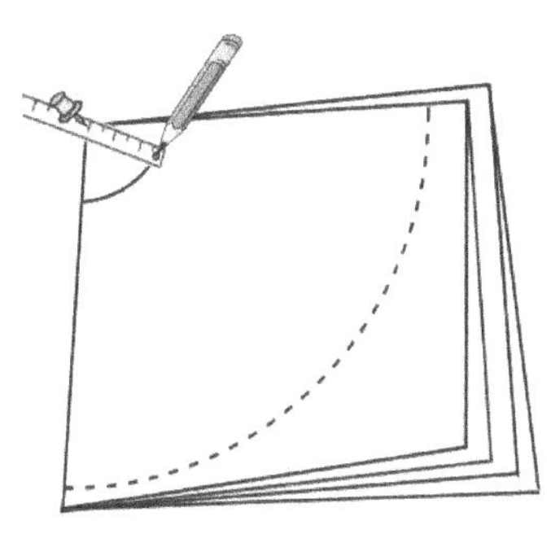

Step 4. From the center of the waist, draw a quarter of a circle.

Step 5. For a circular skirt, draw a second quarter circle that is the hem length as measured from the waist circle.

Step 6. Cut the fabric.

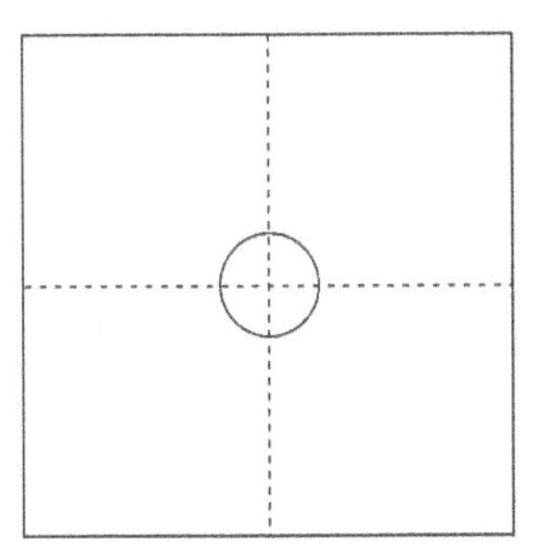

Handkerchief Hem Skirt

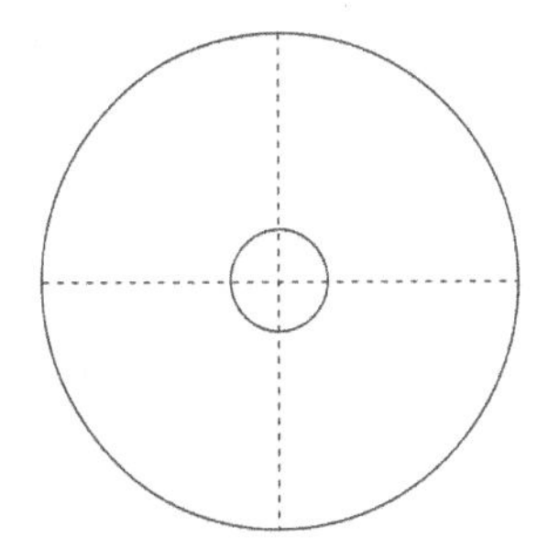

Circular Skirt

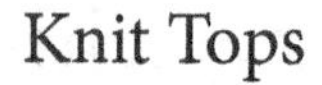

Knit Tops

Knit tops allow you to remove the darts as shaping devices and combine Slopers from both the upper and lower torso to create a garment that can be pulled on without a closure system.

Ease can be adjusted to the stretch of the fabric. The amount of Ease needed depends on the stretch quality of the specific fabric. To test the pattern's fit for the knit, sew the body at the shoulder seam, then sew in the sleeve. You can then baste one continuous underarm and Side Seam and adjust it to the desired fit. When sewing most knits, a 1 mm zigzag stitch will have enough give that it will not break. Always verify this by testing on scrap fabric.

Knits will stretch either across the width of the fabric or the length of the fabric. Some knits stretch equally in both directions. These knits are called four way stretch. The direction of the maximum stretch should always go around the body.

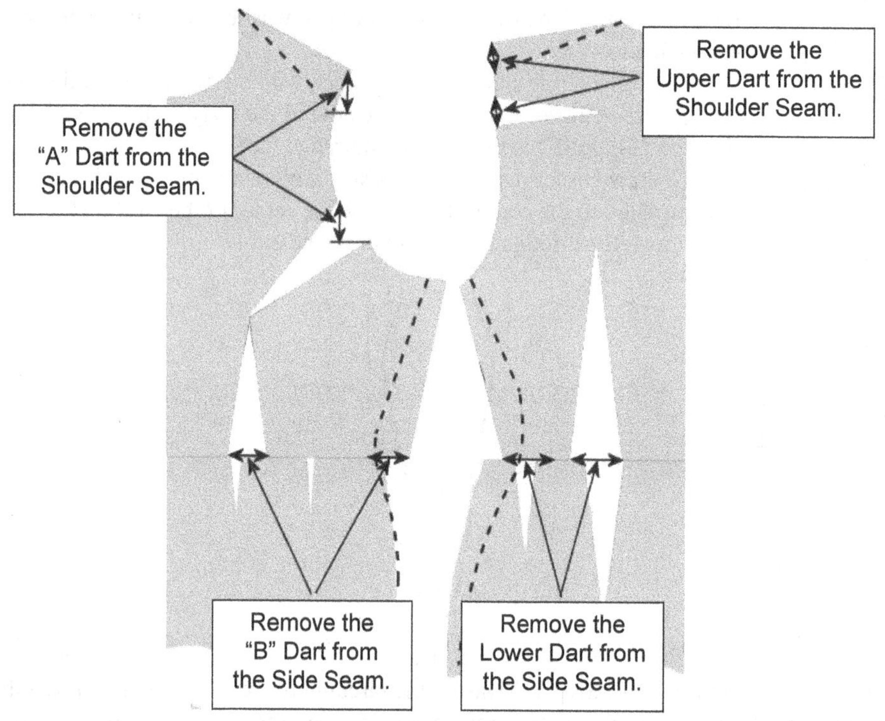

Step 1. Increase the angle of the Shoulder Seam by removing the upper dart widths from the armscye.

Step 2. Remove the lower dart widths of the Bodice Sloper from the Side Seams.

As you adjust the Side Seam, you may need to exercise some discretion. For example, in the illustration above, notice that the Lower Back Dart width is not completely removed from the Side Seam. Adjust the Side seam as necessary during the fitting.

Raglan Sleeve

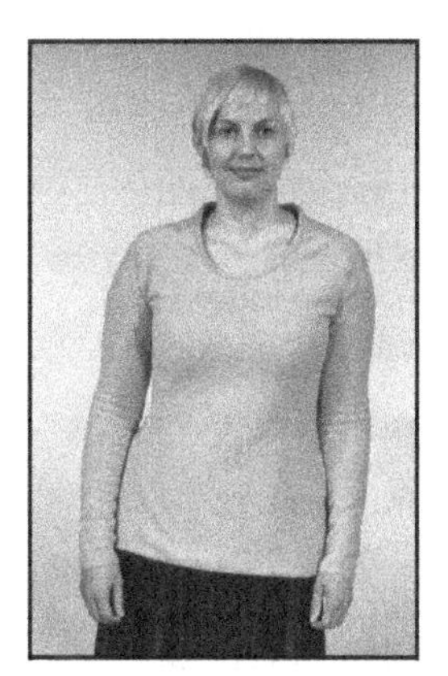

A Raglan Sleeve for woven fabric uses a dart to shape the sleeve over the shoulder, see page 118. When using a knit for a Raglan Sleeve, this dart can be removed.

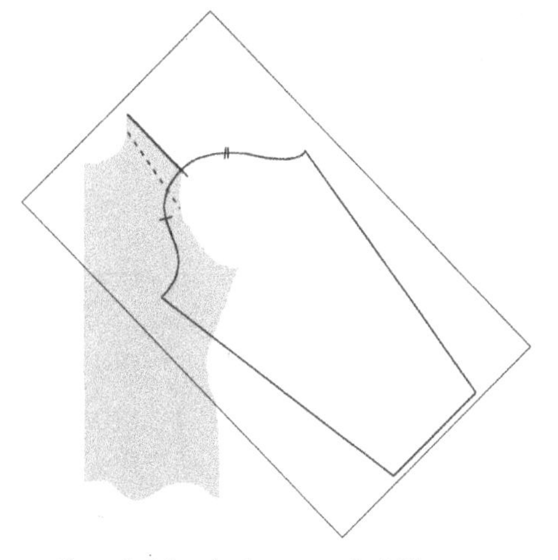

Step 1. Match the extended Sleeve Centerline to the Front Bodice Sloper shoulder seam, then trace the Raglan Seam design line onto the sleeve pattern.

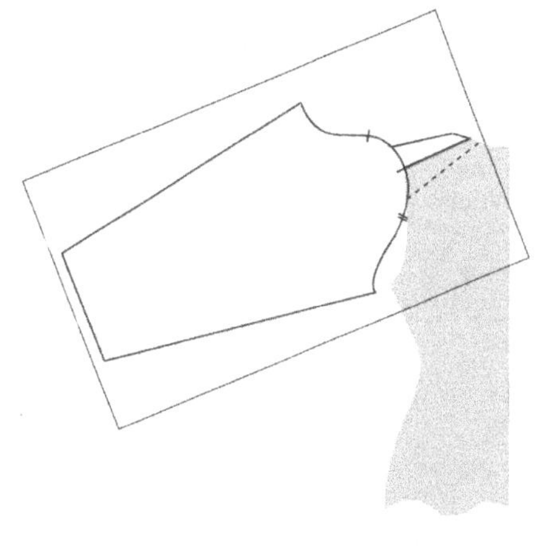

Step 2. Match the extended Sleeve Centerline to the Back Bodice Sloper shoulder seam, then trace the new Raglan Seam design line onto the sleeve pattern.

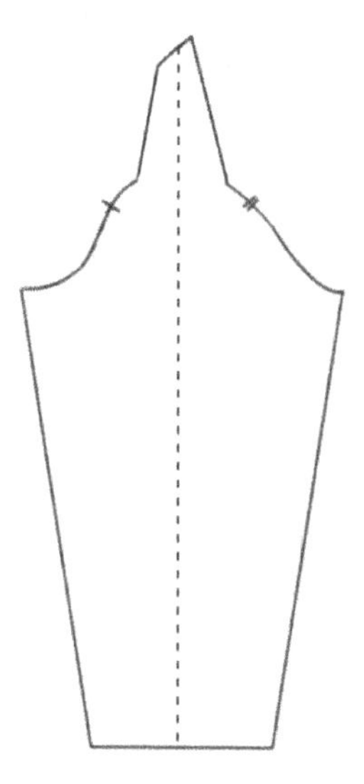

Completed Pattern

Leggings

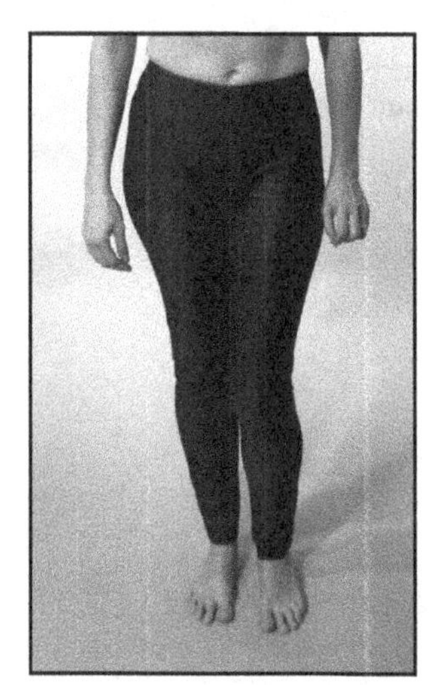

Leggings can be created from the Pants Sloper by removing the darts and the Side Seam. The legs are sewn separately along the Inseam, then sewn together around the Crotch Curve.

When sewing leggings, the direction of maximum stretch should be around the body. The waist is secured with elastic. The leggings may alternatively have elastic or stirrups added to the hem to hold them down. The model in this photo opted not to have any elastic or stirrups.

To create the pattern for leggings as described here, create the patterns for close fit pants described on page 55. The front pattern should be aligned with the back pattern so the distance at the hips from Center Front to Center Back is half the Hip measurement (#13). The front and back Leg Centerlines are parallel. Then draw a vertical line through the hips at the Side Seam from the waist to the hem. This Reference Line will be used to adjust the pattern.

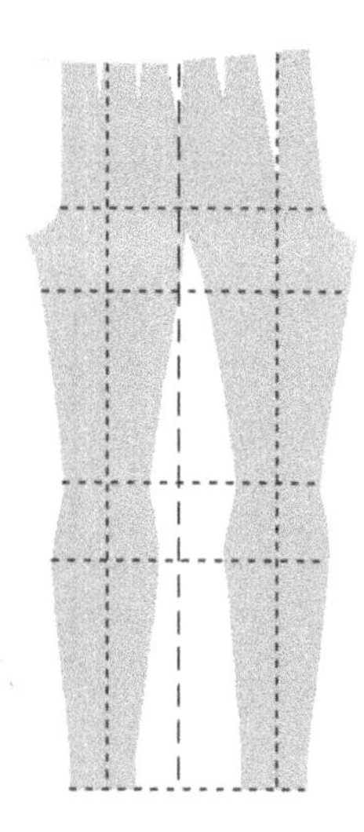

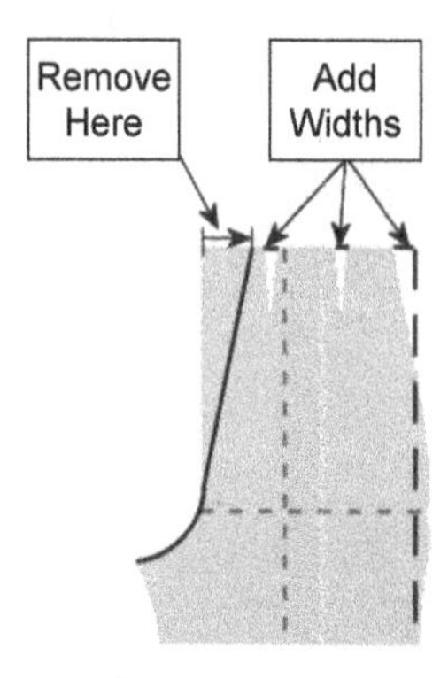

Step 1. Measure the distance between the Side Seam of the Sloper and the vertical Reference Line, then add it to the front dart widths.

Step 2. From Center Front, measure in the distance determined in Step 1 and redraw the Center Front to this position.

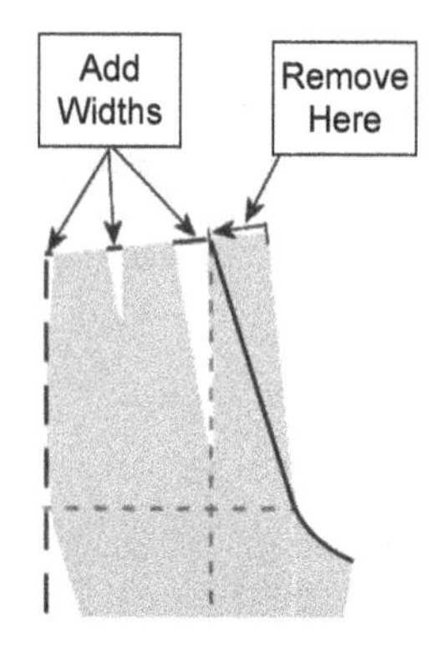

Step 3. Measure the distance between the Side Seam of the Sloper and the vertical Reference Line, then add it to the back dart widths.

Step 4. From Center Back, measure in the distance determined in Step 3 and redraw the Center Back to this position.

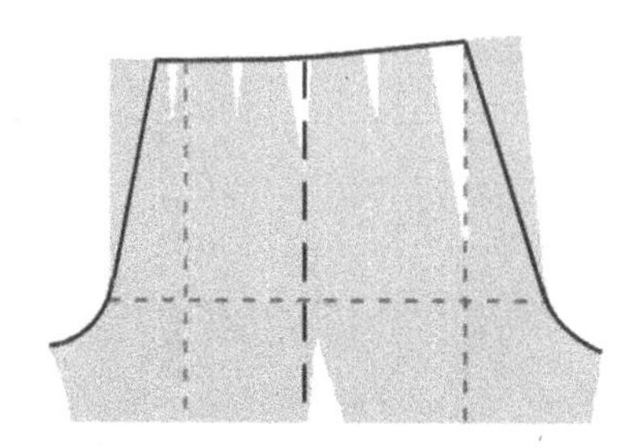

Step 5. Redraw the Waist.

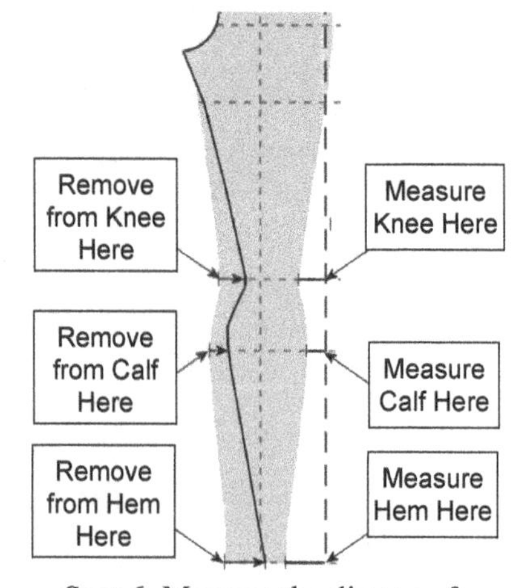

Step 6. Measure the distance from the Reference Line to the front Sloper at the Knee, Calf, and Hem, then remove these distances from the Inseam.

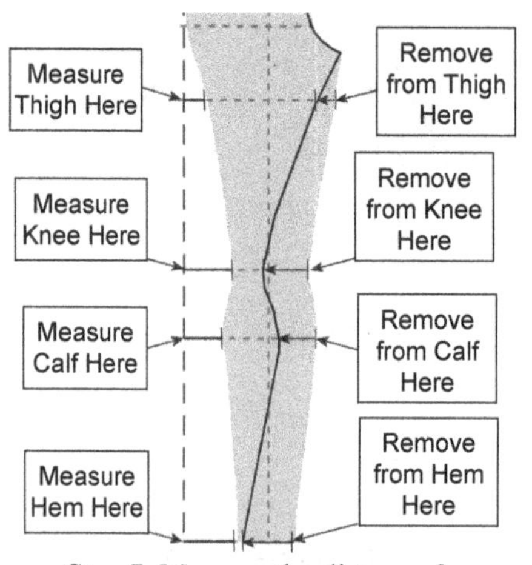

Step 7. Measure the distance from the Reference Line to the back Sloper at the Thigh, Knee, Calf, and Hem, then remove these distances from the Inseam.

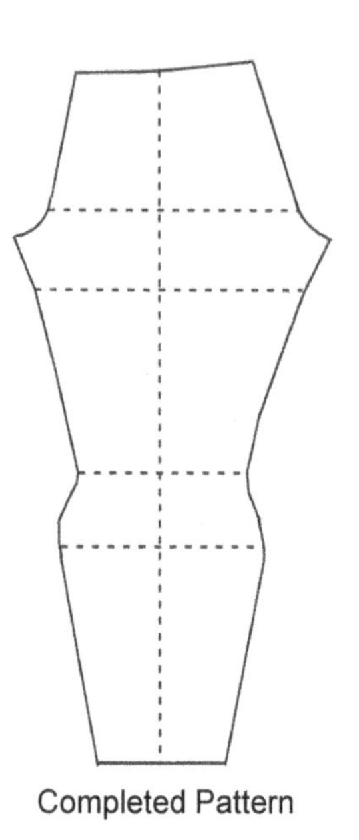

Completed Pattern

Jackets and Coats

Jackets and coats are traditionally the most carefully crafted garments in both styling and construction techniques. The patterns for these designs follow a few simple principles. Once these principles are understood, many different variations can be created.

Jackets, as described here, are garments which are worn over lightweight clothes such as shirts and blouses. Coats, on the other hand, are designed to be worn over jackets and bulkier clothes like sweaters.

Men's suit jackets have a traditional styling which is described in detail in this section. Women's coats and jackets, on the other hand, may be styled in many different ways. The same specifications described here for men may be applied to women's garments.

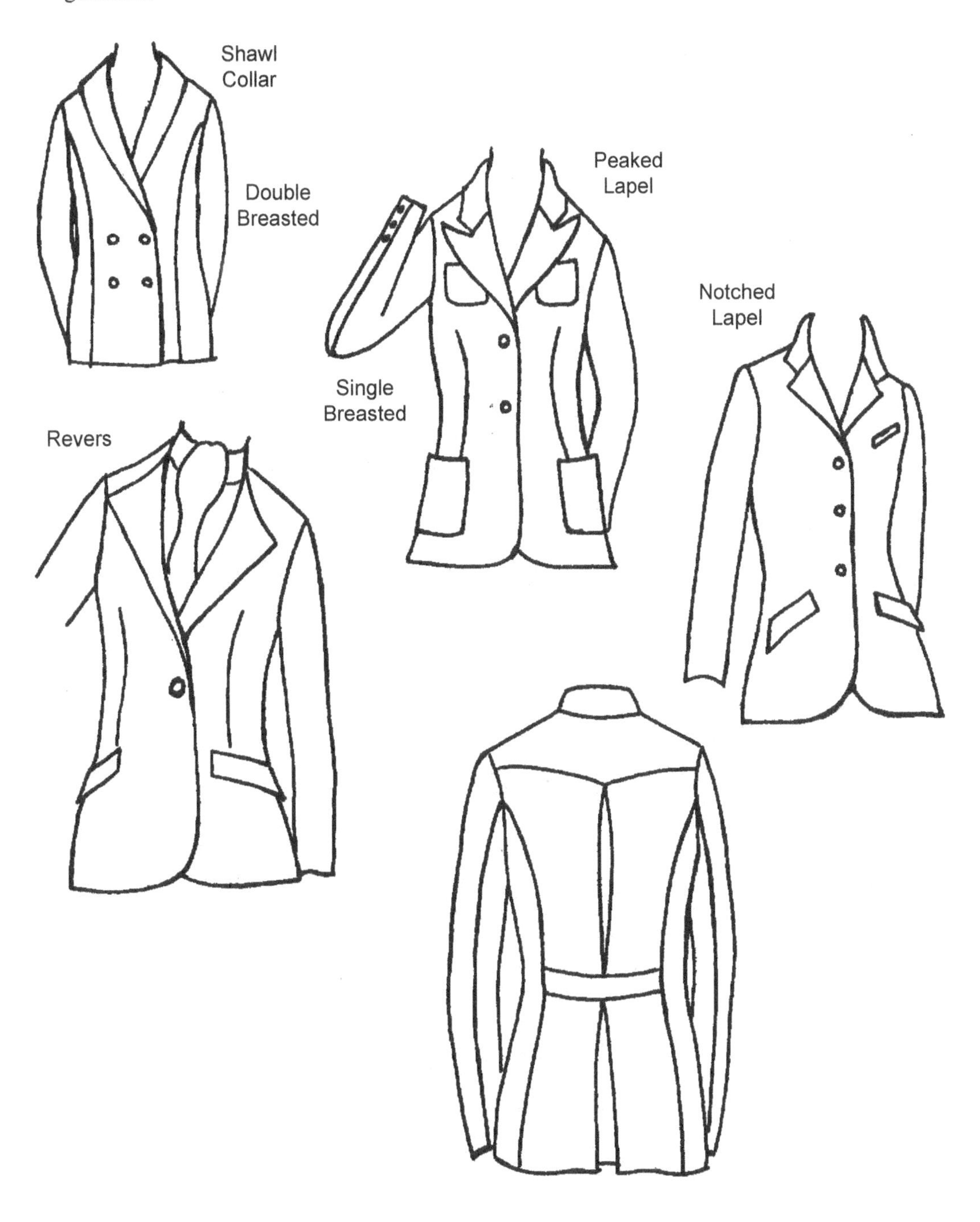

Expanding the Slopers

The fact that jackets and coats are worn over other garments makes it necessary to first increase the size of the Slopers. The seam and dart placements for the particular design may then be established on these enlarged patterns.

The Shoulder Seam must be raised. The Armhole Curve must be made larger. And the Side Seam must be moved out. The dimensions for increasing the Slopers are shown below. Expand the front and the back patterns by the same amount.

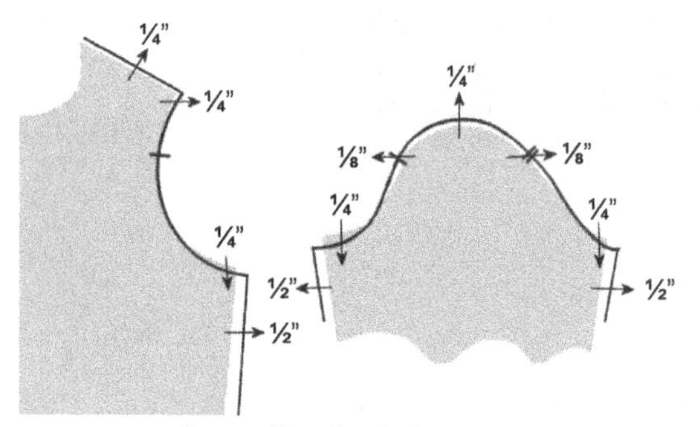

Expanding for Jackets

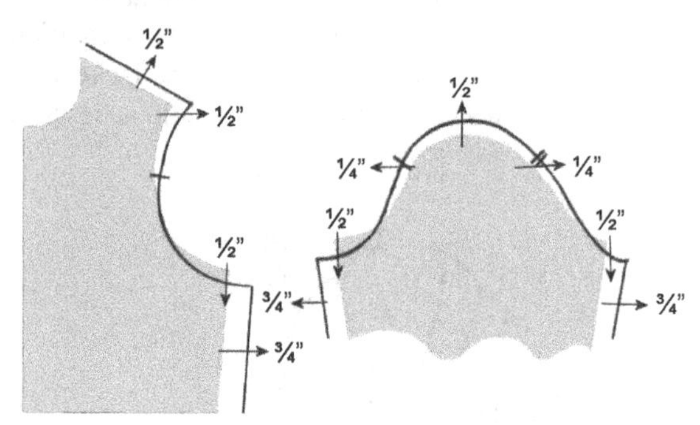

Expanding for Coats

Creating the Body of the Jacket

Suit jackets are designed to hang down far enough to cover the torso portion of pants. Only the leg portion of the pants can be seen below the jacket. The Side Seam on men's suit jackets is normally shifted to a side back location.

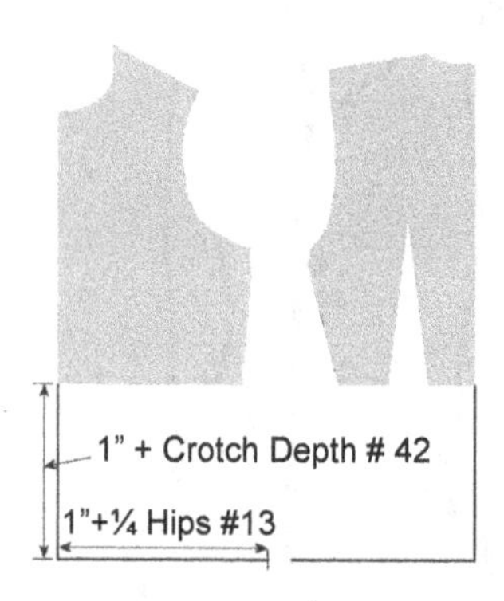

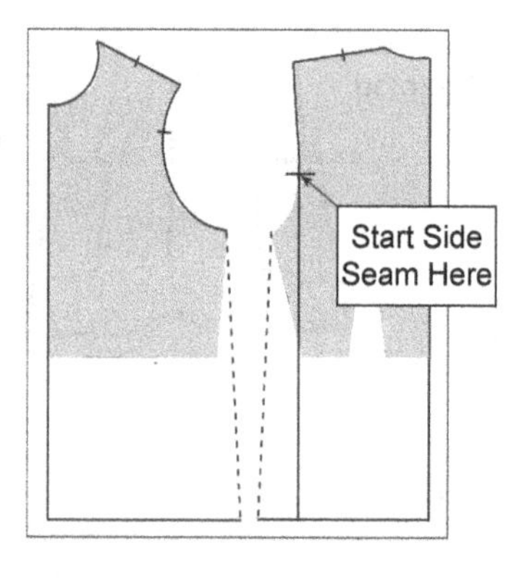

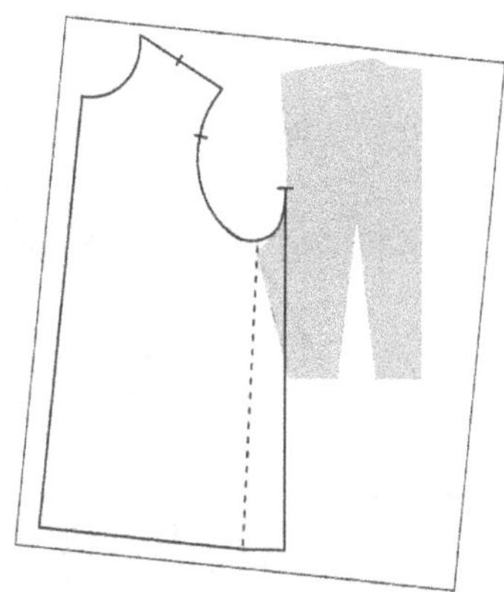

Step 1. On the front Sloper, extend the Center Front line down below the Waist line. On this line, mark off 1" (2.5 cm) plus the Crotch Depth measurement (#42). From this point, draw a line at right angles to the Center Front. This is the Hem line.

Step 2. On the back Sloper, extend the Center Back line down to 1" (2.5 cm) plus the Crotch Depth measurement below the Waist line. From this point, draw in the back Hem line.

Step 3. Add 1" (2.5 cm) to one-fourth the Hip measurement (#13). Measuring out from Center Back, mark this length on the back Hem line. Measuring out from Center Front, mark this same length on the front Hem line.

Step 4. On the front pattern draw a dotted line from the Armhole Curve to the mark on the Hem from Step 3. This is a temporary Side Seam. Draw another temporary Side Seam on the back.

Step 5. Find the point of the back Armhole Curve that is closest to the Center Back line. From here, draw the new Side Seam down and parallel to the Center Back.

Step 6. Place a piece of pattern paper over the Sloper and trace the back pattern to the new Side Seam.

Step 7. Trace the front pattern to the temporary Side Seam. Indicate this line with dashes.

Step 8. Shift the pattern paper so that the temporary Side Seam of the traced front pattern coincides with the temporary Side Seam on the back pattern. Trace the back pattern to the new Side Seam line.

Styling Variations

The shaping of the suit jacket is achieved by curving the Center Back seam and the Side Seam, then adding a dart to the front pattern. The dart is located at the old Side Seam location. The shaping of the seams and dart should be done in a fitting.

A vent may be added either to the Center Back seam or to the new Side Seams. One side of the vent is a facing and the other side is an extension behind the facing. This construction is similar to the plackets described on page 137. The dimensions of this vent should be about 2" (5 cm) wide and 9" (23 cm) long.

The button location of suit jackets is an important part of the garment's styling. It will directly affect the shaping of the lapel.

Three button, single breasted - The middle button is at the waist, the top is 4" (10 cm) above and the bottom is 4" (10 cm) below the waist.

Two button, single breasted - The top button may be 1" or 2" (2.5 or 5 cm) above the waist. The bottom button is 4" (10 cm) below the top button.

Double breasted - The middle buttons are 1" (2.5 cm) above the waist and 2" (5 cm) to either side of Center Front. The bottom buttons are 4" (10 cm) below the middle buttons and 2" (5 cm) to either side of Center Front. The top buttons are 4" (10 cm) above the middle buttons and 3½" (9 cm) to either side of Center Front.

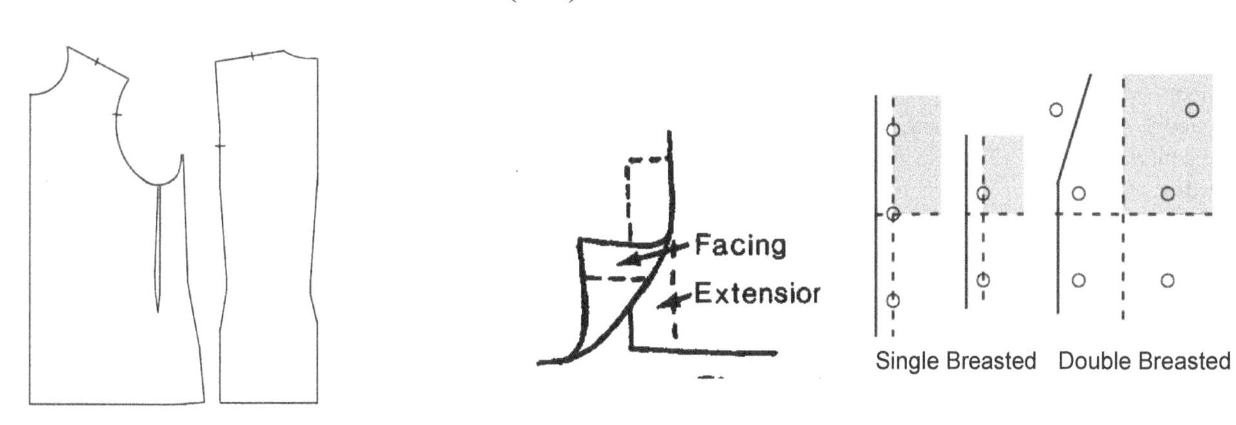

Lapels and Collars

Buttons for men's suit jackets are normally three-quarters of an inch in diameter. The Button Overlap should be this same amount. If buttons larger than this are used, the Button Overlap should equal the diameter of the button.

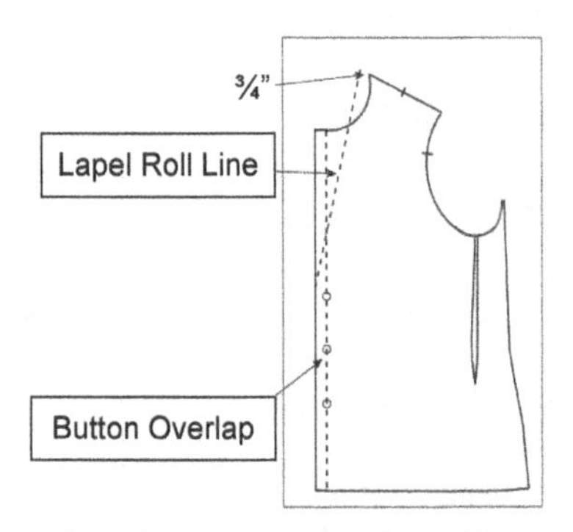

Step 1. Measure out from Center Front the Button Overlap distance and draw a line parallel to the Center Front line.

Step 2. Add the desired button locations.

Step 3. At the Shoulder Seam, make a mark that is ¾" (2 cm) in towards the neck.

Step 4. Make a second mark on the Button Overlap line that is just above the top button.

Step 5. Connect these two marks to form the Lapel Roll line.

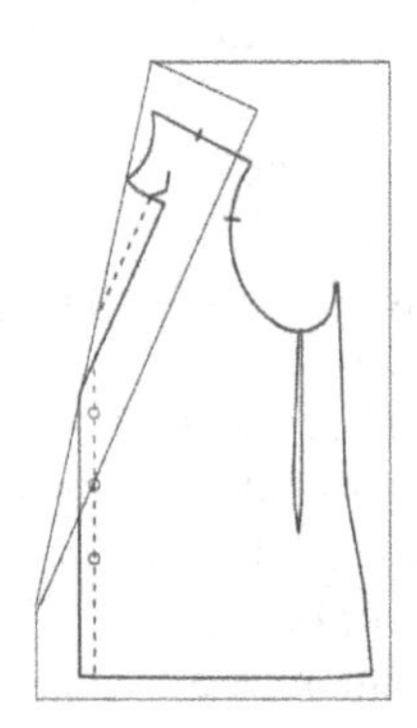

Step 6. Fold the pattern on the Lapel Roll line and draw in the desired shape of the lapel.

A good reference point for the top of the lapel is the point where the Center Front intersects with the Neck Seam. The peak of peaked lapels may start from this point and the notch of notched lapels may be drawn from here.

Step 7. Indicate the front of the collar's shape as it relates to the lapel pattern. Unfold the pattern and transfer these lines to the front side of the paper.

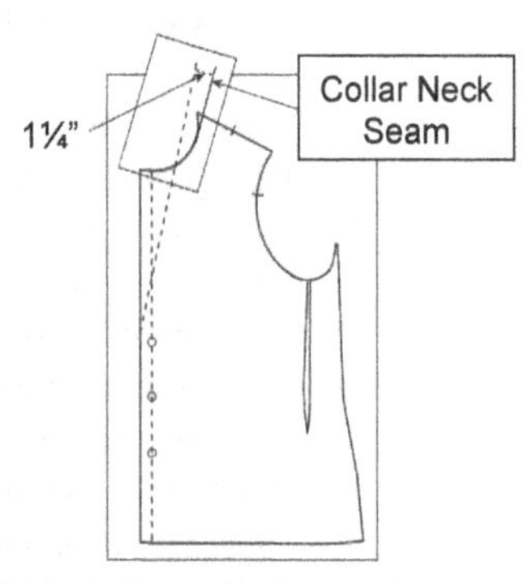

Step 8. Place a piece of pattern paper over the jacket pattern. Trace the Lapel Roll line and extend this line above the Shoulder Seam.

Step 9. Measure out from the Lapel Roll line 1¼" (3 cm) and make a mark. From this mark, draw a line that is parallel to the portion of the Lapel Roll line above the Shoulder Seam. This is the Collar Neck Seam.

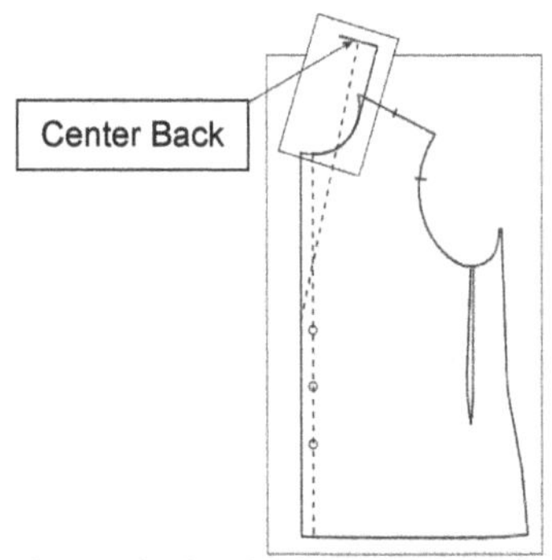

Step 10. On the back jacket pattern, measure the distance around the Neck Seam from Center Back to the Shoulder Seam. Measuring up from the Shoulder Seam, mark this length on the Collar Neck Seam. This mark is the Center Back of the collar.

Step 11. To establish the Center Back line of the collar, draw a line at right angles to the Collar Neck Seam from the Center Back point.

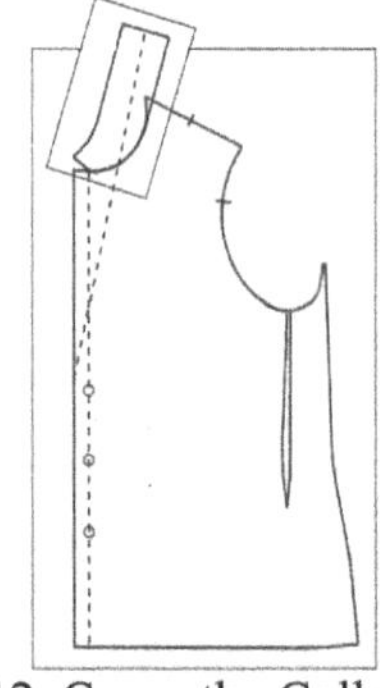

Step 12. Curve the Collar Neck Seam on the front part of the collar from the Shoulder Seam to the point where the Lapel Roll line crosses the front Neck Seam.

Step 13. On the Center Back line, measure up 3" (7.5 cm) from the Collar Neck Seam. Draw a line parallel to the Collar Neck Seam from this point. This is the Collar Top.

Step 14. Draw in the shape desired for the front of the collar.

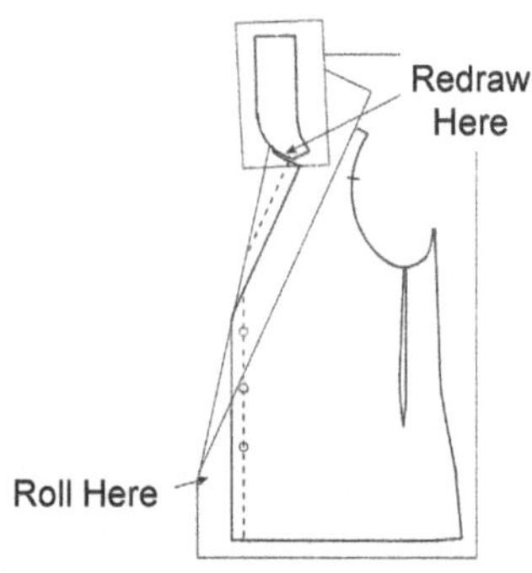

Step 15. To add a roll to the lapel, fold the front pattern on the Lapel Roll line. Matching the Lapel Roll lines, place the completed collar pattern on top of this pattern.

Step 16. Hold the patterns in place and shape a roll in the bottom of the lapel at the top button. This will cause the top of the lapel to pull slightly away from the collar pattern. Even a difference of 1/16" (15 mm) will change the way the lapel lays on the body.

Step 17. Redraw the front of the collar to the lowered lapel top.

The Two Piece Sleeve

The sleeve on men's suits is conventionally shaped with a seam at the back of the arm and another seam approximately 1½" (4 cm) forward of the normal underarm seam position. The sleeve patterns are curved from the elbow to compensate for the angle of the arm as it hangs at the side of the body.

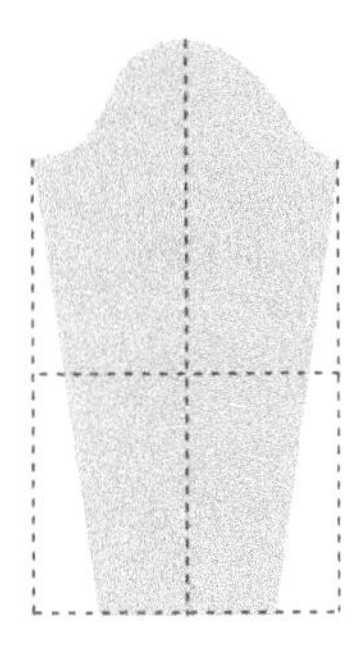

Step 1. On the Sleeve Sloper, redraw the Underarm Seams so they are parallel to the Sleeve Centerline.

Step 2. Measure down the Sleeve Centerline the Shoulder to Elbow length (#34) and draw a line at right angles to the Sleeve Centerline. This is the Elbow line.

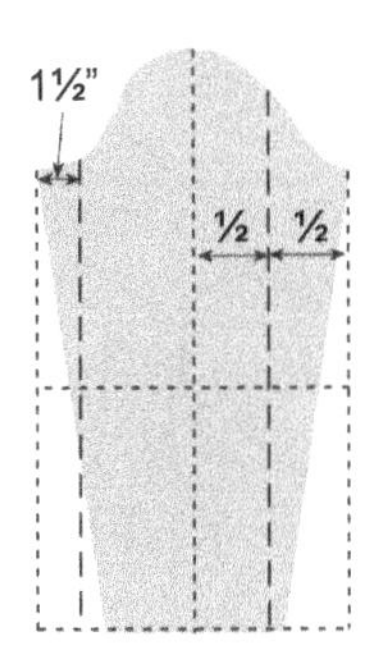

Step 3. Find a point on the Biceps line that is halfway between the Sleeve Centerline and the back Arm Seam of the sleeve. Draw a line of dashes from this point that is parallel to the Sleeve Centerline. This will be the new Back Arm Seam.

Step 4. Mark a point 1½" (4 cm) in from the front Arm Seam. Draw a line of dashes from this point that is parallel to the Sleeve Centerline. This is the new Front Arm Seam.

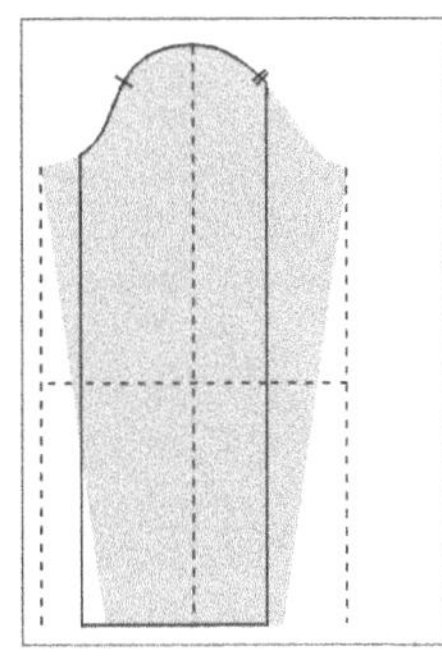

Step 5. Lay a piece of pattern paper over the Sleeve Sloper and trace from the new Back Arm Seam to the new Front Arm Seam. This is the Outside Sleeve pattern.

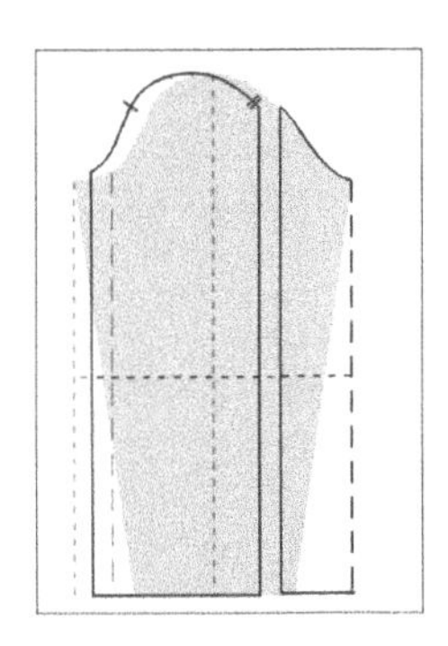

Step 6. Shift the paper to the left to allow for seam allowances and trace from the Back Arm Seam to the right Underarm Seam.

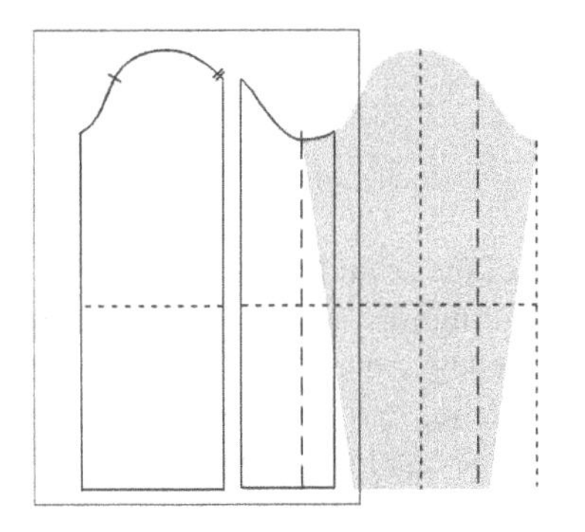

Step 7. Shift the pattern paper so that the traced Underarm Seam from the right side of the Sloper coincides with the left Underarm Seam. Trace to the new Front Arm Seam. This is the Inside Sleeve pattern.

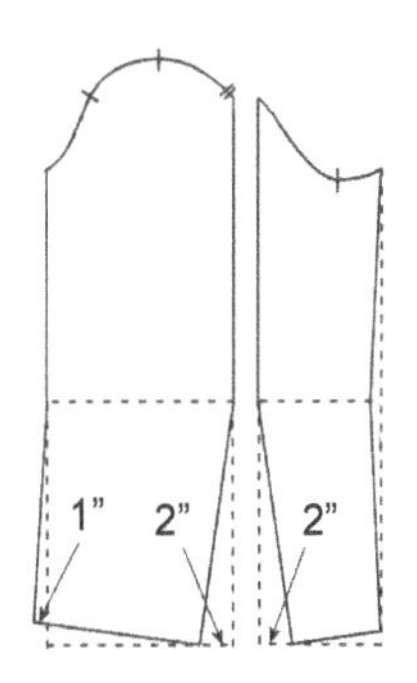

Step 8. Curve the Back Arm Seams of both patterns from the Elbow line to a point 2" (5 cm) in on the Wrist line. Draw new Wrist lines at right angles to the angled Back Arm Seams.

Step 9. Curve the Front Arm Seam of the Inside Sleeve pattern slightly as illustrated. Curve the Front Arm Seam of the Outside Sleeve Pattern from the Elbow line to 1" (2.5 cm) out on the new Wrist line.

Step 10. Measure the length of the Front Arm Seam on the Inside Sleeve pattern and adjust the Front Arm Seam of the Outside Sleeve pattern to the same length.

Fitting the Man's Suit

The Suit Jacket, with the exceptions below, can be fitted by following the same procedures that have been previously described.

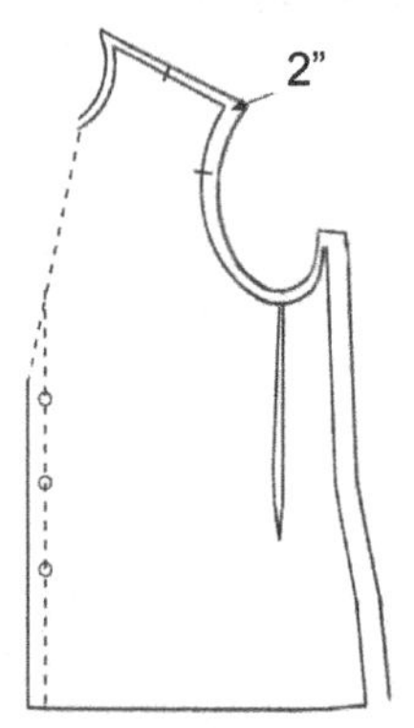

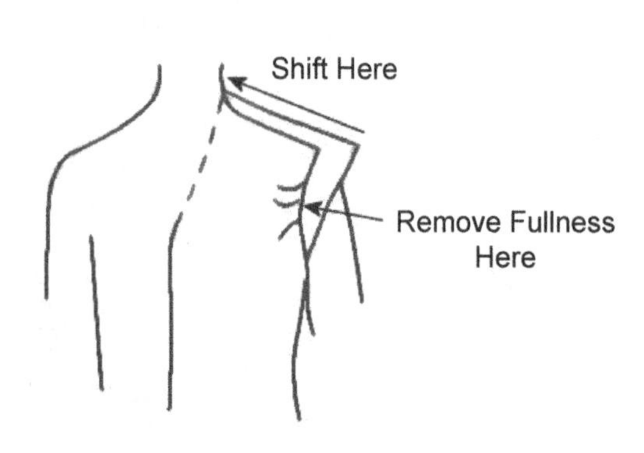

Step 1. Cut out a piece of fabric that is the shape of the front pattern up to the Lapel Roll line. Do not include the shape of the lapel. Add 2" (5 cm) of seam allowance to the top of the Armhole Curve.

Step 2. Place the fabric on the body in the normal manner at the Shoulder Seam.

Step 3. To remove any fullness in the fabric around the Armhole area, shift the Shoulder Seam in toward the Center Front of the body. Correct the Armhole Curve and the Lapel Roll line to this new location. Remember, the Lapel Roll line should be ¾" (2 cm) up the neck.

Step 4. Place the fabric on top of the original pattern aligning the new Lapel Roll line on the fabric to the Lapel Roll line of the pattern.

Step 5. Lay a piece of pattern paper on top of this and trace the fabric for the body and the original pattern for the lapel. This is the pattern for a second fitting.

Facings

Facings are a duplication of the seam lines that are to be faced. They should be taken from the patterns after all the fittings are completed. A facing pattern can be modified slightly by reducing the outside edge, making it ⅛" (3 mm) smaller than the body of the garment. This causes the stitches to roll just to the inside of the garment. Keep in mind that the facing portion of the lapel is the exposed fabric so the seam line must be extended, rather than reduced, by ⅛" (3 mm).

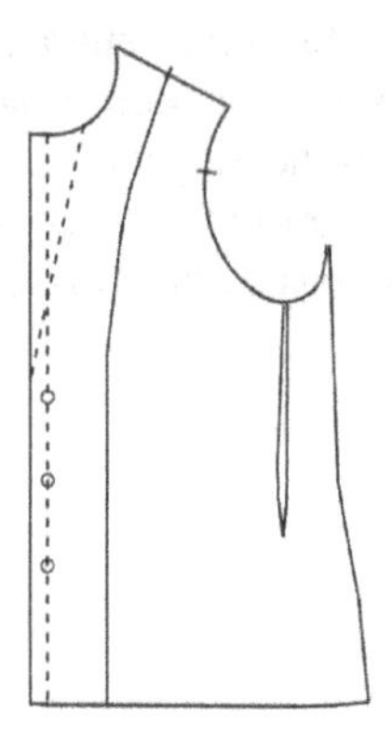

Facing Pattern

Fabric

There are a large variety of fabrics available for clothing construction. Each fabric has specific qualities which establish its character. Some of these qualities, such as color and texture, affect the appearance of the garment but not the fit. Other qualities, such as drape, flexibility, and weight must be taken into consideration during the drafting process. If these qualities are ignored, they can mar the effectiveness of the finished garment.

Understanding the drape, flexibility, and weight of a material is primarily a matter of developing a sensitive touch. There are too many different types of material and too many end uses for each type to make any kind of specific measurement a practical consideration. The material must be aesthetically judged rather than scientifically measured.

The pattern drafter must learn how to respond to each new piece of material as though it had a personality of its own. Two different materials will respond differently to the same pattern and the pattern drafter must learn how to design patterns accordingly. Time and experience are the best way to learn how to handle fabrics, but it helps to know what qualities to look for.

Drape

Drape is the ability of a fabric to fall into even and graceful folds when it is left free to hang. Any design which requires part of a garment to hang from gathered seams should be made from material that drapes well.

A basic procedure for determining how well a fabric will drape is to pick up a corner and let the material hang on the bias. Check to see how easily the material falls into folds. Are the folds deep and do they pick up light to accent the drape? Notice any tendency toward stiffness.

Normally, a fabric's ability to drape may be determined by letting it hang on the bias. However, some materials will drape well on the bias but poorly when hung on the straight of the grain. To check for this quality, gather the top of the material into large pleats or gathers and note whether the material tends to fight the gathers or falls into graceful folds.

Generally speaking, tightly woven fabrics or fabrics using tightly spun yarns will not drape as well as fabrics that are either loosely woven or loosely spun or both. Knits tend to drape well because of the looseness of their construction.

Consideration should also be given to cutting patterns on the bias of the fabric for collars, ruffles, and sleeves that are to have a soft look. In the 1930's whole dresses would be cut on the bias to obtain a softly draped look.

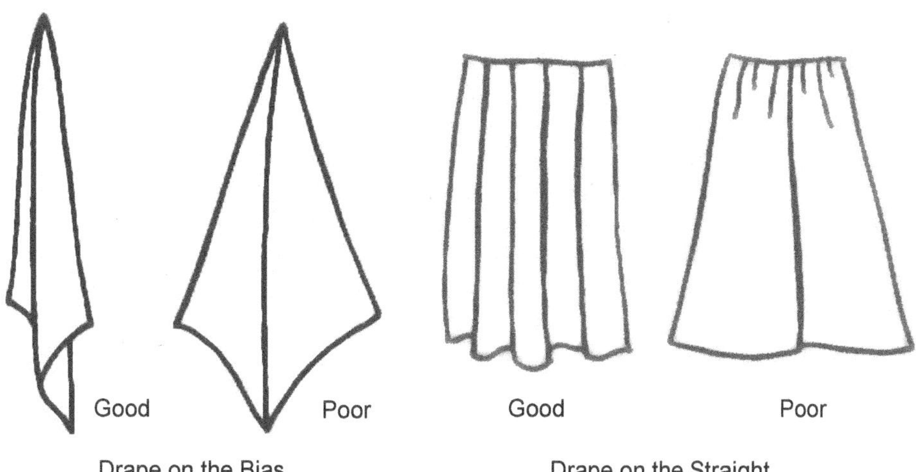

Flexibility

Examining a fabric's flexibility is another means of checking its ability to drape. Flexibility, as the term is used in this book, refers to the ability of a material to fold softly into a swag. Fabric with good flexibility will swag in smooth curves. Fabric with poor flexibility will tend to crack and be uneven when it is swagged. This quality of fabric must be evaluated for garments such as the cowl neckline, see page 147. Good flexibility is also important when a design calls for the material to end in gathers such as in the cuff of a sleeve.

The flexibility of a fabric may be determined by holding the material on the true bias at two points about eighteen inches apart. Move the hands together and notice whether the material drops into graceful curves or whether it tends to buckle and crack.

Some materials will drape fairly well but will not have good flexibility. Other materials will both drape well and have good flexibility. Still others will drape poorly and have good flexibility.

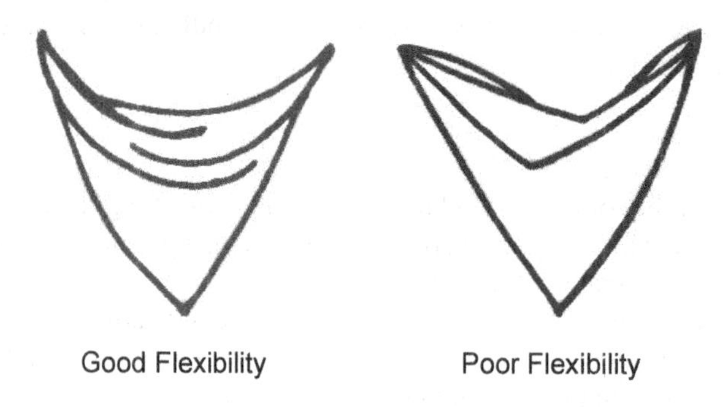

Good Flexibility   Poor Flexibility

Elasticity

Elasticity is the ability of a fabric to stretch. It is not an important quality for most woven goods but it is very important for moderate stretch knits.

To check the elasticity of a fabric, hold it at two points approximately eighteen inches apart and stretch it. This check should be done with the horizontal threads, the vertical threads, and across the bias of the fabric.

Most woven fabrics will not stretch at all on the vertical threads. These are the threads that pull the fabric through the loom. They may stretch slightly on the horizontal filling threads. They will stretch considerably on the bias. The stretch in knits varies according to manufacturing specifics.

Body and Weight

The body of a fabric is its mass or substance. The weight of a fabric is its actual weight in ounces per square yard. Normally the two are related, but some fabrics have more body than their weight would indicate. A thick pellon, for instance, does not weigh that much more than a thin pellon.

The amount of body in a fabric selected for a garment depends on its intended use. Shirts and blouses, for instance, should be lightweight; too much body would be inappropriate for such garments. Pants and skirts, on the other hand, must have more body in order to hang and fit properly. Heavy outer garments, such as coats, should have the most body.

Appendix

The Dress Form

Slopers show the exact shape of the body so these patterns can be cut out of stiff paper and put together to create a duplicate of the wearer's figure for use as a custom dress form.

For women, the dress form should be modified to show bust contours using a bra or the bra Sloper described in my e-Book *How to Make Custom-Fit Bras*.

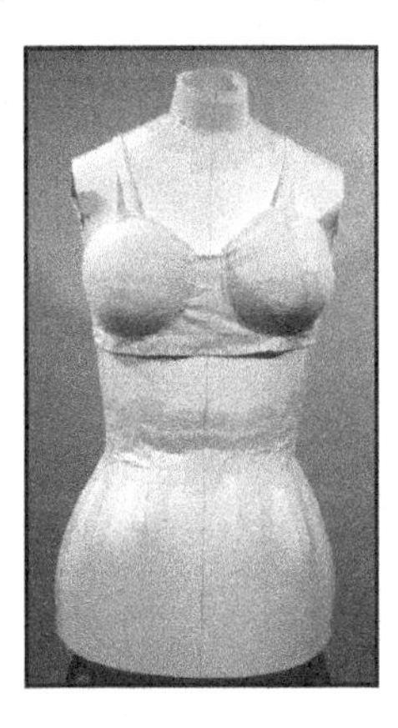

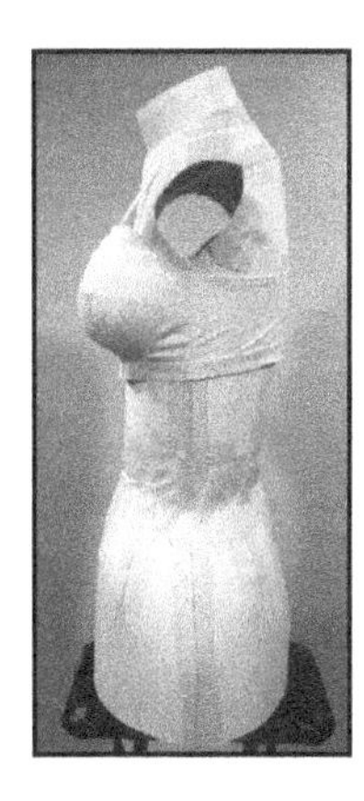

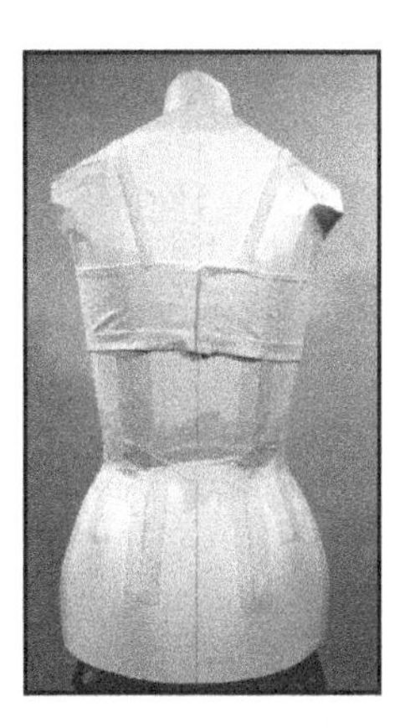

Scale Rulers

When creating Slopers, you are working from circumference measurements for the full body. But Slopers only need to be for half the front and half the back. Measurements are therefore divided by four. A scale ruler eliminates the need for you to do the math, saving time and eliminating potential errors.

Scale rulers can also be used to adjust the fitted patterns and when designing original patterns, such as the circular skirt described on page 149.

You can use the scale rulers either by copying them and cutting them out as strips of paper or make them with a stiffener board that makes a more durable ruler, see the instructions on page 169.

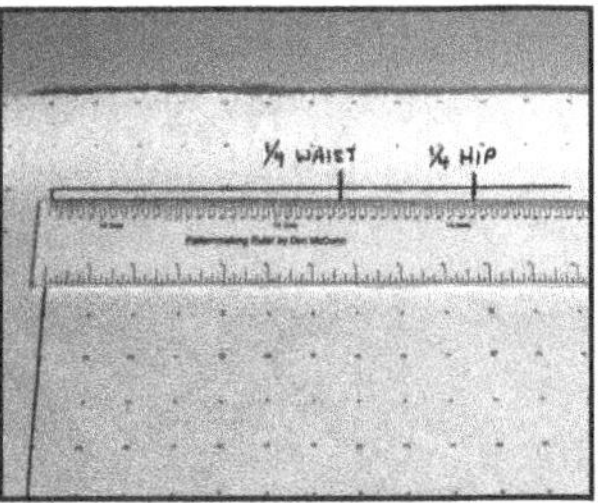

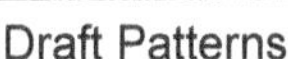

Draft Patterns

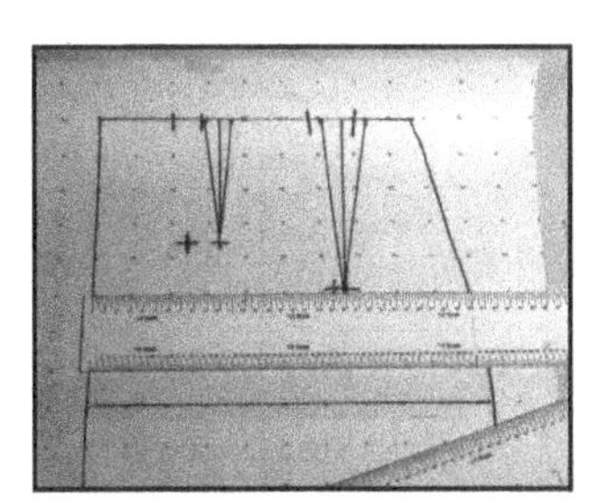

Adjust Patterns

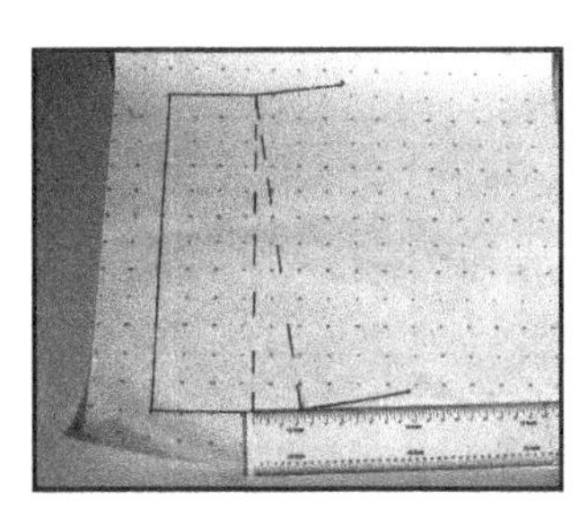

Design Patterns

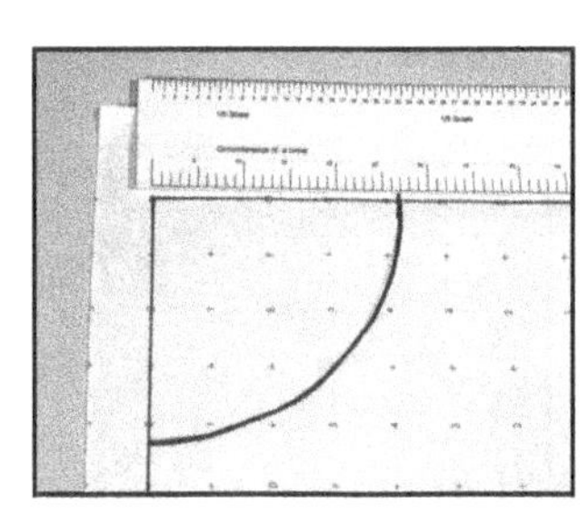

Draft Circles

Working in Quarter Scale

To evaluate the qualities of different fabrics, use the pattern below to cut circular skirts that can be slipped over a bottle, such as a wine bottle.

Working in quarter scale allows you to practice patternmaking and design techniques in the fastest, most economical manner. It is also a good way for beginning sewers to develop their garment making abilities.

One option is to work with quarter scale fashion dolls. You can use the techniques described in this book to create garments for these small dolls. Or you can scale down full-size patterns to create a Mini-Me Dress Form for developing pattern design techniques and evaluating original design ideas, see page 178.

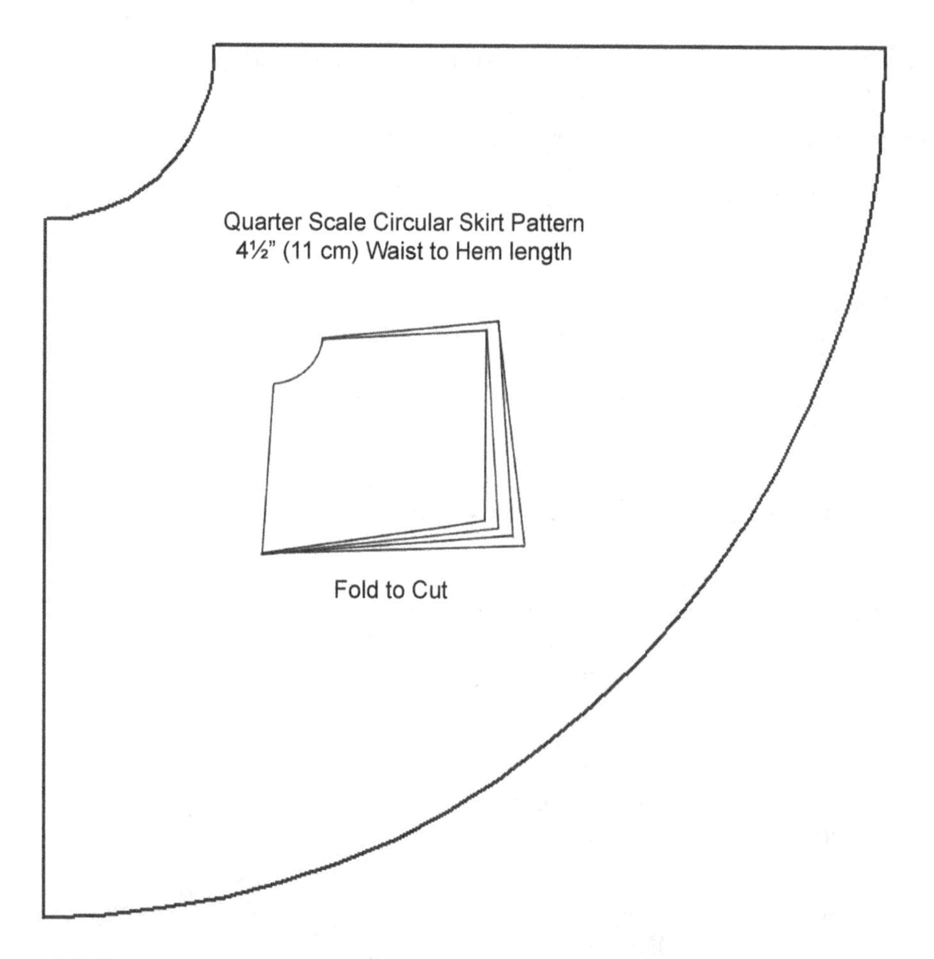

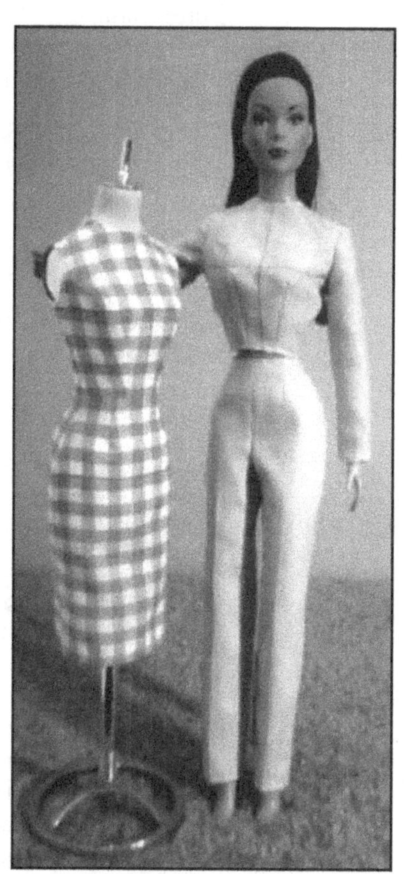

Tyler Fashion Doll

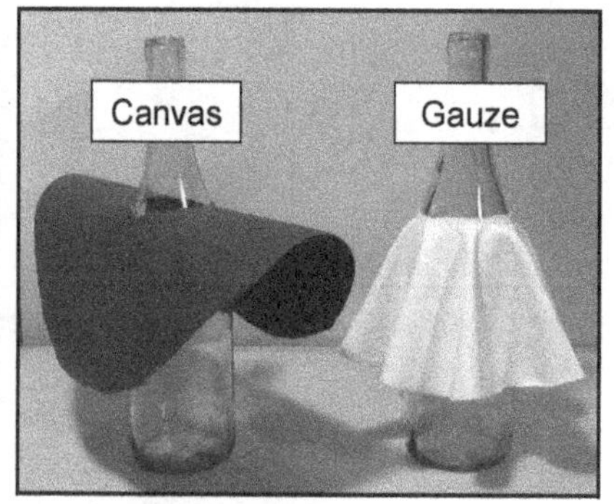

Evaluating Fabric Qualities in Quarter Scale

The Dress Form

The first step in making a dress form is to remove the Ease from the Slopers so that the exact size of the body is established. The patterns for men may then be transferred to the mat board and made into a body form.

For women, an additional step is advisable. The basic patterns do not follow all of the contours of the bust exactly, see page 145. Therefore, the dress form should be made to the size of the rib cage. The shape of the bust can then be duplicated by placing a stuffed bra on the form.

In addition to the Sloper patterns, the shapes of the body's circumference at the waist and hips need to be determined. These shapes are referred to as Cross Sections. They keep the dress form in the elliptical shape of the body.

Once the patterns are established, they can be cut out of mat board and taped together.

Materials and Tools

You will need the following materials and tools to make a dress form.

- Two sheets of 28" by 44" artists' mat board. This is non-corrugated board that is about a sixteenth of an inch thick. It is thin enough to be shaped and heavy enough to keep its shape.
- Lightweight Wire Coat hanger
- Sharp Knife for cutting the mat board
- Table Knife
- 2" (5 cm) Masking Tape
- Cardboard for Cross Sections

The Neck Pattern

For the neck of the Dress Form, use the Mandarin Collar, page 122, adding 2" (5 cm) to the bottom.

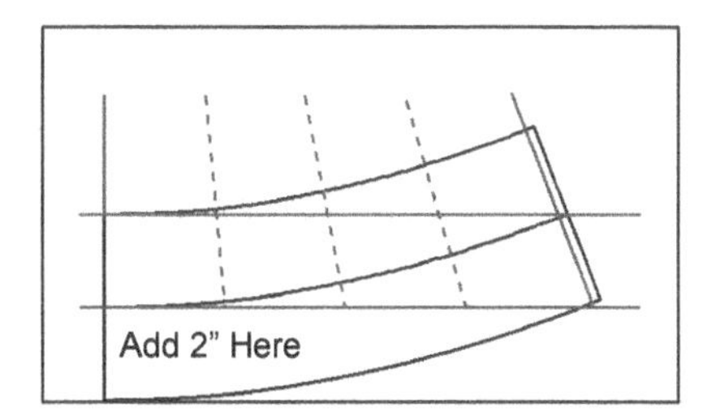

Prepare the Skirt Sloper

When creating the Skirt Sloper, the procedure for making the patterns after the fitting included verifying that there was Ease in the Side Seam, see page 39. This included marking the dimensions of the wearer's body. You can use these measurements to make a copy of the Skirt Sloper that shows the Side Seam without any Ease.

Prepare the Bodice Sloper

For the Bodice Sloper, there are four steps.

1. Remove Ease at the Above the Bust (or Chest) level.
2. Adjust the waist to match the Lower Torso patterns.
3. Adjust the neck curve.
4. For women, adjust the shoulder for the Upper Bust Dart.

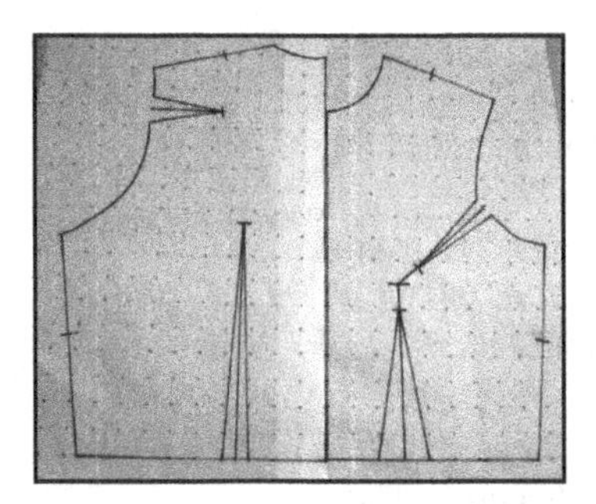

Step 1. Place the Center Front line of the Bodice Sloper along the Center Back line, aligning them at the waist.

Step 2. Tape the patterns together.

Step 3. On a new sheet of pattern paper, trace the Sloper patterns including all the darts.

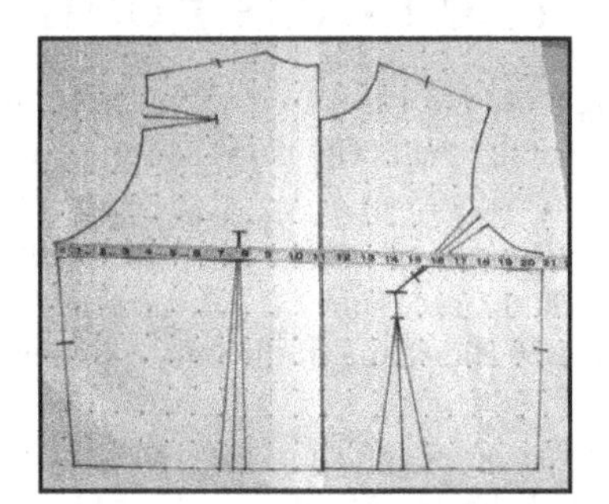

Step 4. At the Above the Bust level, measure from the back Side Seam to the front Side Seam and record in (a) below.

Step 5. Perform the calculations as shown.

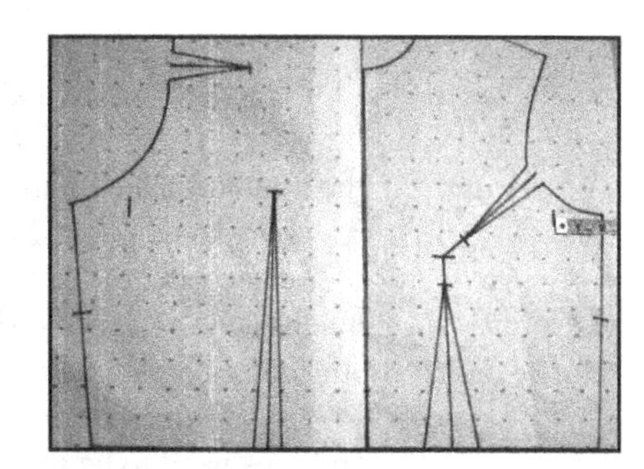

Step 6. Use the amount in (d) below to remove the Ease at the Upper Chest level from the front and back patterns.

	Enter the width of the pattern from Step 4: (a)	
Enter Above Bust measurement #4:	Divide by 2: (b)	
	Subtract (b) from (a): (c)	
	Divide (c) by 2: (d)	

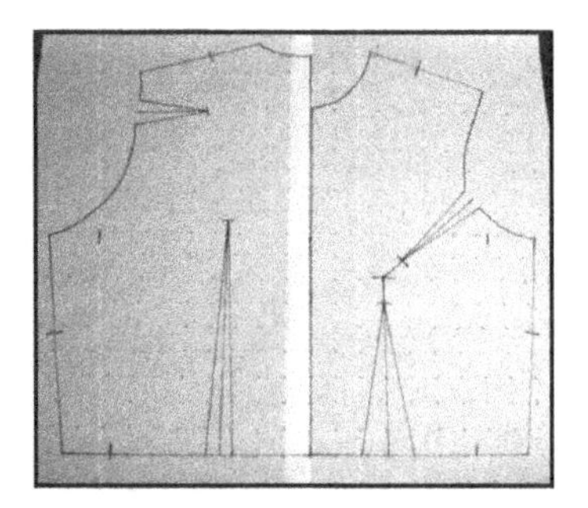

Step 7. Measure the length of the waist on the back pattern of the skirt, skipping over the darts.

Step 8. Apply the measurement to the Bodice back pattern, skipping over the width of the lower back dart.

Step 9. Measure the length of the front pattern of the skirt.

Step 10. Mark off this length on the Bodice front pattern.

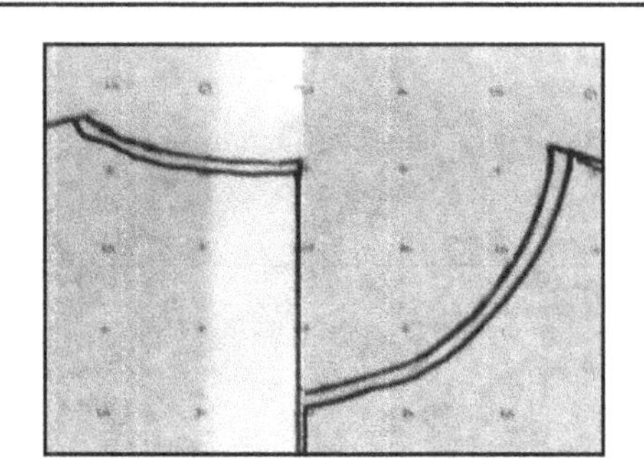

Step 11. Reduce the neck curve until it matches the Neck Circumference measurement (#1) of the body.

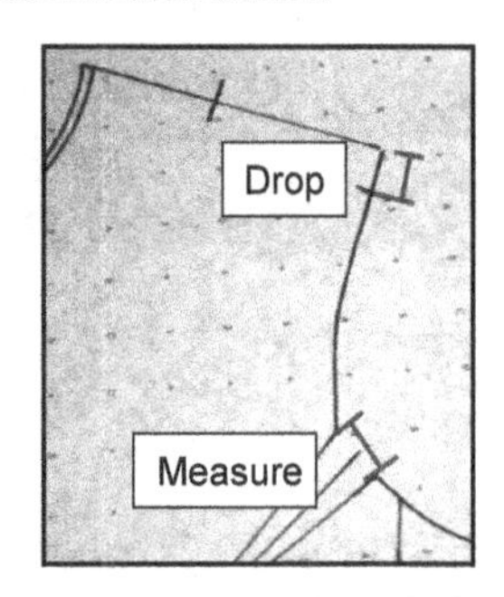

Step 12. Measure the width of the Upper Bust dart, then mark this length by measuring down the armscye from the shoulder seam.

Step 13. Draw in the new Side Seams and front shoulder seam.

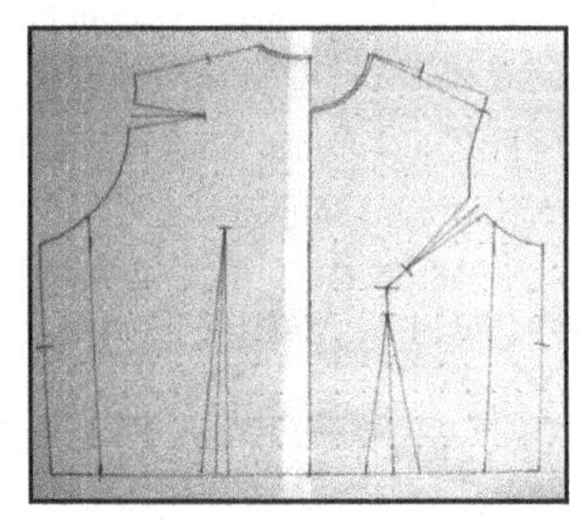

The Completed Pattern

The Waist Cross Section

The Waist Cross Section is used to hold the dress form in an elliptical shape.

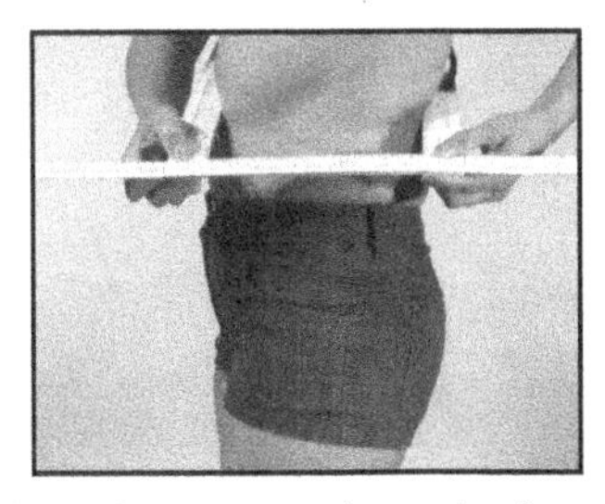

Step 1. Measure the waist from front-to-back and record.

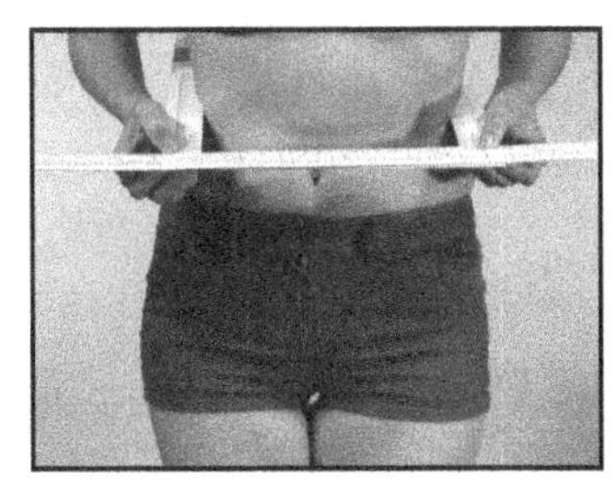

Step 2. Measure the waist from side-to-side, divide the measurement in half, and record.

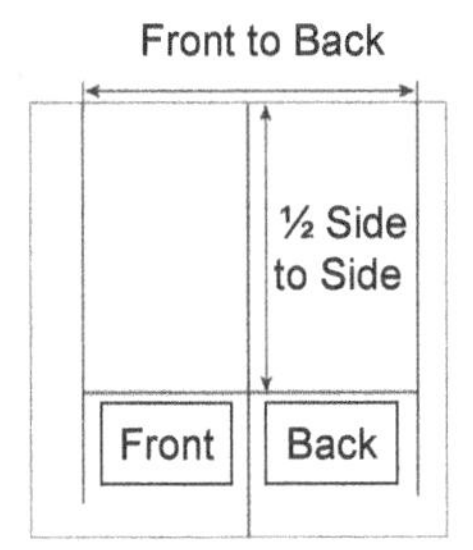

Step 3. On a sheet of pattern paper, mark off the front-to-back length along one edge, then draw lines at these marks that are at right angles to the edge.

Step 4. Use half the side-to-side measurement to draw a line parallel to the front-to-back edge.

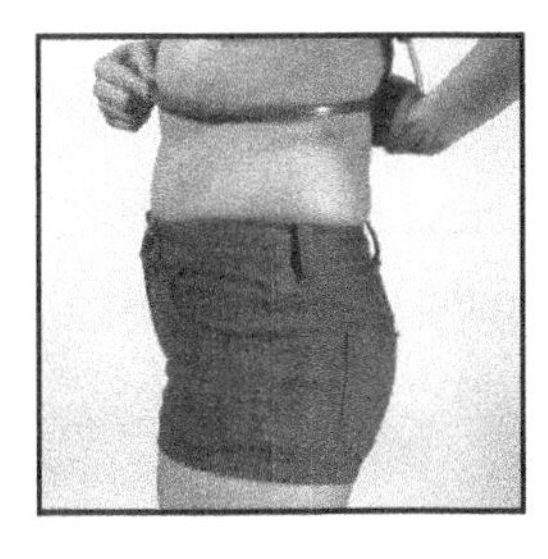

Step 5. To establish the shape of the waist, place a flexible ruler or coat hanger around the waist from Center Front to Center Back.

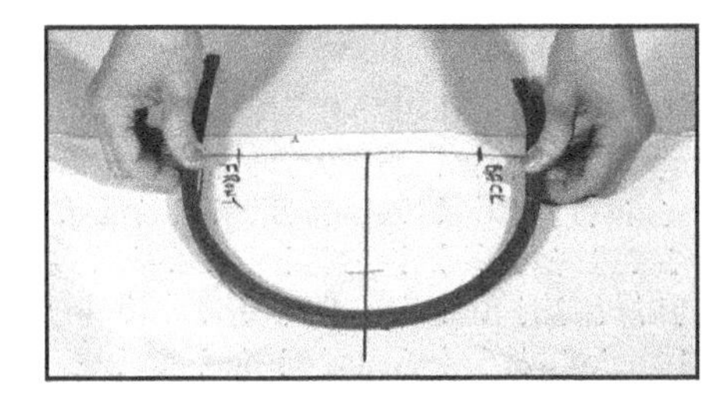

Step 6. Draw that shape on the pattern paper.

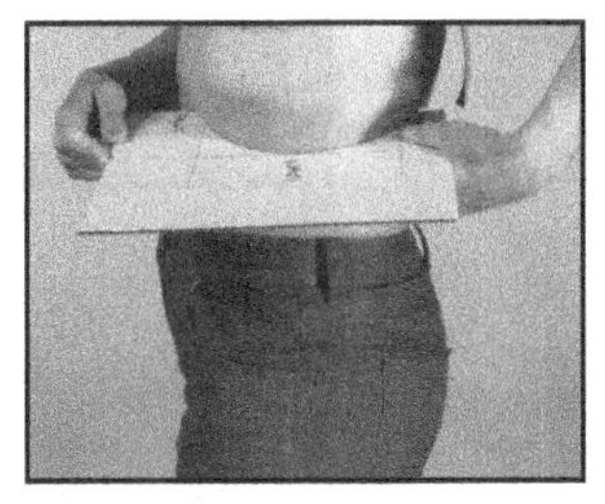

Step 7. Use the pattern to cut a sheet of cardboard using the waist curve shape, then hold it to the body to verify the shape is correct.

Assembling the Dress Form

To create a working Dress Form, transfer the shapes from the patterns to mat board, then tape the mat board sections together.

Tip for Shaping Mat Board: Lightly mist the mat board where you need to bend it, particularly in the shoulder area. After shaping the mat board, dry it before taping the darts or seams.

1. Create the skirt section.
2. Create the bodice section.
3. Add the waist cross section.
4. Complete the Dress Form.

Create the Skirt Section

To create the skirt section, transfer the pattern shapes to mat board. Cut them out. Then tape them together.

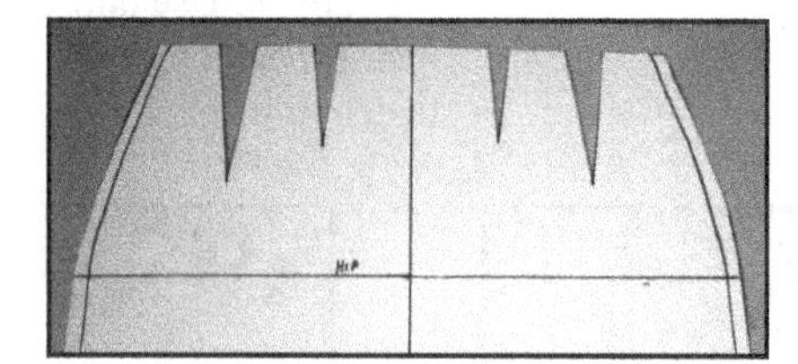

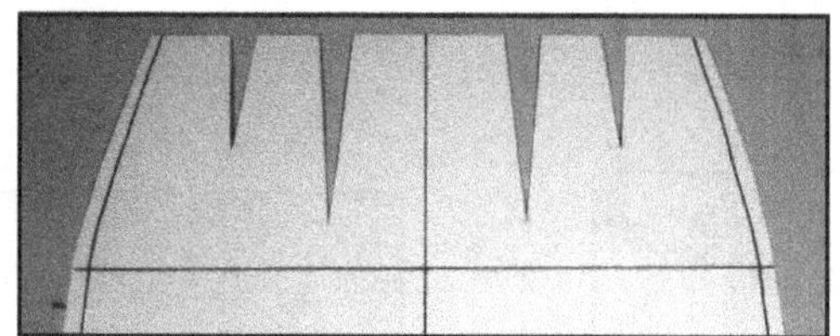

Step 1. Place the front lower torso pattern on the mat board, then draw in the Center Front line and waist line.

Step 2. Mark the position of the hip, then draw in the hip line.

Step 3. Draw in the shape of the Side Seam on one side.

Step 4. Flip the pattern to the other side of the Center Front line, then draw in the other Side Seam.

Step 5. Transfer the darts to the mat board.

Step 6. To transfer the back pattern to the mat board, follow Steps 1 to 5.

Step 7. Cut out the front and back sections of the lower torso, including the dart shapes.

Step 8. To facilitate gradually curved shapes around the body of the form, roll the front and back torso mat boards.

Step 9. Tape the darts closed on both the inside and outside of the form.

Step 10. Rock the dart's points against the table to break them down into a soft curved shape.

Step 11. Tape the Side Seams closed.

Front View

Back View

Create the Bodice Section

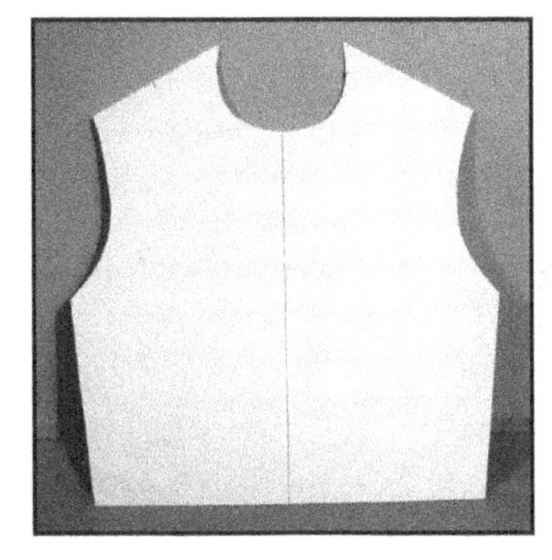

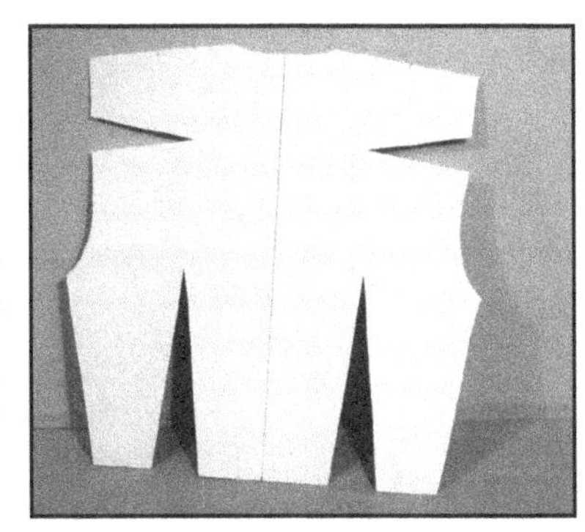

Step 1. Place the front upper torso pattern on the mat board, then draw in the Center Front line and waist line.

Step 2. Draw in the shapes of the neck and arm curves.

Step 3. Mark the locations of each end of the shoulder and Side Seams, then use a straight edge to draw these lines.

Step 4. Flip the pattern to the other side of the Center Front line and draw in the other half of the front upper torso.

Step 5. Follow Steps 1 to 4 to transfer the back pattern to the mat board.

Step 6. Transfer the darts for the back to the mat board.

Step 7. Cut out the mat board.

Step 8. Soften the mat board by rolling the front and back mat boards.

Step 9. Tape the darts closed on both the inside and outside of the form.

Step 10. Rock the dart's points against the table to break them down into a soft curved shape.

Step 11. Tape the Side Seams closed.

Step 12. Tape the shoulder seams closed.

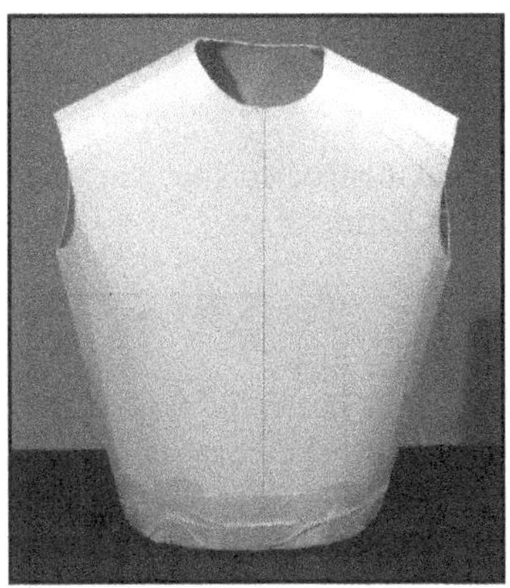

Front View

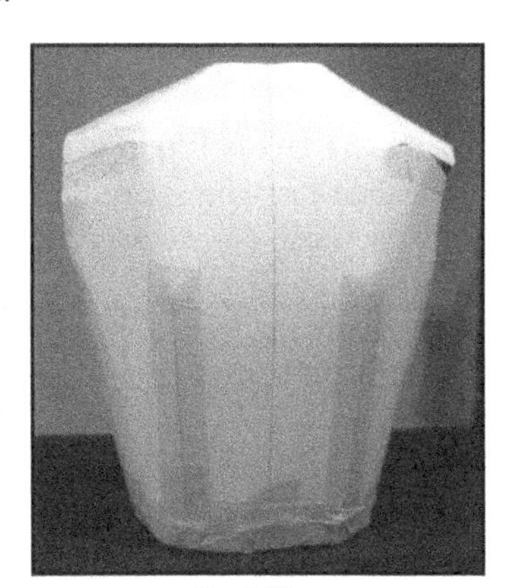

Back View

Add the Waist Cross Section

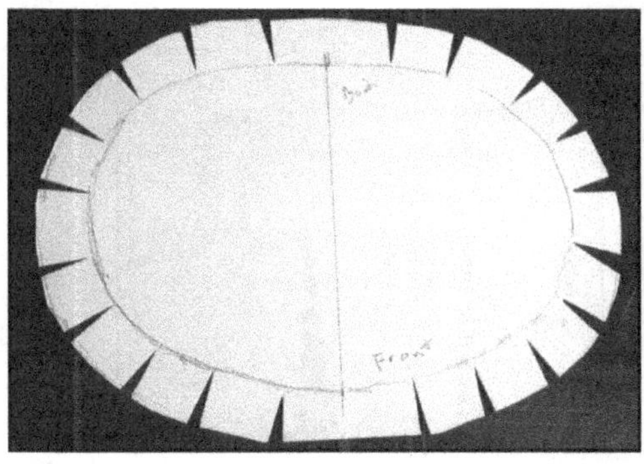

Waist Cross Section

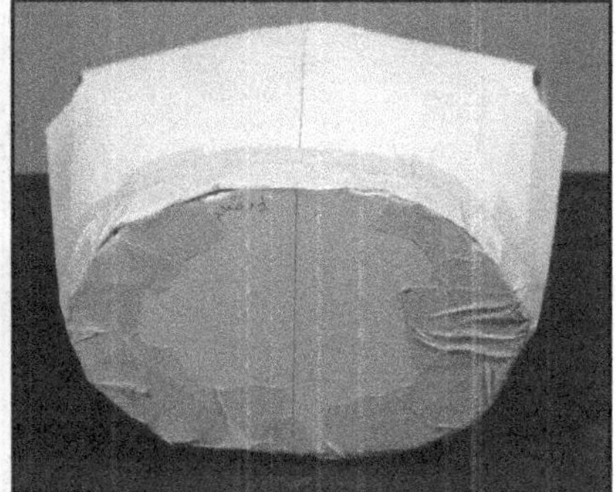

Waist Taped to Bodice

Step 1. Position the Waist Cross Section on the mat board, allowing for a 1" (2.5 cm) flange around the outside of the Cross Section.

Step 2. Draw in a Center Front to Center Back line.

Step 3. Trace the shape of the waist Cross Section.

Step 4. Add a 1" (2.5 cm) flange to the outside of the waist Cross Section.

Step 5. Cut out the mat board.

Step 6. Notch, then bend the 1" (2.5 cm) flange.

Step 7. Align the Center Front of the Waist Cross Section with the Center Front of the Bodice Section, then tape in place.

Step 8. Align the Center Back of the Waist Cross Section with the Center Back of the Bodice Section, then tape in place.

Step 9. Alternate the tabs of the Waist Cross section between the inside and the outside of the Bodice Section, then tape in place. Reach through the neck to tape the tabs on the inside of the form.

Step 10. After all the tabs are taped, run a length of masking tape around the bottom of the upper torso form.

Completing the Dress Form

To complete the Dress Form, tape the neck into the Bodice, then tape the Bodice to the Skirt around the waist. For women, add the Bra Form.

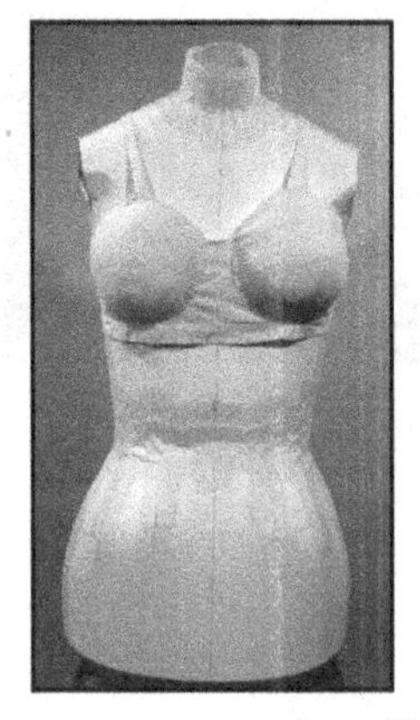

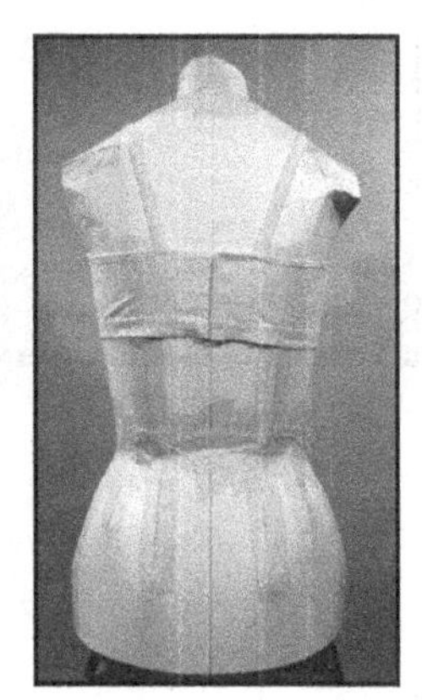

The Completed Dress Form

Scale Rulers

Scale rulers are made by copying the following pages on letter-size label paper (pages 170-173 for inches, 174-177 for centimeters). The top edge of the copied rulers in inches should measure 10". The copied rulers in centimeters should measure 25 cm. Both include the following scales: 1/2, 1/3, 1/4, 1/5, 1/6, 1/8, & the circumference of a circle. They are then made as two separate rulers that can be joined together with a pivot screw. The layout of the rulers is designed so that the most frequently used scales, 1/2, 1/4, and 1/8, are on the outside of the combined rulers. The less frequently used scales are on the inside of the combined rulers.

Materials

Scale rulers can be made from readily available tools and supplies.

- Full sheet permanent adhesive labels (8½" x 11" or A4)
- Clear tape or letter-size laminating sheets from GBC.com
- Pivot screw (optional)
- Two strips of 2" x 22" stiffener board using: mat board or a 2" x 24" c-Thru ruler.

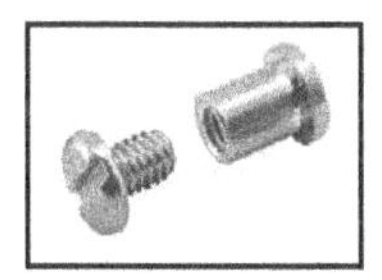

Pivot Screw

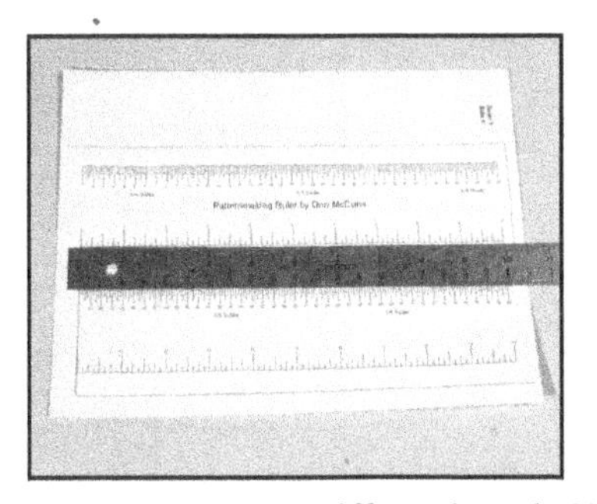

Step 1. Cut two stiffener boards 2" x 22".

Step 2. Copy the scale rulers on label paper. Print at 100% so that each ruler section is 10" (25 cm) long.

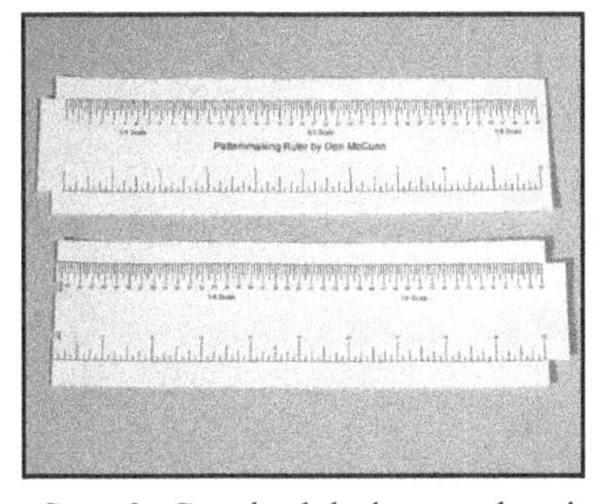

Step 3. Cut the label paper leaving a 1/2" (12 mm) overlap around the outside.

Step 4. Notch the ends of the label paper as shown in the illustration above.

Step 5. Attach the first half of the Side 1 scale ruler to the stiffener board. The horizontal lines of the ruler should align to both edges of the stiffener board.

Step 6. Fold over the ends and sides of the paper to the back of the stiffener.

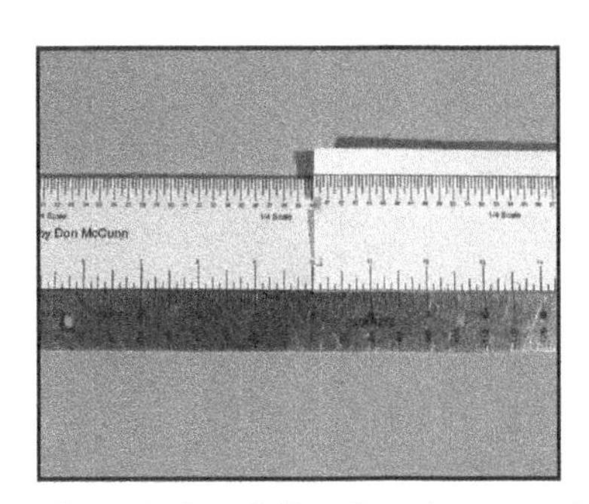

Step 7. Carefully align the second half of Side 1 to the first half. Fold over the sides of the paper to the back of the stiffener.

Step 8. Attach Side 2 of the scale ruler to the opposite side of the stiffener board, then trim off the excess paper.

Step 9. Cover the scale ruler with clear tape or laminating sheet.

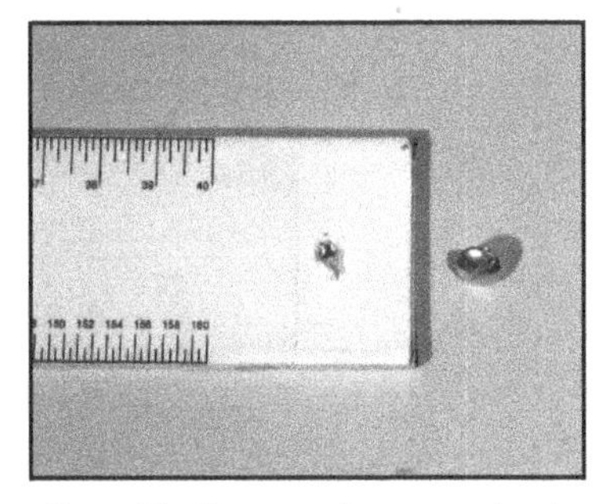

Step 10. Prepare the second ruler the same way.

Step 11. Make a mark 21" (53 cm) from the end of the ruler, 1" (2.5 cm) down from the top, then drill or punch holes at the mark.

Insert the pivot screw through both rulers and secure.

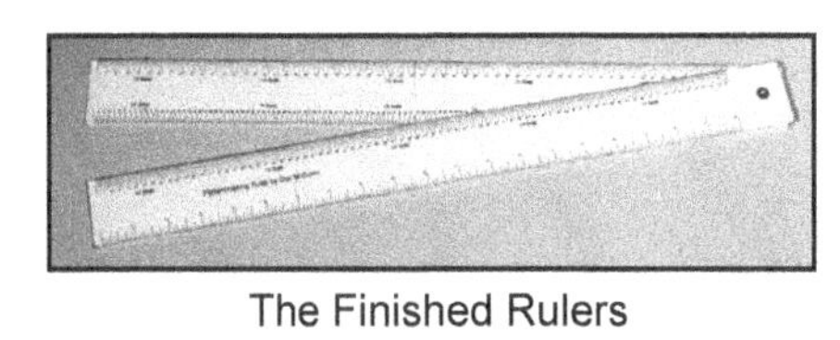

The Finished Rulers

Ruler 1
Side 1
In Inches

Patternmaking Ruler by Don McCunn

1/4 Scale

1/4 Scale

1/4 Scale

1/4 Scale

1/4 Scale

1 2 3 4 5 6 7 8 9 10 11 12 13 14 15 16 17 18 19 20 21 22 23 24 25 26 27 28 29 30 31 32 33 34 35 36 37 38 39 40

1 2 3 4 5 6 7 8 9 10

41 42 43 44 45 46 47 48 49 50 51 52 53 54 55 56 57 58 59 60 61 62 63 64 65 66 67 68 69 70 71 72 73 74 75 76 77 78 79 80

11 12 13 14 15 16 17 18 19 20

Ruler 1
Side 2
In Inches

Patternmaking Ruler by Don McCunn

1/5 Scale

1 2 3 4 5 6 7 8 9 10 11 12 13 14 15 16 17 18 19 20 21 22 23 24 25 26 27 28 29 30 31 32 33 34 35 36 37 38 39 40 41 42 43 44 45 46 47 48 49 50

Circumference of a circle

5 10 15 20 25 30 35 40 45 50 55 60

1/5 Scale

51 52 53 54 55 56 57 58 59 60 61 62 63 64 65 66 67 68 69 70 71 72 73 74 75 76 77 78 79 80 81 82 83 84 85 86 87 88 89 90 91 92 93 94 95 96 97 98 99

65 70 75 80 85 90 95 100 105 110 115 120 125

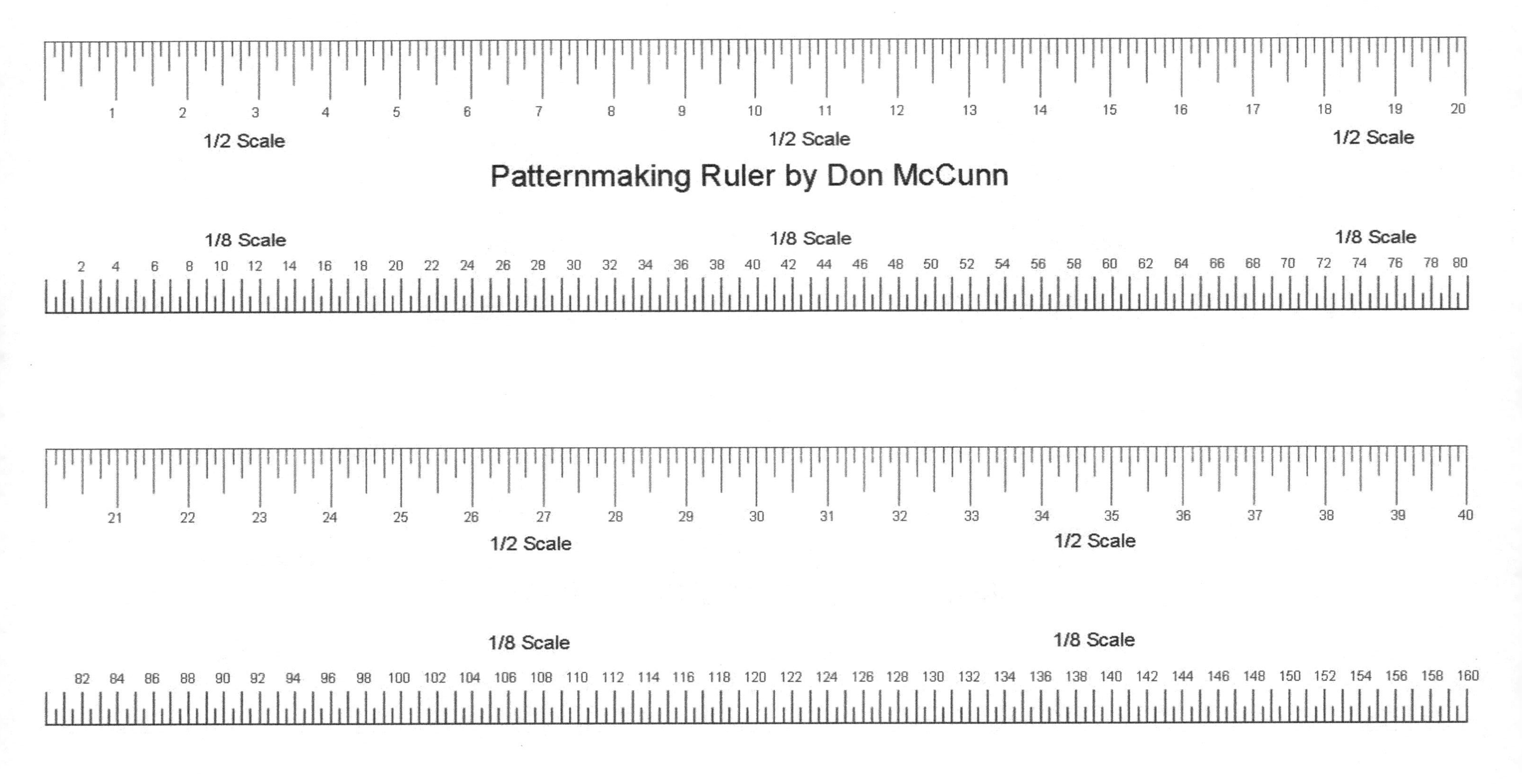

Ruler 2
Side 1
In Inches

Ruler 2
Side 2
In Inches

1 2 3 4 5 6 7 8 9 10 11 12 13 14 15 16 17 18 19 20 21 22 23 24 25 26 27 28 29 30

1/3 Scale 1/3 Scale 1/3 Scale

Patternmaking Ruler by Don McCunn

1/6 Scale 1/6 Scale 1/6 Scale

1 2 3 4 5 6 7 8 9 10 11 12 13 14 15 16 17 18 19 20 21 22 23 24 25 26 27 28 29 30 31 32 33 34 35 36 37 38 39 40 41 42 43 44 45 46 47 48 49 50 51 52 53 54 55 56 57 58 59 60

31 32 33 34 35 36 37 38 39 40 41 42 43 44 45 46 47 48 49 50 51 52 53 54 55 56 57 58 59 60

1/3 Scale 1/3 Scale

1/6 Scale 1/6 Scale

61 62 63 64 65 66 67 68 69 70 71 72 73 74 75 76 77 78 79 80 81 82 83 84 85 86 87 88 89 90 91 92 93 94 95 96 97 98 99 100 101 102 103 104 105 106 107 108 109 110 111 112 113 114 115 116 117 118 119 120

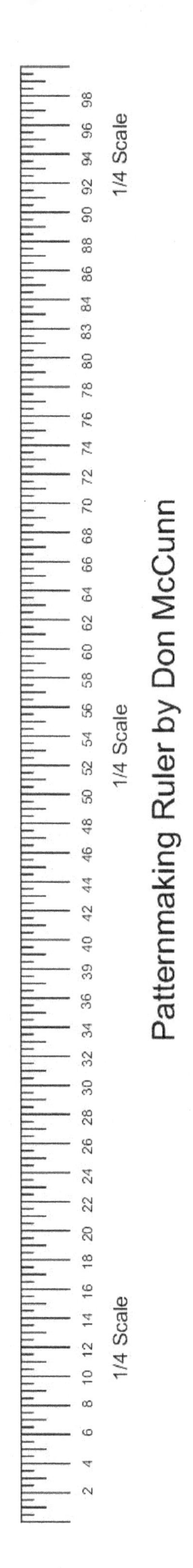

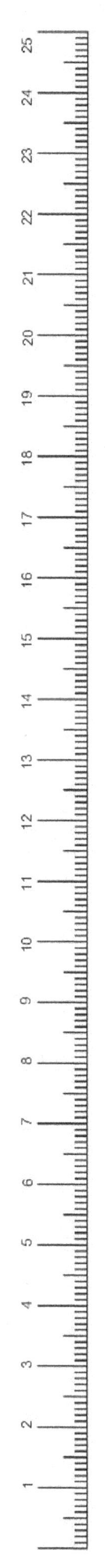

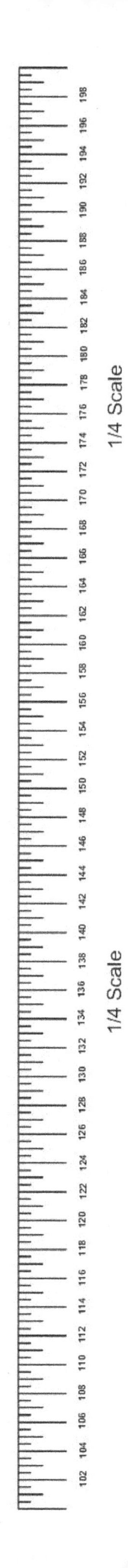

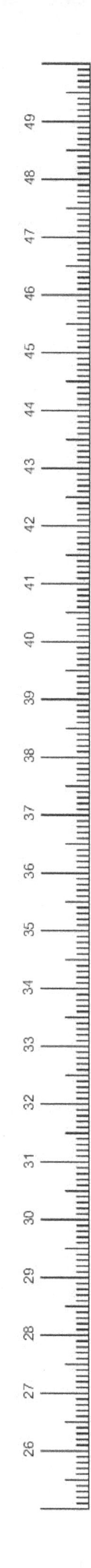

Ruler 1
Side 1
In CM

Ruler 1
Side 2
In CM

Patternmaking Ruler by Don McCunn

1/5 Scale

1/5 Scale

1/5 Scale

Circumference of a circle

1/5 Scale

1/5 Scale

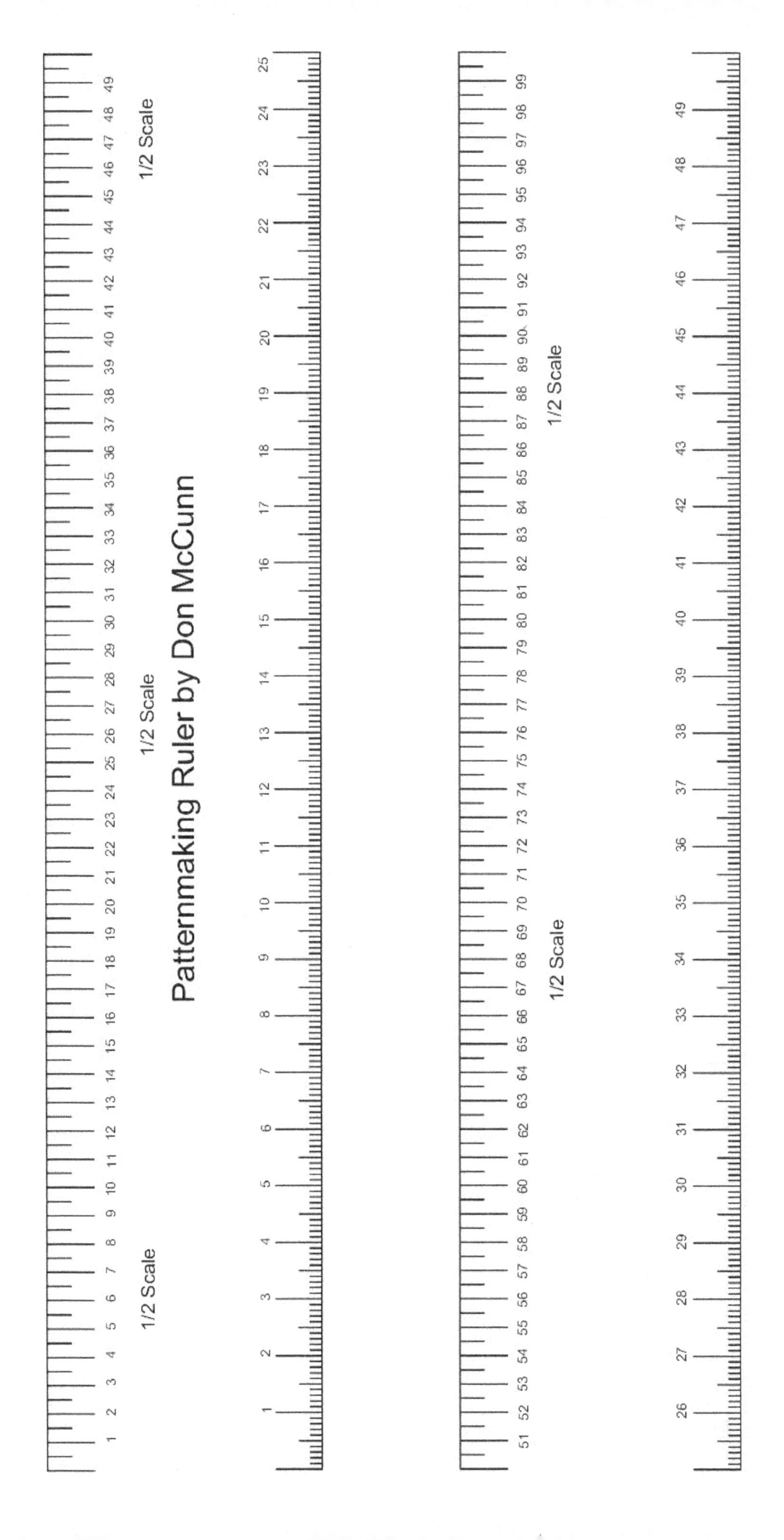

Ruler 2
Side 1
In CM

Ruler 2
Side 2
In CM

Patternmaking Ruler by Don McCunn

1/3 Scale

1/3 Scale

1/3 Scale

1/6 Scale

1/6 Scale

1/6 Scale

1/3 Scale

1/3 Scale

1/6 Scale

1/6 Scale

Working in Quarter Scale

Working in quarter scale allows you to both practise pattern making techniques and create prototypes for your design ideas. It is also a concise way to record original designs both as patterns and as small scale garments. The photo to the left shows full size and quarter scale garments made from the same fabrics. The quarter scale garments are on a Mini-Me Dress Form.

The first step in creating a Mini-Me Dress Form is to scale down the Bodice and Skirt Slopers. The Dress Form can then be created using posterboard paper much the same way the full size Dress Form is created. Posterboard paper is stiffer and thicker than normal letterhead paper but not as thick or stiff as the mat board used for the full size dress form.

While this chapter focuses on scaling down full size patterns to quarter scale, the process can be reversed to convert original quarter scale patterns into full size patterns.

Scaling Patterns

The process for scaling patterns shown here uses pattern making paper with dots every inch and paper with ¼" rules. The ruled paper is placed on the pattern paper at the junction of major reference lines.

The example below shows the front Bodice pattern being reduced to quarter scale. But the same technique can be used for any pattern.

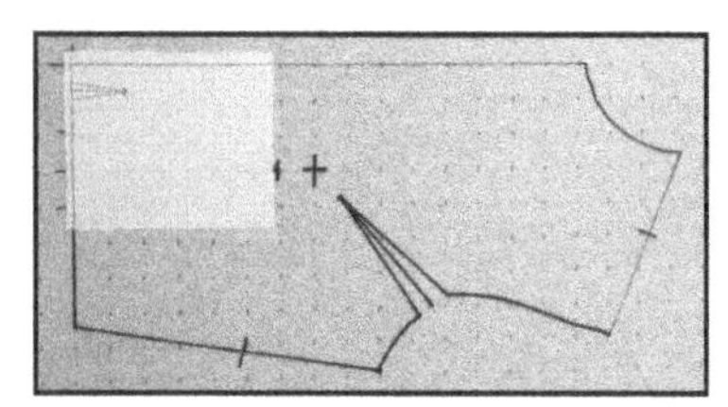

Step 1. Place the quarter ruled paper on top of the Sloper at the junction of the Center Front and Waist lines.

Step 2. Trace the Center Front and Waist lines onto the ruled paper.

Step 3. Transfer the Below the Bust Dart to the ruled squares.

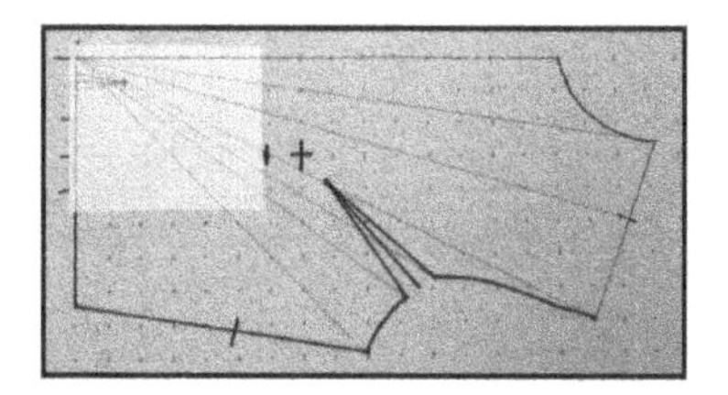

Step 4. Draw lines that radiate from Center Front at the waist to key points on the pattern.

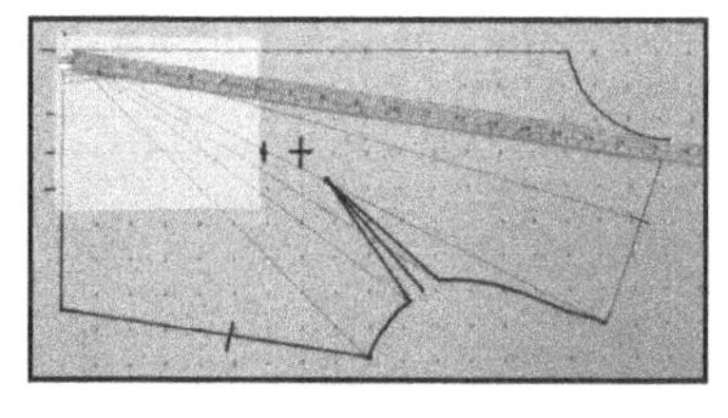

Step 5. Use a tape measure or full scale ruler, measure the length of one radiating line.

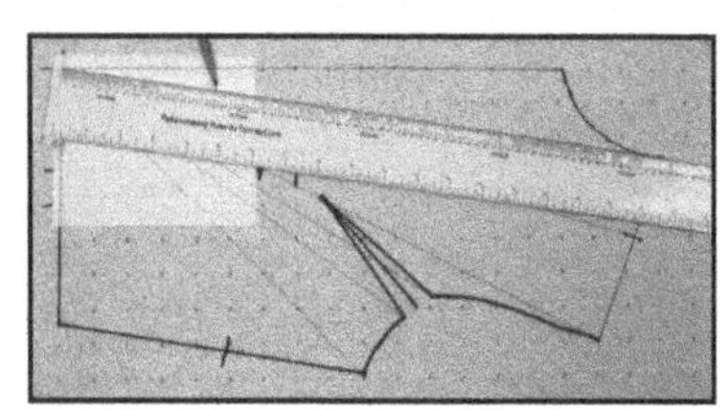

Step 6. Using the Scale Ruler's ¼ scale measurement, mark the length on the ruled paper.

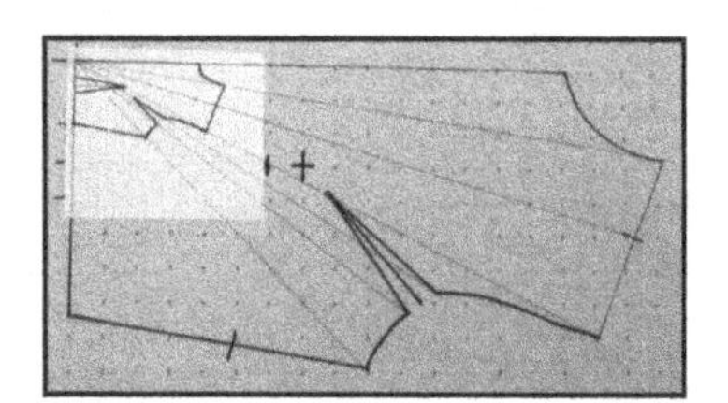

Step 7. Use Step 5 & 6 to mark the lengths on every radiating line.

Step 8. On the ruled paper, draw in the shape of the pattern. If there is any pattern shape that is not clear, use the horizontal and vertical reference points on the pattern to double check the correct locations on the ruled paper.

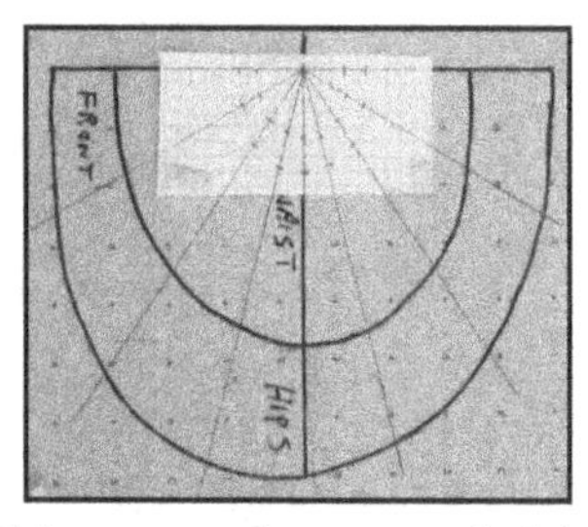

This pattern shows a scaled down pattern for the Waist and Hip Cross Sections.

For the Mini-Me form, create a Hip Cross Section using the same procedure used to create the Waist Cross Section on page 165.

Making a Mini-Me Dress Form

The steps for making a Mini-Me Dress Form are the same as for a full size Dress Form. Patterns are transferred to posterboard, cut out, then taped together. The skirt patterns for this Mini-Me have been extended to the Waist to Floor length (#40).

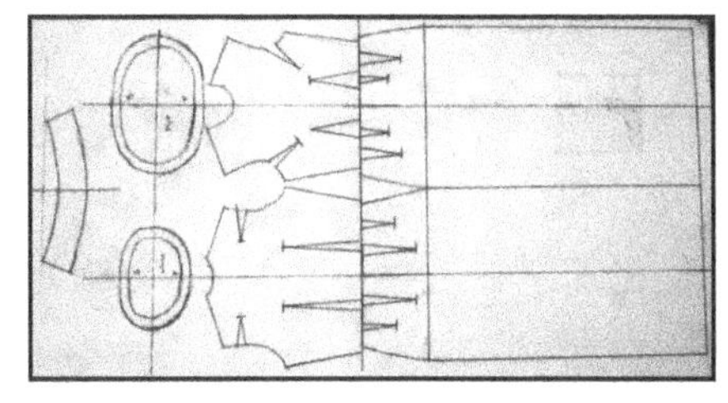

Step 1. Transfer the quarter scale patterns to posterboard.

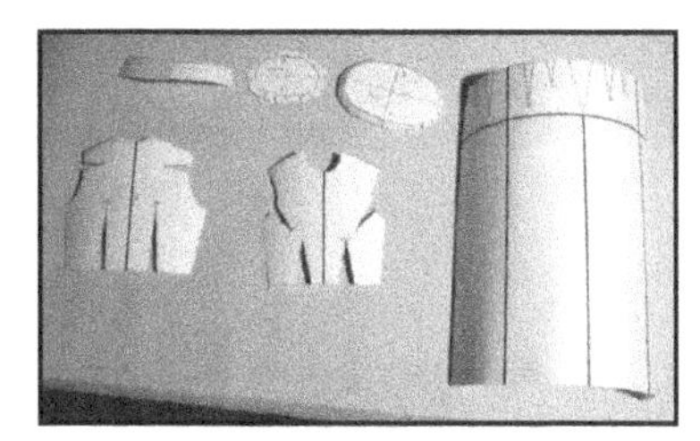

Step 2. Cut out the posterboard, then pre-roll the posterboard to commence the shaping process.

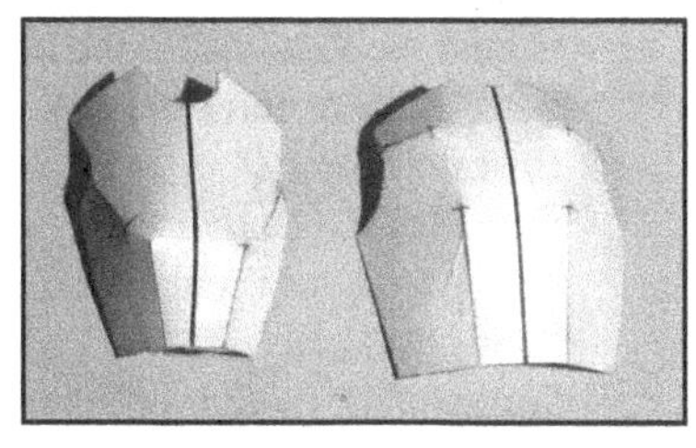

Step 3. Tape the darts closed.

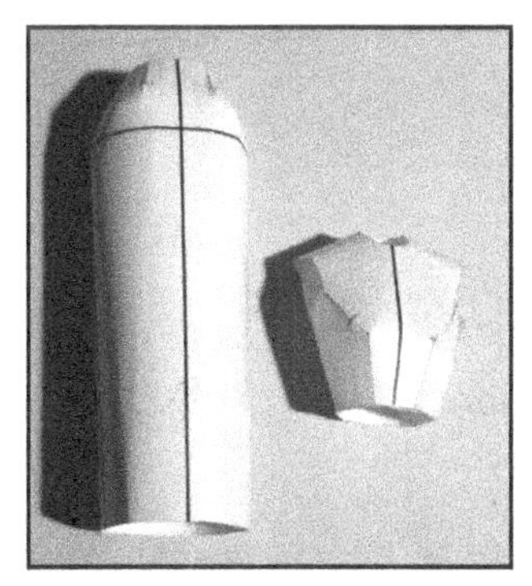

Step 4. Tape the Side Seams.

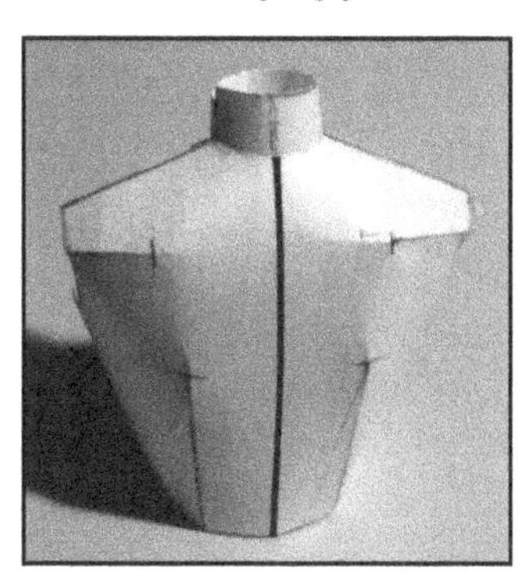

Step 5. Insert the neck and tape it in place.

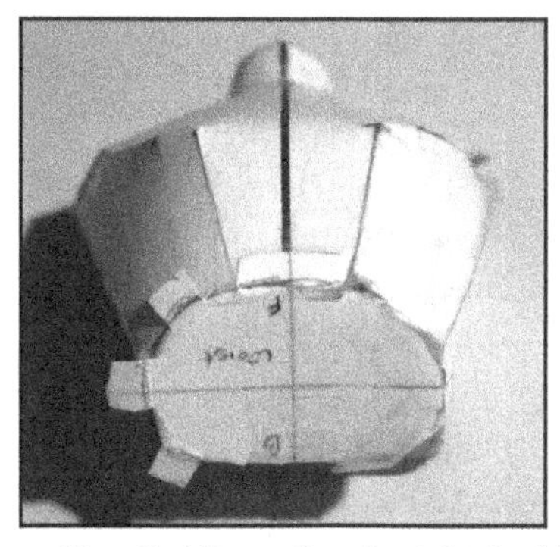

Step 6. Alternating the tabs inside to outside, tape the Waist Cross Section to the Bodice.

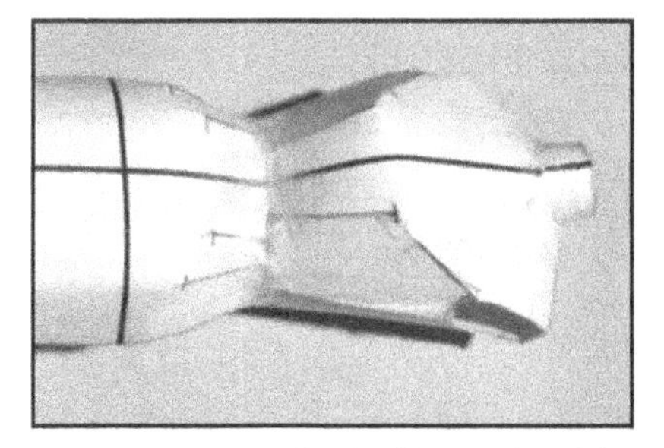

Step 7. Tape the bodice to the skirt.

Step 8. Because the skirt has been extended to floor length, it can be helpful to tape a Hip Cross Section inside the bottom of the Dress Form.

Creating Designs for a Mini-Me Dress Form

The patterns used to make a Mini-Me Dress Form can be used as Slopers for making other designs.

> **Note:** The instructions here did not remove any Ease for these patterns because the Mini-Me does not move and therefore does not require the flexibility of full size garments.

Index

B
- Bodice Sloper, 57
  - Adjusting the Side Seam, 75
  - Adjust the Patterns for the Darts, 72
  - Back Body & Back Pattern, 60
  - Bust Point, 64
  - Fitting of the Bodice, 66
  - Man's Body & Front Pattern, 57
  - Photos to Verify the Fit, 78
  - Woman's Body & Front Pattern, 63
- Body, 12
- Body Silhouettes, 129
- Bust Circle, 74, 90
- Bust Dart Variations
  - Center Front Dart, 92
  - Curved Dart, 92
  - French Dart, 92
  - Shoulder Darts, 93
  - Side Seam Dart, 90
- Button Overlap, 142
- Buttons, Shirt, 142

C
- Collars, 121
  - Adding Fullness to Collars, 128
  - Flat Collar, 126
  - Jacket Collars, 156
  - Mandarin Collar, 122
  - Shirt Collar I, 124
  - Shirt Collar II, 125
- Cuffs
  - Pants, 140
  - Shirt, 143

D
- Darts, 13
- Designing garments, 129
- Dress and Top Designs, 145
  - Cowl Necklines, 147
  - High Waistlines, 146
  - Knit Tops, 150
  - Low Necklines, 146
  - Peasant Top, 145
  - Wrap Around Closings, 148
- Dress Form, 161, 163
- Dropped Shoulder, 119

E
- Ease, 14

F
- Fabric, 12, 159
  - Body and Weight, 160
  - Drape, 159
  - Elasticity, 160
  - Fabric and the Body, 12
  - Flexibility, 160
  - Grain Lines, 14
  - Knits, 13
  - Woven, 13
- Facings
  - Coats and Jackets, 158
  - Shirt, 142
- Fittings
  - Bodice, 66
  - Man's Suit, 158
  - Pants, 50
  - Skirt, 31
  - Sleeve, 82
- Fitting shells, 10

G
- Gingham, 10
- Grain Lines, 14

J
- Jacket and Coat Design, 153
  - Creating the Body, 154
  - Expanding the Slopers, 154
  - Facings, 158
  - Lapels and Collars, 156
  - Two Piece Sleeve, 157

K
- Kick Pleat, 131
- Knits, 149

L
- Leggings, 152

M
- Marking Paper, 10, 16
- Measurement Chart, 20
- Measurements, 10
  - Girth, 21
  - Length, 23
  - Stride, 131
- Mini-Me Dress Form, 179
- Muslin, 10

N
- Necklines, 85, 86
  - Cowl Necklines, 147

P
- Pants Design, 135
  - Cuffs, 140
  - Leggings, 152
  - Plackets, 137
  - Pockets, 137
  - Styling, 53
  - Waistbands, 135

Pants Sloper, 43
Adjusting the Back Crotch Curve, 52
Body and the Pants, 43
Drafting the Pants, 44
Fitting the Pants, 50
Optimizing the Pattern for a Tummy, 48
Pattern Alteration, 83
Changing Back Darts to Seams, 100
Changing Dart Locations, 90
Changing Darts To Seams, 95
Changing External Lines, 85
Changing Internal Lines, 87
Pleats, 110
Principles of Adding Fullness, 101
Procedures for Adding Fullness, 105
Sleeve Variations, 111
Patternmaking Tools, 16
Photos
Fitting the Bodice, 78
Fitting the Skirt, 41
Placket
Pants, 136, 137
Skirt, 132
Pleats, 110
Pockets
Pants, 135
Skirt, 134
Princess Seams, 95
Fullness in Princess Seams, 104

Q

Quarter Scale, 15, 162, 178

R

Reference Lines
Center Back, 17
Center Front, 17
Neckline, 18
Shoulder Point, 18
Shoulder Seam, 18, 19
Waist, 17
Waistline, 19

S

Scale Rulers, 26, 161, 169
Scaling Patterns, 178
Seam Allowances
Back Bodice, 62
Man's Front Bodice, 59
Pants Sloper, 47
Skirt Sloper, 30
Sleeve, 82
Woman's Front Bodice, 65, 82
Seams, 13
Shirt and Blouse Design, 141
Body of the Shirt, 141
Button Location, 142
Button Overlap, 142
Cuff, 143
Facing, 142
Full Sleeves, 144
Shirt Sleeve, 143
Tapered Cuff, 144
Shoulder Yoke, 87
Skirt Designs, 130
Dirndl Skirt, 133
Full Skirt, 132
Handkerchief & Circular Skirts, 149
Pencil Skirt, 131
Placket, 132
Waistbands, 130, 132
Wrap Around Skirt, 133
Skirt Sloper, 27
Body & Skirt Pattern, 27
DIY Fitting, 35
Drafting the Skirt, 29
Fitting the Skirt, 31
Photos for Fitting, 41
Record the Darts, 37
Record the Side Seam, 39
Waist to Hip Contours, 28
Sleeve Design
Bell Sleeve, 116
Cape Sleeve, 117
Dropped Shoulder, 119
Flounced Sleeve, 112
Gathered Sleeve Cap, 113
Gathered Sleeve Top, 112
Leg-Of-Mutton Sleeve, 114
Puffed Sleeve, 115
Raglan Sleeve, 118, 151
Square Armscye Seam, 119
Tunic Sleeve, 120
Two Piece Sleeve, 157
Sleeve Sloper, 79
Slopers, 15
Styling Variations
Jackets and Coats, 153
Men's Shirt Yokes, 89
Necklines, 86
Princess Seam, 97
Shoulder Gathers, 94
Skirt, 134

W

Waistbands
Contoured, 9
Full Skirt, 132
Pants, 135
Skirt, 130
Wrap Around Skirt, 133
Waistline, 19

Printed in September 2021
by Rotomail Italia S.p.A., Vignate (MI) - Italy